Public Relations Techniques

Public Relations Techniques

Todd Hunt
Department of Communication
Rutgers, The State University of New Jersey

James E. Grunig
College of Journalism
University of Maryland, College Park

Harcourt Brace College Publishers
Fort Worth Philadelphia San Diego New York Orlando Austin San Antonio
Toronto Montreal London Sydney Tokyo

Editor in Chief	Ted Buchholz
Acquisitions Editor	Stephen T. Jordan
Developmental Editor	Cathlynn Richard
Senior Project Editor	Steve Welch
Senior Production Manager	Ken Dunaway
Art Directors	Priscilla Mingus/Melinda Huff
Photo Editor	Steve Lunetta

Address for Editorial Correspondence: Harcourt Brace College Publishers, 301 Commerce Street, Suite 3700, Fort Worth, TX 76102.

Address for Orders: Harcourt Brace, Inc., 6277 Sea Harbor Drive, Orlando, FL 32887. 1-800-782-4479, or 1-800-433-0001 (in Florida).

Printed in the United States of America

Library of Congress Catalog Card Number: 93-77649

ISBN: 0-03-046433-1

3 4 5 6 7 8 9 0 1 2   039   9 8 7 6 5 4 3 2 1

Preface

When *Managing Public Relations* appeared in 1984, the authors were gratified that reviewers and educators praised the book for its breadth of coverage and for its marriage of theory with practice. This was accomplished, however, at some sacrifice of detail in the techniques chapters at the end of that volume. This new volume—which can be used as a companion to the earlier book—expands both the number of topics discussed and the amount of guidance provided in managing each communications technique.

We believe that *Public Relations Techniques* will make it possible to expand the content of the traditional course in public relations writing to include all of the techniques used in public relations, including but not limited to written ones. As a new entry in the textbook arena, this book also fits well with the public relations curriculum offered in departments of communication and schools of business. These units typically offer a "campaigns" course rather than a writing course to supplement a principles course and an internship. It is the role of the campaigns course to expose students to all of the techniques used by the public relations practitioner in planning and executing a public relations program—a role that *Public Relations Techniques* addresses.

Not only are introductions to basic activities like writing press releases and public speaking discussed here, but Chapters 1 and 2, "The Roles and Functions of Public Relations" and "Planning and Executing the Public Relations Campaign," provide a thorough grounding for the student or practitioner who needs a framework for understanding how all the various *tasks* and *concepts* used in public relations work come together to shape a *campaign* that is based in *theory*. We highlight these terms because it is important for today's professional communicator to know not only what to do, but when and why to do it.

Chapters on "Media Relations," "Public Relations Writing," "Preparing News Releases and Press Kits," "Catering to the Press," "Using Radio," and "Television and Cable" illustrate the interdependency of the news media and public relations. Other outlets for public relations messages are analyzed in chapters on "Brochures and Direct Mail," "Newsletters and Magazines," "Photographs and Illustrations," "Slides and Films," "Exhibits and Special Events," "Annual Reports and Financial Writing," and "Public Relations Advertising." Another chapter looks at emerging technologies and what they offer: video, computers, and telecommunication services.

Public relations firms work with associates, clients, the media and service vendors to implement complicated programs under pressures of deadlines, budgets, and demands for both group and individual

Photo by FayFoto, Boston

creativity. This all happens in a highly charged setting that is changing as public relations becomes an integral part of management and as the related fields of marketing and advertising bid to join forces with public relations to achieve "integrated" communication. For these reasons two chapters at the end of the book deal with "Business Communication" and "Marketing Communication."

We are particularly pleased that the expanded format of *Public Relations Techniques* permits us to include a great number of illustrative examples. Boxes/sidebars provide an interesting array of exhibits in actual use by companies; a four-color insert sparkles with photographs of recent campaign models; and an appendix furnishes "A Toolbox for Planning and Analysis." Of particular use to both students and teachers alike—and to professionals in the field who use this book to prepare for accreditation exams—are the *checklists* in several of the media chapters that point the reader to the factors that make a message strategy effective. Most of these were prepared by the authors; a few were contributed by practitioners.

We have attempted throughout to keep the focus on the *management* of communication techniques to achieve public relations objectives, particularly the balanced two-way communication that most benefits an organization. This focus will be especially useful in the campaigns course of a public relations curriculum where students sometimes tend to be interested in creative impulses while the instructor appreciates the need for relating every task to the "bottom line."

A textbook, however, is only one of the building blocks of an effective course in public relations techniques. The accompanying instructor's manual includes tools for evaluating student products and programs. It also offers guidance in selecting clients and projects that will maximize student learning. Masters for overhead transparencies are provided for all checklists to facilitate class discussion.

The authors are indebted to those who have helped to shape this book so that it may effectively serve college campaigns courses or seminars in message design, as well as the needs of the professional preparing for the accreditation exam: Neil Alperstein, Loyola College; Jason Berger, Duquesne University; John Butler, Louisiana State University; Michael Cheney, Drake University; William R. Faith, University of Southern California; Mary Lou Galician, Arizona State University; Catherine Pratt, Ohio State University; Charles Rainey, Grossmont College; H. Allen White, Murray State University. Thanks also to the editorial and production staff at Harcourt Brace College Publishers: Stephen T. Jordan, Acquisitions Editor; Cathlynn Richard, Developmental Editor; Steve Welch, Senior Project Editor; Priscilla Mingus and Melinda Huff, Art Directors; and Ken Dunaway, Senior Production Manager.

Contents

5

Preparing News Releases and Press Kits 85

6

Catering to the Press   123

7

Using Radio   137

8

Television and Cable   157

9

New Technologies: Video, Computers, and Telecommunications   179

10

Preparing to Speak   205

11

Brochures and Direct Mail 225

12

Newsletters and Magazines 243

13

Photographs and Illustrations   263

14

Slides and Films   283

15

Exhibits and Special Events   303

16

Annual Reports and Financial Writing   315

19

20

Public Relations Techniques

1

The Roles and Functions of Techniques in Public Relations Theory

Two public relations agencies are preparing to "pitch" for an account. They have been contacted by an electronics manufacturer who feels that employee training and continuing education programs are the key to greater productivity and stability of operations in the workplace. They have asked the agencies to make a presentation on "how they would publicize and promote the education initiative" to employees of the firm.

One public relations agency, which we'll call *Creative Communications,* seizes on the words "publicize and promote" in the potential client's description of the situation. *Creative Communications* has a reputation for producing slick brochures and promotional pieces that use the latest graphic techniques. At the first meeting of the account team that will prepare the presentation, discussion turns quickly to the type of brochure that would be appropriate for the client: what kind of paper, what colors, the art and illustrations—even the kind of slogan or catch-line that might grab the interest of employees.

The competing public relations agency, *Communication Resource Management,* takes a different approach. The principal in the agency who is responsible for acquiring new business sits down at the office computer and logs onto a database service that has access to several business-oriented and education-oriented databases. Within an hour—using key phrases such as "education," "employee" and "training"—the manager has found the titles of almost two hundred articles, studies, speeches, papers, and books that describe and analyze employee training programs. Some of them even focus on organizations just like the electronics firm client. A second hour of work yields print-outs of abstracts for several relevant

Before practicing any of the public relations techniques described in this book, the manager must gather information and analyze the entire communication situation. Online computer databases such as Lexis and Nexis can provide much of the background needed to plan a campaign.

Photo courtesy of Mead Data Central

articles, and the full text of one or two key studies concerning employees' attitudes toward training and continuing education. Armed with the information, the team assigned to pitching the account meets to analyze the data and to draw up a list of goals and objectives for the client. Whether or not there will be a brochure or some other persuasive message isn't even discussed in the first week of research and planning.

There's always the possibility that the client will be dazzled by the mock-ups of sharp-looking publications *Creative Communications* will show them. But because the electronics firm uses research, strategic planning, and management-by-objectives techniques in its manufacturing operations, the chances are much greater that its managers will respond to the approach used by the team from *Communication Resource Management.* In today's sophisticated marketplace, information campaigns are based on careful planning. Their success is measured in terms of whether pre-stated objectives were met, not simply whether the messages produced were aesthetically pleasing.

Most public relations practitioners are the masters of a number of techniques. They know how to secure media coverage, prepare press releases, write speeches, write and design brochures, produce video news releases, negotiate with activists, interview community leaders, lobby legislative representatives in the state Capitol or Congress, stage a special event, or prepare an annual report.

People in other professions must also master the techniques of their work. Physicians perform surgery, dispense drugs, set bones, and deliver babies. Teachers use audiovisual equipment, write tests, lecture, hold discussions, and assign homework. Lawyers write briefs, interview witnesses, present evidence in court, and prepare wills and contracts. In each of these professions, practitioners possess a base of theoretical knowledge to direct the techniques they use. Physicians understand biology, anatomy, and physiology. Teachers understand the psychology of how people learn. Lawyers master legal principles and precedents.

Until recently, public relations was an occupation defined more by its techniques than by its theory. Recently, however, scholars of public relations have developed a body of knowledge that puts public relations on par with other recognized professions. Public relations professionals do not write and design brochures because they think it would be nice for the organization to have one, or strive for publicity because the boss likes to see his or her name in the media. Instead they use such a technique because they decide that it is the most effective way to communicate with a public that is strategic to the success of their organization.

This is a book about the techniques of public relations, but it begins with the idea that public relations is more than technique. Public relations is also theory: of why organizations must communicate with publics, of the nature of publics, of the effects of the techniques employed, and of the ethics of using the techniques. In most public relations curricula, this book will be used in a second course in public relations—a course that generally follows a course in the principles—or theory—of the field.

This first chapter, therefore, reviews public relations theory to help you avoid falling into the trap of thinking of techniques in isolation from a theory that will guide their use. Each time you are asked to write a speech or a news release you should ask "why?" Why is this technique the most effective way to communicate with a public? Why is it necessary to communicate with that public? Why will the public pay any attention to the message? This chapter should help you to supply the answers.

THE TECHNICIAN AND THE MANAGER ROLE

Public relations practitioners and educators often argue among themselves about what public relations is. Does it consist of writing, editing, and the use of other journalistic skills? Or does it consist of research, planning, counseling of management, and other management skills? Many practitioners argue that public relations students emerge from universities able to counsel management about public opinion but unable to write a decent press release. Educators—and many practitioners—counter that too many practitioners have mastered the technical skills of public relations but have little understanding of when and why to use those skills to make the organizations that employ them more effective.

One way to resolve this controversy is to look at what practitioners actually do in their work—at the roles they play in organizations. A long program of research has revealed that both camps are right: public relations practitioners occupy two major roles—technicians and managers.[1] Communication managers plan and direct public relations programs. Communication technicians provide technical services such as writing, editing, photography, media contacts, or production of publications. Both are essential to a public relations program.

The majority of public relations people are technicians, and your first job in public relations probably will be as a technician. Unless you master many of the techniques covered in this book, in fact, you probably never will get your first job in public relations. Without technicians, public relations programs could not be implemented. Without managers, however, public relations programs resemble a perpetual motion machine that churns out press releases, publications, or special events without stopping to think why they are needed.[2]

The same person may be both a manager and a technician in many organizations, especially small ones.[3] Many practitioners will play both roles in their careers, generally beginning as technicians and moving into the managerial role as they are promoted. Many practitioners have satisfying, long-term careers solely as technicians.[4] Many public relations programs, however, have no managers to guide them.

Strategic management is necessary for a public relations program to be effective. This means that the program should be aimed at those publics in an organization's environment that have the greatest effect on the organization. In addition, every person working on a public relations program—whether technician or manager—must look at public relations with a managerial mindset. When everyone has such a mindset, everyone sees the purpose of his or her work and can evaluate when the techniques employed achieve that purpose.

The managerial mindset should include an understanding of what public relations is and what it contributes to an organization—definitions and explanations to which we now turn.

UNDERSTANDING PUBLIC RELATIONS

Why Organizations Need Public Relations

Organizations, like people, must communicate with others because they do not exist alone in the world. If people had no relationships with family, neighbors, friends, enemies, or coworkers, they would have no need to communicate with anyone but themselves. But they are not alone, and must use communication to coordinate their behavior with people who affect them and are affected by them.

Organizations also have relationships—within their "family" of employees and with communities, governments, consumers, financiers, supporters, detractors, and other publics. Organizations need *public relations*, in other words, because they have *relationships with publics*. Organizations are successful when they achieve their missions and goals, and most organizations prefer to choose their own missions and set their own goals. Seldom can they do so alone, however. Publics also have a stake in organizations, and they therefore strive to affect the missions and goals of these organizations.

For example, employees want the organization to provide them with satisfying jobs. Environmentalists want the organization to preserve nature. Government agencies insist on safe products. Communities want clean air, less traffic, and donations to community projects. Organizations probably wouldn't choose these goals if they existed alone in their environment. If they don't choose them, however, publics will pressure them to do so—just as children pressure parents to take them to amusement parks, employers pressure people to work late, or neighbors pressure us to keep our yards neat. Life for both people and organizations, therefore, is a constant process of negotiation and compromise. And communication is one of the most effective means we have to negotiate and compromise.

Organizations that communicate well with the publics with whom they have relationships know what to expect from those publics, and the publics know what to expect from them. They may not always agree or have a friendly relationship, but they do *understand* one another—and achieving *understanding* is the major objective of public relations. Although an organization with good public relations may have to incorporate the goals of strategic publics into its mission, in the long run it will choose better goals and will be able to pursue these revised goals more effectively than it would if it ignored or fought the goals of publics.

As a result, communication and compromise make money for an organization by allowing it to sell products and services to satisfied consumers, secure funds from donors, or expand its operations. Communication and compromise also save the organization money that might be spent on lawsuits, regulations, boycotts, or training of new employees. Communication and compromise, therefore, are the essence of public relations.

Defining Public Relations

Most definitions of public relations—many of which are long and complicated—contain two elements: communication and management. Public relations is the formal way in which organizations communicate with their publics. Public relations, however, is planned—or managed—

communication. Although much communication by an organization happens by chance, public relations is communication that is planned and coordinated by professional communication managers.

Thus, we define public relations as *the management of communication between an organization and its publics.*[5] We define communication as a behavior—of people, groups, or organizations—that consists of moving symbols to and from other people, groups, or organizations. Thus, we can say that public relations is the managed communication behavior of an organization with its publics.

Public relations professionals plan and execute communication for the organization as a whole or help parts of the organization to communicate. They manage the movement of messages *into* the organization, for example, when conducting research on the knowledge, attitudes, and behaviors of publics. Then using the information, they counsel managers throughout the organization on how to make the policies or actions of the organization acceptable to publics. They may manage the movement of messages *out of* the organization when they help management decide how to explain a policy or action to a public and then write a news story or fact sheet to explain it.

Confusion with Other Organizational Communication Functions

Many public relations students—and practitioners—are often confused about the difference between public relations and other organizational communication functions, especially marketing. We can see the difference clearly, however, if we compare both the management and technician roles in public relations and marketing.

At the managerial level, public relations professionals plan programs to communicate with *publics*, while marketing professionals plan programs to communicate with *markets.*[6] Markets consist of people who purchase products or who use the services of an organization. Marketing professionals can create the markets for their products by segmenting the mass market into smaller groups with a particular need for a product. They might group people who are most likely to buy BMW automobiles into a category called Yuppies, for example, or young people in soccer leagues who are most likely to buy soccer balls. Generally, a "market" does not pressure an organization to produce a product. Instead, the organization must identify—or create—the market and exploit it.

Publics are different, however. They create themselves and pursue the organization when they are unhappy. Although we usually think of consumers as markets, they become publics when a corporation supplies unsafe products or products that damage the environment. Other examples of publics are environmentalists who object to air or water pollution or employees who object to low wages or job discrimination. Whereas organizations create markets to accomplish their missions, they must build relationships with publics to keep from being diverted from their missions.

At the managerial level, therefore, public relations is quite different from marketing. Marketing tries to communicate with relatively passive and supportive markets. Public Relations must communicate with active and frequently antagonistic publics. Public relations doesn't just react to publics, however. Practitioners also try to predict what publics the organization will affect in the future—such as employees, communities, or environmentalists—or what publics might support the mission of the organization—such as legislators, stockholders, or donors—and build good relations with them before problems occur or support is needed.

It is at the technical level, however, where public relations most often gets confused with marketing. Advertising, for example, is a marketing technique that can be used to support public relations objectives—such as an advertisement presenting Mobil Oil's position on a policy issue placed on the op-ed page of *The New York Times*. Likewise, public relations techniques such as publicity, media relations, brochures, or special events frequently are used to support marketing objectives. Many of the examples in this book are about public relations techniques used for marketing purposes.

Too often, however, public relations is defined strictly as a set of techniques rather than a body of theory. In that case, an organization sees public relations simply as a set of marketing techniques. When that happens, the organization generally loses the public relations function of managing communication with strategic publics other than consumers and generally suffers severely as a result.

As you study public relations techniques, therefore, you must be able to distinguish whether such use is for marketing or for public relations purposes. If you want a marketing position instead of or as well as a public relations position, you will need to study the theory of marketing as well as the theory of public relations.

In addition to being confused with marketing, public relations sometimes gets defined narrowly as communication with only one public. For example, public affairs is the organization's communication with governments or groups that affect government policy. Employee communication is communication with employees. Community relations is communication with community publics. Media relations is communication with the media. If an organization defines public relations in only one of these ways—as communication with only one public—it typically forgets about its other strategic publics, and suffers as a result. Public relations is a broad term that covers all of these communication functions—an organization's communication with all of its publics.

Models of Public Relations

Communication may be managed in several ways, depending upon the culture of the organization and the way the organization looks at the world. Grunig and Hunt identified four models of public relations that have been practiced in the history of public relations.[7] By "model," they mean four typical ways in which organizations practice public relations. Some of these "models" of public relations are more effective than others, however. Some also are more ethical.

The *press agentry* model describes public relations programs whose sole purpose is getting favorable publicity for an organization in the mass media. P. T. Barnum's promotion of his circus was one of the earliest examples of press agentry. It also is common in the work of publicists who promote sports, movie stars, products, politicians, or senior managers.

The *public information* model is similar to press agentry because it too is a one-way model that sees public relations only as the dissemination of information. With the public information model, an organization uses "journalists-in-residence"—public relations practitioners who act as though they are journalists—to disseminate relatively objective information through the mass media and controlled media such as newsletters, brochures, and direct mail.

Both press agentry and public information are one-way models of public relations; they describe communication programs that are not based on research and strategic planning. Press agentry and public information also are "asymmetrical" or imbalanced models—that is, they try to change the behavior of publics but not of the organization. They try to make the organization look good either through propaganda (press agentry) or by disseminating only favorable information (public information).

Public relations practitioners who take a professional approach base their communication programs on more sophisticated and effective models. The *two-way asymmetrical* model uses research to develop messages that are likely to persuade strategic publics to behave as the organization wants. Two-way asymmetrical public relations is scientific persuasion that uses the services of research firms to plan messages. Because it includes research on the attitudes of publics, it is more effective than press agentry or public information.

Two-way asymmetrical public relations is also a selfish model, however, because the organization that uses it believes it is right (and the public wrong) and that any change needed to resolve a conflict must come from the public and not from the organization. The model seems to work reasonably well when the organization has little conflict with a public and the public stands to benefit from a change in its behavior. For example, even though members of a target public for a health campaign

Characteristic	Model			
	Press Agentry/ Publicity	Public Information	Two-Way Asymmetric	Two-Way Symmetric
Purpose	Propaganda	Dissemination of information	Scientific persuasion	Mutual understanding
Nature of Communication	One-way; complete truth not essential	One-way; truth important	Two-way; imbalanced effects	Two-way; balanced effects
Communication Model	Source → Receiver	Source → Receiver	Source ⇄ Receiver Feedback	Group ⇄ Group
Nature of Research	Little; "counting house"	Little; readability, readership	Formative; evaluative of attitudes	Formative; evaluative of understanding
Typical Uses	Sports, theatre, product promotion	Government, nonprofit associations, business	Competitive business; agencies	Regulated business; agencies

EXHIBIT 1.1
Characteristics of Four Models of Public Relations

may resist changes in behavior to prevent a heart attack or AIDS, they do benefit from changes advocated by the campaign.

Research on these models suggests, however, that two-way asymmetrical public relations—like its fellow asymmetrical models of press agentry and public information—is less effective than a "symmetrical" model of public relations.[8] It is especially less effective when an organization experiences greater conflict with a public. For example, environmentalists seldom can be persuaded that a polluting organization is not polluting. Antinuclear activists seldom are converted to supporting nuclear power plants. Members of employee unions seldom can be convinced that low wages are high or that poor working conditions are good.

Rather, they want the organization's mission to include the problems they consider relevant. They want to participate in the decisions about what to do with the problems. They want balanced, "symmetrical" communication with the organization. They want dialogue rather than monologue. They want the organization to be persuaded equally as often as they are persuaded.

The fourth model, the *two-way symmetrical*, describes a model of public relations that is based on research and that uses communication to manage conflict and improve understanding with strategic publics. Because the two-way symmetrical model bases public relations on negotiation and compromise, it generally is more ethical than the other models.[9] It does not force the organization to make the choice of whether it is right on particular issues. Rather, two-way symmetrical public relations allows the question of what is right to be settled by negotiation, since nearly every side to a conflict—such as nuclear power, abortion, or gun control—believes its position to be right.

During the course of your career you may be asked to use the techniques discussed in this book in support of one or more of the four models. Early in your career you probably won't have a choice. Later on, when you are in a managerial position, you should be able to choose the model you want to practice. In the rest of the book, we provide information that should help you to make that choice. We describe which techniques are most appropriate for which model and how the techniques can be adapted to fit different models.

Public Relations and Public Responsibility

An organization has relationships with publics when it has consequences on those publics or they have consequences on the organization—that is, they affect each other. Preston and Post have described these relationships as those of "interpenetrating systems." They point out that organizations and publics are neither independent nor does one control the other. "Rather their relationship is better described in terms of interpenetration."[10]

Because of the interpenetration of organizations and publics, the organization must be responsible to those publics if it is to have good relationships with them. Thus, Preston and Post use the concept of public responsibility rather than the more frequently used term "social responsibility," which often is cited as a goal for public relations. Social responsibility is a general term that suggests that an organization should be responsible to society. But "society" is a large and vague entity. "Publics" can be recognized more easily: They are groups that the organization affects, such as employees, communities, or stockholders.

Thus, the responsible organization is the organization that is responsible for the consequences it has on its publics. It does so by communicating symmetrically with those publics. Such communication effectively builds good relationships for the organization. As a result, public relations and public responsibility become nearly synonymous terms. An organization cannot practice good public relations without being responsible to its publics: Public relations is the practice of public responsibility.

STRATEGIC MANAGEMENT OF PUBLIC RELATIONS

With these theories and definitions of public relations in mind, we now turn to the process that describes how public relations should be practiced if it is to contribute the most to the success of an organization— the process of strategic management.

Organizations use strategic management to relate their missions to their environments. They use strategic management to identify opportunities and dangers in the environment; to develop strategies for exploiting the opportunities and minimizing the dangers; and to develop, implement, and evaluate the strategies. Without strategic management, organizations have little choice other than to "live from day to day and to react to current events."[11]

An organization should have an *overall strategic plan* to meet its mission—what it strives to accomplish.[12] In addition, each department of an organization should have a strategic plan that outlines its contribution to the mission of an organization, such as a *strategic plan for public relations, public policy, or marketing.* Finally, each level of the organization should have an *operational plan* that states how it should use material and human resources to accomplish its strategic plan.[13]

Earlier in this chapter, we pointed out that public relations contributes to strategic management by building relationships with publics that it affects or is affected by—publics that support the mission of the organization or that can divert it from its mission. Organizations plan public relations programs strategically, therefore, when they identify the publics that are most likely to limit or enhance their ability to pursue the mission of the organization, and when they design communication programs that help the organization manage its interdependence with these strategic publics.

In contrast to this strategic approach, most organizations carry out the same public relations programs year after year without stopping to determine whether they continue to communicate with the most strategic publics. Dozier and L. Grunig have pointed out that at some point in their history, most organizations probably develop their public relations programs strategically—that is, the presence of a strategic public probably provides the motivation for initiating public relations programs. As time passes, however, organizations forget the initial reason for the programs and continue communication programs for publics that no longer are strategic. Public relations then becomes routine and ineffective because it does little to help organizations adapt to dynamic environments.[14]

Exhibit 1.2 provides an overview of the strategic planning process for public relations. We will look at each of the stages in the process in more detail in the remainder of this chapter. First, however, we contrast the strategic planning process for public relations with the strategic process for marketing. Note that the first three steps in strategic planning for public relations are described as "stages" rather than "steps," because they describe the evolution of publics and issues. Public relations practitioners cannot control these stages, although they can manage the organization's response to publics as they evolve and create issues.

Exhibit 1.2

Steps in the Strategic
Management of Public
Relations

1. *Stakeholder stage.* An organization has a relationship with stake-holders when the behavior of the organization or of a stakeholder has consequences on the other. Public Relations should do formative research to scan the environment and the behavior of the organization to identify these consequences. Ongoing communication with these stakeholders helps to build a stable, long-term relationship that manages conflict that may occur in the relationship.

2. *Public stage.* Publics form when stakeholders recognize one or more of the consequences as a problem and organize to do something about it or them. Public Relations should do research to identify and segment these publics. At this stage focus groups are particularly helpful. Communication to involve publics in the decision process of the organization helps to manage conflict before communication campaigns become necessary.

3. *Issue stage.* Publics organize and create issues. Public Relations should anticipate these issues and manage the organization's response to them. This is known as Issues Management. The media play a major role in the creation and expansion of issues. In particular, their coverage of issues may produce publics other than activist ones—especially "hot-issue" publics. At this stage, research is particularly useful to segment all of the publics. Communication programs at this stage usually use the mass media but should also include interpersonal communication with activist publics to try to resolve the issue through negotiation.

Public Relations should plan communication programs with different stakeholders or publics at each of the above three stages. In doing so, it should follow steps 4–7.

4. Public Relations should develop objectives, such as communication, accuracy, understanding, agreement, and complementary behavior for its communication programs.

5. Public Relations should plan formal programs and campaigns to accomplish the objectives.

6. Public relations, especially the technicians, should implement the programs and campaigns.

7. Public relations should evaluate the effectiveness of programs in meeting their objectives and in reducing the conflict produced by the problems and issues that brought about the programs.

The strategic process for planning marketing programs differs from the process for public relations primarily in the first three stages. The components of strategic marketing as described by Kotler and Andreasen[15] and Cravens and Lamb[16] are:

1. Define organizational mission in light of environmental conditions.
2. Define and assess markets that further the corporate mission.
3. Set marketing objectives and strategy.
4. Develop an organizational structure for implementing marketing programs.
5. Execute marketing programs.
6. Evaluate marketing performance.

Steps 3–6 for marketing are essentially the same as Steps 4–7 for public relations. The first three stages for public relations are replaced with the first two steps for marketing. The differences reflect the distinction between public relations and marketing that we described above. The public relations process begins when publics form because organizations have consequences on them. Marketing begins with the organization and its mission, what it wants to accomplish within the constraints of its environment. For marketing, strategic planners can define their own markets—markets that offer the potential for accomplishing the organizational mission.

As a public relations technician, you will probably become involved in the marketing process at Step 4, and in the public relations process at Step 6. If you are a public relations manager as well as a technician, you will be part of the entire strategic management process for public relations. If you function as a marketing manager as well as a public relations technician, you will also be involved in the entire process for marketing.

Our major purpose in this chapter is to provide an overview of public relations theory. Thus, we devote the rest of this chapter to the strategic management process for public relations. As we said earlier, however, public relations technicians often support marketing objectives. Thus, you should study marketing management as well as public relations if you anticipate a career in marketing public relations.

The Evolution of Publics

The first three steps in the strategic management of public relations call for different communication strategies at different stages in the evolution of active publics. Grunig and Hunt have pointed out that a crucial distinction for segmenting a population into publics is the extent to which they passively or actively communicate about an issue and the extent to which they actively behave in a way that supports or constrains the organization's pursuit of its mission. Publics are more likely to be active when the people who constitute these publics perceive that what an organization does *involves them (level of involvement)*, that the consequences of what an organization does is a *problem (problem recognition)*, and that they are *not constrained* from doing something about the problem *(constraint recognition)*.[17]

If none of these conditions fits a group of people, these people constitute a "nonpublic"; they are of no concern to an organization. Whenever an organization does something that has consequences on people or whenever people have consequences on the organization, there is a likelihood that they will perceive an involvement and recognize a problem. Thus, consequences produce at the minimum, a *latent* public—a public that is passive but has the potential to be active. As the level of involvement and problem recognition increases and constraint recognition decreases, however, these publics can become *aware* and *active*.

Publics generally move from the latent to the aware and active stages, therefore, as strategic management of public relations moves through the first three stages of the process.

The Stakeholder Stage

Often the terms "stakeholder" and "public" are used synonymously. There is a subtle difference, however, that helps us to understand strategic planning of public relations. People are stakeholders because they are in a category affected by decisions of an organization or because their decisions affect the organization. Many people in a category of stakeholders—such as employees—are passive. These passive stakeholders also can be called latent publics. The stakeholders who are or who become more aware and active can be described as aware and active publics.

Stakeholders are people who are "linked" to an organization because they and the organization have consequences on each other.[18] People linked to an organization have a stake in it, which Carroll defined as "an interest or a share in an undertaking."[19] A stakeholder, therefore, is "any individual or group who can affect or is affected by the actions, decisions, policies, practices, or goals of the organization."[20]

The first step in strategic management of public relations, therefore, is to make a list of the people who are linked to or have a stake in your organization. Freeman calls this list a stakeholder map of the organization. He suggests that a stakeholder map of a typical corporation consists of owners, consumer advocates, customers, competitors, the media, employees, special interest groups, environmentalists, suppliers, governments, and local community organizations.

You can draw a stakeholder map by thinking through the consequences your organization has on people and those they have on your organization. You can make this map more meaningful by doing what researchers call environmental scanning research.[21] Environmental scanning can be done through public opinion polls, studying the mass media and specialized media, reading scholarly or legal journals, conferring with political or community leaders, or calling upon experts in your organization to serve on "issues management" committees.

After thoroughly researching their stakeholders, public relations managers should rank them or assign weights to them to indicate their impact on the organization.[22] They then should plan ongoing communication programs with the most important—the most strategic—stakeholders, working down the ranked list until the resources available for public relations are used up. Communication at the stakeholder stage—ideally before conflict has occurred—is especially important because it helps to build the stable, long-term relationships that an organization needs to build support from stakeholders and to manage conflict when it occurs.

The Public Stage

As public relations managers develop communication programs for stakeholders, they can improve their chances for successful communication by segmenting each stakeholder category into passive and active components. Active publics affect the organization more than passive ones. When they support the organization, they also support it much more actively than passive publics. Active publics also are easier to communicate with because they seek out information rather than passively waiting to receive it. Active publics are not easy to persuade, however, because they seek information from many sources and persuade themselves more than they are persuaded by others. In other words, active publics make their own decisions. Even passive stakeholders can become active, however, and should not be ignored. Thus, the organization should pay attention to all members of a stakeholder category but should devote most of its resources for public relations to those that can be identified as active publics.

Active publics communicate with and about an organization that affects them, either directly with the organization or through other sources such as the media, other people, community and political leaders, and activist groups. When they feel an organization is unresponsive to their interests, they not only communicate actively but they behave actively in other ways. They may boycott a product, support government regulation, oppose a rate increase, or join an activist group. Other active publics support the mission of the organization, and buy its stock, support its policies, or give it money.

At this stage of the strategic management process, public relations managers should do formative research on publics—research to plan a program. Focus groups are an especially useful technique at this stage.[23] The focus group is a research technique in which several small groups of people affected by an organization are brought together to "focus on" and to discuss the issue that affects them.

Once active publics have been identified, public relations managers should develop programs to involve them in the decision-making processes of the organization—such as committees of employees or community residents or open hearings before decisions are made. If active publics are involved early in the process, their concerns can be addressed before conflict occurs and before they feel they have no recourse other than to pressure the organization to change a decision. When their concerns are not addressed, many join formal activist groups to bring pressure on an organization through lawsuits, government regulation or taxation, boycotts and protests, and media campaigns.[24]

The Issues Stage

If an organization has had effective public relations at each of the previous two stages of the process of strategic management, it will have resolved most of the *problems* with publics before they become *issues*. A public perceives a problem when something is missing that it would like to occur—such as clean air, a good community, or a successful organization. Publics make issues out of problems that have not been resolved.

Robert Heath, an expert on issues management at the University of Houston, has defined an issue as "a contestable question of fact, value, or policy."[25] He added that activist groups play a powerful role in making public issues out of problems.[26]

When publics make issues out of problems, they typically use the mass media to bring attention to their cause. They do this by staging events such as protests, marches, strikes, and sometimes even hunger fasts and violent demonstrations. When publicity mounts, stakeholders and even members of nonpublics hear about the issue—they become "hot-issue publics."

When organizations delay public relations programs until the issue stage, they usually are forced to develop programs of crisis communication. In addition, they begin to campaign against the activists asymmetrically, the activists do likewise, and the conflict degenerates into a shouting match and campaigns to convince passive publics to support each position. Passive publics seldom are involved enough to take a position on the issue, however, although they may form weak, negative attitudes toward your organization.

Sometimes, one side can declare a short-term victory—by defeating legislation or winning a lawsuit, for example—but seldom does the other side give up. The only means of resolving issues at this stage is through negotiation and "horsetrading" with the activist group.[27]

Ideally, however, organizations do not wait until the issues stage to deal with problems. Instead, they set up a program of "issues management" to identify issues while they are still problems and to manage the organization's response to the problems and issues.[28] Issues management programs should be managed by the public relations department in cooperation with a corporate or organizational planning department. When such coordination takes place, strategic management of public relations can be integrated into the overall strategic management of the organization.

The discussion of communication programs at each of the three stages of strategic management suggests that programs should begin at the stakeholder stage. It may be necessary to revise programs as they move into the public and issue stages. All public relations programs should be planned, managed, and evaluated, however—the last four stages of strategic management.

The Objectives Stage

Every public relations program should begin with an objective that it intends to achieve—that is, it should be managed by objectives. Sometimes, public relations practitioners set *process objectives* for their programs, objectives such as the distribution of five press releases, the holding of ten meetings with community leaders, or the staging of an event by a specified date. By themselves, process objectives have little value unless previous evaluation research has shown that these communication processes contribute to desired communication outcomes. Instead, you should specify *outcome objectives* for public relations programs, objectives that specify the kind of effect a program should have.

Practitioners frequently assume blindly that their communication programs will change attitudes or behaviors—that they will persuade publics or management. Public relations programs can change attitudes and behaviors of publics—and of management of the organization—but these objectives often take years to accomplish. Only simple behaviors generally can be changed in the short run.[29] Since changes in attitude and behavior take so long to accomplish, they are not terribly useful objectives to use to evaluate public relations programs or campaigns in a short enough time to make changes in these programs.

Instead, communication theory and research suggests that public relations practitioners should look for changes in the cognitions of publics—in the way people think or in the ideas or beliefs they have—

before looking for changes in attitudes and behaviors.[30] Changes in people's ideas can be achieved shortly after a program or campaign has been completed. The "understanding" that results from cognitive change also contributes over the long run to "agreement" in attitudes and behaviors. Thus, you should choose from the following taxonomy of effects when you develop objectives for a public relations program, emphasizing the first behaviors in the short run and the later objectives in the long run.[31]

Communication   The organization and a public exchange messages. Stories are placed in the media and publics read them; publics read an advertisement, attend a special event, and read a brochure; management has a dialogue with leaders of an activist group and reads the results of a public opinion poll.

Retention of the Message   This objective also can be called *accuracy* of communication. The public or management retains or comprehends a message from the other. Each side can articulate the ideas of the other, even though it does not share the idea, evaluate it in the same way (attitude), or behave in the same way.

Acceptance of Cognitions   The public or management shares the ideas or beliefs (cognitions) of the other about the nature of a problem or issue. They do not necessarily agree about what to do about the problem or even behave in the same way. Thus, this objective also can be called *understanding*, which is different from the next objective of agreement.

Formation or Change of an Attitude (Agreement)   The organization and public evaluate solutions to a problem in the same way—they share attitudes or intend to behave in the same way. One has persuaded the other or both have mutually persuaded each other—that is, they *agree*.

Complementary Behavior   The organization, the public, or both change their behavior in a way that improves the relationship between them.

The Planning Stage

At this stage, public relations managers translate objectives into actual programs or campaigns. Creativity is important at this stage. One should ask what kind of technique will communicate most effectively with a public and how the technique should be executed. At this stage, also, practitioners often find cases and examples of the public relations programs of other organizations to be useful in stimulating ideas for their own programs. In looking at cases, however, practitioners should look for examples of programs that have achieved the objective they seek for the kind of public with which they are dealing. No program should be copied simply because someone else did it before—or because it worked in achieving a different objective for a different public.

The Implementation Stage

Communication technicians take over from managers. Managers may change hats and take on the technician role. Or they may supervise technicians who specialize in executing the program. In all cases, however, technical work must be guided by management strategy and objectives.

The Evaluation Stage

A public relations program that is managed strategically should not end when technicians have executed the program. Instead, the objectives of the program should be measured before and after the program to determine if a change has occurred. Or the effects specified as objectives can be measured on two groups—one exposed to the program and another that has not been exposed.[32]

Practitioners often use "seat-of-the-pants" or informal research methods to evaluate programs, such as using one's previous experience to judge whether a program is going well or listening to a few people who have participated in a communication program. Ideally, however, public relations should be evaluated formally, and each program should be evaluated as though it were a scientific test of a communication theory.[33]

THE MANAGERIAL CONTEXT

Although this is a book about the techniques of public relations, you should not develop these technical skills without understanding the managerial context in which they are used. Public relations practitioners play two roles in the organizations that employ them, either in part or exclusively. Communication managers plan, direct, and evaluate public relations programs. Communication technicians write, edit, make media contacts, produce publications, or use similar techniques of communication.

Organizations need public relations to build relationships with publics that enhance or constrain their ability to pursue a mission and goals. Public relations helps an organization achieve its mission and goals by managing communication with these strategic publics. Public relations differs from marketing, which communicates only with the "markets" that use the organization's products or services. Public relations communicates with all of the publics that affect or are affected by

the organization. Public relations technicians, however, often work in support of marketing objectives as well as public relations objectives.

Public relations should be practiced according to the principles of the two-way symmetrical model of public relations or of that model in combination with the two-way asymmetrical model. The press agentry and public information models are ineffective, in large part because they limit public relations to the technical rather than the managerial role. Public relations practiced according to the symmetrical model makes the organization more responsible to its publics at the same time that it makes the organization more effective in achieving its mission. To meet these dual purposes of public relations, however, communication programs must be managed strategically. Strategic management of public relations passes through seven stages and steps: the stakeholder, public, and issues stages and the objectives, planning, implementation, and evaluation steps.

With this overview of public relations theory in mind, we now step down one level of abstraction to specific public relations campaigns before moving on to specific techniques.

1. See Glen M. Broom and George D. Smith, "Testing the Practitioner's Impact on Clients," *Public Relations Review* 5 (Fall 1979), pp. 47–59; Glen M. Broom, "A Comparison of Sex Roles in Public Relations," *Public Relations Review* 8 (Fall 1982), pp. 17–22; David M. Dozier, "The Organizational Roles of Communication and Public Relations Practitioners," in James E. Grunig (ed.), *Excellence in Public Relations and Communication Management* (Hillsdale, NJ: Lawrence Erlbaum Associates, 1992), pp. 327–356.

2. Glen M. Broom and David M. Dozier, *Using Research in Public Relations* (Englewood Cliffs, NJ: Prentice-Hall, 1990), p. 14.

3. Jennie M. Piekos and Edna F. Einsiedel, "Roles and Program Evaluation Techniques Among Canadian Public Relations Practitioners," *Public Relations Research Annual*, Vol. 2 (1990), pp. 95–114.

4. Pamela J. Creedon, "Public Relations and 'Women's Work': Toward a Feminist Analysis of Public Relations Roles," *Public Relations Research Annual*, Vol. 3 (1991), pp. 67–84.

5. For more discussion of the origin of this definition, see James E. Grunig and Todd Hunt, *Managing Public Relations*, 2d ed. (Fort Worth: Harcourt Brace & Company), Chapter 1.

6. James E. Grunig, "Publics, Audiences, and Market Segments, Models of Receivers of Campaign Messages," in Charles T. Salmon (ed.), *Information Campaigns: Managing the Process of Social Change* (Newbury Park, CA: Sage, 1989), pp. 197–226.

7. Grunig and Hunt, Chapter 2.

8. James E. Grunig and Larissa A. Grunig, "Toward a Theory of the Public Relations Behavior of Organizations: Review of a Program of Research," *Public Relations Research Annual*, Vol. 1 (1989), pp. 27–63.

9. Ron Pearson, "Beyond Ethical Relativism in Public Relations: Coorientation, Rules, and the Idea of Communication Symmetry," *Public Relations Research Annual*, Vol. 1 (1989), pp. 67–86.

10. Lee E. Preston and James E. Post, *Private Management and Public Policy: The Principle of Public Responsibility* (Englewood Cliffs, NJ: Prentice-Hall, 1975), pp. 24–27.

11. Rogene A. Buchholz, William D. Evans, and Robert A. Wagley, *Management Response to Public Issues*, 2d ed. (Englewood Cliffs, NJ: Prentice-Hall, 1989), pp. 38–39.

12. Robert L. Heath, "Corporate Issues Management: Theoretical Underpinnings and Research Foundations," *Public Relations Research Annual*, Vol. 2 (1990), p. 33.

13. Heath calls the operational plan a "business plan."

14. David M. Dozier and Larissa A. Grunig, "The Organization of the Public Relations Function," in James E. Grunig (ed.), *Excellence in Public Relations and Communication Management* (Hillsdale, NJ: Lawrence Erlbaum Associates, 1992), pp. 395–418.

15. Philip Kotler and Alan R. Andreasen, *Strategic Marketing for Nonprofit Organizations*, 3d ed. (Englewood Cliffs, NJ: Prentice-Hall, 1987).

16. David W. Cravens and Charles W. Lamb, Jr., *Strategic Marketing Cases and Applications* (Chicago: Irwin, 1983).

17. Grunig and Hunt, Chapter 5. Greater detail on this "situational theory of publics" can be found in this chapter. Marketing researchers use other techniques to segment markets, such as demographics, psychographics, values and lifestyles, and geodemographics. These techniques also are used in public relations, although they work better in marketing. They can be used most effectively in public relations as a means of identifying and describing active and passive publics. For a discussion of segmentation techniques, see Grunig, "Publics, Audiences, and Market Segments."

NOTES

18. James E. Grunig and Todd Hunt, *Managing Public Relations* (New York: Holt, Rinehart and Winston, 1984), pp. 139–143.

19. Archie B. Carroll, *Business & Society: Ethics and Stakeholder Management* (Cincinnati: Southwestern, 1989), p. 56.

20. Carroll, p. 57; F. Edward Freeman, *Strategic Management: A Stakeholder Approach* (Boston: Pitman, 1984), p. 25.

21. For a review of research on environmental scanning, see David M. Dozier, "The Innovation of Research in Public Relations Practice: Review of a Program of Studies," *Public Relations Research Annual*, Vol. 2 (1990), pp. 3–28.

22. Grunig and Hunt, *Managing Public Relations*, Chapter 8.

23. For a description of the technique, see Larissa A. Grunig, "Using Focus Group Research in Public Relations," *Public Relations Review* 16 (Summer 1990), pp. 36–49.

24. James E. Grunig, "Sierra Club Study Shows Who Becomes Activists," *Public Relations Review* 15 (Fall 1989), pp. 3–24.

25. Robert L. Heath and Richard Alan Nelson, *Issues Management: Corporate Public Policymaking in an Information Society* (Newbury Park, CA: Sage, 1986), p. 37.

26. Heath and Nelson, p. 195; Heath, "Corporate Issues Management," p. 36. See also Richard E. Crable and Steven L. Vibbert, "Managing Issues and Influencing Public Policy," *Public Relations Review* 11 (Summer 1985), pp. 3–16.

27. See, for example, Chapter 25 on special interest groups by the CEO of Hill and Knowlton, Robert L. Dilenschneider, *Power and Influence* (New York: Prentice-Hall Press, 1990).

28. Heath and Douglas, Heath, and W. Howard Chase, *Issues Management: Origins of the Future* (Stamford, CT: Issue Action Press).

29. Garrett J. O'Keefe, "'Taking a Bite Out of Crime': The Impact of a Public Information Campaign," *Communication Research* 12 (1985), pp. 147–178.

30. David M. Dozier and William P. Ehling, "Evaluation of Public Relations Programs: What the Literature Tells Us About Their Effects," in James E. Grunig (ed.), *Excellence in Public Relations and Communication Management* (Hillsdale, NJ: Lawrence Erlbaum Associates, 1992), pp. 159–184.

31. Grunig and Hunt, *Managing Public Relations*, Chapter 7.

32. Grunig and Hunt, *Managing Public Relations*, Chapter 9.

33. Broom and Dozier, *Using Research in Public Relations*, pp. 14–20; Dozier, "The Innovation of Research in Public Relations Practice."

ADDITIONAL READING

Broom, Glen M., and David M. Dozier, *Using Research in Public Relations* (Englewood Cliffs, NJ: Prentice-Hall, 1990).

Dilenschneider, Robert L., *Power and Influence* (New York: Prentice-Hall Press, 1990).

Grunig, James E. (ed.), *Excellence in Public Relations and Communication Management* (Hillsdale, NJ: Lawrence Erlbaum Associates, 1992).

Grunig, James E., and Todd Hunt, *Managing Public Relations*, 2d ed. (Fort Worth: Harcourt Brace & Company, 1994).

2

Planning and Executing
the Public Relations Campaign

Because planning is such an important part of public relations, it is useful to understand the different requirements of an *event*, a *campaign*, and a *program*.

An *event* is a one-shot occurrence. It happens in one time frame—an hour, a day, or perhaps as long as a week—and it serves one prime purpose with one or more selected publics. (In marketing terminology, a "promotion," such as a contest, giveaway or celebrity visit, is similar to a PR event.) If an organization's leader retires and a banquet is held in conjunction with the retirement, that would be an event. A special tour set up to enable the trade press to visit a new facility is an event. If the President of the United States invites the leader of your organization to the White House, you will gain publicity from the event.

A *campaign* has at least one thing in common with an event: a specific beginning and ending point. But because those two points are separated by weeks or even months, and because several different events will be part of the process, we call it a campaign. Obviously, an election campaign is a good example. If the legislature is due to vote on a bill that affects your organization, the ways you target your publics with information add up to a campaign. Campaigns necessarily build to a decision point such as an election or a vote.

A *program* is like a campaign in that it consists of several events. But it differs from a campaign in that it has no pre-set end point. A program is put in place because of an anticipated need for continued dissemination of information. The program is reviewed periodically to determine whether its objectives are being met. All or parts of it will be continued as long as there is a need for more communication with target publics.

Drug education, driving safety, blood donation, adoption, nutrition—these are all social situations that call for continuing programs, because complete resolution of the problem is never achieved.

When public relations people and their counterparts in marketing and advertising sit down to define a situation and begin the planning process, temporary chaos can result if no one defines whether an event, a campaign, or a program is in order. The deciding factor may be the types of *objectives* desired by the client. We discussed five general objectives of communication in Chapter 1: communication, accuracy, understanding, agreement, and complementary objectives. The following are some specific examples of those objectives.

Objectives for an event include: Attendance by a certain number of people. One-time dissemination of information to a target public. Putting something "on the record" for an organization and its publics. Gaining press attention. All are examples of the communication objective.

Objectives for a campaign might be: Delivering a positive vote or reaction at the proper time (behavior). Building support for an issue that will be resolved in due course (agreement). Raising funds for an organization so that it can proceed with growth (behavior). Attracting enough support to guarantee continuance or survival of an organization at a critical time (understanding).

Objectives for a program could include: Creating and maintaining a level of support for an ongoing program (understanding). Opening and maintaining contact with other organizations that enable your organization to continue its functions (communication).

Any organization can be involved in events, campaigns, and programs simultaneously. An example would be a community blood bank:

■ Getting the governor to donate a pint of blood at the beginning of the holiday season, when donations typically lag, would be an *event* that could attract press attention and inform people about the need to help.

■ At the same time, the blood bank might kick off a *campaign* to enlist 1,000 people who would agree to schedule their donations for the weeks before New Year's Day, Memorial Day, the Fourth of July and Labor Day—the times each year when the blood supply reaches a critical low.

■ Meanwhile, the blood bank could launch a *program* to involve more companies and their employees in twice-a-year donations conducted in the workplace, with the companies rewarding each employee a day off with pay for every two donations.

Typically public relations people are working on many projects at one time. Understanding the difference between events, campaigns

Exhibit 2.1
Du Pont Celebrates
Innovation

At the 1939 World's Fair in New York, E. I. du Pont de Nemours and Co. introduced nylon to the public by showing coal, air, and water going into one end of a mythical machine and delicate nylon stockings coming out of the other.

Fifty years later, Du Pont saw the golden anniversary of its product as an opportunity not only to celebrate, but also to remind consumers that the company's global reputation is based on its leadership in product innovation.

In a wide-ranging program, the firm prepared video news releases that were pegged to the anniversary of nylon but focused also on current and planned research. The news media tended to use the historical footage in its reports, but Du Pont is satisfied that it will reap long-term benefits because it took the opportunity to remind editors and program producers of its role in science and business.

Source: "Nylon Anniversary Du Pont's Chance to Talk Up New Research," *PR STRATEGIES/USA*, Vol. 1, No. 1, Feb. 1–15, 1988.

and programs is one way they can allocate their resources of time and money more effectively.

MISSION, GOALS, AND OBJECTIVES

When a football team steps out on the field, the players have no control over the strategies and tactics the other team will use. Nobody can predict the breaks that will alter the course of the game. In the face of these uncertainties, the coaches develop a "game plan" around which they can organize their actions. The game plan might call for maintaining a deliberate, controlled ground game using certain players to run certain patterns at the perceived weaknesses of the other team. Specific plays are selected because they will deliver what the general game plan calls for. The main idea, of course, is to win by doing what your team does best.

Successful organizations also base their actions on a game plan. The process starts with the enunciation of a *mission statement*. This is an important part of strategic planning, as it was discussed in Chapter 1. For a manufacturing company, the mission statement might include "making a fair profit for our stockholders by developing and distributing the highest-quality goods to a national market." The mission statement also might cover "treating our consumers and employees fairly and being good citizens of the communities where our facilities are located." A nonprofit organization's mission statement might call for "Increasing

Mission statements may also take the form of a company creed, such as the now-famous Johnson & Johnson Credo that guided the firm during the Tylenol tampering crisis. Public relations managers at Warner-Lambert analyzed the mission statement of other companies before writing this creed, which is included in press kits distributed to the media and is disseminated to all employees.

WARNER-LAMBERT CREED

OUR MISSION is to achieve leadership in advancing the health and well-being of people throughout the world. We believe this mission can best be accomplished by recognizing and meeting our fundamental responsibilities to our customers, employees, shareholders, suppliers and society.

To Our Customers

WE ARE COMMITTED to providing high-quality health care and consumer products of real value that meet customer needs. We are committed to continued investment in the discovery of safe and effective products to enhance people's lives.

To Our Employees

WE ARE COMMITTED to attracting and retaining capable people, providing them with challenging work in an open and participatory environment, marked by equal opportunity for personal growth. Performance will be evaluated on the basis of fair and objective standards. Creativity and innovation will be encouraged. Employees will be treated with dignity and respect. They will be actively encouraged to make suggestions for improving the effectiveness of the enterprise and the quality of work life.

To Our Shareholders

WE ARE COMMITTED to providing a fair and attractive economic return to our shareholders, and we are prepared to take prudent risks to achieve sustainable long-term corporate growth.

To Our Suppliers

WE ARE COMMITTED to dealing with our suppliers and all our business partners in a fair and equitable manner, recognizing our mutual interests.

To Society

WE ARE COMMITTED to being good corporate citizens, actively initiating and supporting efforts concerned with the health of society, particularly the vitality of the worldwide communities in which we operate.

ABOVE ALL, our dealings with these constituencies will be conducted with the utmost integrity, adhering to the highest standards of ethical and just conduct.

Reproduced courtesy of Warner-Lambert

knowledge about Huntington's disease among the people of California and raising funds for the state chapter of the Huntington's Disease Society to support research at state and national levels."

Out of the mission statement grows a list of *goals*—somewhat more specific than the mission statement, but still general in nature and unspecific as to time frame or numerical targets. Goals for the manufacturing company might be "to be a market leader in the small appliance field." For the nonprofit organization, a goal might be to "offer assistance to all families in the state that are affected by Huntington's disease."

Only when a mission statement and goals are in place can the management of an organization move to the necessary task of setting *objectives*. What makes objectives different from mission and goals is their specificity. An objective should specify the desired *effect* as specifically as possible: "To increase the number of senators who understand the Leukemia Society of America's position on research funding from forty-five senators to seventy-five senators by November 1" (understanding), or "To decrease the number of newspapers in the state that oppose rate reforms for the insurance industry from 60 percent to 40 percent by the first of the year" (agreement).

Well-articulated objectives specify a time frame and the number of people or projects affected. When objectives contain specific times and numbers, they are measurable. Management can determine regularly whether objectives are being met. If they are not, either more realistic objectives must be set or more effective events, campaigns, or programs should be developed.

ELEMENTS OF THE COMPLETE PROGRAM

Once goals and objectives are in place, they can be drawn upon to plan campaigns and programs. Marston's well-known RACE formula for public relations programs described four distinct phases:

> *research* on the problem or opportunity,
>
> *action* that includes evaluation and planning,
>
> *communication* of the messages from organization to publics, and
>
> *evaluation* of the effects of those messages.[1]

Grunig's "Behavioral Molecule" further broke the management steps down into:

> *detecting* a problem,
>
> *constructing* a possible solution,
>
> *defining* alternatives,
>
> *selecting* the best course of action,
>
> *confirming* the choice by pre-testing,
>
> *behaving* by enacting a program, and then returning to the process of
>
> *detecting* whether the program met the desired objectives.[2]

LOS ANGELES WATER CONSERVATION CAMPAIGN

Because of continuing drought conditions, the Los Angeles Department of Water and Power conducted a public relations campaign to reduce water usage.

Research consisted of a survey of consumer attitudes that showed only 55 percent of consumers realized that a drought existed and only 38 percent thought that water conservation was "extremely important."

Planning began with setting an objective of informing all customers about the drought conditions and the importance of water conservation, with a target of 10 percent voluntary reduction in water use during the high-usage period of June through September.

Execution focused primarily on getting the weather forecasters from the twelve television stations in the area to include mentions of the water shortage in their daily weathercasts, and to urge citizens to conserve water.

Evaluation included tracking (repeated surveying) of six hundred customers as well as monitoring of water usage. Awareness of the problem and the need for conservation rose, and water consumption dropped 6 percent. While the objective was not met completely, the goal of reducing water consumption was met sufficiently to carry the area through the drought.[4] ■ ■ ■

Perhaps the most prevalent model in the field for judging the effectiveness of a public relations program is the one prescribed for organizations that compete for the Silver Anvil Awards presented by the Public Relations Society of America (PRSA). Each entrant in the PRSA competition must organize its presentation under four required categories:

Research—Quality of original and secondary research used to identify the problem or opportunity and the approach likely to be successful.

Planning—Objectives, originality and judgment in selecting strategy and techniques, accuracy of budget, and difficulties encountered.

Execution—How the plan was implemented, materials used; in-progress adjustments to the plan; techniques in winning management's support; other techniques; difficulties encountered; and effectiveness of the program's employment of dollar, personnel, and other resources.

Evaluation—Efforts made to identify, analyze, and quantify results and to what degree a program has met its objectives.[3]

While the PRSA Silver Anvil criteria clearly are aimed at assisting with the task of preparing and presenting a contest entry, they indicate very strongly the methods accepted in the field for organizing and executing a program. Before we consider each step in the process, let's look at some Silver Anvil winners that followed each step of the process effectively. (See the Case Studies on pp. 28–30.)

In these three case studies, the research methods included:

SELECTING RESEARCH METHODS

- surveys (to determine customer attitudes about water conservation, and to ascertain the way people view raisins);
- focus groups (to determine the level of knowledge people have about AIDS, and also to gauge reactions to designs for a brochure); and
- analysis of data gathered by an industry (to determine slack sales periods for raisins).

Research can be extensive and expensive, or, if the situation warrants, it can involve simply poring over existing information already gathered for another purpose and analyzing the relevance the data have

---

Congress mandated that the U.S. Department of Health and Human Services produce a brochure on Acquired Immune Deficiency Syndrome and mail it to every household in the country. Over 100 million brochures on the disease were mailed, including a Spanish-language version.

Research consisted of focus groups that determined the level of knowledge about AIDS among representative groups. Focus groups also were used to get reactions to the design and content of the brochure before it was produced.

Planning began with outlining objectives that called for ensuring that all Americans would read, understand, and discuss the information about AIDS, that an information network would be set up to handle questions resulting from the mailing, and

that the media would increase coverage of AIDS issues.

Execution included not only the mailing of the brochure to all homes, but also print releases and public service announcements calling the attention of all citizens to the fact that they would be receiving important information meant for family discussion.

Evaluation by the Gallup Poll and the National Center for Health Statistics showed that "Understanding AIDS" was the most widely-read publication in the country in June 1988, with a total adult readership of 86.9 million. Eighty-two percent read at least part of it, and two-thirds discussed it with friends or family members. The brochure was effective in reaching two target groups with a low level of information about AIDS—young people and blacks.[5] ■ ■ ■

Case Study

THE NATIONAL AIDS BROCHURE MAILING

CALIFORNIA RAISINS GRASSROOTS CAMPAIGN

The advertising campaign for California Raisins made the dancing Claymation figures popular, but the California Raisin Advisory Board needed a public relations campaign to gain the desired purchasing behaviors.

Research included a customer attitude survey showing that most consumers know raisins are nutritious, but consider them "wimpy" and "uncool." Analysis of industry data showed that raisin sales are lowest in the summer months.

Planning included specific objectives for increasing raisin sales during the summer, making the product "cool," and promoting membership in a fan club for the California Raisin characters. Costumed characters were to be sent on a tour of the country from New York to Los Angeles to give daily performances.

Execution involved events where the mayor of each city presented a proclamation to the Raisin characters. Product giveaways and media appearances were held in conjunction with the performances. The tour culminated in Los Angeles with a birthday party benefitting the favorite charity of Ray Charles, who inspired a famous raisin character. The party resulted in a ninety-second video news release distributed by satellite to television stations nationwide.

Evaluation showed an increase in raisin sales of 20 percent by the end of the summer, three thousand members for the fan club, a total of ten hours of television air time for the promotion, and 110 million print impressions. Most of the media coverage mentioned that raisins are "hip" and "cool." Follow-up focus groups revealed that people felt more positively about raisins.[6] ■ ■ ■

for the current public relations situation. You will recall that the head of the small public relations agency in the anecdote at the beginning of Chapter 1 used a computer database to find all sorts of research that already had been done by others. Analysis of that information was sufficient to give the agency an understanding of how to present its ideas to a potential client.

Surveys

Surveys often are performed by opinion measurement specialists, although increasingly people with college training in public relations are able to prepare, administer, and analyze the data from their own questionnaires. As the public relations grad learns in the PR research course, samples of target audiences must be scientific and random if the results are to be valid. Questionnaires must be constructed carefully to rule out bias and to assure the validity of each item, which involves pre-testing. If done properly, the survey may take weeks to design, test, administer, and analyze—often at considerable expense. Fortunately, new software packages designed for the personal computer make it possible for the researcher to glean a wealth of data, including interesting correlations between various responses on the survey. That richness may make the expense of time and money worthwhile.

Focus Group Interviews

Focus group interviews are a marketing research technique that has been successfully adapted to the needs of public relations practitioners. They do not yield the strictly quantitative data that can be gotten from a survey. But they have the advantage of being open-ended and permitting members of target groups to speak in their own terms of understanding, provide their own emphasis, and respond to the views expressed by other members of the same group. The focus group interview requires trained moderators and equipment for recording the sessions. Audio and/or video tapes have to be put in transcript form, and then the transcripts must be summarized and analyzed. Sometimes focus group interviews are used as the basis for designing the questionnaires used in survey research, creating a valuable linkage between the two devices and enhancing the value of both. An example is the focus group research done by Larissa A. Grunig at the University of Maryland that sought to learn the attitudes of adults toward the housing of mentally ill people in apartment buildings within the community. "The focus groups were considered formative research, to be conducted before a telephone survey of a sample of all county residents and well ahead of the public relations plan to be developed and implemented by the consulting firm," the report said.[7]

Analysis of Data

Analysis of data that already exist can be the fastest, and often the least expensive, means of acquiring information that can help with the planning of a public relations campaign. Some examples:

- When Macomb Community College in Michigan wanted to approach taxpayers for increased support, analysis by the public relations firm of Bock and Associates of previous votes on public issues showed that a large turnout meant the greatest likelihood of success for the college's fund request. As a result, the public relations campaign and vote were timed to coincide with the next presidential election.[8]
- When the Children's Hospital Medical Center of Akron sought to position itself as specializing in the emotional and social

well-being of children and their families during medical treatment, secondary research included studying the admissions and functions of all twenty-seven hospitals in the area, and also an analysis of national statistics on "latchkey" children who return from school to their homes without parental supervision—a phenomenon that has a bearing on the independence and/or the emotional needs of many children who are treated.

■ When *Time* magazine decided to help increase voter turnout in the 1988 presidential election by staging a "National Student/Parent Mock Election," it started by analyzing census and population statistics, sociological studies of voter turnout and apathy, and characteristics of nonvoters in the United States.

■ When Hill and Knowlton was engaged to counter the negative publicity directed by AT&T and others at the Open Software Foundation—a nonprofit group formed by leading computer manufacturers, including IBM—the public relations agency hired a media research firm to perform in-depth content analysis on 450 news stories to learn exactly which were the most frequent and the most damaging negative statements made about the client and its mission. Objectives were drawn specifically to counteract those negative statements.

TAILORING IT TO YOUR PUBLICS

As we saw in the introductory chapter, identifying your key publics—those groups that are most likely to seek and process information and to behave in a way that has consequences on your organization—is a fundamental aim of the process we call public relations management.

Two programs planned by public relations students at Rutgers University for outside clients supposedly had "all Rutgers students" as the audience. The downtown merchants association wanted a campaign to attract students to their stores; the area's blood bank wanted to increase donations. Both clients assumed that all students at the university would be the target group. Surveys and focus groups conducted by the public relations students indicated otherwise. Upperclassmen were already set in their ways. If they had not previously shopped in the stores near campus, and if they had not previously donated blood, the indications were that it would be very difficult to change their behaviors with a one-shot information campaign.

Instead, the student-run agencies decided to target incoming freshmen for long-range programs aimed at creating and maintaining behaviors favorable to the clients' goals. First-year students have not fully formed their attitudes and behaviors. They are more susceptible to persuasion than upperclass students who already have set patterns. The program prepared for the blood bank, for example, aimed not merely to get the first-year students to donate once, but to pledge a donation every semester while they are in college—an expected eight times during their career for a total donation of one gallon of blood. (The reward: a special symbol next to their names in the graduation program.)

Once target audiences have been selected, it is important to decide what message each group needs to receive from your organization. Rarely does an information campaign give precisely the same message to each of its publics. That's because careful analysis shows that each public has a different stake in the organization. When Cleveland Scholarship Programs, Inc., an organization that helps disadvantaged inner-city students attend college, used the occasion of its twentieth anniversary to highlight its contributions to the community, its public relations agency specified three key publics and a slightly different message for each of them:[9]

Audience	Message
Donors	"We've earned your support."
Educators	"Our types of programs work."
News Media	"The programs are worthy of news coverage."

Similarly, when the Crafted with Pride in U.S.A. Council—an industry coalition dedicated to promoting American-made apparel and fashions—planned a campaign associated with the Miss America pageant, it spelled out three different audiences and distinct messages for each:[10]

Audience	Message
Retailers	"The Made in U.S.A. label is a valuable selling tool."
Manufacturers	"Producing at home is good business."
Consumers	"Made in U.S.A. means quality."

Formulating different messages for different publics is worth the extra expense. A sophisticated management team knows it is important to tune in to the needs of each public and make certain that those needs are met.

FITTING IT TO THE BUDGET

We have learned to identify key publics and make sure that their information needs are served before we concern ourselves with the so-called "general public." It follows, then, that the campaign or program aimed at the most important public is *fully funded* before additional money is

Exhibit 2.2
Essay Contests
Build Awareness

One of the tried-and-true public relations devices for creating aware-ness is the essay contest. When the competition for prize money, trips, or scholarships is offered to teachers as a way of getting students in-terested in writing, the campaign gains credibility by becoming a school-sanctioned activity.

At one point in the mid-1980s, both sides in the controversy over cigarette smoking were holding national essay contests. Philip Morris asked students to write essays discussing the effects of advertising bans on "free expression in a free market economy." The company of-fered a $15,000 grand prize, plus smaller awards for the best entry in each state. A coalition called Doctors Ought to Care (DOC) countered with a $1,000 essay contest that asked law students to write on the subject of "Are tobacco company executives criminally liable for the deaths, diseases and fires that their products cause?"

The Cox Cable Company in San Diego wanted to make teachers aware of the services it offered to schools, including C-SPAN coverage of Congress. The cable company used a county-wide essay contest with the topic "How Does TV Promote Freedom of Speech in Amer-ica," and offered a grand prize of a five-day, all-expenses-paid trip to Washington, D.C.

Sources: Associated Press, "Both Sides in Cigarette Fight Hold National Es-say Contests," *The New York Times,* Nov. 5, 1986, p. A–18; Case Study No. 2,195, "Using an Essay Contest to Increase Public Awareness of a Company's Iden-tity," *Public Relations News,* Vol. 45, No. 46, Nov. 27, 1989, p. 3.

spent on programs aimed at secondary publics—a concept explored fully in *Managing Public Relations.*

If key publics have not been identified in the planning stage, there is a likelihood that "a little money will be spent on this, and a little on that"—an advertisement here, T-shirts there, and probably an all-purpose brochure just because somebody says "we ought to have a brochure." Budgeting must follow the setting of goals and objectives, and it also must follow the identification of key publics. It precedes me-dia selection and message design.

If budgeting is done at the wrong point in the process, it is difficult for public relations people to explain their financial needs to management. If, on the other hand, the "homework" has been done, management can bet-ter understand the request for the dollars needed to accomplish the objec-tives set for the key publics.

An example is the dean of a college who willingly appropriated $5,000 for a dinner to be held for 100 selected alumni. The school's de-velopment staff could demonstrate that the $50 per head tab would be

Bacon's publishes several specialized directories that help public relations people to target the media and the specific editors they wish to reach with their news releases, photos, and story ideas.

Photo courtesy of Bacon's Information, Inc.

well spent. Research and personal contacts had identified each alumnus as a person likely to support the school with a continuing annual contribution of $100 or more.

Many of the chapters that follow in this book focus on the workings of various channels or media of mass communication. ("Channel" is the term used by communication theorists; it usually is synonymous with the popular term "media.") In these chapters we will try to show the strengths of each medium and the ways public relations people shape a message to fit a medium's technical requirements.

During the planning of a campaign or program, part of the analysis of each key public should include such questions as:

- ■ Where do members of our key publics get their information?
- ■ Which media do they rely upon to make decisions about what is important and how to behave?
- ■ Which channels provide the two-way communication that enables key publics to provide information to our organization about their needs and concerns?

SELECTING CHANNELS AND MEDIA

Case Study

THE CRUSADER BABY CAMPAIGN

The General Health Care Corporation of Piscataway, New Jersey, had seen its market slipping away as parents increasingly chose the perceived convenience of disposable diapers over the use of a diaper laundering service. When the issue of the environmental impact of using disposable diapers grew in importance, General Health Care Corporation saw an opportunity to regain market share. It turned to Gaston & Gordon Associates, Inc., of Flemington, New Jersey, for help.[11]

Research by Gaston & Gordon showed services that launder and return cotton diapers for reuse had been losing business for two decades as disposable diapers became ever more popular. But there was an increasing interest in environmental concerns, and the negative impact of

disposable diapers on landfills could be documented. Gaston & Gordon Associates conducted surveys of current and former customers of diaper services to determine levels of awareness concerning the environmental impact of using disposables. They compiled a media list of editors who were interested in environmental topics, as well as a list of legislators, environmental leaders, and heads of parents' organizations—all people who could help bring the issue to target publics.

The public relations firm then began to think about a way of dramatizing the issue for its publics. Recalling that the cartoon character Smokey the Bear had been successful in getting people to be concerned about forest fires, the creative team came up with their own symbol: *Crusader Baby.* In

Another level of analysis focuses on the characteristics of each medium and their relationship to the campaign or program:

- Which media allow us to get our point of view across most effectively?
- Which media are best suited to the information requirements of our campaign, such as the presenting of visual images, the need for two-way communication, or the ability to tell a story in depth?
- Which media are most cost-effective for this type of information?

Some of the data about media effectiveness can be obtained by checking the various guides, such as *Bacon's Publicity Checker,* for each type of medium. They list circulation for print media, audience breakdowns for broadcast media, and geographic regions where penetration is greatest. Most every state has media guides produced specifically for the local or regional areas. Specialized references such as the annual *Media Guide* published by Polyconomics, Inc., analyze the audience for each publication in terms of liberal or conservative bias and involvement in various social issues.

the words of agency principal Cheryl Gaston: "On paper and in person, 'our nation's newest superheroine' would present the environmental issue on behalf of babies everywhere who were entitled to the legacy of a healthy planet. She would point out that the solution was 'only an attitude away,' that 'disposable diapers are a no-no,' that 'just because you toss them doesn't mean they go away.'"

Crusader Baby appearances were scheduled at shopping malls, and with legislators. Every item sent to the media in news releases and press kits included the Crusader Baby graphic. The results were rewarding: use of diaper services in the test market of Philadelphia increased dramatically, information about the program was requested from around the world, legislators sought information from the public relations agency on drafting legislation encouraging the use of diaper services, and Crusader Baby received mail and requests for personal appearances from all over the country.

The six-month Crusader Baby campaign that ended in April 1989, cost the client only about $65,000 and resulted in increased sales that overwhelmingly justified the expense of the public relations effort. The campaign came at a time when the entire nation was beginning to be aware of the problem, and on the twentieth anniversary of Earth Day in April 1990, the revival of diaper services was hailed by the media as an example of the growing concern about the environment. ■ ■ ■

Focus group interviews are another important tool for discovering where members of key publics get their information and which people are most influential in shaping the opinions of constituent groups. Analysis of letters written to an organization sometimes provide an indication of where involved and information-seeking audience members are getting their data, and which members of the community are influencing them through which channels of communication.

If the objective is to inform the greatest number of people so that they (1) know about a program your organization is conducting, and (2) have a positive view of that program, then the *news* media—television, radio and newspapers—may be the best channel. But if you must convince the leaders of influential but small professional organizations to support an issue, then articles in specialized business or public affairs magazines may better explain the complex issue and convince the leaders to "deliver" the support of the members of their organizations.

Careful analysis often shows that mass media are not sufficient. Direct, face-to-face communication with key individuals may be the necessary channel.

"CREATIVITY" HAS ITS PLACE

We suspect that some faces fell at the beginning of this book when we suggested that an agency called "Creative Communications" might not take the most thorough approach to analyzing the needs of a client. After all, many of the people who go into public relations as a line of work do so because they consider themselves "creative."

The majority of public relations programs involve the application of tried-and-true devices: plant tours, informational brochures, press briefings, speeches, news releases, and audio-visual presentations. Mastering the preparation of standard message formats is, in the long run, more important than coming up with clever gimmicks for capturing the attention of publics and the media.

All that aside, creativity has its place in public relations, and we would be remiss if we failed to acknowledge that many a campaign takes off because somebody comes up with a clever concept on which to pin a solid program. An appropriate example is a Silver Anvil award–winning campaign by a small agency working on behalf of a small firm with a specialized service: laundering baby diapers. In this campaign, "creativity" was not a panacea in itself. It was the frosting on the cake for a public relations idea whose time had come.

Some other examples of creative boosts for public relations campaigns: Ralston Purina used a doggie beauty pageant hosted by Bert Parks to introduce its new Dog Chow for small dogs; Procter and Gamble held a Sing-Off in shower stalls to promote Coast soap, with the finals at Radio City Music Hall hosted by, again, Bert Parks; to increase sales, the Rockport Shoe Company founded the Rockport Walking Institute to study walking and the Rockport Fitness Walking Test to promote the Institute's findings that walking is America's most popular form of cardiovascular exercise; because transatlantic bookings were down, British Airways arranged a lottery for Americans who booked passage to London, with the winners joining Prime Minister Margaret Thatcher at home for tea.

NOTES

1. John E. Marston, *Modern Public Relations* (New York: McGraw-Hill, 1979), pp. 185–203.
2. James E. Grunig and Todd Hunt, *Managing Public Relations* (New York: Holt, Rinehart and Winston, 1984), pp. 104–108.
3. The criteria here are reproduced verbatim from the PRSA materials distributed to Silver Anvil Awards applicants.
4. The Los Angeles public relations firm of Gumpertz/Bentley/Fried prepared many elements of the campaign for the Los Angeles Department of Water and Power.
5. The National AIDS Mailing was accomplished with the assistance of Ogilvy and Mather Public Affairs, Washington, D.C.

6. The California Raisins grassroots promotion was designed and executed by Ketchum Public Relations, San Francisco.

7. Larissa A. Grunig, "Using Focus Group Research in Public Relations," *Public Relations Review* 16 (Summer 1990), pp. 36–49.

8. The Macomb Community College case and others in this section are 1989 Silver Anvil winners.

9. Edward Howard & Co. was the public relations agency for the Cleveland Scholarships Programs, Inc. fiftieth anniversary campaign.

10. The Rowland Company, New York, was the public relations agency for the "Made in the U.S.A./Miss America" campaign.

11. Gaston & Gordon Associates, Inc., is located in Flemington, NJ.

ADDITIONAL READING

Brody, E. W., *Public Relations Programming and Production* (New York: Praeger, 1988).

Broom, Glen M., and David M. Dozier, *Using Research in Public Relations: Applications and Program Management* (Englewood Cliffs, NJ: Prentice-Hall, 1990).

Cantor, Bill, *Experts in Action: Inside Public Relations,* 2d ed., edited by Chester Burger (New York: Longman, 1989).

Lindenmann, Walter K., ed. "Using Research to Plan and Evaluate Public Relations," *Public Relations Review* 16 (Special Issue, Summer 1990).

Nager, Norman R., and T. Harrell Allen, *Public Relations Management by Objectives* (New York: Longman, 1984).

Simmons, Robert E., *Communication Campaign Management: A Systems Approach* (New York: Longman, 1990).

3

Media Relations

In a book on public relations written by thirty-eight practicing experts, Carole Howard, vice president of public relations and communication policy at *Reader's Digest,* titled her chapter "Media Relations: Public Relations' Basic Activity."[1] Media relations does indeed make up the core of most public relations programs—in part because of the historical development of public relations as an attempt to control and influence media coverage of organizations.

Although the media are critical to public relations, many practitioners become so preoccupied with media coverage that they forget why relationships with the mass media are important. Many practitioners consider the media to be *the* public for their organization and believe that media coverage automatically means that they have *reached* and *influenced* a large audience. Nothing could be further from the truth. The media are conduits to strategic publics of the organization. But there are other conduits as well—such as face-to-face communication or specialized publications. Nevertheless, the mass media probably are the major channels to publics; and they certainly are the channels most familiar to practitioners.

Water pipes under your streets also are conduits. They bring water from a pumping station to homes and businesses throughout a community. Just because water travels through the pipes doesn't mean that people drink it, however. Nevertheless, the pipe must be open before the managers of the pumping station can get water to users.

The media serve the same function for public relations. If the pipe is open, your messages can get to members of your publics—if they choose to open the faucet at the other end. But if a "gatekeeper" shuts the system, the water can't get through. As a result, the job of the media relations manager is to build open and trusting *relationships* with reporters and editors so that they keep the media channel open to your publics.

Media relations occupies a central position in public relations because the media serve as "gatekeepers" who control the information that flows to publics in a social system. Media workers really aren't publics in the sense that they are affected by organizational consequences that do not affect other people.

But, in another sense, journalists are publics. They seek and process information just like other people, then pass on that information to their readers and viewers. The communication behavior of journalists, therefore, sets limits on the information available for other publics to seek and process.

Although journalists communicate like members of other publics, they are not strategic publics in themselves. Strategic planning should drive media relations in the sense that journalists are not important unless they are gatekeepers in media used by the strategic publics of the organization. A public relations department should have a strategic plan in which it has identified the publics that most affect the organization (see Chapter 1). Then it should build relationships with the media that offer the potential of communicating with these strategic publics.[2]

The key word to remember about media relations is "relationship"— "a positive, ongoing, long-term relationship with the media."[3] Carole Howard and Wilma Mathews, of *Reader's Digest* and AT&T, respectively, explained the importance of relationships in this way:

> The emphasis in a media relations program should be on the relations aspect—working to build long-term relationships with the people who cover your organization. Good media contacts proliferate once they are established. As is true with many good relationships, they are built only gradually, based on a variety of contacts over time, and strengthened by experiences that foster growing knowledge and respect.[4]

Robert Dilenschneider, the former chief executive officer of Hill and Knowlton and now head of his own firm, also emphasized viewing media relations as the building of relationships:

> Look at your dealings with the press as relationships. You need to establish credibility with reporters over time. They may want to talk about a very routine press release, not a breakthrough announcement of some new product, but it may tie into some other story they are working on. Make a point of being available for the commonplace. If reporters call looking for insight or reactions when a major news event breaks, or they are doing an industry roundup, cooperate.[5]

Many practitioners have bad relationships with the media, in large part because they are guided by the press agentry or public information models of public relations (see Chapter 1). This chapter begins, therefore, with a discussion of the conflict between journalists and public relations practitioners and the practices that produce the conflict. Then it turns to positive, symmetrical practices that produce good relationships with the media.

An Area of Conflict

To listen to journalists and public relations practitioners talk about each other is to get the impression that the field of media relations is a battleground. Journalists feel besieged by hordes of press agents and publicists—"flacks," as they call PR people—who dump unwanted press releases on their desks and push self-serving stories that have little news value.

Public relations practitioners, on the other hand, feel they are at the mercy of reporters and editors who are biased against their organization, who would rather expose than explain, and who know little about the complexities of their organization.

The Media's Side   Newspaper editors frequently form their impressions of media relations specialists from the press releases they get in the mail. One sharp-tongued editor vented his frustration this way:

> *When I moved from managing editor . . . I took my desk-height wastebasket with me. I can slide the press releases into it while talking on the phone. I don't need to crumple anything, or even aim carefully. I seldom need to read anything.*[6]

The *Washington Post* once declared itself off limits to all public relations people. In an article entitled, "'Post' Stabs PR in the Flack," *Advertising Age* reported on a memo written by editorial page editor Meg Greenfield to executive editor Benjamin Bradlee:

> *Ms. Greenfield's memo to Mr. Bradlee is replete with phrases which indicate she feels she is being used. She wrote: "Why should we be in their campaign plans as something 'deliverable' by their various agents who can 'reach' us?" She insisted: "We don't want any of that damn crowd around here, and if people want to get to us they need only know two things: It's easy as pie, so long as they don't come in (or send their manuscripts in or make their request) via a flack firm. . . . We have adopted a rule of simply refusing to deal with these people—period."*[7]

A study of Texas journalists and public relations practitioners showed a wide gap between the two on the value of media relations specialists to newspapers.[8] Of the journalists surveyed:

59 percent thought public relations and the press are partners in the dissemination of information, contrasted to 89 percent of the PR practitioners.

48 percent thought public relations people help reporters obtain accurate, complete, and timely news, contrasted to 91 percent of the PR practitioners.

78 percent believed public relations has cluttered channels of communication with pseudo-events and phony phrases, contrasted to 42 percent of the PR practitioners.

82 percent said PR people obstruct reporters from seeing people they should be seeing, contrasted to 38 percent of the PR practitioners.

84 percent said PR material is usually publicity disguised as news, contrasted to 29 percent of the PR practitioners.

89 percent believed PR people do not understand such journalistic problems as meeting deadlines, attracting reader interest, and making the best use of space, contrasted to 39 percent of the PR practitioners.

Pointing up the fact of their negative feelings about public relations people, only 10 percent of the journalists agreed that public relations is a profession equal in status to journalism; 76 percent of the PR people surveyed agreed with that statement.

In another part of the same study, journalists and public relations practitioners ranked six news values.[9] Both journalists and practitioners ranked "accuracy" and "interest to the reader" as the two top values. When asked to predict how the other group would rank the six values, however, the journalists predicted that the PR people would put accuracy and interest among the lowest three values and that they would rank "depicting the subject in a favorable light" and "prompt publication" as the most important values. The PR people, in contrast, accurately predicted the news values of the journalists.

The PR Side The *Washington Post*'s Meg Greenfield seemed to think she had the obvious answer to her frustration with public relations representatives: Get rid of them and let organizational executives speak for themselves. That answer is oversimplified, PR people would respond. Executives fear the media and would be crucified without PR help. According to PR counselor Carlton Spitzer:

High-level executives, who coolly manage the affairs of multi-million-dollar international corporations, crumble at the sight of an unfavorable story in a newspaper and reach instant boiling point when confronted with a mislead-ing headline. . . . The news media are the most powerful outside force in the life of a business executive. An uncontrollable, unpackageable force, seemingly out to get business . . .[10]

Managers of large organizations, particularly business leaders, be-lieve the media have a definite bias against them.[11] At least one public relations director has attributed this alleged media bias to a shift from an "objective" to an "interpretive" style of reporting.[12]

In a survey of 470 members of the Public Relations Society of Amer-ica, 53 percent of the respondents said they had been misquoted during the past year.[13] When asked, "What do you believe is the major cause for a lack of fairness in news reporting?" the respondents cited either individual or organizational bias as the major reason:

Personal bias by reporter	43.8 percent
Bias of paper, magazine, etc.	31.1 percent
Sloppy reporting	27.0 percent
Poorly trained reporters	22.3 percent
Haste in reporting	20.6 percent

The last three answers to this survey also suggest that reporters and editors frequently misinterpret or fail to understand the informa-tion they get from public relations sources. The Weyerhaeuser Co., for example, told *Time* magazine that the Mount St. Helens volcano had de-stroyed 4 percent of its St. Helens Tree Farm—a farm that made up 8 percent of the company's worldwide timber holdings. *Time* reported, however, that the volcano had destroyed 4 percent of all of Weyer-haeuser's holdings.[14]

Public relations scholars have not been content to accept this re-puted adversarial relationship between reporters and public relations practitioners. They have researched the relationship between the two and concluded that it is not as hostile as the anecdotes we have re-viewed here suggest. Pavlik concluded, for example, that "there tends to be a fairly high level of mutual respect—journalists tend to think most PR people do a good job and vice versa. Further, members of each group tend to hold the same news values."[15] In contrast to the beliefs of executives, Pavlik also reported, most stories about organizations are positive or neutral; and fewer than one in five has a negative slant.

L. Grunig studied the relationship of public relations departments with several publics of organizations and found: "Surprisingly, across organizations the most autonomous, cooperative relationship was be-tween the mass media and the organization."[16]

Cameron reviewed this same research and concluded that reporters and public relations practitioners have a better impression of the people they actually have contact with than of the public relations or journalism profession in general.[17] Most reporters and practitioners have similar training in journalistic techniques and similar values. They also depend on each other in their work—the media for story ideas and contacts with news sources and public relations people for access to the media needed to communicate with their publics. Thus, their relationship is more one of interdependence than of conflict.

INTERDEPENDENCE OF MEDIA AND PUBLIC RELATIONS

When he was Secretary of Health, Education, and Welfare in the Nixon Administration, Caspar Weinberger (then called "Cap the Knife") cut the number of public information specialists in the department. He calculated that there were 2,400 public relations people in the department, serving only two reporters covering HEW full-time. He thought a 1,200-to-1 ratio was overkill!

Weinberger ignored the fact that most of those public relations people did not work in media relations, and that many other reporters covered HEW part-time. Most importantly, however, he ignored the fact that a handful of reporters could not begin to cover a department as huge as HEW then was without the assistance of public relations practitioners.

A series of studies of news media in Milwaukee in 1963 and 1975 showed the extent to which the media depend on public relations sources.[18] Those studies showed that about 45 percent of the news items in newspapers and about 15 percent of news items on radio and television originated in one way or another with public relations sources. A somewhat lower percentage of the actual column inches and airtime came from public relations sources, because PR-originated material usually resulted in shorter stories than media-originated material.

A 1977 survey of business and financial editors by the Hill and Knowlton PR agency showed that these editors considered public relations people to be their most important source of information.[19] And, it is common knowledge that most community newspapers could not exist—and definitely could not cover their communities adequately—without the help of public relations people.

More recently, researchers have examined the extent to which editors accept "information subsidies" from public relations sources. Gandy coined the term "information subsidies" to describe material provided to the media by public relations people without any effort or expense by the media.[20] In essence, public relations people act as journalists without being paid by the media when they produce subsidies.

These studies show that public relations people are quite successful in one sense but unsuccessful in another. On the one hand, as the Milwaukee studies of the 1960s and 1970s showed, a large portion of media content comes from public relations subsidies. Berkowitz summarized the results of several studies as showing that from one-half to two-thirds of all news stories were "source-originated."[21] That is, news sources did something to get coverage in the media; reporters and editors did not originate the story. Many, if not most, of those sources had media relations professionals working with them to get coverage—although the studies did not determine how many.

On the other hand, research shows that the media reject a large proportion of the "subsidies" such as press releases that public relations people try to place there. Turk found that newspapers used 51 percent of the information subsidies produced by six state government agencies in Louisiana.[22] As a result, 48 percent of all the stories about the six agencies in newspapers came from these subsidies. Turk also studied the use of handouts from the White House press office and found that about one-third appeared in the media.[23] In contrast, Morton found that daily newspapers used only 7.6 percent of the news releases sent by Oklahoma State University, although weekly newspapers used 9 percent and twice-weeklies 21.6 percent.[24]

The research, therefore, suggests several reasons why the media reject so many of the attempts of public relations practitioners to place stories.[25] Daily newspapers have more reporters and thus less need for subsidies than weekly or twice-weekly newspapers—as Morton's study showed. Second, stories are more likely to be used if they are centered on events. Third, the media use more stories from government than from more "self-serving" organizations such as corporations. Fourth, media use stories with a local angle or similar source of news value. Releases that lack newsworthiness, contain self-serving information, are verbose, and are delivered after deadlines seldom get published.

In short, you will be successful in media relations most often if you think and act as though you were a journalist and if you see your job as one of helping reporters and editors do their job—the title of a chapter in Howard and Mathews' book on media relations.[26] You will be most successful, that is, if you look at your job from the vantage point of the two-way symmetrical model of public relations that was described in Chapter 1.

What Helps and What Hurts Media Relations

It's impossible to supply much more than a cursory list of the tips that experienced media relations specialists have developed for dealing with the media. Many of these tips relate to specific techniques, which are covered in the next five chapters.

You will probably find it easier to learn a few principles, however, from which you can derive more specific rules of press relations. Our four models of public relations provide such principles.

CHECKLIST ✔ Ten Tips for Surviving a Media Interview

---

1. Develop a brief statement of the company's position on the topic or issue. The statement should present the situation in a positive light and have the approval of company management.

2. Identify and coach your spokesperson and others who may be called by the news media. Rehearse them to avoid answers that can be taken out of context, and have them practice aloud, converting tough questions to positive points.

3. Never issue a "no comment" statement.

4. Never lie. Discuss positive actions, but stick to the facts.

5. If you don't know the answer to the question, find out the reporter's deadline and call back with the appropriate information.

6. Never repeat the negative. If a reporter asks a negatively phrased question and you repeat the negative words, the negative impression will survive long after the facts. Positive responses are best.

7. Use transition techniques to give a straight answer to the question and move the conversation in the direction you desire. Bridge to positive points.

8. Speak in a conversational tone. Avoid jargon, and provide examples or anecdotes to illustrate your points.

9. In television or radio interviews, frame responses in quick bites. Do not provide a lengthy background in order to reach a conclusion.

10. Remain calm, courteous, and cooperative regardless of where the reporter is headed.

(Prepared by the public relations firm of Coleman & Pellet, Inc., Union, New Jersey, for counseling their clients. Used by permission.)

Press Agentry Abuses   Most of the abuses of the press that taint PR's relationship with the press stem from the press agent/publicity model.[27] Some other examples:

Promises to "deliver" the media—decried by the *Washington Post*.

Threats to withhold advertising if editors do not use an item, or a promise to buy advertising if they do use it.

Calling an executive of a newspaper or broadcast station to pressure a reporter or editor to use a story.

Sending reams of news releases with little news value to an extensive mailing list of media that have no use for them—often done to show your superiors or clients that you are keeping busy and promoting their pet projects.

Taking the attitude that the more releases sent, the greater the chance that they will be used, in the belief that editors use them randomly when they have a space to fill.[28]

Catering to television at the expense of the print media, especially at press conferences.

Mailing releases to out-of-town media, when the information has no local relevance to those media.

Sending multiple copies of the same release to different departments or individuals in the same publication or broadcast outlet.

Offering to take reporters or editors out for a drink or meal, when the meeting does not help the reporters or editors get the information they need for a story and instead wastes valuable time.[29]

Holding press conferences or parties, which waste a journalist's time, when a simple press release or phone call will convey the necessary information.

Name-dropping; trying to set up conferences with editors on routine news releases; phone calls to see if the editor got a news release in the mail.

Failing to understand how the news media work—not being aware of deadlines, news values, and beats.

Public Information Abuses   Media relations specialists who follow the public information model, you will recall, function essentially as "journalists in residence." Most worked previously as journalists and can avoid the abuses of the press agents just discussed. Two errors are common to practitioners of this model, however:

The jargon error. Often, public information specialists write in the coded language of their organization, frequently because their work must be cleared by superiors who want the information disseminated in specialized language.[30]

The Parkinson's Law error. Parkinson's famous law of bureaucracy states that "the work expands to fill the time available." We suggest the Hunt-Grunig corollary to this law: "Production of press releases expands to fill the time available." When the major skill of the practitioner is writing news articles, that is how he or she will fill his or her time. There may be no objective reason to write many of the articles, and many of them will have limited news value.

Two-Way Press Relations   Media relations practitioners of both the two-way asymmetric and two-way symmetric models of PR approach their task more systematically, make fewer errors that alienate journalists, and do more research and planning.

Asymmetric practitioners set objectives for what information they want the media to disseminate. In contrast to press agents, however, they understand news values and package that information in ways journalists will accept. They:

> Stage events or write releases that have legitimate news value, in which they articulate the position of their organization.
>
> Rebut what they consider to be erroneous or misleading information in the media, often by purchasing advertising if necessary.
>
> Understand the behavior of journalists, so that they can tailor their messages to the communication habits of journalists.

Conflict may still result from the asymmetric model because media relations specialists usually try to control coverage of their organization and to limit it to organizational public relations objectives. Journalists frequently want open access to an organization, something the asymmetric model may try to limit.

Symmetric practitioners think less about controlling the content of information that flows from their organization to the media. Their objective is to open up their organization to the media and to help journalists cover it, in the belief that such openness and assistance will result in more accurate and less biased coverage.[31]

Research does support the idea that two-way symmetric media relations improves the relationships with the media and the accuracy of the coverage that results. Habbersett sent a questionnaire to science reporters containing items describing media relations techniques typical of each of the four models of public relations and asked them to evaluate the practice described by the items.[32] The reporters' responses indicated a strong preference for two-way symmetric media relations.

Theus tested the symmetric principle of openness to the media by sending a questionnaire to public relations directors of organizations cited in newspaper stories in the Middle Atlantic region.[33] The questionnaire asked the public relations people to estimate the extent to which the stories differed from the organization's view of what happened. It also asked several questions about the openness of the organization to the media. In contrast to much conventional wisdom among public relations people, the more the organization tried to control the information going to the media, the less accurate the stories were. If the organization opened itself to the media, the stories were closer to the organization's view of reality.

The two-way symmetrical model, therefore, seems to be the most effective approach to media relations. To understand the model better, it helps to describe some specific symmetrical techniques.

Public relations consultant Richard Detweiler has described the role of what we call a two-way symmetric press representative as a middleman or arbitrator between management and the press.[34] "There is much of the irresistible force/immovable object confrontation involved here. 'Torn apart' may be putting it mildly," Detweiler said.

> . . . *seldom does either press or management comprehend the arbitrator role of the press officer. In the executive's generally simplistic view he wants a propagandist, a docile functionary who can hawk the party line precisely the way it is given, without a lot of bother and backtalk or expenditure of his time and thought. The two-way street of public relations—the response obligation—generally eludes him.*
>
> *To the press, of course, the public relations professional is a nuisance or worse. He or she is an irritating obstacle to unfettered access to the primary news source, an unwelcomed watchdog at the gate of truth.*

Detweiler then added: "The key to good press relations strategy is to make the newsman's job easy. That is, give him news of substance, with facts he can rely on—all this conveniently packaged and delivered in good time."

Howard and Mathews elaborated on the implications of making the reporter's job easier:

> *One fact that few executives or organization leaders seem to appreciate is that your role is to make a reporter's job easy, help that reporter meet his or her objectives and, at the same time, help your organization meet its objective.*
>
> *This tightrope-walking exercise means that when you speak to a reporter you are representing the organization; when you speak to the people in your organization you are representing the reporter.*[35]

There are many ways in which a media representative can make the journalist's job easier—the objective of symmetric press relations. Here are just a few suggestions:

Send out fewer press releases and rely more on direct contact with journalists, at both their initiative and yours. Be available to the media: Wes Christensen, a Washington public relations consultant, estimated that when he was PR director at Georgetown University, he received about five hundred calls from the media each month. Call reporters when you think you have a story that interests them. Make sure, however, that the story has a local angle or content relevant to the reporter's publication.

Set up interviews for journalists with management or specialists in your organization. Help reporters cover your organization. Don't try to do it for them.

Instead of press releases, send the media a sheet of one-paragraph news tips that they can follow up themselves.

Interview people in your organization yourself and record the interview on cassette tapes. Provide these tapes to journalists so that they can integrate the interview into their own stories.

Set up an information storage and retrieval system (on a computer, if possible) in which you maintain fact sheets, complete articles, interviews, and background information. Tell journalists what is in this system, and that they can have access to it whenever they wish. Update the information regularly.

Robert Dilenschneider counsels against the press agentry or two-way asymmetric practice of striving for splashy, favorable stories in the media in favor of the more symmetric practice of "developing a constant, positive, and low-key press presence."[36] Reporters typically look for the other side of a positive story, he explained. Thus, "good news begets bad news." You may be successful in placing a prominent positive story, but another reporter soon will investigate the other side; and a negative story often follows. Be open to the media when they call, Dilenschneider recommended, but don't push coverage because pushing can produce bad coverage as often as good.

On the other hand, stonewalling can be disastrous, especially when there are rumors circulating about your organization or client. A good example occurred in 1991 when Monica Seles, the top-ranked women's tennis player in the world, withdrew from the Wimbledon Tournament because of an undisclosed injury. She dropped from public view and refused to talk with the media until two weeks after the tournament, when she issued a statement in which she said that her injury "was shin splints and a slight stress fracture in my left leg." The *Washington Post* reported that by that time "there have been Seles sightings in Colorado and Florida and rumors about her physical status, including reports that she is pregnant and recovering from an auto accident."[37]

According to Dilenschneider, "Solidly built, long-term relationships with the media are your only protection against the kind of damage that rumors can do."[38] Solid, long-term relationships come from openness and honesty with the media. Openness and honesty are especially important when the organization is involved in activities that carry a risk for people.

The Environmental Communication Research Program at Rutgers University developed a set of guidelines for the New Jersey Department of Environmental Protection for communicating about risk through the media. These guidelines provide an excellent example of two-way symmetrical media relations. In essence, the Rutgers Center recommended being open with the media and the public whenever possible. When you cannot be open, it added, you should tell when you will be able to release information and what you are doing to investigate a risk. Here are a few of the specific recommendations:

If people are at risk, do not wait to communicate—and to act on—risk information. If a hazard is putting people at immediate risk, the agency should follow its mandate to protect public health without hesitation.

If the agency is investigating a potential risk that people aren't aware of, the agency should seriously consider making known what it is doing and why. When an agency announces findings from an investigation people have not been aware of, the agency is forced to defend its delay in announcing the investigation, and to justify the possibility that people were exposed to a risk longer than necessary. The public, in its anger over not being told, is more likely to overestimate the risk and far less likely to trust any recommendations that the agency makes concerning the risk itself.

If it seems likely that the media or someone else may release the information before you are ready, release it yourself. When information is leaked, agencies lose the ability to shape the issues and are instead engaged in playing "catch up" at the expense of their credibility and the accurate portrayal of information.

If it is likely that the media will "fill in" with information concerning an on-going story while they are waiting for you to speak, speak first. When you wait to communicate about an issue that is already news, the press will shape the issue without you. You may spend more time defending your views or your credibility.

If you really don't trust your data, talk to the public about your procedures but don't release the data. Obviously, hold onto data for which your preliminary review shows serious quality control or methodological flaws. However, be up-front and tell citizens what has happened and when they will be able to get some results.

If you have decided that you can't communicate right away about the risk, talk to the public about the process you are going through to get the information. Don't merely remain silent. In the absence of information from the agency, people may fill in the blanks of missing information themselves, or they may become more fearful thinking that the truth is too awful to be told.[39]

If you practice two-way symmetric media relations, you must take a chance on the accuracy and responsibility of the news media. The more open you can make your organization, the greater is the likelihood of fair and accurate media coverage. Sometimes, however, you may get burned. If you do, don't be afraid to provide a rebuttal. Symmetric communication is give and take. If the media err, provide them information to clarify the error. If you have had good relations with journalists, they won't mind your rebuttal. Never, never threaten or beg, however.

Symmetrical relations with the media and trusting relationships are especially important during a crisis. Thus, we turn to some guidelines for crisis relations with the media.

Media Relations in a Crisis

Although many organizations base their ongoing media relations strategy on the press agentry, public information, or two-way asymmetrical model of public relations, they usually must give them up at the time of a crisis—as a study of managers at several chemical plants in West Virginia showed.[40] They usually give them up because they have little choice.

The three asymmetrical models work from the assumption that the flow of information to the media can be controlled. During a crisis, the media become so active in seeking information about the crisis that organizations cannot control the information going to the media even though they try mightily to do so.[41] If the organization uses asymmetric media relations, the media go to sources other than the organization experiencing the crisis. The resulting coverage is worse than if the organization had been open and forthright about what happened and what it is doing about the crisis.

On the one hand, organizations should be open in a crisis because it is the responsible thing to do. In Troester's words: "When organizational operations result in a crisis that may adversely affect the community, organizations and their spokespersons have an obligation to communicate."[42] In addition to being ethical, however, open communication during a crisis also is more effective. Howard and Mathews explained why:

> . . . *your objective in such "bad news" situations usually is clearly enunciated by the top management of your company or client: Make it go away. The question is how. Your role is to convince them that often the best way is to initiate contact with reporters—or, at the minimum, to respond promptly to questions—so your story is told once and for all. Bad news will not go away if you refuse to comment on it. In fact, lack of cooperation with the media may expand the story and make it last longer than if you handle the crisis and get it over with.*[43]

Many manuals and books provide checklists for media relations during a crisis. Howard and Mathews included a list of seventeen components of a crisis plan in their chapter on crisis planning.[44] For example, they recommended keeping a supply of informational kits available for reporters who need instant background on an organization. They also recommended having a procedure ready for setting up a press conference and briefing the press. And they called for a plan to brief employees since employees often become news sources.

Likewise, the Bank of America's Ron Rhody recommends providing managers with media training in anticipation of crisis and preparing talk sheets for them to refer to if they are interviewed during a crisis.[45] He also recommends calling media that reach strategic publics of the organization to brief them on what the organization is doing about the crisis. Every organization should have such a manual with such a checklist, although many do not.

Although a crisis plan is important, research for a doctoral dissertation at the University of Maryland showed that having a symmetric "communication ideology" is even more important than a predetermined plan during a crisis. Marra conducted case studies of one organization that had dealt successfully with a crisis and one that had not.[46] Neither organization relied heavily on a crisis plan, although the successful organization had one and the unsuccessful one did not.

However, the successful organization had a long-standing tradition of symmetrical public relations and good relationships with the media and its strategic publics. As a result of this symmetrical ideology, media relations people and managers throughout the organization immediately communicated openly with the press and publics. The unsuccessful organization had no tradition of open communication. As a result, it closed itself from the press and the crisis snowballed.

In short, organizations seldom are able to develop good media relations during a crisis if they have not had good media relations habits before. Organizations with ongoing symmetrical communication, therefore, usually respond well in a crisis.

One of the tips for crisis communication—keeping employees informed—also has implications for media relations during normal times.

Media Relations through Employees

Remember that two-way symmetrical communication during a crisis or during the normal course of events means that you open your organization to the media. Opening the organization means that you encourage reporters to interview your employees and that you help arrange interviews.

It's important, therefore, to keep your employees informed[47]—for two reasons. First, they may become news sources. But you also do not want your employees to learn news about the organization through external media if you can help it. Thus, an active and symmetric program of employee communication supports and complements a symmetric program of media relations.

At this point in the chapter, we have provided some guidelines on how to structure and manage media relations programs within a public relations department. To increase your understanding of the theory behind this advice, we turn to theories of the behavior of journalists and effects of the media.

MEDIA PUBLICS In Chapter 1 we argued that public relations people could communicate with publics more often and more effectively if they understood the communication behavior of those publics. Active publics can be reached in one way, passive publics in another. If journalists behave as publics, then the theory of publics described in Chapter 1 could be used to type and classify journalists—and to help the media relations specialist communicate with each journalist public.

Journalists Seek and Process Information

The dependent variables from our theory of publics—information seeking and processing—seem to fit the behavior of journalists well. Most of us think of journalists as communicators who disseminate information. But they also seek and process information when they cover events, interview news sources, or assign stories.

You also may think of journalists mostly as active seekers of information—enterprising reporters. But more of their behavior can be described as the passive processing of information: rewriting press releases, routinely covering events or hearings, reacting to the initiative of news sources.

Sigal, for example, classified the sources of 1,146 stories in *The Washington Post* and *The New York Times* and found that about three-fourths of the stories resulted from what we would call passive information processing.[48] Fifty-eight percent of the stories came from such routine sources as official proceedings, press releases, or press conferences. Another 16 percent came from informal sources such as briefings, leaks, meetings, or conventions. Only 26 percent resulted from the active seeking of information, or what Sigal called enterprise reporting: from interviews or the reporter's own analysis.

Hess found that Washington reporters got 80 percent of their news from "events" that occurred within 24 hours.[49] Quite clearly, the reporters "processed" the news from those events.

And, when reporters process information more than they seek it, media relations specialists can influence their communication behavior much more than they could if reporters actively sought information.

Do Journalists Report According to Personal Interests?

To apply our theory of publics to journalists, we must also ask whether their information seeking and processing—like the behavior of other organizational publics—can be explained by personal perceptions that reporters have of situations created by organizational consequences.

Do journalists, for example, report about pollution from a steel mill because they personally recognize that problem, feel involved with it, or feel unconstrained about doing something about it? Or, do journalists simply report situations or events that are assigned to them by an editor, that other journalists are reporting, or that journalists perceive readers and viewers of the media have an interest in?

Theoretical Explanations of Journalists' Behavior

We can answer these questions by turning to a domain of mass communication research called "communicator analysis"—study of the behavior of professional communicators.

Researchers first tried to show that journalists seek information and write stories that reinforce their attitudinal biases, just as many media relations specialists have assumed that journalists are motivated by antiorganizational biases.

David Manning White conducted the first "gatekeeper" study in 1950, when he asked a newspaper wire editor he called Mr. Gates to explain why he accepted or rejected each wire story.[50] White concluded that Mr. Gates's decisions were "biased and subjective."

Similarly, Janowitz classified journalists as either neutral "gatekeepers" or subjective "advocates" of a position.[51] Starck and Soloski typed journalists as either "neutrals" or "participants" in a news event.[52] Culbertson, similarly, found three types of journalists—traditionalists, interpreters, and activists.[53] You will also recall from the discussion earlier in this chapter that public relations practitioner Donald Van Deusen attributed antibusiness reporting to what he termed a switch from "objective" to "interpretive" reporting.[54]

Recently, researchers have looked for better explanations of the behaviors of journalists than bias.[55] Whitney reviewed studies of communicators and concluded that organizational and institutional variables explain communicator behavior better than individual variables. "Real news," Whitney concluded, "is an organizational product born of routines."[56] Likewise, Shoemaker and Mayfield found that the financiers of media—advertisers, governments, or interest groups—shape the style and content of the news more than the values and interests of individual reporters.[57]

David Manning White's "Mr. Gates," for example, did not appear to be so subjective and biased when McCombs and Shaw analyzed

White's data in a different way.[58] They found Mr. Gates's selections of stories to be highly correlated with the numbers of stories that came over the wire. The more stories in a given category, the more of those stories Mr. Gates chose, regardless of his biases.

Levels of Analysis in Journalistic Behavior

Mass communication researchers, therefore, now do not think the behavior of journalists can be explained by a concept as simple as "bias." Instead, they have developed theories that include three "levels of analysis."[59]

> **Individual Level.**   The extent to which journalists' behavior results from their own interests, as well as their biases, values, or ideals.
>
> **Organizational Level.**   Organizational factors that constrain the behavior of a reporter, such as assignments given by editors.
>
> **Institutional Level.**   The constraints that the larger society places upon a journalist, such as the requirement that a medium be profitable, the perceptions journalists have of their readers, the traditions of journalism, and the unconscious influences that reporters have upon each other.

The institutional level may be the most difficult for you to understand, because it represents influences most reporters may not be aware of. For example, research shows that most reporters cover what other reporters cover to protect themselves from being scooped. The wire services play an especially important role, because editors use wire reports to determine whether their reporters have missed a story. Reporters, therefore, do not try to get stories their competitors don't have. They make sure they get the same stories as their competitors. The result is an institutional routine.[60]

By now, you should realize that press representatives would use a different strategy to deal with journalists for each of these levels of analysis.

> At the individual level, they would try to channel stories to reporters who have either a personal interest in the story or a bias that favors the organization's position.
>
> At the organizational level, media specialists would work with editors to get a story assigned to a reporter.
>
> At the institutional level, they would stage events and cater to the tendency of one reporter to copy others.

Public relations people seem to stress the individual level when they deal with the media, especially when they try to counteract what they perceive to be media bias. Mass communication research, however, suggests that organizational and institutional factors may be more important.

Let's turn next to two studies that combine these levels of analysis to develop a typology of journalistic publics.

Two Studies of Journalist Publics

Grunig has done two studies, one of student journalists and one of Washington reporters, to determine how many types of journalist publics exist. These two studies show that attitudes and biases explain little about journalistic behavior. They also show that some journalists are motivated by individual variables, while others are motivated by institutional and organizational variables.

Journalists Aren't Biased; They Have Different Interests The first study was designed to examine the effect of economic-education programs designed for college and university journalism students.[61] That study is relevant because it compares the attitudes and communication behaviors of journalism students with those of business students—from which we can derive some implications about professional journalists and businesspeople.

When Grunig used two questions to measure general attitudes toward business and government, he found the business students to be slightly more probusiness than the journalism students. Both, however, were antigovernment. The business students also said they were more liberal than did the journalism students.

When Grunig measured what he called cognitive strategies on three specific business issues—pollution, government regulation, and the effect of the law of supply and demand—he found little difference between the two groups. Both business and journalism students accepted an antibusiness position on pollution and "wedged" out a probusiness position. On the impact of government regulation on business, both groups "hedged"—they believed both a pro- and antibusiness position. When presented a pro- and antibusiness statement about the effect of the basic economic law of supply and demand, neither group had much of a cognition (much of an idea) at all—the issue wasn't really relevant to them.

Thus, "bias" didn't seem to separate the journalism students from the business students. Individual communication behaviors did separate them, however. The theory of publics described in Chapter 1 was used to identify publics in the two groups of students on three sets of issues—

three basic economic issues (size of corporate profits, capitalism vs. socialism, and supply and demand), three business consequences on publics (quality of goods and services, prices of goods and services, and pollution), and three governmental relationships (regulation of business, taxation of business, and government spending).

Statistical analysis isolated two publics—one made up mostly of the business students and one made up of journalism students. The business student public was an active public on all nine issues. The journalist public, however, was an active public only for the three business consequences.

The study suggests, therefore, that journalists aren't really biased against business—and probably are not biased against other large organizations either. More likely, they take an interest in business only when it has consequences on publics.

Journalists behave like most other publics. They don't worry about business unless it has an adverse consequence upon them. From the business viewpoint, however, this means that journalists concern themselves mostly with the negative side of business.

Businesspeople, however, take an interest in the general workings of business and its role in the economy. They seek that information. Journalists and most other publics do not—as other research has shown.[62] Publics, including journalist publics, just aren't interested in all aspects of business, and public relations practitioners must deal with that fact. Antibias campaigns probably will affect behavior of journalists very little.

Washington Reporters, Too   It's wise to have reservations about generalizing from students to practicing journalists. However, a similar study of practicing Washington reporters showed almost identical results. Grunig included four business policy issues in this study: breakup of the Bell telephone system, deregulation of natural gas, chemical disposal sites, and acid rain.[63] Again, he could find no consistent pattern of bias.

However, he did find, as he had in a study of nonjournalist publics,[64] that the journalists generally believed an antibusiness statement on each issue as well as a probusiness statement on some issues. Most publics—journalists and nonjournalists—believe business has negative consequences outside the organization. They don't drop those beliefs when they learn positive things about business; they hold both beliefs.

A 1982 study of 240 elite journalists and broadcasters working for influential media such as *The New York Times, The Washington Post, The Wall Street Journal, Newsweek,* and the TV networks demonstrated the same media pattern of "hedging."[65] Although these journalists generally were more liberal than other people on religious and social issues, they combined liberal social views with many beliefs favored by business.

Most of the journalists surveyed supported environmental protection and women's and minority rights. But most also said they believed that free enterprise gives workers a fair shake, that deregulation of business would be good for the country, and that private enterprise is fair to working people.

Which Levels of Analysis Explain Best?   Although attitudes or bias did not explain the behavior of Washington reporters well, Grunig still asked whether individual interests of the reporters explained their behavior or whether organizational or institutional factors did. What he found was five reporter publics, three of which were motivated by individual interests and two by institutional forces.

So, reporters don't all behave in the same way. Neither do other people. That doesn't make the job of the media relations specialist easy—but it doesn't make it impossible. The media relations specialist must treat different kinds of reporters differently.

Grunig's results suggest that you will usually deal with some enterprising reporters seeking out stories in areas in which they take personal interest. Most likely, they are specialized reporters—in science, the environment, business, regulatory agencies, and the like. These reporters are well informed about the issues in which they are interested. You should help them to get complete, factual information on your organization's position on the relevant issues—as you should help all active, information-seeking publics.

Other reporters process information passively. These reporters still can communicate an organization's information to other publics, as long as it is made available for them to report. They won't seek it out. The media relations specialist must "put it on the agenda" for the reporters.

That takes us to a final media concept, agenda setting, which is essential for you to understand if you are to set objectives for and evaluate media relations.

When mass-media theorists first began studying effects of the media, they believed in a hypodermic-needle theory, which assumed powerful media effects on attitudes and behavior. They gave up that theory for a limited effects theory when they learned that media seldom had strong effects.

In the early 1970s, researchers realized that the mass media may not change attitudes and behavior, but they thought the media must have some other important effects. In 1972 mass communication researchers Maxwell McCombs and Donald Shaw coined a term that is now widely accepted as the major effect of the media. They found a strong relationship between the amount of space given to different issues in the media and the importance people think those issues have. The media, McCombs and Shaw concluded, "set the agenda for public discussion."[66]

MEDIA RELATIONS OBJECTIVES AND EVALUATION

McCombs and Shaw took a phrase from Bernard Cohen's book *The Press and Foreign Policy* that distinguished the agenda-setting effect from effects on attitudes and behavior.[67] The media, according to Cohen, do not tell us what to think, but they tell us what to think about. Without the media people would not be aware of many issues—from pollution in their hometown to an invasion in Afghanistan. After the media create awareness, however, people go on to form many different cognitions, attitudes, and behaviors from the information they get from the media.

Recall now the five effects outlined in Chapter 1: communication, retention of messages, acceptance of cognitions, formation or change of an attitude, and overt behavior. The agenda-setting effect entails the first two effects. When the media choose to put certain issues on the public agenda, the public can communicate about those issues and become aware of them (retain messages about the issues).

Agenda-setting research suggests that media relations specialists can choose communication and message retention as realistic objectives for their programs. First, they should work with the press to put an organization's message about an issue or program onto the media agenda (to make communication possible). Once the message is on the media agenda, they want it to be there long enough for the public to be aware of it (retain the message).

After achieving those objectives, the media relations specialist has little control over what publics do with information on the media agenda. Publics use the information for many purposes and get many benefits from using it. This is the domain of another contemporary approach to mass communication—the uses and gratifications approach.[68]

Ongoing Research on Agenda Setting

Research on agenda-setting today occupies many researchers and has isolated many relevant theoretical variables.[69] We can't review all of that research here, but we can present a few highlights:

A story must be on the media agenda for some time—about three to five months—before people become thoroughly aware of it.

Newspapers seem to set the public agenda more than television. Television introduces issues but doesn't stay with them long enough to affix them on the public agenda; newspapers do.

Not all people pick up personal agendas from the media to the same degree as other people. In particular, the more involved people are with issues, the less the media affect how important these people think the issues are. Involved people actively seek information from many sources. They don't just process it passively from the media. Also, people with a "high need for orientation"—a great deal of uncertainty about a problem they recognize—accept the media agenda more than people with less uncertainty. When people don't have cognitions about important issues, in other words, they develop them from the most ubiquitous source of information—the media.

In addition to studying the extent to which the media set the agenda for public attention and discussion, other researchers have examined who puts problems or issues on the media agenda—what has come to be called "agenda building." Sociologists Kurt and Gladys Lang began that program of research by theorizing that issues "build" when organizations, politicians, activists, news sources, *and* public relations practitioners—do or say something to get the attention of the media.[70]

News sources and journalists, in other words, interact to build agendas for public discussion—as we saw earlier in this chapter when we looked at the amount of information in the media that comes from public relations sources. This means that the media aren't the all-powerful manipulators of public opinion that many senior managers and public relations practitioners believe. In fact, as Rogers and Dearing have concluded, organizations, the media, and policy makers interact to set the agenda for public discussion and policy—each affecting the other to a different extent in different circumstances.[71]

The key point for media relations specialists is that they are not at the mercy of the media; nor can they control the media agenda. Skillful media relations people can get issues of concern to their organizations on the agenda for public discussion, and they can be involved in the discussion when other groups build the agenda. Media relations people cannot control the outcome of the discussion, but they can interject the organization's position and get people to pay attention to it if they communicate well.

The next question, then, is how media relations practitioners can determine objectively if they are getting their message on the public agenda.

How to Evaluate the Media Agenda

Most media relations specialists already use a commercial clipping service so that they can evaluate their work—but they usually monitor the clippings haphazardly. A clipping service is a specialized company that, for a fee, will clip all articles that mention an organization from media specified by the media relations specialist. Media relations people peruse these clippings and frequently mount them carefully to present to management as a demonstration of the effectiveness of their efforts.

If we define the objective of press relations as "getting the proper message on the media agenda," then the clipping service isn't really such a bad idea. The clippings show how frequently and in what context the organization has appeared on the media agenda. The media relations manager must set objectives for the kind of media coverage desired and then systematically analyze press clippings to see if those objectives have been met.

Several commercial research firms and public relations firms—such as PR Data, Inc. and Ketchum public relations—have developed systems for analyzing press clippings.[72] To evaluate media relations, the organization specifies what themes it wants to stress in articles that appear in the media and the media in which it would like those articles to appear. Researchers analyze the content of press clippings or tapes of radio and television broadcasts and use a computer to determine how frequently the desired themes actually appeared in desired media.

AT&T also had researchers classify clippings as to whether they were positive, negative, or neutral, charting the results year by year to monitor progress in media relations. When stories were unfavorable, AT&T looked for a "rebuttal ratio"—the relative proportion of times the media relations person got a later rebuttal to an unfavorable article onto the media agenda. It also looked for the relative number of stories initiated by the company's media relations people compared to the stories initiated by the media themselves—to see if the same coverage would have resulted without media specialists.

Many organizations cannot afford a commercial firm to analyze their press clippings, but they can do it themselves with a little knowledge of content analysis. A computer makes comparisons and calculations easier, but it is not essential. Any organization, in other words, can go one step beyond what it is doing—collecting clippings—to do a much more adequate job of evaluating media relations.

At times, media relations managers may also want to determine whether target publics retain the media agenda as their own. In other words, they want to know whether publics remember the themes of articles that appeared in the media. To measure such public agendas requires a survey of the publics. The survey should measure message retention—recall of the themes stressed in the media—not attitudes or behaviors.

NOTES   1. Carole Howard, "Media Relations: Public Relations' Basic Activity," in Bill Cantor and Chester Burger (eds.), *Experts in Action: Inside Public Relations* (New York: Longman, 1989), pp. 258–267.

2. Carole Howard and Wilma Mathews, *On Deadline: Managing Media Relations* (Prospect Heights, IL: Waveland Press, 1985), p. 23. For a discussion of the importance of segmentation in media relations, see Mary Sabolik, "Print Media Placement Strategies for the New Segmentation," *Public Relations Journal* 45 (November 1989), pp. 15–19, 35.

3. Rod Troester, "The Corporate Spokesperson in External Organizational Communication: What We Know and What We Need to Know," *Management Communication Quarterly* 4 (1991), p. 529.

4. Howard and Mathews, p. 43.

5. Robert L. Dilenschneider, *Power and Influence* (New York: Prentice-Hall Press, 1990), p. 188.

6. Charles Honaker, "News Releases Revisited," *Public Relations Journal* 37 (April 1981), pp. 25–27.

7. *Advertising Age* (April 26, 1982), pp. 3, 74.

8. Craig Aronoff, "Newspapermen and Practitioners Differ Widely on PR Role," *Public Relations Journal* 31 (August 1975), pp. 24–25.

9. Craig Aronoff, "Credibility of Public Relations for Journalists," *Public Relations Review* 1 (Fall 1975), pp. 45–56.

10. Carlton E. Spitzer, "Fear of the Media," *Public Relations Journal* 37 (November 1981), pp. 58–63.

11. See, for example, S. Prakash Sethi, "The Schism Between Business and American News Media," *Journalism Quarterly* 54 (1977), pp. 240–247; S. Prakash Sethi, "Battling Antibusiness Bias: Is There a Chance of Overkill?" *Public Relations Journal* 37 (November 1981), pp. 22–24, 64; Joseph R. Dominick, "Business Coverage in Network Newscasts," *Journalism Quarterly* 58 (1981), pp. 179–185.

12. Donald T. Van Deusen, "The 'Shrinking News Hole' Syndrome," *Public Relations Journal* 31 (October 1975), pp. 16, 19.

13. Frank W. Wylie, "Attitudes Toward the Media," *Public Relations Journal* 31 (January 1975), pp. 6–7.

14. W. W. Marsh, "Public Relations and the Big Blow Up, Part II," *Public Relations Journal* 36 (November 1980), pp. 38–42.

15. John V. Pavlik, *Public Relations: What Research Tells Us* (Newbury Park, CA: Sage, 1987), p. 60.

16. Larissa A. Grunig, "Variation in Relations with Environmental Publics," *Public Relations Review* 13 (Fall 1987), p. 55.

17. Glen T. Cameron, "Research in Source-Reporter Relations: Where We've Been, Where We Ought to Go," paper presented to the International Communication Association, San Francisco, May 1989.

18. Scott M. Cutlip, "Public Relations in the Government," *Public Relations Review* 2 (Summer 1976), pp. 19–21.

19. Lucien Toney File, "How Business Editors View Public Relations," *Public Relations Journal* 34 (February 1978), pp. 8–9.

20. Oscar H. Gandy, Jr., *Beyond Agenda Setting: Information Subsidies and Public Policy* (Norwood, NJ: Ablex, 1982).

21. Dan Berkowitz, "Information Subsidy and Agenda-Building in Local Television News," *Journalism Quarterly* (in press). See also Dan Berkowitz, "TV News Sources and News Channels: A Study in Agenda-Building," *Journalism Quarterly* 64 (1987), pp. 508–513, and Jane Delano Brown, Carol R. Bybee, Stanley T. Weardon, and Dulcie Straughan, "Invisible Power: Newspaper News Sources and the Limits of Diversity," *Journalism Quarterly* 64 (1987), pp. 45–54.

22. Judy VanSlyke Turk, "Information Subsidies and Media Content: A Study of Public Relations Influence on the News," *Journalism Monographs* No. 100 (December 1986).

23. Judy VanSlyke Turk, "Between President and Press," paper presented to the International Association of Business Communicators and published in the official conference proceedings, London, July 1987. For a comparison of information

subsidies by governments in the United States and the United Kingdom, see Judy VanSlyke Turk and Bob Franklin, "Information Subsidies: Agenda-Setting Traditions," *Public Relations Review* 13 (Winter 1987), pp. 29–41.

24. Linda P. Morton, "How Newspapers Choose the Releases They Use," *Public Relations Review* 12 (Fall 1986), pp. 22–27.

25. Berkowitz, "Information Subsidy and Agenda-Building"; Craig E. Aronoff, "Predictors of Success in Placing Releases in Newspapers," *Public Relations Review* 2 (Winter 1978), pp. 43–57; Bill L. Baxter, "The News Release: An Idea Whose Time Has Gone?" in Ray E. Hiebert (ed.), *Precision Public Relations* (New York: Longman, 1988), pp. 219–223.

26. Howard and Mathews, Chapter 4.

27. One can find many articles in professional public relations journals that report how journalists react to the excesses of press agents. Among these are Paul Poorman, "Public Relations—The Newsman's View," *Public Relations Journal* 30 (March 1974), pp. 14–16, 40; Chuck Honaker, "Why Your Releases Aren't Working," *Public Relations Journal* 34 (March 1978), pp. 16–19; Honaker, "News Releases Revisited"; Gary B. Bassford, "The Tube vs. the Pencil Press," *Public Relations Journal* 35 (May 1979), pp. 16, 21–22; "An Editor's 10 PR Commandments," *Public Relations Journal* 33 (1977), p. 26.

28. An empirical study, using sophisticated statistical techniques, showed that editors do not select news releases randomly. Generally, they select articles that have a local angle. Craig Aronoff, "Predictors of Success in Placing Releases in Newspapers," *Public Relations Review* 2 (Winter 1976), pp. 43–57.

29. One study showed that contact with journalists decreased the likelihood that a news release would be used. Phillip J. Tichenor, Clarice N. Olien, and George A. Donohue, "Predicting a News Source's Success in Placing News in the Media," *Journalism Quarterly* 44 (1967), pp. 32–42.

30. For example, most of the information released by public relations people after the Three Mile Island nuclear accident was written in technical jargon. Sharon M. Friedman, "Blueprint for Breakdown: Three Mile Island and the Media Before the Accident," *Journal of Communication* 31 (Spring 1981), pp. 116–128.

31. For a detailed discussion of the symmetrical approach to media relations and its relationship to the strategic planning of public relations, see James E. Grunig, "Theory and Practice of Interactive Media Relations," *Public Relations Quarterly* 35 (Fall 1990), pp. 18–23.

32. Carolyn A. Habbersett, *An Exploratory Study of Media Relations: The Science Journalist and the Public Relations Practitioner* (master's thesis, University of Maryland, College Park, 1983).

33. Kathryn T. Theus, "Organizational Ideology, Structure, and Communication Efficacy: A Causal Analysis," in Larissa A. Grunig and James E. Grunig (eds.), *Public Relations Research Annual*, Vol. 3 (Hillsdale, NJ: Lawrence Erlbaum Associates, 1991), pp. 133–149.

34. Richard Detweiler, "What Every Successful Executive Should Know About His Press Officer's Terrible Secrets," *Public Relations Journal* 32 (August 1976), pp. 20–23.

35. Howard and Mathews, p. 15.

36. Dilenschneider, pp. 191–193.

37. The *Washington Post*, July 16, 1991, pp. E1, E6.

38. Dilenschneider, p. 202.

39. Caron Chess, Billie Jo Hance, and Peter M. Sandman, *Improving Dialogue with Communities: A Short Guide for Government Risk Communication* (Environmental

Communication Research Program, Rutgers University, New Brunswick, NJ, January 1988), pp. 11–13.

40. Rae Lynn Cupp, *A Study of Public Relations Crisis Management in West Virginia Chemical Companies* (master's thesis, University of Maryland, College Park, 1985).

41. See some of the advice on how to control information cited in Troester, pp. 531–535, for example.

42. Troester, p. 531.

43. Howard and Mathews, pp. 129–130.

44. Howard and Mathews, pp. 157–160.

45. As reported in *pr reporter,* July 17, 1989, p. 2.

46. Francis J. Marra, *Crisis Public Relations: A Theoretical Model* (doctoral dissertation, University of Maryland, College Park, 1991).

47. Howard and Mathews, p. 67.

48. Leon V. Sigal, *Reporters and Officials* (Lexington, MA: Heath, 1973), p. 121.

49. Stephen Hess, *The Washington Reporters* (Washington: The Brookings Institution, 1981), p. 15.

50. David Manning White, "The Gatekeeper: A Case Study in the Selection of News," *Journalism Quarterly* 27 (1950), pp. 383–390.

51. Morris Janowitz, "Professional Models in Journalism: The Gatekeeper and the Advocate," *Journalism Quarterly* 52 (1975), pp. 618–626.

52. Kenneth Starck and John Soloski, "Effect of Reporter Predisposition in Covering Controversial Story," *Journalism Quarterly* 54 (1977), pp. 120–125.

53. Hugh M. Culbertson, "Three Perspectives on American Journalism," *Journalism Monographs* No. 83 (June 1983).

54. Van Deusen.

55. For a review of this research, see Phillip J. Tichenor, Clarice N. Olien, and George A. Donohue, "Gatekeeping: Mass Media Systems and Information Control," in F. Gerald Kline and Phillip J. Tichenor (eds.), *Current Perspectives in Mass Communication Research* (Beverly Hills, CA: Sage, 1972), pp. 45–79.

56. D. Charles Whitney, "Mass Communicator Studies: Similarity, Difference, and Level of Analysis," in James S. Ettema and D. Charles Whitney (eds.), *Individuals in Mass Media Organizations: Creativity and Constraint* (Beverly Hills, CA: Sage, 1982), pp. 241–254.

57. Pamela J. Shoemaker with Elizabeth Kay Mayfield, "Building a Theory of News Content: A Synthesis of News Content," *Journalism Monographs* No. 103 (June 1987).

58. Maxwell E. McCombs and Donald E. Shaw, "Structuring the Unseen Environment," *Journal of Communication* 26 (Spring 1976), pp. 18–28.

59. Paul M. Hirsch, "Occupational, Organizational, and Institutional Models in Mass Media Research: Toward an Integrated Framework," in Paul M. Hirsch, Peter V. Miller, and F. Gerald Kline (eds.), *Strategies for Communication Research* (Beverly Hills, CA: Sage, 1977), pp. 45–79.

60. For an example, see Sharon Dunwoody, "The News-Gathering Behaviors of Specialty Reporters: A Comparison of Two Levels of Analysis in Mass Media Decision-Making," paper presented to the Association for Education in Journalism, Houston, 1979.

61. James E. Grunig, "Developing Economic Education Programs for the Press," *Public Relations Review* 8 (Fall 1982), pp. 43–62.

62. James E. Grunig, "The Message-Attitude-Behavior Relationship: Communication Behaviors of Organizations," *Communication Research* 9 (1982), pp. 163–200.

63. James E. Grunig, "Washington Reporter Publics of Corporate Public Affairs Programs," *Journalism Quarterly* 60 (1983), pp. 603–615.

64. Grunig, "The Message-Attitude-Behavior Relationship."

65. "The Media Elite: White, Male, Secular, and Liberal," *Washington Post* (January 3, 1982), p. C3.

66. Maxwell E. McCombs and Donald L. Shaw, "The Agenda-Setting Function of the Mass Media," *Public Opinion Quarterly* 36 (1972), pp. 176–187.

67. Bernard Cohen, *The Press and Foreign Policy* (Princeton, NJ: Princeton University Press, 1963).

68. See, for example, Jay G. Blumler and Elihu Katz (eds.), *The Uses of Mass Communications* (Beverly Hills, CA: Sage, 1974).

69. For reviews of research, see Everett M. Rogers and James W. Dearing, "Agenda-Setting Research: Where Has It Been, Where Is It Going?" in James A. Anderson (ed.), *Mass Communication Yearbook/11* (Newbury Park, CA: Sage, 1988), pp. 555–594; Everett M. Rogers, James W. Dearing, and Soonbum Chang, "AIDS in the 1980s: The Agenda-Setting Process for a Public Issue," *Journalism Monographs* No. 126 (April 1991); Maxwell E. McCombs, "The Agenda-Setting Approach," in Dan D. Nimmo and Keith R. Sanders (eds.), *Handbook of Political Communication* (Beverly Hills, CA: Sage, 1981), pp. 121–140; and Maxwell E. McCombs, "Agenda Setting Function of Mass Media," *Public Relations Review* 3 (Winter 1977), pp. 89–95.

70. Kurt Lang and Gladys Lang, *The Battle for Public Opinion: The President, the Press and the Polls During Watergate* (New York: Columbia University Press, 1983). For a discussion of the effect of activist groups on the media agenda, see David L. Paletz and John Boiney, "Interest Groups and Public Opinion," in James A. Anderson (ed.), *Communication Yearbook/11* (Newbury Park, CA: Sage, 1988), pp. 534–546.

71. Rogers and Dearing.

72. These systems are described in James F. Tirone, "Measuring The Bell System's Public Relations," *Public Relations Review* 3 (Winter 1977), pp. 21–38; Robert K. Marker, "The Armstrong/PR Data Measurement System," *Public Relations Review* 3 (Winter 1977), pp. 51–59; Klaus Krippenforff and Michael F. Eleey, "Monitoring a Group's Symbolic Environment," *Public Relations Review* 12 (Spring 1986), pp. 13–36; Glen M. Broom and David M. Dozier, *Using Research in Public Relations: Applications to Program Management* (Englewood Cliffs, NJ: Prentice-Hall, 1990), pp. 53–55.

ADDITIONAL READING

Dilenschneider, Robert L., *Power and Influence* (New York: Prentice-Hall Press, 1990), Part 5.

Grunig, James E., "Theory and Practice of Interactive Media Relations," *Public Relations Quarterly* 35 (Fall 1990), pp. 18–23.

Howard, Carole, "Media Relations: Public Relations' Basic Activity," in Bill Cantor and Chester Burger (eds.), *Experts in Action: Inside Public Relations* (New York: Longman, 1989), pp. 258–267.

Howard, Carole, and Wilma Mathews, *On Deadline: Managing Media Relations* (Prospect Heights, IL: Waveland Press, 1985).

Jamieson, Kathleen Hall, and Karlyn Kohrs Campbell, *The Interplay of Influence: Mass Media and Their Publics in News, Advertising, Politics*, 3d ed. (Belmont, CA: Wadsworth, 1992).

Mathews, Wilma, "Media Relations," in Carol Reuss and Donn Silvis (eds.), *Inside Organizational Communication* (New York: Longman), pp. 223–234.

4

Public Relations Writing

Good writing is clear, concise, correct, and complete.

Clear writing presents ideas logically and explains terms that may be unfamiliar to the reader.

Concise writing takes the shortest path to understanding, using words and sentences that are economical—but not at the expense of style and grace.

Correct writing follows the rules of spelling, grammar, and syntax. It is accurate and does not obscure or bend the truth.

Complete writing does not leave readers unsatisfied or uncertain whether they know all they need to know about the subject.

In this chapter we shall see that the style and form of public relations writing differs according to the needs, interests, and capabilities of the target audience. The nature of the medium and the context in which the message is disseminated also may dictate different approaches to the task of writing.

Whatever the situation, the underlying principal is that public relations writing performs its intended purpose only if it meets the minimal definition of "good writing"—clear, concise, correct, and complete.

To understand the variety of types of writing a public relations practitioner must be prepared to do, let's look at the case of a company listed on the New York Stock Exchange that intends to streamline its manufacturing process by introducing electronic robots on the assembly line

ONE CLIENT— MANY WRITING TASKS

and in the packaging and shipping operations. The public relations department—perhaps aided by freelancers or an agency brought in to augment the regular staff—must consider the information needs of several different audiences:

- *Managers* within the company must receive memos, plans, announcements, timetables, operating manuals, and guidelines to help them prepare for the changeover to automation. Complex information in large quantities must be organized and explained following company procedures and using the terminology particular to the specialized field.
- *Employees* of the firm—including many not affected by the changes—must learn of the impending adjustments in timely fashion, and in ways that do not cause stress or concern. They must be persuaded that the change will improve the company's competitive position, and thus strengthen its ability to provide continued employment for its workforce. Because many employees can neither understand the technical terms involving the automated systems, nor comprehend the economic necessities involved in modernizing, the information must be made accessible and understandable to everyone.
- *Suppliers and customers* of the firm must be told at some point how the changes will affect them, sometimes in general terms, but in the case of some suppliers, perhaps in very technical terms.
- *Trade publications* will want very complete and technical explanations of the new systems that will be informative for others in the same line of business.
- *Stockholders and the investment community* who are concerned with the "bottom line" of profitability will want to have the changes explained in terms of the company's balance sheet, its cash position, its competitive stance, and its projections for the future.
- *Community leaders and government officials* will be concerned about the impact on employment, the social welfare of the community, the effect on labor relations, and implications for the future of the industry. They may be interested in the legal ramifications of the move, and the lawyers for the company may counsel very careful handling of all public pronouncements.
- *The news media*—local, regional and perhaps even state or national—will expect an announcement story for the news pages, a more economics-oriented story for the business section, and eventually "feature" or "human interest" stories about the impact of the change on employees of the company. If there is a suggestion of resistance by employees and their unions, the press may seek information for "investigative" pieces.

The needs of all these audiences should be anticipated by public relations people who are prepared to write to satisfy each one in its own way.

Selecting the Appropriate Style

The public relations writer must know the appropriate style for the intended audience before beginning to write. If it is not intuitive, then the writer must consult with the public relations manager to determine which of the following approaches will be most effective.

Business Style is appropriate for reports, executive summaries, and memos that will be distributed to personnel at many levels of an organization. (See Chapter 18 for information on the content and style of business writing.) Contrasted with other styles, business writing may be more impersonal and formal, especially if the communication is between personnel who normally do not speak to one another in the organization.

Personal Style is appropriate for notes and memos between members of a staff who work regularly together, including those on equal footing as well as supervisors who have an informal working relationship with those they supervise. Written in the first person, these messages may make use of colloquialisms and "shop talk" to get their points across.

Familiar Style often is used in employee publications and memos intended to build a team and gain compliance with management objectives. Not unlike a coach, the writer may exhort the readers to action and call upon sports or family imagery to foster a "let's all pull together" sense of togetherness.

Trade Style assumes that the readers are all familiar with the jargon of a sector of the market or workplace, and thus technical terms and industry norms are not explained or defined in every instance. Articles sent to trade magazines do not insult the readers by talking down to them and assume that they are up-to-date on processes and procedures found in the industry or field.

Straight-News Style is used for releases to the general news media and to the financial press. Journalistic norms of story organization, objectivity, explanation of terms, use of quotes or paraphrase, ethics, and avoidance of libel are followed in preparation of the straight-news story. These will be discussed in the chapters that follow on preparing news releases and working with the media.

Feature Style is used for articles prepared for both internal and external audiences where the format of the newsletter or magazine calls for luring the reader with a catchy lead, then relating the information in a tone that is more casual and light than one would expect in a straight-news story. "Human interest" material including informal quotes, illustrative passages, and sometimes even a first-person approach to telling the story are all permissible when the topic and the communication channel make the feature style appropriate.

Legal Style may be necessary when a crisis confronts an organization and improper statements to external audiences—or even to employee groups—may jeopardize the legal position of the organization. In such cases, the legal department of a corporation, or counsel hired by a public relations agency, will recommend the proper approach and, if so empowered, dictate the exact phrases to be used in answering inquiries from the media.

The writing style might be determined by the needs of the particular medium:

The Broadcast Media use significantly fewer words than the print media and thus require tighter writing that is tailored for reading aloud by an announcer or newscaster. Radio, unlike television, prizes "visual" writing that helps the listener to picture what is happening.

Trade Magazines, as we noted, have their own style. They also have departments such as "Trends" and "New Products" with special formats that may include a standard number of words and a standard headline or caption. The public relations writer aiming at an influential trade magazine department can increase the chance of placing an item by crafting the information to fit the standard space and style.

Commentators and Columnists have their idiosyncrasies, and catering to them increases the chances of placing a story with them. Think of the different whims and fancies of, say, Charles Kuralt, Charles Osgood ("The Osgood File"), Dan Rather, and Walter Cronkite. They all do commentary for CBS radio and/or television. But each has a different style and outlook. Make it folksy for Kuralt. Point out the oddity for Osgood. Make it full of portent for Rather. Take the historical perspective for Cronkite.

Regional Media may require a nod to local terminology and shared culture values. Articles on a new product or service might be prepared in different versions for audiences in New England, the Southeast, Texas, California, and the Great Plains. Subtle differences might include different images and names of the people described as using the product or service.

CHECKLIST ✔ Selecting the Right Writing Style

✔ What is the relationship of the target public to your organization?
   Internal or external?
   Friendly, hostile, indifferent, or unfamiliar?

✔ What is the level of expertise of your public?
   Well-informed, partially informed, or uninformed?

✔ What is the interest level of your public?
   Motivated to seek information and read it?
   Mildly interested in the topic?
   Unaware of the need to be informed on the topic?

✔ What are the style requirements of the medium/channel selected?
   Straight-news style required?
   Feature style is an option and may be desirable?
   Trade or business style required?
   Special requirements (broadcast)?

✔ To what style does the subject matter lend itself?
   Serious, straightforward subject?
   Human interest angle?

✔ To what extent do management objectives dictate the writing style?
   Personality and style of sources used for the article?
   What facet of the organization is being featured?
   Are there legal requirements for the information communicated?

✔ What was the style of past communications with the target public?
   Should the new message strike a new tone?
   Must the message be consistent with past communications?

Consult Your Stylebook(s)

So far we have used "style" to mean the fashion in which words are arranged to fit a certain mindset or approach. The word "style" also is used by those with journalistic training to refer to the specific set of rules laid down for capitalization, punctuation, and handling of the identification of persons and things. Style, in this second sense, is spelled out in a *stylebook*—a manual prescribing the forms a writer must follow when preparing articles.

The standard manual used by the print news media is the *Associated Press Stylebook and Libel Manual* (AP Stylebook, for short). Broadcast media and some print media may use the *United Press Stylebook,* and larger newspapers such as *The New York Times* have their own style manuals.

Most newspapers have their own supplements to the AP Stylebook to cover local terms and institutions that may not be covered by the standard style manual. By studying local media, public relations firms and departments can determine special cases where rules differ.

Individual companies may publish their own style manuals for use by the public relations people in their headquarters offices and in the field. Amoco Corporation, headquartered in Chicago, prepares its own stylebook that follows AP style in standard situations. In addition, Amoco spells out for its public relations writers the special usages of the oil industry: tank farm and tank truck are two words, but tankwagon is one word; TBA (for tires, batteries, and accessories) is acceptable in headlines for oil-industry readership, but not for articles released to the general media. Special rules are provided for mentions of Amoco services and subsidiaries: The Amoco Foundation, Inc. may be referred to as "the Foundation" in second reference, and it must always be described as "financially supported by Amoco Corporation," not as a "unit" or an "arm" of the Amoco Corporation.[1]

Directors of public relations for many organizations also prescribe other manuals for writers in their organizations, the most popular being *The Elements of Style,* Third Edition, by William Strunk, Jr., as edited and expanded by E. B. White—the "little book" that has influenced two generations of writers who want to achieve clarity and correctness of expression. Fowler's *Modern English Usage* and *New York Times* editor Theodore M. Bernstein's *The Careful Writer: A Modern Guide to English Usage* are also favorites of public relations executives who encourage their writers to uphold the highest standards of writing.

The most important reason for learning style and using a style manual to look up what you have not yet learned is to achieve *consistency* in writing and to fit your written product to the norms that editors expect will be followed. The aim of stylebooks is not to stifle creativity, which is fortunate because most public relations writers prize the opportunity to use creative approaches to get attention for their client's message.

Editors Expect Correct News Style

In another of its many public-spirited gestures, the Goodall Company has announced that once more it will take the lead in community betterment by donating a generous gift of $10,000 worth of playground equipment to the city so that the little children of the low-income Helmsley housing development can enjoy their summer. . . .

The donation of playground equipment certainly is a newsworthy occurrence. Most media gladly would give the story space—unless, that is, they learned of the event through a news release filled with such

---

CHECKLIST ✔ Public Relations Writing

✔ Has the target public been defined specifically enough so that the best channel of communication and the best style of writing can be selected?

✔ Is the selected channel of communication the one that will best reach and influence the target public?

✔ Is the writing style—including vocabulary and amount of background information—appropriate to the target public?

✔ Is the story complete enough to satisfy the information needs of the target public? Are fundamental questions left unanswered?

✔ Is the correct stylebook followed for the channel selected? (AP Stylebook or other media stylebook; organizational stylebook?)

    ___ Punctuation   ___ Handling titles and IDs of individuals
    ___ Spelling   ___ Identifications of groups and organizations
    ___ Numbers   ___ Proper handling of quotes and paraphrases

✔ Is the length of every element appropriate for the audience and channel?

    ___ words   ___ sentences   ___ paragraphs   ___ the entire item

✔ Is the use of jargon and specialized vocabulary appropriate to the situation?

✔ Is reader interest maintained throughout?

    ___ Does the opening section identify the topic and attract attention?

    ___ Does the information flow logically throughout the piece?

    ___ Does the item indicate how or where more information can be obtained?

✔ Does the piece satisfy the information needs of the target public?

Instructors and students: A grading version of this checklist is found in the instructor's manual and may be used for evaluation of class assignments.

---

puffery as "public-spirited gesture," "taking the lead once more," and "generous gift." The gratuitously sentimental image of "little children enjoying their summer" only compounds the error.

News editors rankle at such blatant and self-serving phrases. On a slow day, they might be willing to edit the offending news release. But, then again, they might not have the time or the inclination. It is up to the writer of the news release to know what the editor is looking for in style and format.

Exhibit 4.1
Avoid "Hype" Words
That Editors Hate

Wall Street Journal reporter Michael W. Miller—who one day received sixty pieces of mail from high-technology companies hoping he would write stories about their products—analyzed the words that are used most frequently to "hype" an article and make the new product seem worthy of news coverage. His analysis provides an example of the press agentry approach to media relations.

Miller catalogued and analyzed 201 new-product releases received in the period of one month. Based on that study, here is his list of the most overused words by public relations writers for high-tech firms:

1.	Leading	(88)
2.	Enhanced	(47)
3.	Unique	(35)
4.	Significant	(30)
5.	Solution	(23)
6.	Integrated	(23)
7.	Powerful	(20)
8.	Innovative	(18)
9.	Advanced	(17)
10.	High-performance	(17)
11.	Sophisticated	(17)

Source: Michael W. Miller, "High-Tech Hype Reaches New Heights," *The Wall Street Journal,* January 12, 1989, p. B–1.

Getting legitimate news stories published or broadcast in the community news media is a major public relations goal for any organization. It's no wonder, then, that newswriting experience is a prime requisite for a well-rounded practitioner. A study of two hundred PRSA members showed that 90 percent of the professionals in the field say basic newswriting is the most important course required of the PR student, even ahead of the basic introduction to public relations course.[2]

Writing and Public Relations Models

Not all public relations techniques require writing skill, but the majority of them do. In addition, writing represents a crucial skill in each of the four models of public relations practice described in Chapter 1.

Many of the practitioners who stress the importance of writing practice the public information or press agentry models. Writing is critical to practitioners of those models, whose main objective is to place stories in the news media—where unclear writing cannot be tolerated—or to produce brochures and other publications.

Yet writing is equally critical for the two-way asymmetric and symmetric models. The persuasive communicators of the asymmetric model often look for motivations of readers or for writing devices that will make persuasion possible. What they ignore is the simple fact that people cannot be persuaded to accept an idea unless they understand it—and that clear writing is a key to understanding.[3]

In the two-way symmetric model, the public relations person uses many interpersonal communication channels. But even in this model, practitioners communicate most often with their publics through print or broadcast media, and those messages must be written. Messages to management about publics generally are written, too, as memos or reports. A two-way symmetric practitioner who wants to be understood must be able to write well.

REQUIREMENTS OF PUBLIC RELATIONS WRITING

Several specific categories of public relations writing including press releases, speeches, radio announcements, and scripts, will be examined in later chapters. At this point, however, it is useful to take a general look at the special requirements of the field, including maximum objectivity, source review, long-range implications, consistency, achieving maximum impact, and special style considerations.

Although we speak frequently of public relations writing as if it were a subfield of its own, we must acknowledge that the best PR writing blends into context by adopting a style and tone consistent with the medium chosen for its dissemination. The practitioner must learn to emulate straight news style for a basic news release, then shift gears into a "feature" style for a magazine article, or a conversational tone for the script of a welcoming speech. In other words, PR writing is doing its job when the audience never stops to think, "This is good PR writing!"

Maximum Objectivity

Objectivity sounds like an absolute: A writer either is biased or unbiased. But the best news reporter or editor knows that every sentence is a compromise. Every choice of adjective presents a problem of drawing a completely "accurate" picture of the truth.

The beginning reporter is taught that objectivity begins with keeping himself out of the story. Instead of writing, "I observed an oddly dressed procession outside the courthouse," which suggests a response based on personal values, one learns to write, "Eleven young men dressed as colonial elders marched up the steps of the courthouse carrying anti-taxation placards." The reader can decide whether that scene is "odd," or moving, or whatever.

Reporters may keep their own views out of a straight news story, but they are often identified with a byline. That simple device has the effect of informing the reader that one person's eyes and mind have filtered the facts in the article. But the public relations writer works anonymously. PR writing must stand on its own merits, divorced from the identity of the author. For the reader to accept anonymous information, the words and sentences must carry self-evident authority and integrity.

How do PR writers reconcile the need for credibility with the need to be loyal to their employer? It is a matter of keeping the employing organization in mind when gathering the information, and then keeping the editor—and, by extension, the reader—in mind when organizing the information and writing it for publication.

In other words, the writer who is planning an article on new engine developments for General Motors probably would gather information only from GM's research and testing facilities, whereas the newspaper reporter would be obligated to interview GM's competitors as well as independent researchers and auto industry critics such as Ralph Nader. However, when the PR writer sits down to assemble the article, the information is developed in the same way as the news reporter would do it, looking first for a lively angle to get the readers thinking about what sort of car they'll be driving in a decade, and then summarizing the types of propulsion envisioned by the engineers.

Both the news reporter and the PR writer would rely on the same elements to carry the story along: visual description, anecdotes about testing of the new systems, quotes from engineers who know the capabilities and drawbacks of the test engines, and simple statistics that give an idea of the cost savings or other benefits of the technological developments.

Source Review

Despite deadline pressures, material written by the news reporter is subjected to some scrutiny before it is printed. A city editor or news editor reads the piece to ensure that the content is complete, adequately explained, free of libel, and attributed properly to knowledgeable sources. Next, a copy editor checks spelling and grammar, verifies addresses and proper identification of sources, attempts to remedy any lack of clarity that results from careless or complex writing, and, finally, assures that the newspaper's style for figures, quotations, titles, and punctuation has been followed. Rarely does an editor double-check the reporter by telephoning a source to verify a fact or a quote. The assumption is made that the reporter got the basic facts straight. If the source complains, the remedy may be a small correction notice the next day or a subsequent story that clarifies the matter. If the editors feel no great harm was done by the slight inaccuracy or misplaced emphasis, nothing will be done.

The PR writer finds a different reality. One professor puts it this way:

> *It is considered a breach of journalistic ethics for the source of a story to review the copy prior to publication. Journalists do not wish to render themselves vulnerable to pressure from the source, even at the risk of getting the facts wrong.*
>
> *In public relations, on the other hand, review of written copy by a source is frequent. It is one reason that the factual accuracy of press releases is far superior to media-generated stories; press releases have been checked by someone other than the writer who is thoroughly familiar with the facts. Most practitioners know by experience what embarrassment such checking can save them.[4]*

So, in addition to the omission of a byline as a reward, we now note that the PR writer's pride of authorship must be subjected to another burden—the approval of others who may not be appreciative of good writing. One of the crucial interpersonal skills a PR practitioner must develop is the ability to take the criticism of a piece of writing from a superior who knows the technical facts better than the writer does, incorporate the necessary changes into the written message, and still maintain the style, interest, and integrity of the words so they will attract a media audience.

To sensitize nonwriters in an organization to what you are doing, it may be useful to show them models of media stories you intend to emulate in order to get space in the news media. A superior who has no mental picture of the final product may instead visualize a dry technical report. If, on the other hand, you can show examples of the kind of "spread" you're aiming for, the superior may grant the creative leeway you need in order to write an article that will attract an editor's attention.

Long-Range Implications/Consistency

Newswriting is ephemeral. The reporter usually worries only about the current twenty-four-hour cycle of news production. If the facts appear to change tomorrow, it's simply a matter of updating the story by "finding a new angle."

The PR writer enjoys no such luxury. Access to the public media cannot be taken for granted. And when a story does appear, the impression it leaves with the public may last until such time as it is again your organization's "turn" to get news space, or until you have another item of fresh and legitimate news interest. The PR writer must review past articles about the organization, determine how the public perceives the organization or program, and then write a piece that will be consistent with how the writer wants the public to view it. Advertisers talk of "maintaining market position" for a product. Similarly, it is useful for the PR writer to view articles in the media as a way of maintaining position in the marketplace of ideas, or of "repositioning" the organization's programs, if that is needed.

Another parallel between advertising and public relations writing is the need for consistency, so as to reap the effects of repetition. Imagine if the Coca-Cola people said "Things go better with Coke" one time and "Coke makes everything taste better" the next time. You have to work hard to get an idea to remain in the reader's mind after the act of receiving the message is over. Develop a concept, work out the written expression of it, and then use it faithfully without alteration.

For example, the publicist, the director, and the president of the board of trustees of a museum must agree to refer to the institution in all public messages as "a regional arts facility serving the citizens of the tri-county area" if they want to implant the notion that the museum does not belong to the city in which it is located, and is not restricting itself to use by cultural elites. The payoff comes when the organization notes in articles and editorials initiated by news media personnel that the phrase has caught on as the proper identification. Sometimes the goal may seem simple, like making certain that people say "Health Systems Plan" instead of merely "Health Plan" when they refer to an agency. But the discrimination may be subtly important in terms of the public's ability to identify the role and contribution of that agency.

You'll especially want to use repetition when your analysis of publics shows that people will be passively processing rather than actively seeking out the message you have written. People who actively seek information tend to remember it because they need to use it to guide their behavior. But when they don't really need the information—which is true of most public relations messages—they will not go out of their way to remember what you said. You have to repeat your message over and over so that they not only process the message, they remember some of it as well.

Achieving Maximum Impact

Simplicity versus completeness.

That, in a nutshell, is the dilemma PR writers face every time they sit down at the keyboard.

Simplicity is vital because "the news system is a relentless process of progressive simplification and oversimplification," as one PR consultant has pointed out.[5] Faced with thousands of worthy stories competing for attention each day, editors and readers alike distill it all down into bite-sized chunks:

> The local hospital has a new CAT-scanner that will save many lives through faster, better diagnosis.

Poor people can get help with their rent from the county housing authority.

The local auto assembly plant expects rising car sales to result in the recall of laid-off workers.

In reality, each of those important stories is much more compli-cated. Because the hospital was designated to house the CAT-scanner, it will not be given permission by the state to become a center for car-diac analysis and therapy. The requirements for county rent aid are complex, and it may be more advantageous for low-income tenants to receive pass-along rent savings from a landlord who qualifies for ren-ovation assistance under a less-well-known federal program. The re-turn to full auto employment may be temporary, pending the manufacturer's long-range plans to phase out the local facility.

Simplicity or completeness? The PR writer tries to have it both ways by giving the news media a concise and understandable twelve-paragraph press release summarizing the story in a way that is readable and interesting. And then the reporter or editor is provided with an accompanying press packet that includes fact sheets that go into greater detail about specifics.

The hope is that the news organization, once it has used the succinct version of the story, will see the need for an in-depth report and will use the press packet as background for a Sunday feature or magazine piece. Another technique is to distribute the simplified press release at a news conference where organization officials with the necessary expertise are ready to answer the press's more probing questions. If the media want to go with the concisely digested version, fine. If they want depth and breadth, the opportunity is there.

Involving the Reader

By this point, communicating with some sort of flair may seem to be totally out of the question, so complicated is the PR writer's task. But no. Once all those other thorny problems are addressed, PR writing, like all good writing, must capture the attention of the reader, engage the imagination, and eventually, one hopes, gain approval.

Begin any writing task by identifying—and then identifying with— the readers. In an institutional advertisement sponsored by the Interna-tional Paper Company, author Kurt Vonnegut pleaded with writers:

Pity the readers. They have to identify thousands of little marks on paper and make sense of them immediately. They have to read, an art so difficult that most people don't really master it even after having studied it all through grade school and high school—twelve long years.[6]

People tend to read or listen to messages for one of two reasons. Sometimes, the message has practical relevance to them. At other times, the message has no relevance, but if it is written well, they will read it because the message arouses interest or curiosity.

What involves your readers? How will a development change their lives? What's in it for them?

An article that introduces a new product shouldn't focus on the fact that the company "has announced" marketing of the product. It should focus on what the product can do for the consumer: "The drudgery of fertilizing the lawn can be greatly reduced with a spreader attachment that spreads pellets at the same time the homeowner is mowing the lawn. Introduction of the GREEN-SPRED device was announced this week by . . ."

You got the reader's attention by bringing the story close to home, literally and figuratively. Keep that attention by humanizing the story, which means having people talking. Use quotes from those who are most affected by the program or product your organization is promoting. Don't let them ramble; synthesize what they have to say into a brief, memorable sentence or two: "My customers used to groan when I told them it was time to attack the dandelions," smiles hardware store owner Hy Becker, "but GREEN-SPRED means they can do two jobs at once and not drop over from exhaustion."

If there is really no way to show the relevance of your message because the reader's involvement is low, then you've got to simplify and brighten your writing. Packaging information in digestible portions makes the message more palatable. The writer may find that a forty-word sentence in a memo to the boss has the effect of adding importance and apparent substance to the message. But a forty-word sentence in an article may be just the turnoff the reader needs in order to justify returning to the program on the tube.

So, write short. Short words. Short sentences. Short paragraphs . . . with an occasional long one for variety.

Read your material out loud, and punctuate where the sentence compounds or where you insert an explanatory phrase. The resulting "visual relief," which supplements the required structural punctuation, helps the reader's eye.

Avoid overcapitalization. Organizations have a tendency to capitalize the name of every little subcommittee and program. The news services, in the interest of speed and clarity, have taught us to expect only proper names and the names of full organizations to be capitalized (Consolidated Edison, for example, but "Con Ed's rate advisory board" rather than "Rate Advisory Board").

When you have written enough, don't be afraid to end neatly and swiftly. Like this.

Evaluating Your Writing

Many people think that writing is an art, that it can't be evaluated. Don't be misled. Only stream-of-consciousness writers fail to evaluate their work.

Because the principal objective of writing is message retention, you can evaluate your own writing by putting it aside for a few days and then reading it over by yourself. Have you retained your own messsage? Do you understand what you want to say? Ask someone else to read what you have written and tell you what you said. You'll be surprised at how often the other person fails to retain the message.

If you want to use formal evaluation devices, refer to the appendix on evaluation research. The readability tests outlined there will help you to determine whether you have written simply enough for your audience. You'll probably find the signaled stopping technique (SST) to be the most useful technique to evaluate your writing. That's where you or someone else reads your writing, and whenever you or the reader feels like stopping, you or he note the reason for stopping—such as confusion, rereading, or disagreement. It's an excellent technique for finding what goes on in the reader's mind (or your own mind). The reasons given for stopping will help you when you rewrite or edit your work.

Remember this axiom: Good writing is not merely written; it is rewritten.

NOTES

1. *WritingStyle: A guide to writing style and usage for Amoco communicators.* The authors are indebted to Michael E. Thompson, Director, Corporate Media Relations, Amoco Corporation, Chicago, for providing us with a copy of the firm's stylebook.

2. Mike Shelly, "PR Professionals Pick News Writing as Priority Course," *Journalism Educator* (January 1981), p. 16.

3. See, for example, Richard E. Petty, Thomas M. Ostrom, and Timothy C. Brock (eds.), *Cognitive Responses in Persuasion* (Hillsdale, NJ: Lawrence Erlbaum Associates, 1981).

4. John S. Detweiler, "Public Relations Writing Is Different," paper presented to the Association for Education in Journalism, Boston, 1980, p. 16.

5. Richard M. Detwiler, "Executives Make 10 Great Mistakes Mis-Coping with News," *Public Relations Journal* (December 1975), p. 17.

6. Kurt Vonnegut, "How to Write with Style" (reprints available from International Paper Company, Dept. 5-T, P.O. Box 900, Elmsford, NY, 10523).

ADDITIONAL READING

Bivins, Thomas, *Handbook for Public Relations Writing* (Lincolnwood, IL: NTC Business Books, 1988).

Flesch, Rudolf, *The Art of Readable Writing*, rev. ed. (New York: Macmillan, 1986).

Gunning, Robert, *The Technique of Clear Writing*, rev. ed. (New York: McGraw-Hill, 1986).

Kessler, Lauren, and Duncan McDonald, *Mastering the Message: Media Writing with Substance and Style* (Belmont, CA: Wadsworth, 1989).

Newson, Doug, and James Wollert, *Media Writing: Preparing Information for the Mass Media* (Belmont, CA: Wadsworth, 1988).

Pesmen, Sandra, *Writing for the Media* (Lincolnwood, IL: NTC Business Books, 1983).

Pickens, Judy, Patricia Walsh Rao, and Linda Cook, *Without Bias: A Guidebook for Nondiscriminatory Language* (New York: John Wiley, 1982).

Strunk, William, and E. B. White, *The Elements of Style*, 3d ed. (New York: Macmillan, 1979).

Zinsser, William, *On Writing Well*, 3d ed. (New York: Harper & Row, 1988).

5

Preparing News Releases and Press Kits

At first glance, the daily newspaper serving your region or city and the weekly newspaper covering your town or neighborhood appear to be written by staff reporters. Magazines, trade publications, and other specialized periodicals also carry the bylines of staff writers and editors. Indeed, the final versions of the stories and articles we read each day are assembled and packaged by journalists. But often the raw materials—the ideas, facts and figures, quotes, and even tables or charts—are prepared by public relations professionals working for their companies or their clients.

The free information comes to the media in the form of news releases, sometimes in multi-part press kits that include fact sheets, biographical sketches of persons mentioned in the main release, photographs, other graphic materials, and reprints of earlier articles on the same subject. This "subsidization" of the media, where companies and clients foot the bill for preparation of information for use by reporters and editors, works to keep the cost of the mass media low.[1]

Read critically and you will discern the large amount of information that the media do not create, but merely pass along. This chapter helps you know how to prepare such information for use by the media.

Four members of management have just been named vice presidents. That's newsworthy to the readers of weekly newspapers in the various suburban communities where each of the officers lives. It also is of

RELEASES SERVE MANY PURPOSES

interest to those who keep up with your field through a biweekly trade journal.

Your company has shifted to a new advertising agency in preparation for bringing out a new line of products. Advertising trade columnists will want to know about it, and the products also should be written up in the public media.

Plans for modernizing your plant mean profitable construction contracts for many other area firms—a development that will be important news in the regional Chamber of Commerce magazine.

Other occasions for issuing news releases include:

- Milestones, such as anniversaries of a company's existence, the millionth customer, or a decade since the introduction of a successful product or service.
- New savings or economies, such as institution of an energy-conservation or recycling program, or the achievement of productivity goals.
- Selection of the company by another institution or by a government agency to produce a component or service a new program.
- The winning of achievement awards by the company or its individual employees. Also, completion of training programs by managers or other employees.
- Opinions of company officials regarding the economy, pending legislation affecting business, or other public issues in which the firm has an interest.
- The results of research.
- Announcement of a contest.

The list could be virtually endless, and so far it includes only *good* news. Obviously, it also may be useful to issue a press release if you fire four vice presidents, lose an anticipated contract, decide to close a plant instead of modernizing it, or if your plant burns down and the fire chief states allegations of improper storage of combustible materials.

At holiday time, a beverage company distributes a feature release describing how to entertain large groups of people, complete with a photograph depicting the ideal setup (with the company's products prominently displayed, of course). Any company involved in high technology probably can arrange for a panel of its scientists and engineers to predict the future a decade or a century hence, resulting in an interesting article for the Sunday newspaper.

Editors Depend on Releases

Some editors say they never look at the piles of "handouts" that cross their desks each day.[2] But usually even the largest news organizations sort out the releases that offer tips, ideas, data, or other starting points for staff reporters, who will assemble and write a story in their own style. Routinely, certain columns in almost every paper are put together by pasting up news releases: business promotions, military personnel activities, and cultural and entertainment events. Similarly, many of the short "bulletin board" items about meetings and social events carried by local newspapers and radio stations come to them as news releases.[3]

Most weekly and small daily newspapers with limited resources depend heavily on news and features provided by governments, educational institutions, and trade associations to fill their columns. Similarly, radio station news personnel receive taped feature materials from public relations departments, and they have the phone numbers of "daily feed" systems that permit them to tape a minute or more of "live quote" information from spokespersons for various organizations. The amount of information in the media that has its origins in news releases cannot be underestimated.

First, we will look at the format for the standard news release. Then we shall examine the difference between broadcast and print releases, the matter of timing a release, and methods of submission.

THE NEWS RELEASE

A small electronics company was proud of its letterhead, printed on a cream-colored, heavy linen paper with burgundy ink. The firm's officers were listed down the side of the stationery, and superimposed in the middle of the sheet was a faint image of a computer data display. It was enough to make recipients of a letter squint. When an unsophisticated public relations person decided to use the letterhead to carry news releases, it made editors see red.

Ideally, a release is prepared so that the news editor can hand it quickly to a rewrite person for light editing. The copy desk then quickly writes a headline in the available white space left at the top of the first page.

Flyers Aren't Releases

The Neptune Swim Club's flyer publicizing its upcoming regional swim meet is a perfectly legitimate example of a *flyer* intended to arouse interest and gain support from an *internal audience*. The folksy style is appropriate for members of a club, including the direct appeal to "come out and show your support." The extravagant use of capitalization, quote marks, and underlining is probably the simplest way to build excitement in a flyer that is prepared on a typewriter. The crude drawings add to the fun for an internal audience. Even the fact that the

Exhibit 5.1

<u>COME ONE, COME ALL TO THE GOLDEN STATE'S BIGGEST SWIM MEET!!!</u>

The coaches have been working <u>hard</u>, and the kids have put in <u>long</u> hours, and now THE NEPTUNE SWIM CLUB is ready once again to say: "Welcome, Southern California!" It's time for the "Pop" Smith trophy to be awarded once again, and once again THE NEPTUNE SWIM CLUB contingent is strong and competetive.

<u>You</u> can be there to join in the excitement! Now is the time to order your tickets for the annual swim meet that pits the finest Southern California talents against once another. Of course we'll be rooting for NEPTUNE, favored hosts of the meet, and the swim team that has given the Golden State its finest champions in the past.

THE NEPTUNE SWIM CLUB is <u>proud</u> to have a trophy named after our illustrious coach, who has gone on to coach the Olympic team. <u>Come out</u> and show your support for NEPTUNE and coach Bob Smith!

NEWS
FOR IMMEDIATE RELEASE

Contact:
J. Y. Young
Neptune Swim Club
1234 Route 56
West Suburba, CA
(213) 123-4567

NEPTUNE SWIM CLUB HOSTS
REGIONAL COMPETITION

Swimmers from 11 Southern California swim clubs will compete for the Robert "Pop" Smith Trophy Saturday at the Neptune Swim Club on Route 56 in West Suburba.

Boys and girls age 6 through 11 who have qualified through the summer-long "Splash and Dash" program will take part in relays, diving competition, and individual events. First place winners qualify to compete in the state meet next month in Santa Clara.

The "Pop" Smith trophy is named for the longtime coach of the Neptune Swim Club who stepped down last year to coach the U.S. Olympic team. This is the third time in the past five years that the Neptune Swim Club has been the site of the regional competition.

Admission to the meet is $2 for adults and $1 for children under 12. For more information call club manager J. Y. Young at 123-4567.

#

flyer is printed on shocking pink paper is defensible: that way it will stand out from other announcements on the bulletin board and when it is mailed to club members.

But what happens when a copy of the flyer is sent to the local newspaper? An editor—presuming he or she isn't turned off by the corny art, the loud color, and the cheerleading style of writing—is faced with the task of doing a complete re-write to put the item into news style. And once that task is begun, it becomes apparent that some important information is missing: Is there an admission charge? What are the ages of the competitors? Where can interested parties obtain more information about the event?

Not-for-profit groups usually can't afford the services of a professional public relations agency. But even a volunteer with basic experience writing a release can work on the simplest typewriter or personal computer to turn out a competent release that will make it easy for the editor to use the information. (In many states, *pro bono*—"for the good"— programs are run by chapters of public relations organizations for the express purpose of mentoring members of nonprofits so that they can turn out an acceptable news release.)

The reincarnation of the Neptune Swim Club flyer as a proper news release (page 89) contains most of the elements of the basic release format: the "News" banner, identification of a contact person with address and phone number, the standard "For Immediate Release" line, a sample headline, the body of the article, and the end sign (#). We'll discuss the reasons for each of these conventional items below and include them on our checklist for this section as well.

ELEMENTS OF THE STANDARD NEWS RELEASE

If news releases really were "standard," there would simply be forms for public relations people to complete, or perhaps a software program calling for information in a fixed format. In fact, practitioners follow conventions that have been developed over years of relations between the news media and their information providers. The "rules" that follow may be bent if circumstances are unusual, but they are the tried-and-true way of packaging your client's story so that it has the best possible chance of attracting the attention and interest of the target editors.

Paper and Typeface

Print on one side only of plain white paper. Double-spacing is standard for news copy, and triple-spacing is not uncommon. In order to conserve the taxpayer's money, some government agencies double-space the first few paragraphs and then single space, on the theory that a rewrite person will rework the information in any case. Keeping the release all on one page also permits the editor to see all of the information at a glance.

Use a standard, clean typewriter face or one of the basic computer fonts for body text. Under no circumstance should script or any informal typeface be used. If your release is for radio use only, you may wish to render it in the quarter-inch-high typeface that is available on special typewriters (18-point on the computer). Use mylar (film) ribbons with a typewriter or a laser printer with a personal computer for crispness of type.

"News" Flag

To make it absolutely clear that the information is intended as a news release, the large single word NEWS in plain black or red letters is printed in large type (36-point is typical) near the top of the page.

Release Date

Floating clearly above the text, below the news flag, appears the underlined and capitalized phrase FOR IMMEDIATE RELEASE. In rare situations, you may wish to indicate a specific date and time of release, such as: For release at 6 p.m. Friday, Oct. 23. If you want to indicate that it is for release in time for morning newspapers and drive-time radio, say: For release AMS Tuesday, May 3. (The appropriateness of such an "embargo" is discussed later in this chapter.)

Contact Person

The name, address and phone number of the person to contact for additional information should appear in a block near the upper-right-hand corner of the page. Ordinarily the contact would be the person who prepared the release—either a member of the in-house staff or the practitioner at the agency that prepared the release for the client. In some cases, an agency puts the name of the client as the contact. Occasionally, on a new-product release or a story involving technical information, the public relations department will decide it is useful to list the product manager or the chief engineer as an alternate contact person. For the trade press, that eliminates the need to wait while the public relations department passes on the information request.

Exhibit 5.2
Sample News Release

Public Relations
Society of America

33 Irving Place
New York, NY 10003
(212) 995-2230

Contacts: Donna Peltier, APR
         Public Relations Director
         office: (212) 995-2230
         home: (212) 838-2870

         H.J. (Jerry) Dalton, Jr., APR   Joe Epley, APR
         1990 President   1990 President-elect
         (214) 979-7964   (704) 522-1220

PRSA REAFFIRMS PHOENIX CONFERENCE

CHICAGO, December 17 -- The Public Relations Society of America's
Board of Directors today unanimously reaffirmed its decision to
hold the Society's 1991 National Conference in Phoenix, Arizona,
November 3-6.

PRSA President H.J. (Jerry) Dalton, Jr., APR, said, "The
scheduling of our meeting in Phoenix and the recent defeat of the
Martin Luther King state paid holiday issue in Arizona converge
as a catalyst for PRSA to re-examine our profession's role as a
facilitator of change.

"The PRSA board strongly supports the concept of Martin
Luther King Day as a paid holiday nationwide. Consistent with
that and effective immediately, a PRSA presidential task force
will be appointed to support our PRSA chapters in Arizona in
efforts to achieve a state paid Martin Luther King holiday. This
task force will include members of our national Minority Affairs
Committee, PRSA members from Arizona, and members of the PRSA
College of Fellows.

- More -

Source: Courtesy of PRSA

Serial Number

Many organizations assign a code number to each release and include it
either in the heading, under the contact person area, at the end of the
first page of the release, or at the very end of the last page of the release.
The code number includes a few numbers representing the date of
release (93-11-3 might mean the third release in November, 1993), the

```
PRSA Reaffirms Phoenix Conference
2 - 2 - 2


     "Beyond  this,  we  will  undertake  other  programs  consistent
with  the  values  represented  by  the  life  of  Dr.  Martin  Luther
King,  Jr.    In  that  process,  we  will  look  first  at  our  own
professional society and its ability to bring people together."

     Today's  decision  was  made  in  a  specially  called  meeting  of
the  PRSA  Board  of  Directors  here.    During  the  day-long  meeting,
the  PRSA  board  heard  views  from  the  Minority  Affairs  Committee,
the  Phoenix  Chapter,  the  National  Conference  Committee  and  other
PRSA  leaders.

     Board  members  also  reported  on  views  expressed  to  them  about
the  conference  site  issue  by  the  presidents  of  most  of  the  101
PRSA  chapters  nationwide  and  by  chairmen  of  several  PRSA
professional  sections.

     The  Public  Relations  Society  of  America,  headquartered  in
New  York  City,  is  the  leading  professional  association  for  public
relations  practitioners  and  educators.    The  Society's  15,000
members  represent  business  and  industry,  counseling  firms,
government,  associations,  hospitals,  schools  and  nonprofit
organizations.


                              ###
```

initials of the person who prepared the release, and perhaps a few letters representing the type of release (NP might mean new product;
P could stand for personnel).

The serial number serves two purposes for organizations that prepare a large number of releases. If a reporter calls and inquires about a
topic for which there has been more than one release, the public relations
department can ask for the serial number to identify the release to which
the reporter is referring. The code system also is useful at the end of the

year or any other time when management requests an "audit" of the public information operation, or when budget-planning requires that the public relations manager prepare a recap of the numbers and types of releases prepared during the past year.

Headline

The headline on a release serves the same purpose as the headline on a story in a newspaper: to capture the reader's attention and to summarize the information in the article. This time the audience is the editor or reporter. The headline should be simple, direct, and written in the active voice:

```
Wheeling Steel Appoints Jones
  To Head Pittsville Foundries
```

Exhibit 5.3 shows the many variations possible when crafting a basic headline, and the pitfalls of writing a head that tells too much or too little.

The headline you provide won't necessarily be used. Usually editors will write a headline to fit their own specifications, so the sample is primarily a means of suggesting the important point of the story. If no headline is provided, leave approximately one-fourth of the page blank to allow the editor to write one right at the top of the release. Often the decision on whether or not to use a marginally newsworthy release is simply the ease with which it can be processed by the editor.

Dateline

Start the story with a so-called "dateline" which, in most cases today, no longer carries a date as it did a century ago when news traveled slowly. The dateline today usually carries the name of the place where the release originates. (Note that the Neptune Swim Club release did not carry the optional dateline.)

While many newspapers will move the name of the town into the body of the story, others still prefer a dateline. Some organizations use boldface to highlight names of towns mentioned throughout the article—**Green Bay,** for example—not because they will appear that way in final print, but in order to highlight them for editors who skim through looking for local names and places. You can even re-fold a release and mark town names with color so that a mention of Belleville on the second page of a list of appointments or awards will jump right out at the editor of the weekly *Belleville Bugle.*

Headlines look so simple sitting atop their stories. That is, they do if they are written well. Achieving both clarity and simplicity takes practice, however. One way to simplify the task is to offer a one-line headline:

Health Fairs to Explain Benefits

That does the job of catching the editor's attention and summarizing the main point of the release. It also doesn't look much like the headline the editor is likely to use on a story that runs one or two columns wide in a newspaper. So, if you have the time and patience, you'll try to offer a multi-line head similar to those used by the news media.

Here are some tries by various members of a public relations class, along with the instructor's comments:

Annual Health Fair to Benefit
Boeing Employees

(Lines should be more balanced in length. "Benefit" is used in a different way from the body of the story, which talks about "employee benefits." Head sounds too general, and the word "annual" makes it mundane.)

Health Fairs to Be Held
At Local Boeing Plants

(Acceptable, but ho-hum. "To be held" is an uninspired verb form that doesn't involve anyone.)

Boeing Employees to Explore
Health Benefits at Fairs

(This one fits the model of the classic headline: noun and verb in the first line, and an explanatory phrase in the second line. "Employees explore" is active. Clear and concise.)

Alternate Health Plan
For Boeing Employees

(Called a "label" head because it has no noun or verb. The story mentions alternatives to the standard health plan, but that fact is too complicated to be understood in a headline.)

Exhibit 5.3
Try Not to Lose
Your Head . . .

Exhibit 5.3 (*continued*)
Try Not to Lose
Your Head . . .

Employee Benefits Department to Sponsor
Health Info Fairs at Boeing Plants

(Too much information to absorb—heads should be brief. Focuses on the department rather than the employee—on the *sender* of the message instead of the *audience* for the message. "Sponsor" is an uninteresting verb.)

Boeing Health Fairs to Help
Employees in Making Choices

(Nice try, but ends up being unspecific, and it's complicated to read and retain the message. "Fairs/help" is a strange noun-verb combination.)

Boeing to Hold Health Fairs
To Enlighten Its Employees

(Well-meaning, but puts the emphasis on the company's action and sounds condescending toward the employees. For all the verbiage, it doesn't get at the angle of employees making choices.)

Boeing Plants to
Hold Health Fair

(Bare-bones. Splitting of verb between lines is a no-no, as would be a preposition at the end of the line. An editor might have to settle for this if the story called for a small one-column-wide head. But for the news release to carry such a condensed headline would be counterproductive.)

Come One, Come All to the Boeing
Employee Benefits Health Fairs!

(Restrain yourself: public relations isn't the same as advertising. Cut the ballyhoo.)

Slugline, Continuations, and End Sign

Standard newspaper copyediting marks and symbols should be used throughout. Follow the Associated Press style manual.

If a release runs more than one page, the word "more" should appear at the bottom of each page except the last. An end sign such as "30" or "#" indicates that there are no more pages.

The second and successive pages should be "slugged" at the top in the following manner:

PROMOTIONS—add one, or PROMOTIONS—2

PROMOTIONS—add two, or PROMOTIONS—3

The slug word ("Promotions," in this case) is selected from the first paragraph of the story and keys the most important aspect to the news.

These journalistic conventions signal that you are "playing the game" and that you know what the editor wants.

The news releases on pages 92–93 and page 112 provide models to follow. Before we look at them, however, it is important to understand the roles and functions of three key parts of any release: the lead, the main quote, and the "boilerplate" paragraph.

KEY COMPONENTS OF THE MAIN TEXT

The Summary Lead

Imagine you had just run the marathon and you were asked to explain your company's plans to open a new plant to make a new product. Knowing you had the breath for maybe fifty words, you'd make sure every syllable counted. That's the task the writer faces when drafting the first paragraph—the *lead*—of a news release. If the editor, and by extension the target audience member, isn't clear about what the story involves and why it is important after the first paragraph, the subsequent paragraphs will never be read.

(You must realize, too, that even though you send out a three-page news release, the editor may deem the story worth only a single paragraph in a "round-up" of similar news items. That single paragraph that makes it into print will be your lead. So, you have to write the lead with the objective of making it a story that can stand alone.)

Let's examine some leads and what they are trying to accomplish. In addition to standard summary leads, we'll look at a few snappy ones

---

CHECKLIST ✔ Print News Release

✔ Is the release printed on one side only of plain paper?
   14-inch paper okay, but 11-inch paper is standard.
   Double-spaced typing.
   Plain, easy-to-read typeface.
   No decorations, lists or excessive use of logos and slogans.

✔ Is the release plainly marked with the word "NEWS" or "News Release"?

✔ Does the phrase "For Immediate Release" signal the editor?
   Embargo ("For release at . . .") only if necessary.

✔ Is the name and phone number of a "Contact" person provided?
   Should be someone capable of answering inquiries from the press.

✔ Is the released datelined with information useful to the editor?
   City of news origin should be provided.
   Date of release also may be provided in the opening line (optional).

✔ Is a headline provided?
   Should be one or two lines, with noun, verb, and explanatory clause.
   If no headline, capsule summary may alert editor to the news.
   Use plain typeface.
   Avoid hype.

✔ If there is more than one page, is a running slug line used to label pages?
   Provide a key word and successive numbers.
   Write "more" at end of each page; put end sign at end of last page.

✔ Are bias, opinions, and "hype" avoided?
   All opinions should be in the form of quotations.
   All quotes should be attributed to a fully identified source.

✔ Is the information presented in order of importance (inverted pyramid)?
   Explain terms and concepts that appear in quotes.
   Alternate paragraphs with basic info, context, data, and quotes.

✔ Are illustrative materials provided with the article to enhance its use?
   Cutline for photo or graphic should identify all persons depicted.
   Art materials should be identified with same slug line as the article.

that aim to pique the reader's interest. In such cases, the second explanatory paragraph is considered part of the lead.

NEW YORK, April 2, 1991 – Two of New York's largest thrifts intend to file for approval to merge into what would be the nation's fourth largest mutual savings bank, it was announced today.

The Metropolitan Savings Bank and The Brooklyn Savings Bank would have combined assets in excess of $3.9 billion . . .

This straightforward "hard news" lead summarizes the main point of the story. Because the names of the two banks involved in the proposed merger would tend to clutter the first paragraph with too much information, they are saved for the second paragraph.

CHICAGO, November 12, 1990 – American Excelsior Company, a leading manufacturer of innovative, natural packaging materials, announced today its latest environmentally-sound packaging product--corn starch-based Eco-Foam™ loose fill.

Made from a special hybrid corn, Eco-Foam loose fill is composed of over 95 percent corn starch. Due to its high starch content, it begins to decompose on contact when saturated with water. Unlike polystyrene "peanuts," Eco-Foam loose fill does not use CFCs (chlorofluorocarbons) in its production process . . .

The opening paragraph tells the story in microcosm. The second paragraph provides greater detail and explains the benefit of the new product. The "science" is explained in layman's terms, but scientific terms are spelled out. Note that the release calls attention to the trademark status of the new product the first time that it is mentioned.

The fifth consecutive season of THE CHEMICAL BANK NEW JERSEY MET IN THE PARKS SERIES of free concert opera in the parks of New Jersey will open on June 25 for four performances. The soloists, orchestra, and chorus of the Metropolitan Opera--close to 200 artists in all--will present two performances each of Mozart's "Don Giovanni" and of Verdi's "Un Ballo in Maschera." This 1991 series, sponsored by Chemical Bank New Jersey, will see the New Jersey debut of the new state-of-the-art Carlos Moseley Music Pavilion containing a band shell, stage, computerized theatrical lighting system, and a revolutionary new distributed sound system.

This 100-word lead tries to include several angles: the beginning of the annual concert series, the size of the opera company, the names of the works to be performed, the debut of a new staging system, and not one but two plugs for the sponsoring bank. Few newspapers used the complex lead as written. Newspapers in the towns where the concerts were to be given wrote leads featuring the night the Metropolitan Opera would be in their area and the work to be performed. Because pictures of the new staging system were provided with the release, many newspapers rewrote the lead to feature that fresh angle. The names of the operas and the size of the company were saved for the second and third paragraphs. Music editors tailored the release to their pages by leading with the names of the operas to be performed. And most editors moved the mention of the sponsoring bank—one time only—to the second paragraph or lower.

SAN FRANCISCO - War and peace. Love and death. Pomp and circumstance. And to top it all off, a parade that includes horses and an elephant. Verdi's spectacular "Aida" will open the San Francisco Opera season October 5.

The "ballyhoo" style is an appropriately exciting way to kick off a story that could have been humdrum with a standard "hard news" lead.

FORT MYERS, June 5, 1990 - A Lee County executive is calling for the State of Florida to mount an effort to assure national businesses once and for all that the Sunshine State will not pass a tax on advertising and public relations services.

"At least three companies expressing interest in doing
business in this region have 'chilled out' on us in recent
months, and it's hurting our chances of luring firms from
other states," said Business Council chairman . . .

The summary lead does the job, but the quote is more interesting.
There would be nothing wrong with switching the two paragraphs and
leading with the "chilled out on us" quote. The second paragraph then
could be used to explain the context of the story.

(City. State. Date) — Spring is here and the buzzing in
the air is due to the upcoming spelling bee for grown-ups
which will be held on (Date) at the (name of shopping mall).
Not since the golden days of grade school has there been a
chance to "bee" a part of such a competition.

This is a dummy press release to be used when promoting a local
spelling bee that is part of the Olsten Corporation's series of contests
for grown-ups in support of its adult literacy program. The local
public relations office provides the date-time-place data before sending the release to the media. Similar dummy releases were prepared
for announcements of the winners of the spelling bees. The lead
writer has some fun with the word bee, because the shopping center
promotions included helpers dressed as bees to draw attention to the
competition. The tone is consistent with the public relations program's objective of injecting some fun into the serious topic of adult
literacy.

KENILWORTH, N.J., June 4, 1986 — For the first time in
the United States, interferon has been approved for use in
treating cancer.
     'Intron A', the genetically derived alpha-2 interferon
developed and produced by Schering-Plough Corporation,
has been approved in the United States for treatment of
hairy cell leukemia, a form of cancer, and is being marketed
immediately.

Stories about medicine usually involve unfamiliar words and terms that boggle the mind of the lay person. Schering-Plough delayed specifics—including its own identification—until the second paragraph of the release in order to write a clear, hard-hitting lead that emphasizes the importance of the announcement.

SAN DIEGO, June 6, 1991 //PRNewswire// – Citing mental stress as the main factor in an increasing number of court awards for sexual harassment, Donald T. DeCarlo, vice president and general counsel for Commercial Insurance Resources, underscored that such claims will continue to mount unless corporate management begins to take seriously the underlying pervasiveness that precipitates such behavior.

This is the type of "trend" lead that is favored by consulting firms, professional associations, opinion research organizations, and others who wish to call societal problems to the attention of business and education leaders. The main elements are a bit of news (stress is factor in sexual harassment), a prediction (claims will continue to mount), and a call to action (management should take the problem seriously). The spokesperson's credentials are offered, and in doing so the client organization gets mentioned in the lead.

EL SEGUNDO, Calif., June 6, 1991 //PRNewswire// – In all the lands Down Under, independent travelers can "do as they please" with Air New Zealand's new 1991 Hotpac Planner and choose from hundreds of freewheeling holiday programs starting from only $25 per person per day for motorhomes in New Zealand.

Marketing public relations comes close to advertising style, as this lead attests. The amount of hype and commercialism permitted in travel releases far exceeds the norm for typical news releases.

CHICAGO – What stretches from Chicago to Cairo, comes in strawberry, orange and grape, contains only 19 calories, and pops in your mouth?

It's over six million packages of an old favorite--Pop Rocks™, the carbonated candy that is being launched in Illinois by Wirth-Daniels Corporation of Rosemount and Carbonated Candy Ventures.

The question lead is criticized by some editors, who see it as a lazy or too cute way of getting into a story. But consider how a "straight" version of this marketing release might begin: Wirth-Daniels Corporation of Rosemount and Carbonated Candy Ventures today announced the launch in Illinois of the sale of Pop Rocks, a carbonated candy. . . . Most editors would find that dull.

"Boilerplate" Paragraphs

When preparing a release about your organization or a client, you will draw upon "stock" paragraphs—sometimes called "boilerplate" by editors—to identify the organization and the products it makes or the services it provides. These chunks of information are stored in your mind (or, more likely, on the hard disk of your computer), ready to be dropped into every release you prepare. Some examples:

The Wyatt Company is an international consulting firm specializing in the areas of human resource, systems, and financial management with 3,700 employees working in 71 cities.

■

Multisoft Corp. is a privately owned software corporation which develops and markets performance enhancement technology internationally. The company produces retail products which are currently distributed in major world markets and licenses technology to hardware and software clients.

■

Open Company Ltd., founded in 1984, is a worldwide, independent open systems organization dedicated to developing an open, multi-vendor Common Applications Environment (CAE).

■

```
    Schering-Plough is a $2 billion company engaged primar-
ily in the discovery, development, manufacture and market-
ing of pharmaceutical and consumer products worldwide.

                              ■

    NutraSweet™ brand of aspartame (APM) is the low-calorie
sweetener for foods and beverages developed by G.D. Searle
& Co.
```

Handling Quotes

As we have seen from some of the examples of leads, quotes from authoritative persons are important elements of a news release. A short release containing routine material may not call for quotes. But when the subject is a new product or service, an organization's stand on an issue, or your company's response to changes in the marketplace, quoted material from your chief executive officer or another spokesperson can dramatize and emphasize ideas much more effectively than a recitation of information or data.

In fact, quotes permit you to inject passion and opinion into a release that otherwise must be "factual" in order to appeal to the editor as "news." Putting quote marks around ideas and attributing them to a spokesperson enables you to state your organization's view unabashedly and with vigor.

You may be able to take quotes from statements the leaders of your organization have made in public or at meetings within the organization. More likely, however, it is the responsibility of the public relations people to sift through the opinions, ideas, statements, records, and reports of management, then *create* the neat, pithy quotes that will appear in the news release. Once these "quotes" are crafted, they are shown to management in the form of news release drafts, for approval or rewritings or suggestions or questions from the intended speakers of the quotes. Through a process of internal negotiation, the exact text of the final quote as it will appear in the release is worked out. If the public relations people are persuasive and good listeners, the resulting quotes will be efficient and effective reflections of management's opinions—in a form that the ordinary reader can understand and believe.

Quotes rarely serve as the lead paragraph. Editors consider it a gimmick. They prefer a summary lead that sets the context. The second paragraph is the most likely position for displaying the potent quote. If considerable contextual information is necessary to set the stage, the quote may not fit in before the third or fourth paragraph.

Follow newspaper style for the quote: Open with quote marks, then end the first sentence of quote with an attribution. Usually the attribution is "said," unless a more descriptive verb is appropriate (demanded . . . suggested . . . asked . . .).

"We do not think the time has come for higher taxes," Mayor Jones said, "but we are willing to listen to all views."

■

Acme president Smith said he would support the council. "If merchants in Peoria don't stand together, the whole city will fail," he said.

■

"The fate of the urban renewal program is in our hands," said Coalition 2000 chairman Ray Brown. "If we don't do it, who will?"

Restrain yourself from using more than a short sentence or two of quoted material. Paraphrase continued thoughts: Brown said he has the support of 200 other members of the Chamber of Commerce. Quotes are like icing on a cake: a small amount is sweet and rewarding; too much and you begin to choke.

Apply the "read-aloud" test: Quotes should look good to the eye, but read them aloud to make sure that they sound like something your CEO or spokesperson really could and would say in a television interview or a speech. Readers can detect when a quote sounds phony or contrived. The best quotes read well and simultaneously transport the attitude your organization wants to cultivate.

Feature Style

Journalists talk about "straight news style," meaning unbiased information presented straightforwardly using the summary lead to open the story and the classic inverted pyramid organizational structure with facts presented in descending order of importance.

On the other hand, "feature style" treatment is considered appropriate for news about trends, interesting people, and product information that is part of a marketing public relations campaign.

"Teasers" are one kind of feature lead, and sometimes they take the form of a question:

Why is John Milgram moving for the third time in three years . . . and why has his family decided to stay behind this time? (Article on special real estate services for corporate and military personnel.)

■

A salad with seventeen ingredients, including not only lettuce and other greens but fruit, meat, and cheese as well. That's what you'd have to eat for every meal if you followed your doctor's advice while dieting. (Article about a new weight-loss program that provides all basic nutrients in a "liquid salad.")

"Suspended interest" feature leads tell a story in chronological order:

Mary Angelinas was on time, as usual. Her car pulled out of the driveway exactly at 8 and she was on the freeway headed for Center City by 8:10. The deejay on the radio kept her mind off all distractions . . . including the slight pain in her chest. (Article about heart attacks in working women, sponsored by a pharmaceutical company.)

Marketing public relations features often speak directly to the reader in order to involve him or her with the information:

Let's face it, you have better things to do with your time than remodel the entire house. But try getting a tradesman to work for you on the weekend when you can be home to supervise the painting, carpentry and plumbing. (Feature on do-it-yourself remodeling shortcuts, sponsored by a home improvement products company.)

■

> Every year you vow to "try something new" for holiday meals. But then your family requests all the *traditional* fare: turkey, mashed potatoes, stuffing, and pies for dessert. This year you can have your cake (or creamed onions) and eat it too. New recipes and menus developed by General Foods artfully blend something new and something old for your festive table.

Feature treatment usually makes liberal use of quotes, as well as lists, charts, and other items that make the information more interesting and useful to the reader. Use of a spokesperson—such as home repair expert Bob Villa for Sears, or home decorator and party planner Martha Stewart for K mart—allows for feature releases written in the speaking style of the personality associated with the product or service. Articles may even be written in the first person and carry the byline of the expert spokesperson.

The family living section of the newspaper welcomes feature treatment. Nationally distributed features sometimes come with a list of suggestions for ways the editor can localize the story by adding information from area businesses or personalities. The public relations agencies that package such features are more than happy if columnists or editors absorb the information (and the feature writing style) into their own columns or features, since that adds extra credibility to the information being placed.

The public relations department or agency is fortunate if a news release is used in its entirety. Often several news releases from various organizations are combined by the editor into one piece. The mention of your organization may be brief and at the end, instead of lengthy and high in the article as you envisioned it. That's the tradeoff for getting "free" publicity.

Many times you can enhance the placement of your news release by actually offering *more* information—or at least information that is broken into more than one news release. We'll see now how the sidebar and the press kit can increase your chances of getting a news release placed.

OFFERING AUXILIARY MATERIALS

Sidebars

Editors use the term "sidebar" to refer to a shorter article that appears alongside the main article and offers greater detail about one aspect of the main piece. Good reporters learn to think while they are writing an article: "Would this information stand out better in a sidebar?" Stop and think about how you look at spreads in a newspaper or magazine: often the information in a sidebar is so interesting that it convinces you to go back and read the main article. In other words, sidebars are not afterthoughts—they can and should be the best information in the article. (Notice, for example, that in this book there are boxed items along with the main text. The authors could have included the information in the basic discussion, but they thought it would interest the reader more as a "sidebar.")

Suppose you are planning a new product release. You have enough material to provide three, four, or five pages of information. What would you break out into a sidebar?

- A list of special applications of the product.
- A history of advancements and developments that preceded this product.
- Comments from researchers, testers, and trial users of the product.

You are announcing the centennial of your organization—one hundred years of serving the community. Sidebars to the main article might include:

- A capsule history, with major events and the dates they occurred.
- Profiles of the major leaders of the organization in the first century.
- Statements of congratulation from other groups in the community.
- Statistical information about the number of individuals who have been involved in the organization over the first century.

Your organization has announced that it will support legislation to protect the environment from air and water pollution. Think of these sidebars:

- A list of other organizations supporting the same legislation.
- Major pollution events in the history of the area that led to support for the current legislation.
- A breakdown of costs for cleanups from past pollution events.

Sidebars are a mindset. Effective public relations practitioners who know from experience how complicated a multi-page news release can be (and how reluctant readers are to wade through long articles) think instinctively: "What information can I put into a sidebar in order to make the story more attractive to the editor and to my target publics?"

Press Kits/Information Packets

The "sidebar" concept can be expanded into the full information packet that includes a master release, sidebars, fact sheets, biographies of principals in the organization, charts, reprints of comments from other media, photographs, and even samples of products. When such a packet is developed especially for a news conference or a special event to which journalists have been invited, it is called a press kit.

Most organizations develop an all-purpose, two-pocket folder with the group's logo or other identifying marks on the cover. That way a press kit or information packet can be assembled on short notice. For special events such as an anniversary or the launch of a new product line, however, most organizations choose to go to the extra expense of designing a special folder featuring the event on the cover. Another solution is to prepare a standard folder with a rectangular area blocked out on the cover for application of a label. A more expensive variation is the die-cut (hole) through the cover that shows the words and graphics of the first item inside.

To get an idea of the variety of content possible in a press kit, we'll catalog the contents of a few examples.

The introduction of "Touch-Banking" by the Brooklyn Savings Bank:

■ A master release announcing the new electronic banking service.
■ A sidebar describing the ad campaign planned to announce the launch.
■ Samples of print ads for the new service.
■ A backgrounder on the history and growth of the bank.
■ A profile of the CEO.
■ A glossary of terms used in electronic funds transfer systems (EFTS).
■ A photograph of customers using a new electronic banking center.

Schering-Plough's kit for the introduction of Intron A:

■ An agenda for the press conference introducing the product.
■ The main news release.
■ A forty-eight-page backgrounder on interferon.
■ A six-page backgrounder on hairy cell leukemia.
■ A glossary of medical and scientific terms used in the materials.
■ Reprints of two medical journal articles about interferon.

Exhibit 5.4
Sample Press Kit

NEWS FROM:

American Excelsior Company
AN EMPLOYEE OWNED COMPANY

850 AVENUE H EAST, P.O. BOX 5067, ARLINGTON, TEXAS 76005-5067, (817) 640-1555, TLX 735298 AMEXCO, FAX (817) 649-7816

CONTACT: Deborah Aikey
Allan Fliss
Francioli, Richartz
Weiman & Fliss
(201) 299-8090

For Immediate Release

AMERICAN EXCELSIOR COMPANY INTRODUCES
ENVIRONMENTALLY-SOUND PACKAGING MATERIAL

Eco-Foam™ Loose Fill Seen as an Alternative to Polystyrene

CHICAGO, November 12, 1990 -- American Excelsior Company, a leading

manufacturer of innovative, natural packaging materials, announced

today its latest environmentally-sound packaging product -- corn

starch-based Eco-Foam™ loose fill.

Made from a special hybrid corn, Eco-Foam loose fill is composed of

over 95 percent corn starch. Due to its high starch content, it

begins to decompose on contact when saturated with water. Unlike

polystyrene "peanuts," Eco-Foam loose fill does not use CFCs

(chlorofluorocarbons) in its production process. Nor, does it release

any harmful substances when it decomposes.

- more -

■ Biographical sketches of the company CEO and two research scientists.
■ Details of the marketing plan for the product.
■ Photos of the product, the developers, and a leukemia cell.

The U.S. Department of Commerce's packet detailing plans for the 1990 Census:

■ A letter of introduction from a representative of the Census staff.

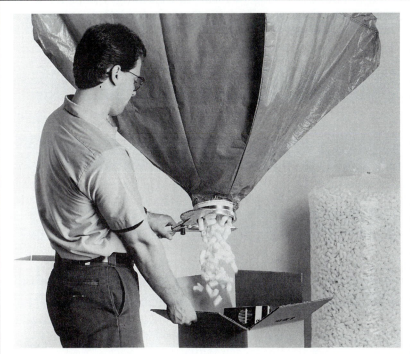

This shot of a worker filling boxes with Eco-Foam was among the photos included in American Excelsior's press kit.

- ■ Reprint of a historical article explaining the role of the census in democratic government.
- ■ A brochure: "USA Statistics in Brief."
- ■ Several free-standing fact sheets carrying the special Census 90 logo:
  - ☐ Your Introduction to the 1990 Census—An Overview
  - ☐ Census Facts—Size and Scope of the Operation
  - ☐ Why Census Information Is Vital to Communities
  - ☐ Local Governments Are Vital to a Successful Count

□ Education Project—Ideas for Classroom Involvement
□ The Census Is Strictly Confidential—Your Answers Are Protected
□ How Census Information Is Used
□ Questionnaire Subjects for the 1990 Census
□ Your Help Is Needed—How Individuals Can Get Involved

General Media, Inc. announcement of its minority internship program:

■ A cover letter from the coordinator of the internship program.
■ A release about the program.
■ Application forms for the program.
■ America's Leading Radio Groups—fact sheet showing General Media's ranking as the eighth largest radio communications company in the U.S.
■ Five related fact sheets detailing the scope of the company in general as well as its divisions—radio, cable, telecommunications, and publishing.

American Excelsior's rollout of its Eco-Foam loose fill packing material:

■ Three essays printed right on the multi-fold packet organizer:
□ The use of corn starch, a natural product.
□ Use of the product in industry.
□ A profile of American Excelsior Company.
■ Other items held in the center of the multi-fold by a horizontal flap:
□ The main news release.
□ Fact sheets about the product and the company.
□ Reprint of a technical article describing the scientific principles.
□ Map of the U.S. showing scheduled rollout dates for various regions.
□ Photos showing the ease of using the product.

BROADCAST RELEASES

We already have noted that the requirements of radio differ from those of the print media. Radio has much tighter space–time requirements than print. News items are usually only a few sentences long.

Here are the requirements of the broadcast release:

■ Type the information entirely in large capital letters to facilitate reading.

- Keep the item to no more than two hundred words, which is about one minute of reading time.
- Use short paragraphs; it may be useful to display each sentence as a separate paragraph.
- Separate clauses, or the parts of long sentences, with ellipses (. . .) to give the newscaster an indication of where to pause or take a breath.
- Avoid contractions, hard-to-pronounce words, abbreviations, or anything else that may trip the tongue.
- Provide pronunciation help in parentheses immediately following any unfamiliar word or name: Tomas Arguea (toe-MAS ar-GWAY-ah). Note how the accented syllable is indicated.
- Do not put names, figures, or other critical information in the opening phrase or sentence. The first sentence should "index" the story for the listener and catch attention by naming the general topic.

> *Wrong:* Deputy Director of Finance Hiram Williams today submitted a $4.2 million budget to city council . . .
>
> *Right:* It will cost less to run the city next year.
> A budget of over four million dollars was . . . etc.

Of course you would not go to the bother of preparing a separate broadcast release if your distribution was primarily to print media, with only a few local radio stations included. But if your subject will interest many radio outlets, it is worth the extra effort to cater to their needs.

Make a Spokesperson Available

One of the things that may "sell" a release to radio is the availability of a spokesperson who is willing to be interviewed over the phone. At the bottom of the release or on an attached page, indicate if the person named in the release is "available for phone interview" and provide the telephone number. Make sure the spokesperson has been provided with a copy of the release and an outline of material that might be discussed in the interview. Typically, a reporter from the radio station will conduct the interview in just a few minutes, using the phone "beeper" system.

If your source is available for an appearance on a radio or television talk show or public-affairs program, attach a very brief note to the release summarizing the spokesperson's expertise and availability, and include your number so that you can arrange the appearance.

TIMING
THE RELEASE

When an important event happens, or when something will be news-worthy for only a day, you might have to phone local editors and send a courier quickly to carry a "perishable" release to the media. Ordinarily, however, sufficient lead time must be allowed when submitting a news release, especially if it is accompanied by photographs. Only when you have alerted an editor or news director in advance are you likely to get a major news item in the paper or on the air with a lead time of less than a day.

That means anticipating an event with positive PR value. You must allow yourself ample time for preparing the release and processing photographs. Plan at least two or three days for mail delivery, unless the release is important enough to deliver by courier. Then allow two or three days for the media to process the material.

Using an "Embargo"

In order to have information in the hands of the media at the proper time, it may be necessary to divulge facts before your organization desires to have them distributed. The names of scholarship or contest winners, destined to be announced on a certain date, must be provided to the newspapers ahead of time if the long list of names, addresses, and hometowns is to be set in type. Drawings and charts depicting the plans for a new plant and its impact on the community must be in the hands of the newspaper's art department early in order to have suitable illustrations ready on the day when the expansion is announced to the public at a news conference.

In such situations, it is understood by the news organization that the preparer of the news release will "embargo" the item, meaning that a release date is put on the material, and the media are expected to hold the information until that time. The public relations department must be extremely sensitive to the requirements of all the media when using an embargo.

A reasonable embargo that most media would agree to observe would be the 6 A.M. release, which means that the item could appear in all morning papers and be included in the drive-time radio broadcasts.

An embargo for almost any time of the day is acceptable when the press release is based on the text of a speech, as long as it is made clear that the release time coincides with the precise time when the speaker will be appearing before the audience. Similarly, a "September 15" embargo on the results of a research study is understandable when the release indicates that the findings will be presented at a conference on that date.

Unfortunately, some organizations arbitrarily assign release dates to items for no apparent reason. The media may ignore such an embargo or, more likely, simply toss the release in the wastebasket.

Exhibit 5.5
An Editor
Requests . . .

A trade magazine editor who reads approximately 1,000 news releases a month makes these suggestions:

- Date your release so we know when you sent it, and when it's up-to-date. (We work months in advance.)
- Don't call to see if we received your release. If I have any questions, I'll call you.
- Send one and only one release, not one to every editor of our magazine. We'll make sure a useful release gets passed to the right editor.
- Know the publication. Read the magazine to make sure we use the type of information you're sending.
- Don't ask the editor to send you a tearsheet (a copy of the article as published). Use a clipping service, go to a library, or buy the magazine.
- Follow up after an article is written. Send me a thank-you note sometimes. I'm only human, and it's nice to hear when you liked the write-up.

Source: Marcia S. Clark, "Checklist: Getting Your News Releases Through," *Public Relations Journal,* November, 1986, p. 57. Ms. Clark is assistant editor at *Progressive Grocer* magazine.

Hand Delivery May Be Necessary

Some releases call for extraordinary handling. When announcements of major personnel changes mean that some people will be big winners and others big losers within the organization, it is not unusual for the head of the public relations department personally to write and reproduce the press release, hold it for safekeeping, and hand deliver it to the media when word comes from the chief executive officer that the affected parties are being notified.

Similarly, in crisis situations, such as when a company has been charged by the government with wrongdoing, or when an accident destroys a facility and causes injuries, the rules change. The press shows up at the organization's doors, and the public relations chief must set up a press briefing and issue a statement. The underlying facts and the essence of the statement should be ready for distribution in the form of an on-site press release:

A spokesman for the Acme Rubber Products Company today denied charges that the firm had engaged in price-fixing. Public relations director Carl Baker called a press conference at the main plant on For-dam Road and distributed information showing that Acme has engaged in a vigorous competition for its approximately 25 percent share of the market in sports diving equipment.

We have focused mainly on the daily news media. Except for weekly trade publications, which function much like newspapers, most magazines have deadlines of two or three months, rather than days or weeks. Releases about new product lines or seasonal material must be prepared far in advance if they are to be of use to magazines.

SUBMITTING THE PRESS RELEASE

If your press release is aimed at all of the media in the area, you can find the addresses in standard directories, such as the *Editor and Publisher Yearbook* for newspapers and the *Broadcasting Yearbook* for radio and television stations. Address the release to "Editor" for the print media and "News Director" for broadcast media.

Because of the large volume of releases, however, it is useful to target the release more specifically when possible. On most daily newspapers, the managing editor oversees the daily operation of the newsroom, and the city editor is in charge of local coverage. It is worthwhile to check the yearbook for listings of specialized editors. If your news belongs on the business page, aim it at the business editor. Your item may get better play on the education page or from the women's editor. Familiarity with the paper is useful.

When to Be Selective

Ordinarily, it is of no particular help to contact the media personally if your release is a routine one that you are sending to dozens of outlets. However, if you are being selective and sending the release to only a handful of media with a particular interest in the story, or if you have taken the time to prepare a special article or photo for each paper, it is useful to alert the editor by phone about the "exclusive" material. Over time, the editor will come to recognize and appreciate when you provide material that is different from what the general media are receiving.

Always analyze the benefits of selective mailings of releases. Features about people or programs in your organization can get major play if the editor senses exclusivity. On the other hand, routine announcements should be sent equally to all media in order to keep your organization's name in the minds of all publics and all editors. The PR director of a state-run summer arts facility, for example, sends the same release to every paper, but selects different shots and poses of the star celebrities for use in various competing media. That way, no editor jettisons the picture, and the release along with it, simply because the same shot appeared in other papers.

Note that the role of "art"—photographs, tables, graphs, or diagrams—in selling a news release cannot be underestimated. See Chapter 13 for information on how to prepare photographs and cutlines for submission along with the print release.

Using Directory Services

While the general directories mentioned above are useful for finding names and addresses of the media as well as the names of top editors, you may want more specific information covering a broader range of media. The leading source serving the industry is Bacon's. The Chicago firm used to refer to itself as "Bacon's Media Directories," but its promotional literature now identifies the company as "Bacon's PR and Media Information Systems." That reflects the broadening of the number of directories published and services offered. The Bacon's reference shelf now includes separate Publicity Checker volumes for newspapers and magazines, a Radio/TV directory, an International Publicity Checker focusing on Western Europe, and Media Alerts—a resource book for planning campaigns that lists calendars and lead times for 1,900 magazines and 200 major daily newspapers. Bacon's now maintains a computerized media bank listing 130,000 editors; the firm can print and distribute releases and maintain specially targeted mailing lists for clients.

Major states and cities are serviced by specialized firms that not only publish directories, but offer mailing and distribution services as well. Resource Communication Group, Inc., of Florham Park, NJ, for example, sells directories of the media, government, and businesses for the State of New Jersey and also for the Atlanta region. RCG maintains a computerized mailing list of all the media, agencies, and firms in its directories, updated constantly. If you wish to generate releases and personalized cover letters to all the editors in a specified region and/or category, the mailing will be assembled for you. Many public relations agencies find that process to be more effective than using outdated directories and burdening office staff with complicated mailings.

Exhibit 5.6

Sample page from
Bacon's Publicity
Checker—Magazines

*Coding system along the
right margin (keyed at
bottom) alerts public
relations people to special
requirements or formats.
Number codes within each
entry are keyed to specific
editorial needs.*

18C-3490 P C COMPUTING, 4 Cambridge Center, 9th Fl., Cambridge, MA 02142-1494; Michael Edelhart—Editor In Chief; John Dickson—Editor; Michael Kolowich—Publisher; Monthly; 450,000; Ziff-Davis Publishing Company; 1,3,5,7,9,10; Fax: (617) 497-2587. **(617) 492-7500**

18C-3495 P C GAMES, 80 Elm Street, Petterborough, NH 03458; Dan Muse—Editor In Chief; Paul Boule—Publisher; Quarterly; I D G Communications; 1,3,6,7,11,14. **(603) 924-9471** ★

18C-3510 P C HANDS ON, 52 Domino Drive, Concord, MA 01742; Mike Harvey—Publisher; Lisa Stern—Mng. Ed., Monthly; 20,000; Mind-Craft Publishing Corp.; 1,2,3,5,6,7,8,10. **(508) 371-1660**

18C-3515 P C LETTER, 3 Lagoon Drive, #160, Redwood City, CA 94065-1558; Steward Alsop, Editor; Semi-Monthly; P C World Communictions, Inc.; 1,3,4,7,8. **(415) 592-8880** ■

18C-3520 P C MAGAZINE, One Park Avenue, New York, NY 10016-5802; Bill Machrone—Editor In Chief; Ronni Sonnenberg—Publisher; Paul Ross—Mng. Ed.; Bill Howard—Features; Robin Raskin—New Products; Gerald Kunkel—Technical; Bi-Weekly; 750,000; Ziff-Davis Publishing Company; 1,3,6,7,9,10,11,14; Fax: (212) 503-5519.**(212) 503-5100** ▲

18C-3540 P C NOVICE, 120 West Harvest Drive, Lincoln, NE 68521; Cletus Pillen—Publisher; Ronald D. Kobler—Mng., Ed.; Monthly; 100,000; Peed Corporation; 1,2,3,6,7,10,11; Fax: (402) 477-9252. **(402) 477-8900** ★

18C-3580 P C PUBLISHING, 950 Lee Street, Des Plaines, IL 60016-6556; Robert Mueller—Editor; Michael Angelo—Mng. Ed.; Maryann Meyenberg—New Products; Monthly; 50,000; Hunter Publishing Ltd. Partnership; 1,2,3,5,6,7,9,11; Fax: (708) 296-1302. **(708) 296-0770** ✔

18C-3600 P C RESOURCE, 80 Elm Street, Peterborough, NH 03458; Paul Nesdore—Editor In Cheif; Stephen D. Twombly—Publisher; Marilyn McMaster—Mng. Ed.; Eric Greustad—Features, New Products; David Arowell—Technical; Monthly; 165,000; I D G Communications; 1,2,3,6,7,10; Fax: (603) 924-9384. **(603) 924-9471**

18C-3660 P C WEEK, 800 Boylston Street, Boston, MA 02199-8001; Sam Whitmore—Editor In Chief; Claude Sheer—Publisher; Wendy Maxfield—Mng. Ed.; Weekly-Mon; 117,112; Ziff-David Publishing Company; 1,3,5,6,7,8,9,11; Fax: (617) 536-8307. **(617) 375-4000**

Selected Editorial Offices/Bureaus

18C-3660 P C WEEK, 110 Marsh Drive, #203, Foster City, CA 94404; Russell Glitman—Bureau Chief. **(415) 378-5540**

18C-3680 P C WORLD, 501 Second Street, San Francisco, CA 94107-1431; Richard Landry—Editor; Ed Bott—Mng. Ed.; Eric Knorr—Features; Mike Hogan—New Products; Karl Kessel—Technical; Monthly 500,000; P C World Communications; 1,2,3,6,7,9,10; Fax: (415) 442-1891. **(415) 546-7722**

1. New Products	8. Financial	< Charges for Cuts
2. Trade Literature	9. Letters	★ New Listing Since Previous Edition
3. General News	10. Questions & Answers	✔ Uses Color Publicity Photos
4. Personnel	11. Books	▲ Does Not Use Publicity Photos
5. Events	12. Contacts	■ Newsletter Format
6. Articles, By-Lined	13. Films	C Canadian Publication
7. Articles, Staff	14. Entertainment	R Regional Publication

Distribution of press releases involves maintaining an up-to-date mailing list, photocopying, addressing, and stuffing envelopes, and affixing postage stamps. As we noted above, the *Editor and Publisher Yearbook* and regional media directories are useful for finding addresses of weekly and daily newspapers, but names of department editors listed in such directories can get out of date quickly. And what if a release sent to a particular editor sits in the in-basket past the point of usefulness simply because the editor is on vacation? Yet another problem facing the PR department is the often undependable service of the increasingly expensive U.S. Postal Service.

For the PR department that regularly sends out news releases with "time value," the answer may be to use the PR Newswire service or a regional service such as the Southeastern Press Relations Newswire, which serves twelve southern states.

USING PR WIRE SERVICES

How the Service Works

For a fee, PR Newswire and the various regional PR wire services process your organization's news releases for electronic transmission to computer terminals and/or high-speed teleprinters at many of the leading news and business media. Your news can be transmitted to the PR Newswire by messenger, Telex, facsimile, or telephone dictation. It can be held for transmission at a specific time, or if it has instant news value, it will go out at once. The release can be distributed to all media or only specialized publications.

PR Newswire's special Investors Research Wire carries news about publicly owned corporations to banks, investment firms, and financial publications. The instant and simultaneous transmission of such news by electronic means helps to meet the federal government's requirements for "timely disclosure."

The Information-Retrieval Link

News releases distributed through PR Newswire may also become part of a computer-stored database used for information retrieval by researchers in PR, the news media, and specialized business and industrial publications. The NEXIS database is a news-retrieval service that includes a backlog of information carried in the *Washington Post*, *Newsweek*, *Congressional Quarterly*, the Associated Press, PR Newswire, and many other services and publications.

Using the service, a researcher is able to scan not only news stories and fact sheets concerning an organization, but also the organization's own news releases and statements about its stock offerings,

Exhibit 5.7

The Beginning and End
Sections of a PR
Newswire Transmission

*This reprint from a PR
Newswire brochure
highlights the features
of the specialized public
relations news service.*

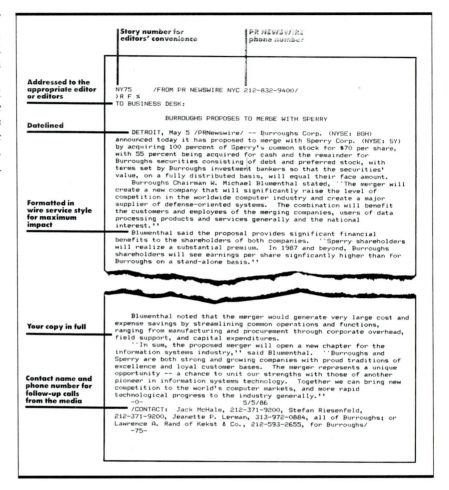

new products, management decisions, or plans for expansion. The president of PR Newswire has pointed out a particularly attractive feature of NEXIS: storage of a press release in the news retrieval system is analogous to publication. In other words, even if no medium prints the story, it still is available to researchers.[4] Clearly, the computer age has provided new and expanded uses for the traditional PR news release.

In 1987, DIALOG—one of the largest database services used by business, educators, and government—added the PR Newswire to its lineup of databases. That means that company earnings reports are readily available to the widest possible number of users.

By the early 1990s, in addition to its basic service, PR Newswire offered:

- a feature news service on the supplementary US2 NewsLine,
- a PR/TV Newswire reaching almost three hundred television stations,
- satellite transmission of photographs,
- a National Affairs NewsLine focusing on Washington, and
- Entertainet, a separate circuit catering to entertainment editors.

Business Wire, which bills itself as the International Media Relations Wire Service, targets investors and the investment community. In addition to the basic on-line database service, it handles photos and faxes, and it offers the BW SportsWire and EntertainmentWire catering to those industries.

Other specialized services handling the needs of public relations people are springing up all the time. Southern New England Telephone (SNET) targets its FaxWorks service at practitioners who have to deliver multiple print messages speedily. Other firms offer electronic transmission of broadcast and cable news releases, as we shall see in later chapters.

Twenty-five years ago, public relations people were on their own when it came to getting news out. The main decision then was whether to add interns or temps to the production and mailing job. Today it's a matter of deciding among (and budgeting for) the many wire and data services available.

After news releases have been disseminated, you will want to document their use. The only practical way to do that—since no public relations staff has time to search through hundreds of publications for mentions of your organization—is to use a clipping service.

For years, Burrelle's in Livingston, NJ, has been synonymous with the phrase clipping service. Now billing itself as a company that provides "Comprehensive Information Services," Burrelle's also offers a clip mounting service for display purposes, radio and television monitoring, same-day NewsExpress service for clients who need instant feedback, analysis of news placements, media directories, preaddressed media labels, and computerized information retrieval. Not surprisingly, since Burrelle's now offers services in Bacon's territory, the media guide firm has countered by offering its own Bacon's Clipping Bureau. At last it is possible to get all your news release services from one source.

CLIPPING SERVICES

NOTES
1. For a discussion of the concept of public relations "subsidization" of the news media, including a useful list of references, see Judy VanSlyke Turk and Bob Franklin, "Information Subsidies: Agenda-Setting Traditions," *Public Relations Review* (Winter 1987), pp. 29–41.

2. See, for example, Mary Sabolik, "Print Media Strategies for the New Segmentation," *Public Relations Journal* (November 1989), pp. 15–19, 35; Gail Bernstein, "Meet the Press," *Public Relations Journal* (March 1988), pp. 28–32; Chuck Honaker, "News Releases Revisted," *Public Relations Journal* (April 1981), pp. 25–27; Chuck Honaker, "Why Your News Releases Aren't Working," *Public Relations Journal* (March 1978), pp. 16–19; Ed Zotti, "Journalists Gripe: Too Much, Too Little," *Advertising Age* (January 5, 1981), pp. S6–S7; Gerald Powers, "For Immediate Release: View From the Editor's Desk," *Public Relations Journal* (September 1971), p. 18.

3. See James E. Grunig, "Time Budgets, Level of Involvement and Use of the Mass Media," *Journalism Quarterly* 56 (1979), pp. 248–261.

4. David Steinberg, letter to the editor, "Press Relations: A New Dimension," *Public Relations Journal* (July 1981), p. 8.

ADDITIONAL READING

Brody, E.W., *Public Relations Programming and Production* (New York: Praeger, 1988).

Howard, Carole, and Wilma Matthews, *Managing Media Relations* (Prospect Heights, IL: Waveland Press, 1988).

Lesly, Philip, ed., *Lesly's Handbook of Public Relations and Communications* (Chicago: Probus, 1991).

Newsom, Doug and Bob Carrell, *Public Relations Writing: Form and Style,* 3d ed. (Belmont, CA: Wadsworth, 1991).

Pesman, Sandra, *Writing for the Media* (Lincolnwood, IL: NTC Business Books, 1983).

Tucker, Kerry, and Doris Derelian, *Public Relations Writing: A Planned Approach for Creating Results* (Englewood Cliffs, NJ: Prentice-Hall, 1989).

Wilcox, Dennis L., and Lawrence W. Nolte, *Public Relations Writing and Media Techniques* (New York: HarperCollins, 1990).

6

Catering to the Press

Jeff Greenfield, who covers politics and the media for ABC, suggested in one of his commentaries that the press must be treated as "a dangerous, but potentially valuable, animal. You must house it, feed it, pet it once in a while. You must never show it fear, or it will turn on you. You must gently, but firmly, guide it in the way you want it to go."[1]

Catering to the press—housing, feeding, and petting—is only an occasional task for most public relations departments. As a matter of course, both sides find it easier to depend on news releases for transmitting routine information.

In fact, some critics contend that corporate public relations people today go out of their way to avoid dealing with press, preferring instead to let their infrequent and highly controlled news releases serve as their only contact with the Fourth Estate. Responding to an article titled "Corporate PR People Retreat from the Press," in a special Corporate PR Issue of *O'Dwyer's Service Report,* L. James Lovejoy, director of corporate communications for the Gerber Products Company, blamed the lack of media relations on various phenomena, including:

1. Public relations people are trying to fill too many other roles and have put media relations on the back burner.
2. Corporate managers prefer people who understand business to those who understand communication.
3. CEOs, who wish to minimalize risk, have shied away from the media.
4. The understaffing of today's media means that reporters and editors have less time for attending press events set up by PR people.[2]

The press conference should be used when it is clear that giving the press an opportunity to question expert sources will result in more meaningful and effective news coverage.

The press party, festive cousin to the news conference, is appropriate when an organization has genuine reason to mark some sort of milestone, such as an anniversary, or when the attendance of celebrities is a cause for excitement, as when astronauts pay a visit to a government contractor.

The Bank of America, whose Broad Street offices are just around the corner from the New York Stock Exchange, regularly calls in the business press for briefings by company economists on topics ranging from interest rates to trends in banking methods. It's a low-key coffee-and-donuts affair, and the emphasis is on providing background information to the writers rather than providing a headline item.

There are many ways for a press event to turn into a disaster:

- The news value may be so weak that the reporters feel duped.
- The release may contain all the information the press needs, so reporters don't show up, and the guest or interviewee is embarrassed.
- The guest or interviewee may not perform as expected, and the press wonders why it was summoned.
- The timing may be wrong, or a breaking news event may pre-empt the attention of the press.
- The broadcast press, with its lights and microphones, may sour the print press, resulting in negative publicity.

All of these potential miscues should be weighed before making the decision to proceed with a press event.

CONSIDER THE LOGISTICS

It should be clear by now that PR professionals should invite the media to attend a news conference or a special event only if there is real news, not just because it "seems like a good thing to do."

If you do have an event of interest and news value, you are ready to address several logistical considerations: whom to invite, how to issue the invitation, where to hold the event, what amenities to offer, and how to assure that the members of the press are able to gather and transmit the information with the greatest possible ease.

Whom Shall We Invite?

At first, it might seem easy. But deciding whom to invite to a press conference isn't automatic. If we send an invitation or release to the

Exhibit 6.1
Synchronizing
Your Stories

Two years after it acquired a large insurance holding firm, Xerox decided to consolidate management by replacing the acquired firm's leadership with Xerox managers. It was not an unusual business move, but one that called for great sensitivity toward all involved. As is usual in business, the announcement—both to employees and to the press—was scheduled for 4 P.M. Friday. That allows the financial press two days before the market reopens to assess the impact of the story. It also gives the fired officers the weekend to clean out their desks without facing other employees.

Public relations people for Xerox and the subsidiary developed a Question-and-Answer script, had it approved by management, and practiced its use before the 4 P.M. announcement. Several staff members would be on the phone simultaneously with members of the business press; the synchronization assured that all reporters would hear the same story.

Sample:

Q. Was the resignation of Mr. A and the retirement of Mr. B requested?

A. The A. decision was a mutual decision that flowed from an understanding of what had to be done. Mr. B. felt he had accomplished all his objectives and that this was a good time to retire.

Source: Personal interview.

managing editor or the city editor, a general-assignment reporter might be sent to the event—that is, a less experienced writer who just happens to be available. It's far wiser to invite business editors if our story involves economics, political writers if we are involved in a legislative matter, the entertainment columnist if we are sponsoring a cultural event, or a member of the "lifestyle" staff if our organization is running a summer camp for underprivileged children.

Shall we invite bona fide reporters only, or a wider list of journalists? If the story has legitimate spot news interest, the presence of press hangers-on may interfere with reporters who must meet a deadline. On the other hand, if our news conference is intended to suggest a continuing story that deserves prolonged coverage, it may be wise to invite managing editors and editorial writers, who have the responsibility of planning long-range news policy.

Should print and broadcast press be invited to the same conference? If so, how can we assure that both are adequately served? Early morning and late afternoon are good times for the print press, but midday usually is better for television. Moreover, if television crews arrive in full force with their lights and microphones, the print press may be pushed to the side. The television reporters may want only a crisp, concise one-minute statement, preferably with visual interest, while the print reporters may prefer to probe for the in-depth stories they have the time and space to cover.

One solution to the dilemma posed by the different needs of the various media may be to hold a split conference, with the television cameras invited for one segment, and the print people given exclusive access to another segment.[3]

Avoid Embarrassing Silences

A news conference may be jeopardized if no reporter is willing to ask the opening question, or if the press—through ignorance or laziness—fails to explore all of the available topics.[4] Some organizations routinely seat one or two members of their own public relations staff or the editor of the organization's magazine with the working press to raise additional questions at the appropriate time, and generally to "keep the ball rolling." Of course, such a maneuver must be handled in a way that is perceived as helpful by the news media, not as a heavy-handed job of "shilling." It probably is better to prepare your speaker to raise and answer his or her own questions if the press is remiss.

If your organization provides a spokesperson who is not adequately prepared, or who does not know how to handle questions from the press, the conference quickly falls apart. Until the Nuclear Regulatory Commission appointed a qualified "point man" to brief reporters covering the Three Mile Island incident, the press complained of "conflicting and contradictory statements" about the nuclear emergency, and the result was confusing and incomplete news coverage.[5]

You must be prepared, too, for reporters who refuse to attend a press conference because, in the words of one journalism news-writing textbook, they "dislike working with precisely the same clay their competitors are using."[6] Some print reporters flatly refuse to raise questions while television cameras are running, saying, "Why should I let my questions get answered on TV before I can put them in print?"[7] If coverage by the reporters who complain is important to you, be prepared to make special arrangements so that they can interview your speaker or obtain the information in another manner.

How to Issue the Invitation

An editor who is contacted the day before a press conference: "Look, all my reporters are busy. You've got to give me greater lead time if you want coverage."

An editor who is contacted well in advance: "Two weeks from now? You know we work on a day-to-day basis. Give me a call the day before."

Exhibit 6.2
An Earful from
the Press

Ask any PRSA or IABC program chair: the best-attended chapter meeting of the year is the session where a panel of newspaper business editors and trade magazine reporters tell public relations people how to increase their chances of making successful media placements. Here are some of the suggestions—most of them of the "no-no" variety:

- Don't look at the sending out of a release as the *end* of the process. For us it's the beginning—we look at your story as a lead into the story that we want to do.
- Don't bombard us with stories about how wonderful your corporation is. These days we're asking, "What does this mean to the consumer?" So pitch us with a consumer-oriented angle.
- Don't send us the same news release two or three times. It's annoying!
- Don't fax anything we haven't requested or given our approval to send. And then send us a page or two, not fifteen pages. Don't tie up our machine!
- Don't send us gifts. We aren't allowed to keep them, so food goes to the local food bank and everything else goes to charity.
- Instead of pitching your stories to us, introduce us to people in your organization who are good story sources. We'd rather have Rolodex cards than news releases.
- Don't send us a huge press kit with a videotape. We don't have time to drop everything and watch your videotape.
- Don't call us the next day to see if we got your release. It just wastes our time.
- Don't hide your news—in fact, summarize it at the top of your release so we can tell at a glance if it interests us.
- Read our publication to know what we publish. Then you won't send us material we don't even use.
- Don't shoot for a major article every time. Your chances are better if you give us a short item we can fit into a department or a listing.
- We read the PR Newswire and the Business Wire. Trust us to find your story there.

Thus, it is difficult to time an invitation. To that, add this dilemma: for every editor who insists on a written record, another runs his entire operation verbally over the phone. The only compromise seems to be sending out a press release (combined with an "invitation" and an RSVP postal card, if you wish) about ten days before the event. Then, plan to call the editor the day before to confirm whether or not a reporter will be sent. Some PR practitioners who feel that their personal persuasive abilities are their main strength may reverse the process, making the phone contact ten days ahead to alert the editor about the upcoming event, then

Exhibit 6.3
Tracking Your
Press Contacts

John Skalko, Director of Corporate Public Relations for AT&T, uses his office computer system to keep on top of his press contacts. He maintains a directory of all the media people with whom he has dealt in the past. When he receives a call, during the opening moments of the conversation he punches in the reporter's name. Up comes a list of what the reporter has written in the past—short takes, unless the comments were hostile, in which case the entire document may be in the file. That way Skalko knows how to handle the caller and he has some idea of what to anticipate.

In the same computer system, he stores information that he can have ready at the press of a key:

■ A list of all AT&T facilities and names of public relations people at each location to which a reporter might want to talk.
■ Position statements on current AT&T stories, so that he or members of his staff can give consistent answers when contacted.
■ Memos from other AT&T public relations people that might help him handle a press contact.

Used this way, the computer can be the media relations specialist's best friend when the telephone rings.

Source: Interview, November 5, 1986.

timing the written reminder to arrive just a day or two ahead of the workshift in which the reporter will be assigned.

Dealing with Journalistic Ethics

When issuing invitations to a press party or social event, special consideration should be given to the ethics codes subscribed to by many newspapers, such as the Associated Press Managing Editors Code. An important clause of the Code of Ethics of the Society of Professional Journalists states: "Nothing of value shall be accepted."[8] This is generally interpreted to mean gifts having intrinsic value (but excluding premiums or mementos such as imprinted ballpoint pens).

Most journalists feel that attendance at a social function where an ordinary hotel-style dinner is served, preceded by a cocktail hour, will not compromise their integrity. However, it is increasingly common for larger papers to require that the charge levied on paying guests be applicable to journalists, with the paper picking up the tab. It is wise for

Exhibit 6.4
Sometimes Firmness Is
the Best Policy

Despite the title of this chapter, companies don't always cater to the press. In fact, sometimes they go out of their way to control the press and deny it access to information. Some examples:

■ Once Chrysler offered photographers a "photo opportunity" with chairman Lee Iaccoca as he toured a stamping plant near Detroit. When radio reporters tried to interview the famous industrialist, their questions were drowned out by the noise of the plant and the chattering of employees. Said the PR people: "It was billed only as a photo opportunity—why would radio people show up?"

■ United Technologies Corporation barred reporters from a meeting of its chairman and board of directors with security analysts. A separate meeting was scheduled with press afterwards. The company defended its action on the grounds that each of the groups complained that the others "hog the officers" after the meetings.

■ The public relations agency for NCR Corporation—realizing that its news releases were right for the trade press but too technical for the business press—drafted "plain language" versions. The company vetoed the move on the grounds that it might look like it was "talking down to" the regular press.

Sources: *Wall Street Journal* "Shop Talk" column, March 15, 1989, p. B-1, and February 23, 1989, p. B-1; Michael W. Miller, "High-Tech Hype Reaches New Heights," *The Wall Street Journal*, January 12, 1989, p. B-1. (N.B.: Page one of the second section of the *Journal* is a must-read for public relations people!)

the public relations practitioner to be sensitive to this trend, even though it may mean that some journalists are paying and others are availing themselves of a free meal.

Ethical considerations also dictate that an invitation not be sent to the private home of the journalist, thereby confusing the issue of whether the reporter is being invited in a professional or a private capacity. Similarly, the invitation of the spouse to attend may raise ethical questions, unless the nature of the event—such as a dinner-dance—clearly dictates that attendance by couples is the norm.

WHERE TO HOLD THE EVENT

If your organization has a large boardroom, auditorium, or general-purpose facility that is equipped with a public-address system and is available to you for at least half a day, you may be able to hold a press conference in your own facility—provided, that is, that you are located within a short drive of the media, and you have adequate parking available.

Aside from the convenience of using your own facilities, there may be another valid reason for bringing the press to your site. If the point of the event is to show off a new plant or piece of equipment, then some inconvenience on the part of the press may be warranted. You may even arrange for the press to congregate at a convenient central location to be bused to the site of your event, but that presupposes an attraction of genuine interest or novelty.

Not surprisingly, hotels, motels, and restaurants frequently are used for press conferences, simply because they are centrally located, offer a full range of catering services, and can provide basic amplification and audiovisual equipment. (How many times does the first item in the evening television news consist of a speaker behind a lectern bearing the name of a well-known hotel!)

Check the Facilities

Representatives of the PR department should make at least one on-site inspection, accompanied by a sales representative of the facility, to check for items such as:

- ✔ Adequate electrical outlets for audiovisual equipment.
- ✔ Sufficient water pitchers and drinking glasses.
- ✔ Phone booths outside the room. (If none or too few are available, you can arrange with the phone company to bring in a temporary portable unit.)
- ✔ Comfortable seating and, if appropriate, tables for writing or for displaying handouts and brochures.

One sure way to ruin the effect is to rent half of a partitioned room, only to find out that a hog-calling contest or a demonstration of stereo speakers has been scheduled for the space on the other side of the flimsy partition. Rent the entire room. You'll not only assure peace and quiet for your meeting, you can arrange to open or shut partitions as necessary to make your meeting appear well attended but comfortably uncrowded.

And finally, if you determine on your scouting trip that the layout of the conference area is confusing, have your art department prepare plenty of signs pointing the way to the proper outside entrance, the conference room, the phones, and, of course, the restrooms. Keeping reporters from getting irritated over logistics is part of what Greenfield means by "petting" the press.

We already have noted that offering gifts or lavish entertainment to journalists may constitute a breach of journalistic as well as PR ethics. However, it is never inappropriate to provide coffee and soft drinks, along with donuts and cookies, in recognition of the fact that those attending a press conference may have hurried from another assignment without time to stop for refreshments.

Similarly, most news reporters carry their own paper and pencils, but it is useful to have a supply on hand at a press table for the benefit of those who have exhausted or misplaced their supplies.

Anticipate the special needs of journalists. Radio people often wish to record a speech or presentation, and even print journalists use portable tape recorders as a backup note-taking device. Prevent the scramble that occurs when they all try to place microphones around the lectern. Avoid discomfort to your speaker, and leave the view uncluttered for photographers, by arranging to have a single microphone leading not only to the public address system, but also to a box below the platform or on a table to one side where each journalist can "jack in" to the sound source. That way, those who need to pop up and flip cassettes every thirty minutes won't distract the speaker or destroy the decorum.

Offer Helpful Handouts

The issue of how much printed material to provide, and where and when to distribute it, is always a complex one. If you pass out transcripts of the presentation and plenty of background data, the press will be pleased— but they may also disrupt the proceedings with their paper-shuffling, or, worse, they may determine that they can get a story from the handouts and decide to leave early. On the other hand, they may be irked when they realize they have taken copious notes throughout the presentation, only to be presented with a transcript immediately afterward. The answer may be a combination of techniques: a one-page outline of material to be covered (placed on every chair), a selection of fact sheets (placed on the press table), and a text of the main speaker's prepared statement (passed out at the door as reporters leave).

In addition to smoothing the way for reporters, you must keep your own selfish interests in mind: Did everyone attend, and did they get all of the information? By stationing a member of the PR staff at the door with a checklist of invitees and an envelope of prepared material, it should be possible to keep track of which media received the material. An important part of the press conference plan should be to assure that, as soon as possible, all printed materials get in the hands of invited reporters who did not attend—by courier delivery, if necessary.

CHECKLIST ✔ News Conference / Press Event

✔ Does the invitation list include the people we want to target for this info? General reporters, or specialized reporters such as those from trade media? All media? Different setups or meetings for print and broadcast media? Separate event for financial and business reporters?

✔ Has a kit been prepared for those who attend the event? Will same kit be delivered subsequently to those who cannot attend?

✔ Has the best spokesperson been selected for the conference or the event? Will there be adequate training and practice sessions? Are there audience members who will get and keep the momentum going?

✔ Are the room facilities adequate for the technical needs of the press? Lighting? Ability to jack tape recorders and microphones into the main microphone? Good sight lines? Post-meeting access to the speakers? Telephones nearby? Copy machines? Fax? Computer modems?

✔ Have the ethical concerns of the press been considered? Opportunity to pay for lunch or services?

✔ Have transportation needs been arranged for remote locations? Bus or cabs to site of special event, plant tour, etc.

✔ Have the basic amenities been provided? Water and drinking glasses? Paper and pencils?

✔ Is there adequate signage to prevent confusion?

✔ Are all speakers and participants adequately identified with panel signs, nametags, listing of participants on handout, projection of IDs on slides?

✔ Are staff members present and identified to assist reporters in finding information, sources, or services they need to report the story?

✔ Is there a press room for longer events? Resource materials: handouts, directories, staff members, computers, typewriters, phone lines, paper and pencils? Don't forget refreshments.

✔ Has a single spokesperson been assigned for complex situations?

✔ Has follow-up been arranged to take care of the needs of the media after the news conference or special event is over?

PROVIDING A PRESS ROOM We would be remiss if we failed to mention that something called the "hospitality room" frequently is set up in a suite adjacent to the area where the press is covering a conference, convention, or the proceedings of an organization. Typically, such a room is well stocked with ice and a variety of beverages. It is "the American way of doing business," and the custom wouldn't be continued if all parties didn't find it advantageous. Reporters enjoy talking informally with sources and other journalists in such an atmosphere. The result frequently is a frankness that can't be found on a convention floor or in the formal atmosphere of a press conference. From the PR practitioner's point of view, the value of the social situation cannot be discounted, but it is generally useful to follow up any discussions in the hospitality room with a more businesslike contact.

Whenever journalists are required to spend a prolonged period far from home base, they need the services of a temporary press facility—the working press room. Of course, at large political conventions the major media set up their own operations, with direct electronic links to home base. But for other events, including trade shows or expositions, professional or union conventions, and natural disasters or calamities such as Mount St. Helens and Three Mile Island, the press expects the sponsor of the event, or the organization most closely involved with it, to set up a press room—sometimes on the spur of the moment.

Organizations such as the military, public utilities, and large corporations that routinely hold events far afield find it advantageous to equip a trailer or bus with phones, typewriters, water cooler, and perhaps even bunks for quick naps. Typically, though, space is rented from a hotel. Or arrangements may be made to use a public facility in order to set up a temporary news operation with links to the wire services and major media.

PR Staff Relations with the Press

Occasionally, the room where convention materials are mimeographed for distribution to delegates must double as the press room. That gives reporters the advantage of getting information as it rolls off the machines—though this may not serve the interests of the public relations department. In addition, the working habits of the organization's public information staff and the working press may not coincide. So, it is best to have a separate room for each function. As we have already noted, television and print press have different needs, so it also is advantageous to set up a room separate from the print people where TV crews can store their equipment and hold electronic interviews.

It is a good idea to designate one or more members of the PR staff to be available in the press room regularly—holding briefings, providing background information, or simply hearing the suggestions and complaints of the reporters concerning services they need.

It is extremely important that knowledgeable members of the PR staff, and not just go-fers and clerks, be assigned press-room duty. Having good-quality information available to the press is important, and

Exhibit 6.5
Shaping Up
the Press

Is it ever proper—or even possible—to call a news conference for the pur-pose of criticizing the press and telling it to clean up its act? Will the or-ganization that tries it regret the decision to take an adversarial stance?

Brown University's Robert A. Reichley, vice president for university relations, did just that when the media were having a field day with the story that female students at the university posed nude for photographs and were arrested on prostitution charges in an off-campus apartment. Tabloid coverage implied that Brown itself was where criminal activity took place.

The university's top spokesperson took it straight to the press in his news conference. Saying reporters had a "magnificent inability to focus on what the real issues were," he attacked the media for placing undue emphasis on the university's role in the affair. At root, he pointed out, was an ongoing belief by the media that Brown University is an un-orthodox place.

Reichley's approach worked. Most reporters were more careful of their facts in succeeding coverage, and the university got better press as a result. In this case, the intelligent demeanor of the spokesperson paid off, along with a consistent pattern of handling the press fairly.

Source: Zoe Ingalls, "Telling the Story of a University 'Completely, Frankly, Honestly,'" *The Chronicle of Higher Education*, July 12, 1989, p. A3.

the staff also must have the authority to cut red tape and expedite ac-cess of the press to important sources.[9]

As far as equipment is concerned, even a minimal press room should be equipped with typewriters, telephones, typing paper, pencils, storage space, a dictionary, press kits, publicity photos, drinking water, and—if the budget permits—envelopes, stamps, and simple refreshments.

FOLLOW-UP IS IMPORTANT

Carefully keep track of those who attend every event or press confer-ence. Good records help you decide whom to invite to your next brief-ing, press conference, or special occasion.

Be sure that each person who attends one of your organization's events has been greeted properly by a member of the organization, and either introduced to a sufficient number of other guests or provided with an identification badge. Similarly, assure that someone is at the door to offer a farewell to each guest and to determine if transportation has been arranged.

For the PR department, the event does not end as the press de-parts. Whether it was a simple news conference or a one-hundredth-anniversary ball, the next morning the staff should conduct a full review of the event's success or problems. A checklist with the names of every member of the press should be maintained to note who attended, who did not, and what reasons were given. Follow-up mailings should be ready to go within days, along with additional fact sheets in the case of a developing news story, and perhaps souvenir photographs in the case of a gala reception.

And finally, the media must be monitored to find out whether the event generated news coverage (and thus is worth repeating in the future).

NOTES

1. Jeff Greenfield, "A Charm Book for Candidates," *Columbia Journalism Review* (July/ August 1980), pp. 34–37.

2. L. James Lovejoy, "PR's Job: Media," *O'Dwyer's PR Services Report*, September 1989, p. 12; see also Jack O'Dwyer, "Corp. PR's People Minimize Face-to-Face Press Contact," *O'Dwyer's PR Services Report*, July 1989, pp. 1–3.

3. John L. Normoyle, "Split Media Press Conferences," *Public Relations Journal* (May 1979), pp. 14–15; see also Gary B. Bassford, "The Tube vs. the Pencil Press," *Public Relations Journal* (May 1979), pp. 16–22.

4. Lou Cannon, "Nessen's Briefings: Missing Questions (and Answers)," *Columbia Journalism Review* (May/June 1975), pp. 12–16.

5. Peter M. Sandman and Mary Paden, "At Three Mile Island," *Columbia Journalism Review* (July/August 1979), pp. 43–58.

6. Mitchell V. Charnley and Blair Charnley, *Reporting*, 5th ed. (New York: Holt, Rinehart and Winston, 1979), p. 281.

7. Charnley and Charnley, p. 222.

8. Adopted by the national convention of SPJ-SDX, November 16, 1973. See also Todd Hunt, "A Study of Ethics Codes in New Jersey Daily Newspapers," Institute of Communication Studies monograph, Rutgers University (1977).

9. R. Stanwood Weeks, "Setting up the News Room," *Public Relations Journal* (December 1969), p. 18.

ADDITIONAL READING

Brody, E. W., *Public Relations Programming and Production* (New York: Praeger, 1988).

Center, Allen H., and Patrick Jackson, *Public Relations Practices: Managerial Case Studies and Problems*, 4th ed. (Englewood Cliffs, NJ: Prentice-Hall, 1990). See Chapter 7, Media Relations.

Gannett Center Journal, Vol. 4, No. 2, Spring, 1990: "Publicity."

Howard, Carole, and Wilma Mathews, *Managing Media Relations* (Prospect Heights, IL: Waveland Press, 1988).

Lesly, Philip, ed., *Lesly's Handbook of Public Relations and Communications* (Chicago: Probus, 1991). See Chapter 21, Relations with Publicity Media.

7

Using Radio

Radio, the first of the electronic media, was "new" in the 1920s, when it began to offer an alternative to print information media. Subsequently, broadcast television became the novel medium—then cable and the VCR, along with the computer and the many programs and database services that turn a personal computer into a medium of mass communication.

Does that mean that radio's days are past, that the medium is a relic of a bygone era when people listened to it carefully for up-to-the-minute news and to hear events as they unfolded? Not if you think about what radio is and does today. Radio is another person talking to you. Radio is local. And the cost of radio is comparatively inexpensive per message, which permits an organization to repeat something until it sinks in.

Radio, in other words, is a very important medium for the public relations practitioner to consider.

Let's begin our discussion of the way radio fits into the public relations campaign by analyzing the formats it offers, from paid advertisements to public-service spots.

Paid Advertisements

If you want to dictate the precise content, time, and date of your message, you'll have to pay for advertising space. The size of your budget will determine what kinds of paid spots you can afford. It costs more to buy drive-time spots, when millions of commuters are listening to the

RADIO INFORMATION FORMATS

radio, than it does to buy late-night time, when insomniacs are the main audience. It costs more to position your spots before the local news broadcast each evening than it does to buy a package deal for thirty or forty repetitions of the same spot when the radio station selects the positions—perhaps guaranteeing that a certain percentage of them will fall in prime time.

Although there are many attractive and useful ways to gain access to radio, the paid announcement is effective enough to be used by such diverse organizations as Planned Parenthood, Inc., the National Milk Council, the International Ladies Garment Workers Union, and the U.S. Postal Service.

Perhaps radio's greatest attribute is its utility in sudden or emergency situations, when it is necessary to get a quickly prepared message to the general public or specialized publics on short notice. When the air traffic controllers' union went on strike, seriously disrupting air service across the nation, the airlines quickly bought time to broadcast simple spots in which a calm and authoritative announcer explained which flights would be operating normally, which service would be curtailed, and what telephone numbers area residents should call for various types of information—one number for flight crews, another for ground personnel, another for passengers with flights scheduled on that particular day, and still another number for general information.

During Hurricane Hugo in the fall of 1989, when power outages knocked Charleston, S.C., television stations off the air, radio stations that were not affected became the main public information source for citizens and rescue workers. Radio also was an important source regarding street closings and public transportation schedules after the San Francisco earthquake that year.

Public Service Announcements

In order to get their broadcast licenses renewed, commercial stations must demonstrate that they have provided the public service of distributing useful information to the community from government agencies, charities, and community betterment groups. When the information is carried in the form of a free advertisement, it is known as a public service announcement, or PSA.

Often the PSA is as slickly and as expensively produced as any paid advertisement and arrives through the mail from national organizations such as those organized to raise research funds to combat diseases or social problems. Other PSAs may come to the station in the form of scripts. Or a spokesperson from the organization may come to the studio and record the spot. Stations also take information from news releases or letters and rewrite it into radio format for reading by the station announcer.

Usually only nonprofit groups may expect to get PSAs on the air, although consumer information offered by power companies and professional associations is included in this category. Not surprisingly, the organization that submits a PSA in any form should expect to hear it aired mainly in time periods when paid advertising cannot be sold—which is to say, when only some segments of the radio audience are listening.

Usually, more than one version of a PSA is submitted to the station, both to provide variety for the listeners and to give the station flexibility in scheduling spots.

In its booklet *Making PSAs Work—A Handbook for Health Communication Professionals*, the U.S. Department of Health and Human Services points out that PSAs are limited in their impact. They alone are not likely to cause long-term behavior changes. They are most useful for creating awareness or heightening the public's sensitivity to a health problem or issue. They do generate requests for health information, and they can increase the public's recognition of a health program aimed at the community.[1]

Community Bulletin Board

Many stations offer a variation on the PSA, variously called "Community Bulletin Board," "Around the Town," or "In (our town) Today." For decades, citizens of the Minneapolis-St. Paul area have tuned to CBS affiliate WCCO around 9 A.M. every morning to hear a cheery woman read a listing of fundraising events, free senior citizen attractions, health clinics, the Bloodmobile schedule, and educational or cultural goings-on. Most stations limit the bulletin board to nonprofit organizations or to nonprofit events sponsored by businesses.

In the largest markets, bulletin board announcements usually are limited to county-wide events, and are sprinkled at random throughout the day's programming rather than being assigned a specific time slot. In any case, it is easy for a public relations department to get an item read in the bulletin board format because a simple letter to the station manager will do. It may even be possible to telephone the item in to the promotion manager or to the news desk of the station.

Local News Broadcasts

We saw in the preceding chapters that the press release, especially when it is geared to radio's special needs, can gain you air time when you have a legitimate news story. The staged event is another way to create free news coverage, when the publicity/press agent model is appropriate. On a slow news day, it is not unusual for a midday radio broadcast to devote two or three minutes to a live report from the intersection of Main and

Exhibit 7.1
Meet the Needs
of Radio

Ted Feurey, former UPI Radio Network vice president and a news director for a leading New York radio station, is a consultant to the news industry. Some of his suggestions for meeting the needs of radio:

- Listen to local radio stations, learn the names of the on-air people as well as their approaches, the subjects that interest them, their likes and dislikes. Hooking up with radio personalities is the key to gaining access.
- Don't just go to radio when you have a story to tell. Be a resource: make a spokesperson from your organization available at all times, even when the story angle isn't yours and you'd rather not be called upon for an interview.
- Instead of bombarding the radio station with several spokespersons from your organization, select the one who is most effective on radio—even if it isn't the highest-ranked person in the organization.
- Don't try to set the parameters for a radio appearance. Nothing should be off limits; be ready to answer any and all questions.

Source: Ted Feurey, "Get It on the Radio," in *Media Resource Guide,* 5th edition, published by The Gannett Foundation and The Foundation for American Communications, 1987, pp. 32–33.

Broadway, where a man dressed as a chicken is climbing a light pole. When the ensuing interview reveals that the stunt is promoting "Eat More Chicken Week," everybody has a good chuckle, and the press agent for the poultry association chalks up a success.

Deejay Chatter

Disc jockeys love to "chat" with their listeners while changing records. Most of them command loyal followings. Deejays need new material all of the time and often seize upon an unusual tidbit of information. If you have something intriguing, just phone or drop a short letter.

Talk Shows

Radio must fill endless hours with sound, and one of the cheapest sources of programming is the listener call-in show. The format varies widely. Sometimes, the host announces one or more topics for the day;

other times, it's "open mike." Typically, the participants call in, are placed briefly on hold, then go on the air with a seven-second tape delay, which permits the station to cut off profanity or slander.

Some of the callers are articulate and informed, some are rabid advocates of extreme positions, and others are merely blabbermouths. The longevity of the format attests to the fact that the mix usually is interesting, if only as a barometer as to what the "common person" is thinking and saying. (Research shows that some listeners/callers are strongly motivated by a desire to motivate others to action, while others apparently tune in purely out of loneliness.[2])

The programs can serve a public relations function. Thus, many organizations assign at least one well-informed member to monitor each broadcast. That way, if the conversation turns to gun control, birth control, self-control, or whatever falls within the purview of the organization, an opportunity is provided to offer the group's standard line: "This is Elissa Dandridge from the Lee County Adoption Service . . . I'd just like to reply to the woman who called earlier to say that she had heard there is a two-year wait for adoption. Fortunately, that isn't the case if the party is willing to consider adopting a minority child or a child with a minor birth defect. Anyone who is interested should call this number for information about adoption . . ."

Some radio talk shows use guest panelists to begin the discussion and act as respondents to the callers. Government and social agencies can take the opportunity to get their views across by providing panelists. When topics are announced in advance, it may also be useful to assign members of your organization to join the ranks of the callers.

Public Affairs Programming

As another way of fulfilling the FCC's public service requirements, most stations air two or three programs a week in which a member of the news staff or station management interviews a newsmaker, a representative of government, a spokesman for a community group, or a public relations person from industry. A call or letter to the station manager proposing a program or a segment on a weekly show usually will get a reply. Most of the programs are aired late in the evening or early Sunday morning, but the radio audience is large enough even at those times to deliver thousands of listeners.

Almost a thousand radio stations in the U.S. are sponsored by universities and other educational institutions, or they receive their support from listeners who send in contributions, as well as from foundations. These educational or public stations—most of them found on the FM part of the spectrum—devote much more of their program time to discussion of public affairs issues, and their audiences are more affluent and more educated than those for commercial stations. Your organization may be able to suggest topics for discussion and provide spokespersons for the specific programs. More than two hundred public stations carry programming from National Public Radio in Washington. Your organization, if it has a large budget, may want to seek goodwill from the public radio audience by becoming an underwriter of the quality programming distributed by National Public Radio or American Public Radio.

Right of Reply

Many stations permit "responsible groups or persons representing differing viewpoints" to reply to any opinions put forth by the management in the form of an editorial. The "editorial reply" segment usually is broadcast in the same general time slot and in the same format as the original broadcast, and the station provides its engineer and a director to assist whoever wishes to reply.

Other stations, acknowledging that there may be many opinions differing with the one broadcast by management, prefer to read listeners' letters, or to splice together excerpts from telephone calls from citizens who have voiced their viewpoints. Whatever the system, organizations with political, social, or public affairs positions should monitor local stations and be ready to make use of the access.*

Specialized Opportunities

Radio stations often use programs prepared by others as public information. Universities, for example, call on professors and agricultural extension agents to discuss topics in which they have expertise. The taped programs, a staple of weekend mornings on many stations, enhance the reputation of the educational institution. Trade and professional organizations provide public affairs programs about careers, and businesses provide consumer information. Just as large corporations underwrite cultural programming for public television, they also provide the funding for public radio, in return for a credit at the beginning and the end of the program.

---

* The right of reply to editorial opinions used to be guaranteed by the "equal-time" provision of the Fairness Doctrine, which has been largely dismantled by the Federal Communications Commission. Nevertheless, the FCC expects fairness from broadcasters, and most continue their reply policies.

Journalists and copywriters who are practiced at writing for the eye eventually must learn that writing for the ear is something quite different. Rarely is a message that appeared in print directly translatable to the audio media. Because time is money, audio messages must be more economical. And they must be written in a more conversational style rather than following the more formal structure required by print. Long Island Lighting Company Chairman Charles Pierce refers to himself as "Charlie" in his radio announcements.

At its simplest, the radio spot consists merely of an announcer speaking:

> ANNCR: Today the Red Cross Bloodmobile will visit the Ford Motor Company plant in Edison. Employees and family members will find it in the south parking lot from 8 A.M. until 2:30 in the afternoon. If you have Type O blood, your donation is especially urgent. Help alleviate the critical shortage in our Tri-County area. Donate today!

Every radio station is prepared to have an announcer read any material that is accepted for airing. Many stations also are willing to help advertisers, and perhaps even nonprofit organizations, to add other elements to improve a spot, including voices of actors or "real people" previously taped or recorded in the studio. Most stations have a library of sound effects for which they have been granted radio rights, having paid for them at the time of original purchase. If a script calls for a "lead-in-and-fade-under" of quiet pastoral music or an uptempo "city beat," the engineer can find it quickly in the library of standard music.

These basic elements are readily available for the simple PSA or commercial spot that does not require elaborate sound mixing or split-second timing. But don't expect your local station to help you produce slick spots like those featuring the snappy dialogue of Jerry Stiller and Anne Meara, or Dick (Orkin) and Bert (Berdis). Those award-winning spots are created in special studios with a director and a battery of engineers, and then distributed in recorded form to individual stations.

Getting It Timed Right

Once the basic sound elements have been selected, the critical limiting factor is time. Whereas the print writer may be able to use nine hundred words to get across the message, and the advertising copywriter may be able to "fudge" a bit through the manipulation of type size, the

PREPARING THE RADIO SPOT

radio writer must live with formats as short as thirty seconds (a typical time for PSAs) that cannot be stretched to forty or fifty seconds.

Sixty seconds of copy, read at moderate speed, is about 140 words. Some writers find that fifteen typed lines of seventy characters come out to just a minute of air time. But short, rapid-fire phrases may shrink the reading time, and polysyllabic mouthfuls may slow the announcer down. Thus, the only dependable system is to ask one or two other people to read the script aloud. Be prepared to pare out or add several words or phrases after trial readings and rehearsal in the studio.

The time limitations mean that often an entire idea must be expressed in a single adjective. You might like to explain the reason for the blood shortage mentioned in the spot above, but you have to hope that the adjective "critical" will impress the listeners enough to make them believe the appeal without hearing the specific reason.

It also may mean resorting to stereotypes: a few bars of campfire music, hand-clapping, and the line "Welcome to Camp Wanatsha" may have to set the scene in the listener's mind for a YMCA spot. A picture can be telegraphed to the listener by having the announcer or the first speaker in a dialogue spot use descriptive words:

> *"You there in the jogging suit . . . have you outgrown your need for milk?"*
> *"(Puff-puff) . . . No!"*

The All-Important Opening

You'll remember from our first discussion of radio writing in the chapter on news releases (Chapter 5, p. 111) that we cautioned against loading the opening sentence of a radio spot with specific names, facts, or figures. That's because radio listeners get the "index" for an item from the opening sentence. That is, they find out what the topic is, and they get the sense of why the story is important, and to whom. Then, with their attention raised, they are ready to absorb specific data. The print release might open with an information-packed lead:

```
Weyerhauser announced today that it will lay off 1,600
workers in its Hawthorn, Oregon, mills Friday as a direct
result of the loss of a $4 million U.S. government contract.
```

A release aimed at radio, however, would be better if it gave an overview of the situation and its impact:

```
GOVERNMENT CUTBACKS MEAN MORE LOST JOBS IN OREGON'S PAPER
INDUSTRY. WEYERHAUSER ANNOUNCED TODAY THAT . . .
```

Often the solution is to write a short opening sentence, as short as four or five words. The lead for a print release might read:

```
The Silver City Merchants Association will sponsor its
third annual Oktoberfest, with Main Street closed to traf-
fic all day Saturday, Oct. 3, to make way for food and beer
tents, a sidewalk sale, craft demonstrations, and musical
entertainment at three major intersections.
```

But the radio release is snappier:

```
IT'S OCTOBERFEST TIME AGAIN! MAIN STREET WILL BE CLOSED TO
TRAFFIC ALL DAY SATURDAY, OCTOBER 4 TO MAKE ROOM FOR FUN AND
FOOD. THE SILVER CITY MERCHANTS PROMISE TO PROVIDE PLENTY OF
FOOD, BEER, ENTERTAINMENT . . . AND SIDEWALK SALES, TOO.
```

Some would argue that radio's ability to jump into a story is what the national newspaper *USA Today* is offering its readers. As the amount of time people spend with newspapers continues to shrink, and as taboos against mixing advertising style with straight news style fade, radio's shorter sentences and greater involvement with the subject matter may become common in print as well.

To make the transition from print writing to broadcast writing, make sure to read your releases out loud, with feeling. If they are verbose and flat, rewrite until you feel comfortable reading the words with enthusiasm.

Live Announcer or Taped Spot?

If you have a very small budget, you may only be able to prepare a news release that you hope will be used on the radio. If you have a budget big enough to buy radio time, but not to do creative work, you may choose to write a script for the radio announcer or "talent" (deejay or program host) to read during the commercial segment of programming. If you're on the borderline—that is, if you decide that you might be able to tape your own spots—here are some of the considerations for making the decision.

In Favor of Using the Live Announcer for "Talent"   The station personnel have credibility with their listeners, as well as a rapport that comes from familiarity. When the regular program announcer or talent reads a spot, it blends into the rest of the programming and thus is harder for the regular listener to "tune out." The reader may also become enthusiastic about the spot and add his or her own endorsement. One more plus: if the situation dictates that changes have to be made in a spot, it's easy to call the station and change a sentence in the announcer script.

Drawbacks of Using the Live Announcer   An uninterested or distracted announcer or talent can give your script a lackluster reading. The pace may be off. The personality of the reader simply may not match the content or style of the spot—especially if a substitute takes over for the talent you expected. Goofs in pronunciation or emphasis may destroy the meaning or the rhythm of the script. (Of course, if any of these problems is pronounced and you have paid for the commercial time, you can demand a "make-good" to assure that the spot is aired properly at a later time.)

Selecting Production Values

If you do have a full budget and you decide to produce your own spots for distribution on tape, you will want to hire a production firm to create the product for you. Some production firms merely facilitate the technical production of the tapes, with your department or agency providing the script, talent, and direction. Full-service firms will work with you to develop a concept, produce a script, and take care of all facets of direction and production.

Whether you are a full-service client or your own producer, it helps to know about the script and production values that will make your radio spot interesting, memorable, and persuasive to the listener.

Stylistic Devices   include vignettes, dialog situations, monologs, and announcer copy. They include:

■ *Humorous dialog.* The device here is that one person is the foil for the other. Usually one character is uninformed in a silly or

---

CHECKLIST ✔ Broadcast Script

✔ Is the format suitable for the client's campaign material?
   Use humor, if appropriate, and it helps make the point.
   Use instructive dialog if it gets points across efficiently.
   Use monolog for serious subject and with celebrity spokespersons.
   Announcer copy may be most cost-effective and persuasive.

✔ Is the timing correct for the designated 30-second or 60-second spot?
   Provide several variations in different time formats.

✔ Does the opening get the listener's attention?
   Interesting sound effects, setting, or music.
   Situation that intrigues the listener.
   Relevance to the interests or problems of the listener.

✔ If the script uses an announcer, is the "tag" at the end effective?
   Summarizes the point of the script.
   Repeats important information.
   Tells listener where to get more information.
   Identifies the sponsoring organization.

---

embarrassing way, and the other person—often exasperated or even condescending—sets the dummy straight by providing the needed information. (See example, page 148.)

■ *Instructive dialog.* This is a variation on the humorous dialog, with the main difference being one of tone: the uninformed person is merely lacking information, and the knowledgeable person is helpful. This is a kinder format, but may not be as interesting or memorable to the listener as humorous dialog. (See example, page 149.)

■ *Monolog.* Can be humorous or not, depending on the appropriateness to the subject matter. This device lends itself well to health information campaigns (see example, page 150) and other touchy subjects. A variation, of course, is the celebrity spot, in which a well-known spokesperson talks to the audience.

■ *Announcer copy.* As discussed above, this may be as effective as more expensive and fully produced styles of presentation.

Visualization Devices help the audience for the audio medium to imagine and visualize what is going on. Some argue that radio can be more effective than television because each listener projects the kind

Exhibit 7.2

Sample Radio Script:
Humorous Dialog

PSA: 30 seconds

SFX:	Health club: clanging weights, huffing and puffing, aerobics music, and instructor in background.
1st Man:	You're in pretty good shape, Fred.
2nd Man:	(Exhaling loudly) Thanks!
lst Man:	In fact, you're in *great* shape, Fred.
2nd Man:	(Louder exhaling) Gee, thanks!
lst Man:	So tell me, why aren't you signed up to donate blood next week with the rest of us at the health club?
2nd Man:	(Nervous) Uh . . . I'm overweight.
lst Man:	Fred, look at those muscles!
2nd Man:	I . . . I'm pregnant.
lst Man:	Fred!
2nd Man:	I'll be out of town. I have an appointment on the moon!
lst Man:	Fred, Fred, Fred.
ANNCR:	Everybody has an excuse for not giving blood. But how can you use those excuses when your neighbors, friends . . . and your own family are counting on you? Think of donating blood as part of your physical fitness and well-being. This message brought to you by the American Red Cross in cooperation with this station.

of characters and speakers that appeal to him or her on the voices and sounds heard over the radio. Some visualization devices are:

- *Character voices.* Ethnics, young, old, stereotypes, authoritative announcers (such as the long-famous Don Pardo), gender roles, and even such old chestnuts as the fuddy-duddy professor.
- *Music.* May set the scene (New York Street, wedding) or the mood (romantic, hectic, outdoors) and may recall happy or unhappy situations.
- *Sound effects.* Subways, busy restaurants, construction sites, office settings, kitchens, and the great outdoors all can be suggested by brief sounds or a continuing blend of background noises.
- *Cue words in the copy.* (Shakespeare, whose actors did not wear costumes as they performed on bare stages, was good at this.) "Why are you wearing that loud plaid tie, Hubert?" "I never thought I'd see you in a red sports car." "Don't you know you

Exhibit 7.3
Sample Radio Script:
Instructive Dialog

PSA: 30 seconds

SFX: Health club: clanging weights, huffing and puffing, aerobics music, and instructor in background.

1st Man: So tell me, Fred, why aren't you signed up to donate blood next week with the rest of us at the health club?

2nd Man: (Nervous) I . . . I don't know. I just don't know if . . .

1st Man: It's easy and almost painless. And it takes less time than a good workout.

2nd Man: But I'm not sure if it's completely safe. You know . . .

1st Man: Believe me, it's safe. They take all the precautions. I should know, I've been giving regularly for all these years.

2nd Man: Well, okay, but I . . .

1st Man: If not you, who, Big Guy?

ANNCR: Everybody has an excuse for not giving blood. But how can you use those excuses when your neighbors, friends . . . and your own family are counting on you? Think of donating blood as part of your physical fitness and well-being. This message brought to you by the American Red Cross in cooperation with this station.

can't put those newspapers in the trash?" All of these sentences carry words or phrases that help us visualize the setting and the action, even though we are only hearing words produced by voices.

Memory Devices help us retain information while listening to radio, a medium from which clippings cannot be made at one's leisure. Examples:

- *Repetition.* "What was that number again, Floyd? One more time!"
- *Exaggeration.* "Monday used to mean laundry, but now it means recycling. Monday used to mean back to work, but now it's recycling. Monday is the most important day in my life: recycling day!" (Repetition is also used.)
- *Jingles.* "Put your worries away . . . ride the Metro today!"
- *Forewarning.* "In just a moment, I'm going to give you the number that could save your life, the Heart Lifeline. While you're getting a pencil and paper, let me remind you that one out of five Americans will experience . . . ."

Exhibit 7.4
Sample Radio
Script: Monolog

PSA: 30 seconds

SFX:	Health club: clanging weights, huffing and puffing, aerobics music, and instructor in background.
Talent:	I really like my workouts here at the club. I can see the improvement in my health and my outlook on life. I feel like I can face any of life's challenges when I'm in shape. That's why I felt funny when I kept finding excuses for not donating blood here at the club: too busy . . . whatever. But that's changed now. Once I became a blood donor, I realized that it was the most important part of my routine: helping others to a healthier life . . . and maybe even helping myself.
ANNCR:	Everybody has an excuse for not giving blood. But how can you use those excuses when your neighbors, friends . . . and your own family are counting on you? Think of donating blood as part of your physical fitness and well-being. This message brought to you by the American Red Cross in cooperation with this station.

■ *Humor involving a "dense" foil.* "No, Hubie, I'm telling you for the last time, you've got to register to vote. And you have to do it by March 17. Can't you remember any number bigger than the number of fingers on your hand? It's March 17 if you want to be counted in the primary election."

You may have noted that many of these devices look silly on paper. But they work in radio because people retain simple, entertaining information.

Variation of the Spot

Usually, different versions of the radio spot are written to fit the various standard time slots, from sixty seconds down to ten seconds. In the case of the paid announcement, cost savings can be realized by introducing the campaign with full 60-second spots, and then achieving the desired repetition using 30- or 20-second spots that contain all of the main elements but that have been condensed.

When a nonprofit organization prepares PSAs, it is a good idea to offer 10-, 20-, 30-, and 60-second versions so a station can choose the versions that best fit its format. Here, for example, are different versions of the same PSA written for the George Street Playhouse, a regional nonprofit professional theater:

ANNCR: The spotlight is on the George Street Playhouse. Make sure you get the best seat in the house. Subscribe now. Call 246-7717. (10 sec)

ANNCR: The spotlight is on the George Street Playhouse. You'll see *Tobacco Road, Jacques Brel, Private Lives,* Shakespeare, and two great new American plays. Subscribers have the best seats in the house. To reserve your season tickets, call 246-7717 now. (20 sec)

ANNCR: The spotlight is on the George Street Playhouse. The season begins in September with *Tobacco Road.* You'll thrill to the delightful musical *Jacques Brel.* Rounding out the season are Noel Coward's wonderful and witty *Private Lives,* William Shakespeare's moving *Henry the Fourth,* plus two great new American plays. Our subscribers enjoy the best seats in the house. Reserve your season tickets now. Don't wait. Call 246-7717. (30 sec)

Notice that the extra time is not used to make quantum jumps in the amount of information, but rather to flesh out the basic ideas of the shorter spots by offering more adjectives, filling in a few particulars, and engaging in greater familiarity with the listener.

Time constraints dictate that most radio stations must be selective about which PSAs they use. The main reasons for rejecting a PSA are:

SUBMITTING THE MATERIAL

The material is too dry or dull.

The spot lacks a local angle

The tone of the spot does not "blend" with the station's format.

The tapes submitted are not up to the standards of technical quality required by the station.

Material that is to be submitted to radio stations in tape form should be produced with studio-quality equipment on clean, quarter-inch magnetic recording tape. If only one copy is needed, cut the tape from the master recording reel and rewind it on a small plastic reel. If the station plans to make repeated use of the spot, they will transfer it to a plastic cartridge, or "cart," so that it can be played automatically merely by punching a button.

If duplicates are needed, take the master tape to a studio equipped with a multiple duplicator. The high-speed machinery simultaneously makes as many as half a dozen copies, which can then be rewound on individual reels or carts. PSAs distributed in large quantities for frequent use should be packaged in carts to increase the chances that a station manager will okay the spot because it is conveniently ready to go.

If you are submitting a PSA or other taped information for radio use, and if you have no familiarity with station management, the material may be directed to the general manager, which is the equivalent of sending it to the editor of a newspaper. If it is newsworthy, it will be routed to the news director. If it fits better in another format, it will be routed to the program director.

The organization that plans to make frequent use of radio should endeavor to cultivate a contact in both the news and programming departments in order to be able to deliver material to someone who is directly concerned. Make sure that the name, address, and phone number of someone in your organization who can answer questions or provide additional information is included at the top of the covering letter, on the script, and on the tape reel itself—you never know which they'll have in hand at the moment they decide to call you. Anyone who is unsure of how to submit material, or to whom, usually will be granted a short interview and orientation merely by coming to the reception desk of the station.

RADIO FONE-FEED   When a public relations department begins to notice that it is dealing with radio stations on almost a daily basis—providing quotes from spokespersons within the organization on such topics as the economy, energy, safety, or research—perhaps it is time to institute an "audio feed" system. Then radio stations can call a special number to tape one or two minutes of material recorded for continuous automatic sending. In effect, the radio station's tape recorder listens to and copies the PR department's tape recorder. The advantage to the station is that it receives "live interview" material with only a few minutes of effort and no special arrangements.

Obviously, the feed is not worthwhile for many organizations, but it works well for, say, a sports team that is telephoned daily by dozens of broadcast media people for a word or two from the coaches on the upcoming game. A major university that issues print press releases at the rate of four or five a day finds it natural to offer a supporting audio feed to the many radio stations in the state or region.

Perhaps the most vigorous users of Fone-Feed services are the departments of the federal government. Nearly every agency in Washington has a well-publicized number that reporters can call for transmission of program material. In fact, the practice is so widespread that *The Washington Post* has listed some of the numbers in mockingly humorous stories about the varied materials available at the broadcaster's fingertips.

To be successful, the feed system must be promoted vigorously when it is initiated. Essentially that is done by making personal phone calls to the news directors for all area radio stations, explaining to them how the system works, and then playing sample tapes to them over the phone. A follow-up letter is sent to the station, and along with it a reminder card (or self-stick adhesive label) to be placed next to the news desk phone, listing the special number.

Preparing the Tape Loop

The sender must be prepared to provide one or two short items each day. Usually, these are feature items, but if a spot news story breaks, the feed may be used to provide a statement to the press from the president, the manager, or whichever official is in a position to speak for the organization.

The message is put on a loop of audio tape in playback equipment that is attached to the phone in such a way that it is activated by an incoming call. It automatically rewinds when the connection is terminated. The message consists of two parts, an introduction, and the voice "actuality." Note that the following script is written in the all-capital-letters format favored by radio news personnel.

```
THIS IS ROBERT ROBBINS, SPORTS INFORMATION DIRECTOR FOR
STATE UNIVERSITY. THANK YOU FOR CALLING STATE U FONE-FEED.
TODAY WE HAVE A 40-SECOND STATEMENT FROM FOOTBALL COACH ALEX-
ANDER ANDERSON ON HIS CHOICE OF STARTING QUARTERBACK FOR SAT-
URDAY'S GAME WITH CENTRAL TECH, AND A 50-SECOND STATEMENT
FROM UNIVERSITY PRESIDENT HOWARD H. HOXIE SPEAKING IN SUP-
PORT OF THE BOND AMENDMENT TO BUILD A NEW FIELDHOUSE. IF YOU
DESIRE FURTHER INFORMATION, PLEASE CALL ME AT 999-9999. THE
FONE-FEED WILL COMMENCE AT THE SOUND OF THE TONE.

(Five-second pause, followed by a "beep.")
```

WE . . . UH . . . WE'VE DECIDED TO GO WITH LANCE LARSON FOR
THE TECH GAME BECAUSE THEY HAVE SHOWN A STRONG DEFENSE
AGAINST THE RUNNING ATTACK, BUT WE THINK THEY'RE VULNERA-
BLE TO THE PASS, AND LANCE IS OUR . . . (etc.)

An organization that regularly puts out feature print releases may
find that the feed system will help place more of those stories on radio.
If the tape recorder carries voice actualities to "illustrate" a print release, radio stations should be alerted by a special box at the top of the
release:

RADIO NEWS DIRECTORS, CALL FONE-FEED AT 999-9999 FOR SPO-
KEN VERSION OF MAJOR QUOTES IN STORY BELOW.

To make an audio-feed system work, the public information department must make careful advance plans, and one member of the staff
must be designated to prepare the tapes and maintain the equipment.
Some organizations find that it is not feasible to offer the daily feed
year-round, but it is a useful adjunct at specific times, such as a convention, a state tournament, or another annual event where the media demand extra servicing. In New Jersey, the governor's communication
office provides audio feed on the two days each week when the state
legislature meets and, toward the end of the session, on days when the
governor is scheduled to sign major bills.

**MAXIMIZE
THE IMPACT**

Once the public relations department or agency has placed a story on a
radio program or has paid for a series of spots on local radio, the question begins to nag: Will anybody be listening? The answer is yes, because thousands of people are listening to radio at any hour of the day.
The real question is: Will the radio program have the desired impact?
There are things you can do to assure that it will.

If you have placed a spokesperson for your organization on a talk
show or a public affairs program, use internal and external media to
publicize the fact. Tell employees, stockholders, customers, and any
other publics you reach through print media to listen. If you have paid
for a series of spots promoting your organization's point of view, call attention to it with brief boxed items in your employee newsletters, on

bulletin boards, in notices to stockholders, and even in small print ads on the page of radio and television listings in the local newspapers.

Remember, too, that the appearance of a spokesperson on a radio talk show or public affairs program is news. An advance story to local print news media can cover the information your spokesperson plans to present on the radio show. Have a print release ready to mail to trade and business publications as soon as the broadcast is over, outlining the points your spokesperson made.

NOTES

1. U.S. Department of Health and Human Services, *Making PSA's Work—A Handbook for Health Communication Professionals*, NIH Publication No. 84-2485, pp. 1–2.
2. Jeffry Bierig and John Dimmick, "The Late Night Radio Talk Show as Interpersonal Communication," *Journalism Quarterly* (Spring 1979), pp. 92–96.

ADDITIONAL READING

Broussard, E. Joseph, and Jack F. Holgate, *Writing and Reporting Broadcast News* (New York: Macmillan, 1982).

Fang, Irving, *Television News, Radio News,* 4th ed. (St. Paul: RADA Press, 1985).

MacDonald, R.H., *A Broadcast News Manual of Style* (New York: Longman, 1987).

O'Donnel, Lewis B., Philip Benoit, and Carl Hausman, *Modern Radio Production* (Belmont, CA: Wadsworth, 1986).

Smelyak, Paul G., *Broadcast News Writing,* 2d ed. (New York: Macmillan, 1983).

St. John, Tracy, *Getting Your Public Relations Story on TV and Radio* (Babylon, NY: Pilot Books, 1986).

Weaver, J. Clark, *Broadcast News Writing as Process* (New York: Longman, 1984).

8

Television and Cable

If the print news release is still the bread and butter of public relations techniques, getting your organization's story on television is the peanut butter and jelly.

Partly it's because of the numbers: an article in a print medium may reach up to 5 or 10 million readers in the most popular magazines, but get a 30-second exposure on a network news program or a morning talk-news show, and your "reach" may be as many as 50 million people. Similarly, a local newspaper may reach 100,000, but the evening news show in the same area may reach half a million or more.

Then, too, it's the glitz and glamour of television. A mention in print is nice, but a mention on the tube is exciting. Reading a newspaper is work, and the more educated members of society are willing to do that work. But many target publics—especially those for marketing public relations campaigns and campaigns involving public issues such as health—prefer to receive and process information the effortless and entertaining way, by watching the television set.

In this chapter we consider broadcast television and cable together, because the programs carried by both are conduits for video news releases and other techniques aimed at external publics. Video—meaning recorded visual information for showing to specialized and internal publics, including employees—will be discussed in the next chapter.

**TELEVISION
PROVIDES
RECOGNITION**

Messages seen on television bring instant public recognition, and with it very often comes approval of an idea or program. Many of the award winners in the Public Relations Society of America's annual Silver Anvil competition, as well as the top Gold Quill winners in the annual competition sponsored by the International Association of Business Communicators, cite the importance of television to their successful campaigns:[1]

- In 1990 the StarKist Seafood Co. and H. J. Heinz were being blamed by environmental groups for fishing practices that resulted in the death of dolphins. Consumers began to avoid tuna products. StarKist took the lead in adopting a "dolphin-safe" fishing policy and transmitted a video news release of its press kit by satellite. The story led the ABC evening news and received coverage on the other American networks as well as foreign television.

- Publication of a book criticizing the use of pesticides by the food industry caused the National Food Processors Association and the industry's Food Safety Group to worry about consumer backlash in the early 1990s. The groups' public relations agency videotaped interviews with influential scientists and government officials, who pointed out the book's fallacies and provided an unbiased account of safety practices in the food industry. Footage from the interview tape was used on major national broadcast outlets such as the "Today" show and "CBS This Morning," as well as the popular "Larry King Live" on cable.

- McDonald's responded to attacks for not having environmentally safe products by launching its "McRecycle USA" campaign to create markets for recycled materials. In addition to mailing video releases to television stations, the firm's public relations agency set up satellite interviews so television reporters could question McDonald's executives.

- Concerned that consumers did not know they could charge health care to their credit card, Visa U.S.A. engaged a research firm to conduct a survey that showed people wanted to be able to charge their health care. Material from a video news kit with the results appeared on many cable shows watched by consumers, including CNN's "Business Day" and "Your Money," and on ESPN's "Nation's Business Today."

- The Royal Melbourne Hospital in Parkville, Australia, brought in a film crew to shoot scenes in the emergency room and intensive care unit showing what happened to victims of drinking-and-driving automobile accidents. When the footage was prepared as a 60-second television spot, commercial stations were so impressed with the impact of the message aimed at young drivers that they agreed to run the spot for free.

- When Coca-Cola used an ice-skating robot to publicize its involvement with the Lake Placid Winter Olympic Games, it released two television film clips, which were carried by 136 television stations in 119 cities for a total of 214 telecasts that reached a projected 37 million households. A twenty-three-city tour by the robot attracted further coverage: 125 minutes of television time, reaching an audience of 30 million.
- The British Post Office marked the issuance of a Pony Express commemorative stamp by re-creating the original Pony Express ride from St. Joseph, Mo., to Sacramento, Calif. A 90-second TV news clip, entitled "High Noon in Sacramento" and produced by Carl Byoir & Associates, showed the start and end of a race along the Pony Express trail. The film was used by 185 stations in North America.
- The Houston Parks Department made a persuasive case for increasing park acreage and funding by financing a 20-minute documentary videotape, "No Room at the Park," which was aired in prime time by public television.
- Burger King's "spokesman" for its fire-safety program aimed at children is "Snuffy," a scaled-down replica of an antique fire engine. Following a campaign that included appearances on sixty television shows, and a PSA run by 105 television stations with an estimated audience of 115 million, nationwide market research by Burger King showed that 74 percent of children under age thirteen were aware of the talking fire engine.
- When an Air Force Academy cadet was selected to chaperone a Colorado competitor in the International Special Olympics, the service academy's public affairs office assigned a PR practitioner full-time to assist ABC in preparing a television feature on the relationship between the cadet host and the handicapped athlete. The human-interest angle was a major part of the network's nationwide coverage of the event on its popular "Wide World of Sports."

PUBLIC SERVICE ANNOUNCEMENTS FOR TV

We saw in the preceding chapter that the radio PSA is an important public relations tool. The FCC also requires television stations to provide time for nonprofit public service messages. Some, such as the anti-drug spots donated by the Advertising Council, Inc., are as slickly and expensively produced as those for commercial products. On the other hand, the no-budget PSA may be as basic as an announcer reading a two-hundred-word script while a title card with the name and phone number of the service organization is shown on the screen.

A series of PSAs prepared for the Summit County (Ohio) Association for Retarded Citizens sought to dispel myths about mentally handicapped people by employing new words to describe and depict them, by differentiating between mental illness and mental retardation, and by giving mentally handicapped persons a chance to speak for themselves in the public media—a powerful use of television:

> *A major step in the production process was the use of a 15-person focus group. Eight TV storyboards and scripts were produced and submitted to the focus group for review and discussion. Based upon these findings, amendments were made and final production undertaken. Of greatest significance was the finding that PSAs were most successful if they avoided preaching and stimulated new thinking about mentally handicapped people.*[2]

The PSAs were used in conjunction with a complete media program that also included talk shows and news programs (see following section). Seven television stations aired the PSAs an estimated 133 times during the one-month campaign.

Some Stations Produce PSAs

Before planning the television PSA, it is wise to make contact with area stations to find out what special formats they make available free of charge. In the New York metropolitan area, for example, one station produces a series of "Big Apple Minutes"—news features using the station's own personalities and production crews to highlight attractions such as museums, exhibits, and historic programs. The station prepares spots that would cost the nonprofit organizations thousands of dollars to produce independently.

GAINING ACCESS TO COMMERCIAL TELEVISION

We noted in our discussion of PSAs above that a complete media program seeks every possible access to television, including news coverage and talk shows, as well as cable coverage. In the case of the Summit County Association for Retarded Citizens, the campaign was labeled Project Dawn. The help of radio, television, and print professionals was enlisted to form a media consortium to advise the association how to gain access to the media. Each of the television stations serving the county was contacted, and visits were arranged so that volunteers and the PR firm engaged by the association (Meeker–Mayer) could learn how best to place information in the electronic media. The organization did not pressure the media. Instead, it sought to find out how material could be tailored to the media's needs in order for the association to achieve greater acceptance and usage.

A variety of background material was provided to talk-show hosts, and assistance was given in finding mentally retarded people to appear on the shows as spokespersons. Eventually, six television talk-show appearances were booked, providing a large share of the more than four hours of television coverage in a single month.

Such cooperation is extremely important for an organization that wants to make an impact on television. Often, a failure or unwillingness to accommodate the special needs and desires of television means the loss of valuable exposure. Although the American Academy of Family Physicians received volumes of print coverage for its observance of the tenth anniversary of the establishment of family practice as a medical specialty, it forfeited valuable exposure on both the "Today" show and "Good Morning America." Why? Because it declined to offer either show an "exclusive" prior to the release of a major healthcare research report at a press conference open to all of the news media.

For decades, print news releases prepared by public relations firms on behalf of clients—or prepared by the public relations staffs of corporations and nonprofit organizations—have generated not only print articles, but broadcast stories as well. Sometimes the press release is used in its entirety as written. More often it suggests stories to a news medium and provides information reporters can use as part of their own stories.

By the beginning of the 1990s, video news releases (VNRs) were gaining dramatically in usage. They typically are 30-second to 5-minute video tapes that a television station can show, in whole or part, to provide visual information in stories put together by their reporters. Sometimes the footage provided in VNRs is referred to as "B-roll" material, because it is the information that editors cut to after the taped introduction and before the taped transitions and final wrap-up on the "A-roll" produced by the broadcast news medium.

The tightening of budgets for television reporting has led to increased use of VNRs—and to the growth of the agencies that specialize in producing them for clients. A 1987 Nielsen survey of television news producers showed that nearly a quarter of the stations surveyed had used video releases in their entirety, and two-thirds had used parts of VNRs in conjunction with reports by their own staffs. A follow-up survey in 1990 showed usage increasing, with nearly 90 percent of news directors saying they follow advisories provided by Medialink Video Broadcasting Corporation, the leading distributor of VNRs.[3]

The Nielsen study showed that the majority of television newscasters prefer VNRs under two minutes in length, and most prefer "B-roll"

VIDEO NEWS RELEASES GAIN IN USE

On the evening of April 25, 1989, ABC closed its evening news with a report about the fiftieth anniversary of television. The item was generated by a public relations agency (GCI Group, Inc.) working on behalf of a client (Electronic Industries Association/Consumer Electronics Group).

The airing of the news item is documented here by VMS—the video monitoring service affiliated with Burrelle's news clipping service. The transcript provided by VMS to the GCI Group shows exactly what information was carried on the ABC broadcast.

Peter Jennings, anchor of ABC's "World News Tonight," introduced a pre-packaged segment by ABC correspondent Richard Threlkeld concerning the fiftieth anniversary of television. The Threlkeld footage opened with a film clip of President Roosevelt introducing television at the 1939 World's Fair (shown in the still photo here). The footage, like the clips from early television shows later in the segment, was part of the package provided by the public relations agency.

ABC shaped the material to fit its format for a special item at the end of its news broadcast that salutes a person or industry for some contribution to society. The network used its own resources, but also drew upon footage and ideas provided by the agency on behalf of the client. The result satisfied the client's wish to publicize the fiftieth anniversary of television.

Photo and script courtesy of VMS

130 West 42nd Street, New York, N.Y. 10036
(212) 736-2010
434 West 17th Street, Los Angeles, CA 90020
(213) 380-5011
212 West Superior Street, Chicago, IL 60610
(312) 649-4131
1430 Chestnut Street, Philadelphia, PA 19102
(215) 569-4990
577 Howard Street, San Francisco, CA 94105
(415) 543-3361

17400 Lahser Road, Southfield, MI 48034
(313) 352-9220
745 Boylston Street, Boston, MA 02116
(617) 266-2121
4111 I.B. Freeway, Dallas, Tx 75251
(214) 644-9696
336 National Press Building, Washington, DC 20045
(202) 393-7110
10260 Westheimer, Houston, Tx 77042
(713) 789-1635

2125 Biscayne Boulevard, Miami, FL 33137
(305) 576-3581
100 East Ninth Avenue, Denver, CO 80203
(303) 861-7152
10 Oakwood Avenue, West Hartford, CT 06110
(203) 246-1889
1451 Fourth Avenue, San Diego, CA 92101
(619) 544-1860

A _____ Affiliate

DATE	April 25, 1989
TIME	6:30-7:00 PM (ET)
NETWORK	ABC-TV
PROGRAM	World News Tonight

TRANSCRIPT

Peter Jennings, anchor:

Finally here this evening, thinking about television. This month, we celebrate the fiftieth anniversary of the first public demonstration of a moving picture in a box. Today, three out of four people in the country were born after television was invented.
In Washington, the Smithsonian has just opened an exhibit to mark the half-century. ABC's Richard Threlkeld has been to see it.

Richard Threlkeld reporting:

The first telecast featured President Roosevelt opening the New York World's Fair. (Clip of telecast.) If you think the cameras were something back then, the TV set looks like it's related to R2-D2.
It's now the centerpiece of an exhibit in the Smithsonian Institution of all places, the scholars having decided that the last half-century of TV is a history worth examining, if not necessarily repeating.

Roger Kennedy (National Museum of American History): It's a great mystery whose technology is known but whose psychology is not.

Threlkeld: So, the memorabilia of American TV have been assembled here like artifacts around the sacred totems of some obscure and slightly eccentric civilization: Howdy Doody himself, Timmy's shirt and pants from "Lassie," Groucho Marx's Emmy for "You Bet Your Life," the Mickey Mouse Club lunchbox, the Fonz's jacket from "Happy Days" and the much maligned Nielson meter to find out who out there is watching, and more important, who is not. (Clip of above named shows and the "Milton Berle Show.")
When TV first came out, Fred Allen, the humorist, dismissed it as chewing gum for the eyes. Over the last fifty years though, there's been just enough on TV to hold out at least some hope for the next fifty...if we're lucky.

Edward Emereau [sp] (From Clip): We're impressed with the importance of this medium. We shall hope to learn to use it and not to abuse it. Good night and good luck.

Threlkeld: Richard Threlkeld, ABC News, Washington.

Jennings: Edward Emereau.

Videocassettes are available in any format for a period of 31 days from air date; audio cassettes for 14 days. Call any VMS office.

# # #

material that isn't packaged into a finished news story, although two-thirds of the directors said they would like to receive both a packaged news story and the "B-roll" footage, so they can decide which fits their needs better. Three-quarters of the television news directors received their VNRs by satellite transmission rather than through the mail or by hand delivery.

Medialink—which acts as a go-between serving public relations people whose organizations have a story to tell and television or cable stations that need material—advises its clients to make the best use of the service by observing several requirements:

- The perishability of a story and its uniqueness may lead you to choose live transmission instead of taped and edited footage. Press conferences are of interest to broadcast media because of their immediacy.
- High-speed teleprinters installed and serviced by the Associated Press alert newsroom decision makers to new information and advise them on how to get access to it.
- Stories with a national focus have the best chance of being used by a great number of outlets, but you can use the newswire to alert local media to special angles and tie-ins that may be of interest to their viewers.
- VNRs must be educational, entertaining, and interesting. They should be truthful and should not obscure bad news. Most important, VNRs must be clearly identified as public relations material. Identification must include the source of production, and the name of the sponsor of the VNR.
- VNRs should be produced to be edited. That is, the client should not expect that the entire VNR will be used by all outlets, but rather that some footage will be used.
- Production values must conform to broadcast news standards and should have legitimate news value; they should not be commercials packaged to look like news.
- News producers should be given the choice of using an announcer provided by the sponsor or their own announcer. To facilitate that option, either two versions should be provided, or two sound tracks should be laid on one visual image—"natural" sound as well as announcer mixed with natural sound.[4]

Medialink, which is the largest distributor of VNRs, does not produce them. It does, however, offer its own monitoring service to clients, so that usage of material can be tracked and reported. It offers teleconferencing, satellite news conferences, and other services to its clients.

Dozens of smaller firms offer regional services or specialize in dissemination of science, marketing, health, and educational VNRs to general and specialized broadcast and cable outlets. For the past several years, *Public Relations Journal* has printed an annual listing of VNR suppliers and services.

Target VNRs Carefully

Video workshop features in the industry's leading trade publications stress that because VNRs are expensive to make and distribute, they cannot just be run off and scattered like print press releases. Some producers of VNRs, for example, stress that they prepare up to a half-dozen different versions of each client's video release, each one stressing different content for different outlets.

Business-related shows on cable are more likely to accept VNRs that discuss a product or service, as long as the business aspects are obvious. But news outlets want the focus to be on interesting people, with the name of the product mentioned only once and unobtrusively or casually, if at all. An example is the annual dirtiest sneakers contest sponsored by Odor-Eaters. Television stations love the shots of kids with their scruffy shoes, and they'll play the angle of sponsorship by a company that makes deodorant inserts for sneakers. Sometimes, though, the only way the name of the product makes it on the air is in the form of a sign hanging on the stage behind the contestants.

One producer of VNRs believes the greatest danger is in producing a VNR that looks and sounds like an advertisement. She recommends using the news technique of preparing for coverage of an event, but not to the point of writing a script or shooting footage to "stage" the event. Instead, the VNR production crew should approach the shoot as if they were a broadcast news team, catching the "breaking news" feeling of the event.[5]

Another producer of video releases suggests getting inside the heads of broadcast news directors to anticipate the types of coverage that they will find useful. Holidays are slow news days, so producing a VNR suitable for showing on a holiday may increase your chances of getting air time. An example was the VNR produced for the Irish Tourist Board showing how St. Patrick's Day is celebrated in Ireland. Television is fascinated with celebrities, so involving a well-known personality in your VNR may be the ticket to acceptance. Television likes to be on top of trends and topical issues. Tax time provides a good peg for an investment company's VNR on how to use retirement planning and tax shelters to soften the bite of the Internal Revenue Service.[6]

Still another VNR producer tries to avoid the dullness of "talking heads" by choosing interesting locations for shoots and making sure that there is action in the footage, preferably a demonstration of the product or service that is being promoted. For a paper goods manufacturer's line

A crew from NYTV—a production firm specializing in corporate videos—prepares to shoot a pep talk by Seton Hall head basketball coach P. J. Carlesimo aimed at employees of Public Service Electric & Gas Co. Executives of PSE&G used the video to explain and dramatize the company's long-term strategic goals.

Photo courtesy of NYTV

of party and entertaining products, the videos were shot in homes where the spokesperson for the firm could show table settings and other decorations in use.[7]

VNR producers such as The News Group in Boca Raton, Florida, stress that they use former television news personnel who are familiar with the needs of local broadcast and cable outlets. They price VNRs at a basic rate of $10,000 but stress that an electronic press kit (EPK) with only "B-roll" footage can be produced for under $4,000—and may be even more effective than a slick VNR in getting the message on the screen.[8]

WHO'LL PRODUCE THE MESSAGE?

Television is a highly specialized medium, and messages for showing on television must meet the highest technical and content standards. Many of the largest corporations maintain their own production departments because they have enough work to justify the expense.

Johnson & Johnson, for example, uses outside producers to prepare commercials for its products. But messages aimed at employees, stockholders, and managers of subsidiary companies are prepared in-house, as are training films and cassettes that sale personnel take to hospitals and doctors to "demonstrate" the use of sutures and other products during operations. During the crisis involving tampering with the firm's Tylenol capsules, the video department prepared footage showing production and distribution of the capsules and passed the cassettes out to the broadcast news media following a press conference at company headquarters. Because Johnson & Johnson uses television to keep in contact with managers at its family of 170 companies, its production facility is called WorldWide Video Network. Its logo, WWVN, gives its productions the feel of programs produced by a commercial broadcasting operation.

Organizations that do not have the resources of a large corporation use the services of specialized television production and distribution firms. They're listed in the Yellow Pages in most large cities, and they advertise their services in trade magazines. Some specialize in VNRs; others can produce anything from a 30-second PSA to a half-hour documentary for closed-circuit use in video conferences aimed at investment counsellors.

The Story Conference

Whether the television message will be produced in-house or contracted out, the planning process begins with a story conference—a meeting where the public relations managers and their clients decide what kind of message they want. (Even in-house operations refer to the departments for which they prepare television messages as their "clients," because their working relationship is much the same as if they were an outside agency.)

Here are some of the considerations that must be worked out in the story conference process:

Objectives for the Television Message Why is television the medium to use to reach the target publics for this program? What behavioral outcomes are desired, and are they likely to happen as the result of receiving a television message? Will there be print support for the television campaign? Is it cost-effective?

Budget Even within a corporation, the client department must pay for the cost of the television message, which means the production department must be prepared to figure out its costs and present a budget.

Style and Format Will the message be short or long, serious or humorous, in documentary style or entertainment format? Will there be an on-screen host or only the voice of a narrator? Will we use dramatic storytelling devices, or model the message after a broadcast news story? Will all footage be original for this production, or will file footage, historical material, or clips from other sources be used? Will we need special graphics and titles?

Exhibit 8.2
Television
Script Format

CLIENT: Meals on Wheels
   TITLE: A Friend in Need
LENGTH: 30 Seconds

Video	**Audio**
Open on Elmer, sitting on porch, rocking in rocking chair.	ANNCR (VO): Time passes slowly when you're alone. Meal time's coming . . . but that's nothing special when you've got to fend for yourself. Unless you're Elmer and you've got *Meals on Wheels* to look forward to.
	SFX: Motor sounds. Horn honking.
Cut to station wagon turning onto block.	
Cut to Elmer leaning forward in chair and smiling.	ELSIE'S VOICE: Right on time, Elmer. Are you hungry today?
Elmer rises from chair and waves.	ELMER: Hungry? Sure enough.
Close-up of tray in Elsie's hands.	ELSIE: Your favorite today.
Close up of Elmer's smiling face.	ELMER: Ham and peas?
Close up of Elsie's face.	ELSIE: Ham and peas!
Medium shot of Elmer and Elsie going into the house and screen door swinging shut. Hold on doorway.	ANNCR: Ham and peas . . . and love and attention . . . and something to look forward to each day. Meals on Wheels. It's more than food. It's a reason to go on living.

TITLE CARD:
   To Contribute.
   To Help.
   To Assist a Loved One.
   Call now: (908) 246-1151.
	ANNCR: A public service message provided by Meals on Wheels and Pro Bono Public Relations.

Exhibit 8.2 *(continued)*
Television
Script Format

This sample television script uses the split format with visual elements on left side of the script and the sounds on the right. The heading here identifies the client, gives the script and title, and indicates the length of the spot. Headings may also include the name of the firm that prepared the spot and code numbers, dates, and other identifying information.

Abbreviations are ANNCR for the off-screen announcer voice, VO to indicate that the announcer is heard "voice over" the other material, and SFX to indicate sound effects that help set the scene. Characters may be given names if the names are heard in the script. Otherwise they may be descriptive: Grandfatherly man . . . Middle-aged woman.

The staggering of the final items on either side of the script indicates that the announcer's voice is heard only after the information on the title card has been on the screen for a few seconds. This is a fairly short script for a 30-second spot, indicating that the pace of the vignette is leisurely. Some scripts carry notations on the video side indicating exactly how long each shot is to last—.02 for two seconds, for example.

Writing　Can we produce the script, including visuals and audio, ourselves, or should we hire a specialized freelancer to translate our ideas into a workable concept?

Preparing the Script and Storyboard

Because television has both visual and sound components, the script for a television production, whether a short PSA or a long documentary, must be prepared in a split format. This accounts for all visual elements on the left side of the page and everything audible on the right side. Exhibit 8.2 has many of the standard elements.

After script conferences have been held to determine that the message is meeting PR objectives, the producer will prepare a storyboard for the client and the supervising public relations people to approve. Now the script as been translated into actual drawings or photographs that give an idea of what the eye will see as the words are spoken. (Exhibit 8.3 shows an example of the storyboard format.)

Throughout the conference process, the public relations people must keep the client's aims in mind and assure that the technical people achieve the desired results. Screenings of the "rough cut" are the final part of that process, with the public relations people telling the producers whether or not they think the message has the sound, the

Exhibit 8.3
The Storyboard Is
Your Planning Tool

To help you and your client visualize the "montage" of a television message, and to show how the audio coordinates with the visual, you'll want to translate your script into a storyboard. Pads of blank storyboard sheets like this can be bought at office supply and graphic arts stores in 12-by-18-inch or 16-by-22-inch sizes designed for use on an easel or corkboard. In the preliminary stages, the visuals are pencil-sketched in using stick figures. For the client presentation, you may want to use Polaroid pictures for the visuals. Dialog and sound effects from the right-hand side of the script are pasted in the rectangles below each screen frame.

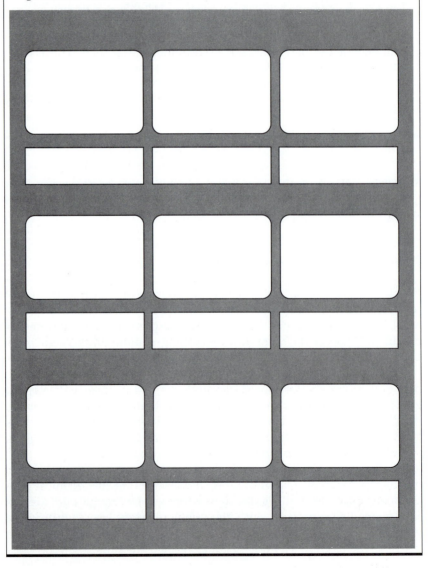

feel, and the impact they expected. And, of course, the client has the final say.

Placing Longer Features

News programs and talk shows may be the most important forms of television communication, but there are plenty of hours to be filled outside of prime time, with millions of viewers watching. If your organization can afford the $20,000 to $100,000 it costs to produce a television-quality program (including five to ten prints, plus distribution and promotion costs), your message may gain air time worth many times that amount.

Here is a sampling of film features, prepared by PR departments and provided free to local broadcast and cable stations, that can be viewed on a weekend morning:

- A depiction of "air strike readiness," with exciting action footage showing pilots scrambling to their planes and flying in formation—prepared, of course, by the U.S. Department of Defense.
- A travelogue depicting life on the arctic tundra, with a soft-sell pitch for the trans-Alaska pipeline—produced by a major oil company.
- An exploration of "miniaturization" in industry, with fascinating microphotography and stop-action sequences—provided by a manufacturer of computers and other high-technology products.
- A dramatic documentary of the life of Alexander Graham Bell—as recounted by (who else?) a telephone company.

These are familiar topics and sponsors, of course, but even a smaller organization can prepare television features. Nonprofit groups, especially, may be able to work with donated equipment and volunteer personnel. An organization can virtually assure itself of local air time if it prepares a historical documentary on the area or a look at a regional public service program such as Meals on Wheels or a halfway house for drug rehabilitation. Typically, these public service tapes and films feature the name of the sponsor only at the beginning and the end, although it may be possible to work in subtle identification of the firm when its employees are shown working as volunteers in the program, or when its donated equipment is being used.

Your chances of getting a feature film used are enhanced if you aim for a length of approximately 24 minutes, which allows for several advertisements, PSAs, and station announcements during the half-hour slot. You can contact the station manager by phone or letter, and even improve your chances by preparing a brochure or fact sheet to promote the tape or film. Include representative still shots and a synopsis of the content, along with notations about running time, format, and narration.

Cable and broadcast stations may also be interested in scheduling the showing far enough in advance so that your organization can promote it in local advertising, stuffers mailed out with monthly bills, and articles in the employee house organ.

Provide Stations with "Stock" Footage

Why wait until a story happens to think about providing visual information to the local broadcast and cable media? Large companies, especially utilities or manufacturers with large plants in a community, provide area stations with stock footage on their key operations.

AT&T, for example, supplies the media with half a dozen 5-minute films on how long-distance dialing works, how fiber optics and satellites handle thousands of messages, and other basic operations.

Consultants suggest that such footage be prepared two ways: with voice-over narration or with a stand-up reporter to simulate television news programs. That way the stations can decide which format blends in with their own material or even adapt the footage. For example, they can use the narrated version and replace the narrator's voice with their own news reporter's voice.

If there's an explosion at your plant, or if the service you provide the community is disrupted, it is better to let the local station use images you've prepared, rather than film a reporter standing outside the gate of your plant and talking about what *apparently* happened.

Getting on the Talk Shows

A broadcast news item may last only a fraction of a minute and get lost among a dozen stories squeezed between two commercials. But get a spokesperson for your organization on a talk show, and you are virtually assured of ten minutes of leisurely and uninterrupted attention. And if the host is a major personality who takes a liking to you or your organization's cause, you can garner an extremely influential "testimonial" at no cost.

Of course, an appearance on "The Tonight Show" on NBC is the top target. The syndicated Phil Donahue, Oprah Winfrey, and Geraldo Rivera shows are also considered prime spots. In addition to the dozens of network and syndicated national shows, local stations have their own formats, including "Dialing for Dollars" programs that mix visiting celebrities and interesting local people with viewer promotions and contests, and perhaps even variety acts or performances by the host talents. The charge can be made that many of these shows are corny and that they deliver lowest-common-denominator audiences. But the cost is low, and the numbers reached are high, which makes them attractive when you are working in the press agent or public information model.

Most talk shows have talent coordinators or assistant producers in charge of screening suggestions for guest spots. One survey of these gatekeepers showed that most prefer to be contacted by telephone, so that they can save time by giving the public relations person an immediate reaction to a proposed guest or topic. If they are interested, they'll ask for a written proposal summarizing what is interesting about the guest. Phil Donahue's producer stresses that all ideas are kept on file in case a guest might fit in well on a later show.[9]

Before grabbing the phone, the PR person should study the format of the target show carefully. Some shows use only celebrities or oddities. Some are so frivolous, or the hosts so inane, that they may not provide a good showcase for your spokesperson. Others may be preferable because they regularly provide a consumer-oriented spot or a serious segment involving representatives of all sides of a current issue. You have a better chance of getting on some shows if you're willing to take a controversial stand. Other shows put a premium on the visual aspect, such as whether a guest is good-looking or whether he or she can bring something to the studio to show or demonstrate. (In Chapter 10, "Preparing to Speak," we look at ways you can help your spokesperson to perform well on television.)

Most talk shows shy away from guests who want to use the opportunity for obvious and heavy-handed product publicity. But they don't mind if someone works in a few "plugs" while discussing trends, consumer issues, technology of the future, or public issues. Many local shows have regular features where new products, unusual gifts, and other innovations are demonstrated.

Touring the Media by Satellite

A media tour for an author, a spokesperson, or someone who had been thrust into the news used to involve a week or more of running for planes, coping with jet lag, and showing up breathlessly at television studios just before air time. Recently, however, the "satellite media tour," often shortened to SMT, has replaced hopping literally all over the country.

A survey by On The Scenes Productions Inc. showed that 90 percent of the television stations in the top-80 markets use satellite interviews in news broadcasts and talk shows.[10] Viewers have grown so accustomed to the format where an interviewer in the studio talks with

To publicize the introduction of Pop Rocks, a candy confection, the public relations agency (Clarke & Company) created the "Popman" character as a spokesperson and sent him on a national tour to promote the product.

The agency provided the client with a complete list of television and radio exposures, indicating an audience of almost 15 million people based on ratings for the shows where the appearance of Popman was covered. Samples from the multipage list of broadcast coverage include:

Date	Media Outlet	Audience	Program
2/3/87	KTVK-TV (ABC) Phoenix	725,000	"5:00 P.M. News"
2/13/87	KSEE-TV (NBC) Fresno, CA	50,000	"6:00 P.M. News"
6/22/87	KREM-TV (CBS) Spokane, WA	50,000	"5:00 Evening News"
7/10/87	KPTV-TV Portland, OR	68,000	"Ramblin Rod Show"
8/21/87	WXYZ-TV (ABC) Detroit	168,000	"Kelly & Company"
9/19/87	WZZM-TV (ABC) Grand Rapids, MI	20,000	"Bozo's Big Top"
9/24/87	WEEK-TV (NBC) East Peoria, IL	52,000	"Live at Five"

Courtesy Clarke & Company

someone on a monitor or split screen that it no longer matters where the interview subject is located.

Medialink, a leader in the field, puts the subject on a set, then takes her or him electronically to one city after another, sometimes to appear "live" on a show as it airs, other times to record a segment that will be edited into a talk show or the evening news broadcast hours later. Medialink usually provides a VNR package or B-roll in addition to the live satellite feed so that stations can prepare a package to introduce the interview subject.[11]

Getting television news directors and talk show producers interested in participating in the SMT involves writing a "pitch letter" that describes the attractiveness of an interview, the timing, the arrangements, and the support materials to be provided in addition to the interview. One of the best selling points might be that the interview subject otherwise would not be available for an "exclusive" interview in smaller markets.[12]

Now that more than half of American homes subscribe to cable—and importantly, that's the more affluent and well-educated half—it can be looked at as a legitimate alternative to broadcast television, even though network programs continue to have the greatest penetration.

Originally cable was used to ensure clearer signals for the existing broadcast stations. Twenty years ago it carried very little original programming. Today, some cable services carry dozens or even scores of channels, many of which offer original programming, and some with programs of local or regional interest. More important, the specialized channels are watched by thin slices of the demographic pie, and thus they may be used to target very specific publics. That's always been difficult with network television and the "me-too" independent stations that carry the same type of programming and advertising as the networks.

CABLE'S GROWING REACH AND INFLUENCE

CNN Provides Placement Opportunities

When Ted Turner began his twenty-four-hour Cable News Network in 1980, skeptics said that it would never find an audience. Who, after all, wanted to watch nothing but news all day?! A decade later, during the Desert Shield and Desert Storm operations in the Persian Gulf, the American viewers—and, in fact, a worldwide audience—delivered their verdict. They did indeed want a service that enabled them to select the time of day for watching news and news-related programming. They welcomed the opportunity to edit their own news consumption using the Cable News Network menu, rather than settling for the 22-minute diet served up once a night by the broadcast networks.

CNN offers literally dozens of shows that are open to suggestions for story ideas from public relations people. In the business area alone, the programs include "Business Morning," "Business Day," "Moneyline," "Moneyweek," and "Inside Business," as well as "Your Money," a weekend program with tips for investors.

Talk shows carried by CNN include "Crossfire," which uses a guest each week from the fields of politics, academia, or government, "Sonya Live" from Los Angeles every day, with topics especially of interest to women, "Larry King Live" weeknights with an eclectic mix of topics, and public affairs shows such as "Evans & Novak," "Newsmaker Saturday," and "Newsmaker Sunday."

Special focus shows include "Science and Technology Today" and "Showbiz." Regular features airing daily or on the weekend focus on medical news, nutrition and diet, travel, and fashion. Each of the shows and segments has a producer, who is the person to approach with suggestions and ideas for shows, segments, or guest appearances.

Exhibit 8.5
Cable Television
"Alphanumeric" Formats

Most cable alphanumeric channels offer a "crawl"—a continuous line of information that moves across the screen from right to left. If this is the format available to nonprofit groups for PSA messages, you should aim to write fewer than twenty words. Abbreviations help keep the message simple:

> *Friday Nite Square Dance—7 PM Feaster Park—Sponsored by Gloucester County Rec Board*

More likely, PSAs will be carried on the Bulletin Board that fills the main part of the screen. The cable company will inform you that the Bulletin Board consists of eight lines of thirty characters. Shoot for less than that in order to surround your message with some "white space"—especially because there may be other material above and below your message, including the "crawl" at the bottom of the screen. The square dance message, six lines long, in this format might read:

FOR FUN!   FOR EXERCISE!

TRY SQUARE DANCING

EVERY FRIDAY NITE   7 TO 9 P.M.

COOK PAVILION—FEASTER PARK

SPONSORED BY YOUR

GLOUCESTER COUNTY REC BOARD

Of greatest importance to some public relations campaigns is the fact that CNN's programming is seen around the world. Trends, new products, and social ideas often receive their first international exposure on CNN. World leaders have been quoted as saying, "All we know about America and about what is happening in the world is what we see on CNN."

Approaching Your Local Cable Operator

Based on their bad experiences trying to report and correct service outages, many consumers assume that local cable companies are as unapproachable as the Wizard of Oz. Public relations people should have no such fear. The cable operator is hungry for "product"—information to put on the screen—and is especially happy when you offer an attractive program at no cost.

PSAs on cable usually take the form of announcements run on the "alphanumeric" channel, the channel reserved for announcements and advertisements and sometimes also for program listings. Time is donated for nonprofit organizations to list their activities, and other groups may purchase advertising message space, which often appears on the same screen at the same time. (See Exhibit 8.5 for examples of cable formats that take advantage of the alphanumeric channel.)

Nonprofit groups also can take advantage of the public-access channels on cable television. As a condition of their franchise, most cable companies must reserve times and channels for community groups. Prepackaged tapes may be shown, or the cable company may make one of its own studios available for production of program materials.

If you purchase a paid advertisement on cable television, you'll find it cheaper than advertising on broadcast television—as low as fifty dollars for a one-shot spot. Cable operators also will talk with you about using their demographics to target people by neighborhoods, or even street by street, for a campaign.

NOTES

1. The Visa U.S.A. and Royal Melbourne Hospital campaigns were IABC Gold Quill Award winners for 1991. The StarKist, McDonald's and National Food Processors' Association campaigns were 1991 PRSA Silver Anvil Award winners. All others were earlier Silver Anvil winners.

2. The Summit County program was a PRSA Silver Anvil Award winner. These remarks are excerpted from the winning entry.

3. Sandra Sugawara, "Putting Out the News on Videos," *Washington Post*, August 10, 1987, Business Section, pp. 1, 9; ——— "Nielsen Survey Says News Shows Air VNRs Weekly," *O'Dwyer's PR Services Report* (May 1990), pp. 46, 48.

4. ——— *The Video News Release Handbook,* promotional piece prepared by Medialink Video Broadcasting Corporation.

5. ——— "Video Workshop: Quality Needed in VNRs for Placements," *O'Dwyer's PR Services Report* (October 1989), pp. 28–29.

6. Margie Goldsmith, "Developing Topics for VNRs," *Public Relations Journal* (July 1987), pp. 29–30.

7. ——— "Wounded Vets of Failed VNR Efforts Get Therapy," *O'Dwyer's PR Services Report* (April 1989), pp. 4–5.

8. The News Group, press release and brochure.

9. Kathy Rand, "How to Work with TV Talk Shows," *Public Relations Journal* (March 1977), pp. 20–21.

10. Kevin McCauley, "Satellite Media Tours Enter PR Mainstream," *O'Dwyer's PR Services Report* (April 1990), pp. 1, 12–14.

11. ——— *Satellite Media Tour Handbook,* Medialink promotional piece, 1990.

12. Darren Bosik, "Satellite Tour 'Tricks' Told in PR Firm's Pitch Letter," *O'Dwyer's PR Services Report* (July 1991), pp. 33–36.

**ADDITIONAL
READING**

Blythin, Evan, and Larry A. Samovar, *Communicating Effectively on Television* (Belmont, CA: Wadsworth, 1985).

Cantor, Muriel, *Prime-Time Television: Content and Control* (Beverly Hills, CA: Sage, 1980).

Fang, Irving, *Television News, Radio News* (St. Paul: RADA Press, 1985).

Hilton, Jack, *How to Meet the Press: A Survival Guide* (New York: Dodd, Mead, 1987).

Lamont, Edward, "Cable Television Offers Many New Choices," in *New Technology and Public Relations* (New York: Foundation for Public Relations Research and Education, 1986).

St. John, Tracy, *How to Get Your Public Relations Story on TV and Radio* (Babylon, NY: Pilot Books, 1986).

Trufelman, Lloyd P., "Workshop: How to Plug into Cable TV," *Public Relations Journal* (September 1988), pp. 43–44.

9

New Technologies:
Video, Computers, and
Telecommunications

At the beginning of the 1980s, public relations managers were just beginning to learn that new technologies soon would be reshaping the way they accomplished their work. By the beginning of the 1990s, the new technologies already had become an accepted part of the workplace and public relations practitioners had powerful new tools to help them accomplish their objectives.

- Studies by the National Investor Relations Institute (NIRI)—an organization of more than 2,200 specialists who serve the information needs of the financial community—showed that just in the four years from 1985 to 1989 the number of NIRI members using electronic databases rose from 57 percent to 76 percent. The number who said they use video or audio tapes to communicate with their publics tripled (from 15 percent to 44 percent). The fax machine wasn't even included in a 1985 survey, but by 1989 the number of respondents who said they used the fax to transmit financial data totaled 94 percent.[1]
- A 1988 survey of public relations professionals by Washington State University showed that an overwhelming majority use a personal computer, and half use a terminal that is connected to another computer. An electronic mail system is used in about one-third of public relations offices.[2]
- The Niberg Corporation, a small advertising/public relations firm near Boston, has created its own database to store all of the information it needs when dealing with clients, many of which are computer companies. News releases and designs for

advertisements and brochures move electronically from computer screen to fax machine to the client and back. Employees who leave the office take laptop portable computers with them and phone their work in. Memos go back and forth among staffers via electronic mail system, and account executives have a special program to manage their daily and monthly schedules. Says a vice-president of the firm: "If it were taken away from us tomorrow, we wouldn't be able to function."[3]

Indeed, many elements of the so-called "new" technology already deserve to be called simply "the" technology. Without the word-processing and graphics capabilities now mastered by many users of personal computers, public relations organizations would have to lengthen the number of days or weeks it takes to produce written and visual material. Many jobs now completed within the office once again would have to be sent out to typographers and printers, increasing the cost as well as the production time.

In this chapter we'll look first at video, which used to be discussed in the same breath with television. The increasing use of video for communicating with internal publics makes it a specialized electronic business tool, not just a variation on the kinds of television used to reach external audiences. After video, we'll visit the electronic office for a demonstration of computer work stations, databases, electronic mail, desktop publishing, and various applications of telecommunications, including faxes and teleconferencing.

NEW ROLES FOR CORPORATE VIDEO

By the beginning of the 1980s, U.S. businesses and nonprofit organizations were producing more television programs for their own use than the programming carried by the networks and public broadcasting combined. Hundreds of organizations produced over 46,000 programs annually, totaling some 15,000 hours of viewing time.[4]

Businesses first adopted video as a training tool, and responsibility for making and distributing tapes initially rested with the personnel departments of many corporations. But increasingly, management is appreciating the potential of video communication, and corporate communication departments are taking greater responsibility for it. Video capability is no longer considered a luxury enjoyed by only the largest organizations: The typical user is a medium-sized company working with a budget of $100,000 and a production staff of two or three people.[5]

One of the attractions of video is that it has many of the elements of "face-to-face" communication, but it cuts down on the cost and wasted

Exhibit 9.1
Recycling "Special
Events" Videos

Sponsorship of special events—from sports tournaments to historical pageants—is an increasingly popular use of public relations to serve marketing goals. When the event is over, a video record can be used to extend the audience beyond those who attended or saw coverage on commercial television news.

- Mercedes-Benz's celebration of the centennial of the automobile was documented on videotape and edited for broadcast on 300 affiliates of the Public Broadcasting Service.
- Schick's "Legends Classic" all-star game was transformed into promotional films, sales videos, corporate documentaries, in-store promotions, video news releases, and photo displays.
- After installing an exhibit at EPCOT Center, Kraft prepared a video version for distribution to junior and senior high schools. The "Food for the Future" video teaches students about technologies that someday may be used to feed the Earth's growing population.
- Timberland, manufacturer of outdoor clothing and boots, videotapes its annual Sled Dog Race in Alaska and uses the footage in sales promotions.

Source: Adam Shell, "Sponsors Stretch the Impact of Special Events With Video," *Public Relations Journal* (May 1990), pp. 12–13.

time of sending managers all over the country or the world. Johnson & Johnson, the health-care company, sends talks by company officers and reports on new developments to its 150 companies and divisions through a worldwide video network. The average cost per program is $10,000— far cheaper than sending company representatives to 170 locations. The programs are distributed on three-quarter-inch videotape cassettes. The home-office public relations department suggests appropriate audiences, but each division has its own video coordinator who decides when, where, and how each tape will be used. The video network is especially useful for announcing personnel changes: Managers in the company's many outposts have an early opportunity to hear and "meet" the new person on video tape.[6]

It is even possible to set up a long-distance video conference using phone lines to carry closed-circuit television. Usually, when a company is about to make a new stock offering, its top executives travel around the country talking to brokers and major investors in key cities about the move. But when AT&T was planning a new offering, its executives appeared on a closed-circuit show carried to twenty cities simultaneously, and viewers were able to phone in their questions during the program.[7]

Video offers an opportunity to bring the annual report to life. Emhart Corp., a metal parts and chemical firm, produced a 22-minute videotape version of its annual report for use on cable stations in eight states. The tape, which cost less than $10,000 to produce, presented company executives, not actors, and gave stockholders a glimpse of components being manufactured in its various plants. Company officials felt the taped report gave a better picture of the firm's activities than could be obtained from still pictures and written copy. The firm's specific public information goal was realized when an estimated audience of 250,000 viewers in fifty-one communities saw the program.[8]

It might even be advantageous for a company to allow its annual meeting to be carried on cable television, with prepared "documentary" film footage inserted. Many stockholders are already accustomed to receiving information about companies on home microprocessors merely by paying a monthly fee and using a telephone hookup to access a satellite that transmits the Dow Jones News/Retrieval service. A logical next step would be for companies to prepare their own materials for direct electronic transmission to the home.

Many companies already use videocassette systems for training employees. Usually, the workers come to a meeting room for playback of the prepared lessons. But there is even greater potential for employee communication: video monitors placed in the lunchroom, so that the employee house organ may be a weekly television program instead of a monthly printed publication.

What Does It Take to Produce Video?

Of course, many organizations have decided they do not have the budget or the personnel to produce video messages, and some organizations have found that television does not address enough of their goals to warrant the high cost.

Approximately 90 percent of those organizations regularly using video have invested in their own in-house production facility. One-third spent less than $50,000 on a studio, and one-third spent more than $200,000.[9] While the cost of video equipment exceeds the cost of making and showing slide shows and films, duplication costs are much less. Copies can be made on any video recording and editing equipment—it is not necessary to send away to a specialized studio.[10] Although technology is changing rapidly, the most popular video format is the three-quarter-inch cassette, which loads as easily into a playback unit as an audio tape cassette loads into a tape recorder.

What does it take to produce video? The sections that follow describe the various components of the corporate video system.

The Studio   It is not necessary to construct or remodel a huge space in order to have a workable video studio. Ideally, it is useful to have 12–15-foot ceilings from which you can hang lights, but lighting can be mounted on tripods or wall fasteners. The studio space should be at least 300 square feet (15 by 20) to permit movement by two cameras mounted on rolling tripods. Yet, one East Coast medical center manages to produce acceptable live programming for its in-house channel using a room measuring no more than 12 by 12—less than 150 square feet.

You'll want to provide the studio space with sound-absorbent material such as acoustic tiles or cork. The velvet curtain you hang on a track or against one wall to form a neutral background will also serve to soak up studio noises. Furniture should include a desk or table, two straight-back chairs for formal narration, and two easy chairs for more conversational settings. Visual-aid equipment should include an easel and a blackboard.

Today's lightweight video cameras can free you from the confines of the video studio. The PR department should look upon the entire physical plant as its studio. Instead of "talking heads" taped in a static setting, strive for real-life situations that show employees on the job.

Cameras   The standard small-format camera is a miniaturized version of the huge cameras the networks use. Mounted on similarly scaled-down rolling tripods, it enables you to duplicate most of the zooms, pans, dolly shots, and switches from general to close-up shots that you are accustomed to seeing on television news and talk shows. Using a two-camera studio setup, you can vary the presentation so that a recorded fifteen-minute talk by your president or the director of training will be visually interesting.

The real excitement in small-format video, however, comes from the Porta-Pak or ENG (electronic-news-gathering) units, which enable a crew of two or three to wander at will in search of information that is live and visual. Battery-powered camera and recorder are housed in portable units connected by cables. The taped material is brought back to a studio for editing.

Recording and Editing Equipment   Unlike motion pictures, where the visual image is recorded on film (and where you can view the images frame by frame), video images are scanned by the television camera and converted into electronic information that can be stored on magnetic tape. No image is visible on the tape. In order to reconstitute the image (and the sound that was recorded simultaneously), it is necessary to place the tape (on a loose reel or in a packaged cassette) in a playback unit connected to a monitor. During production, the same "deck" can be used to record the

Exhibit 9.2
Video Documents
Tylenol Response

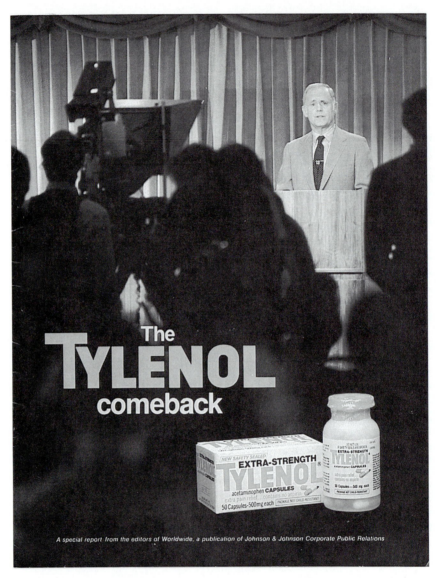

original material and to view it. To ensure quality, more expensive edit-ing equipment should be used to edit the final version.

Special effects such as dissolves from one shot to another, optical effects such as split-screen or the "wipe" transition, and even overlap-ping images can all be created during recording or editing with the use of a special-effects generator (SEG), the most sophisticated and most costly piece of equipment in the small-format video studio.

Johnson & Johnson's Worldwide Video Network (WWVN) got its biggest test when the news of the Tylenol tampering broke. During the first Tylenol crisis, WWVN produced three news conferences at the firm's headquarters in New Brunswick, New Jersey. The news conferences were broadcast nationally by closed circuit and were aimed primarily at television stations and newspapers. (The audio portion of the news conference was carried over 900-service telephone lines to those who could not receive the videocast.)

Reporters who attended the press conference left J & J's conference center with footage showing briefings from the Chairman of the Board and Chief Executive Officer. They also were provided with footage showing the manufacturing operation for Tylenol.

The information in the news conferences also was edited for transmission on the in-house employee "News Channel." A special version of the video that detailed the company's response as well as the cooperation of its distributors was sent to its major wholesalers and retailers.

J & J officials credit their ability to prepare video information quickly in-house as one of the reasons they were able to maintain consumer confidence in the firm and in the Tylenol brand.

Source: Personal interviews with J & J Corporate Vice President for Public Relations Lawrence G. Foster and WWVN Director John Sheahan.

Editing of taped video material can be accomplished with splices, but the preferred system is electronic editing. With this method, various sounds, scenes, and images, including superimposed titles, are assembled electronically by moving each piece of recorded material from the reel on which it was shot. The material is then stored to a master finished reel, which can be duplicated for distribution.

Sound mixers enable background music, separately recorded narration, and other effects to be joined on the single sound track found on standard video tape.

Lighting and Sound   Small-format video doesn't require exotic or expensive auxiliary equipment in order to make a credible product. The standard video lens system is sensitive enough to use in normal lighting conditions. The result is an acceptable cinema verité feeling that we are accustomed to in film documentaries. Most video crews carry one or two lightweight sources of illumination—high-intensity lamps with reflectors, mounted on slender tripods or clamp-on devices—so that they can wipe our shadows, provide good general illumination, and "key" on the faces of speakers.

The standard camera-recorder outfit sold by most video manufacturers includes a unidirectional microphone, with a lavaliere cord to hang it around a speaker's neck or a simple mounting stand to hold it in place on a table. It is also useful to obtain other microphones, including an omnidirectional one for recording general sounds, crowd noise, or multiple speakers. For recording of panel discussions or meetings, it is wise to provide all speakers with their own mikes, all jacked into a microphone switcher—a device that enables several sound sources to be picked up by the sound track on a single recorder.

Playback Equipment   To show video to a small audience, your organization needs a suitcase-sized playback unit that accepts the reel or cassette, and a standard television set or monitor equipped with an input jack. For audiences of more than ten, you can link several monitors together with cables so that no one person sits more than ten feet from a screen. You can also use special optical equipment that enlarges the image and throws it up on a movie screen for viewing by large audiences of as many as 100. Usually, the image is brighter and better focused if it is viewed on the glass-screen monitor.

Videoconferencing: One Big Meeting

Making videotapes for showing to employees, customers, and far-flung managers can be more effective than print, but it remains an example of one-way communication. The audience for prerecorded video tapes is essentially passive, although the showing of the video tape may provide the spark for discussion among audience members after the showing.

Two-way video communication is possible when the technology of videoconferencing is put in place. Video and audio equipment must be installed in the base site for the videoconference and at all remote sites that will be participating. Each site also needs an antenna or satellite

This videoconferencing room—one of two at the Johnson & Johnson worldwide headquarters building—provides a two-way interactive voice and picture link with dozens of company facilities around the world. Equipment in the room includes interactive computer, a facsimile machine, and a VCR so that any information format can be used to transmit data during a videoconference.

Photo courtesy of Johnson & Johnson

dish so that signals can be sent to a commercial satellite, beamed between satellites, and back down to earth—from the "uplink" across to the "downlink" in videoconferencing terminology.

In the 1970s and early 1980s, many organizations tried one-shot videoconferences and found that renting the equipment, setting it up, and establishing clear connections was time-consuming and expensive, whether you did it yourself or hired an outside firm. Today, the one-shot videoconference is still in use for conventions and sales meetings held at hotels and convention centers. But many large companies and some professional associations have realized the benefits of installing permanent videoconferencing equipment to link headquarters with other operating or participating sites across the nation and even the world. "Dedicated" videoconference rooms—meaning that the facility has been designed specifically for that use—are growing more common.

Here are some examples of how groups were linked through video-conferencing technology:

■ The American Diabetes Association held a one-day intensive workshop on the latest developments in diabetes treatment. The national hookup enabled 19,000 doctors at twenty-seven sites in twenty-four cities to interact with a leading expert on diabetes at each site, and those experts, in turn, asked questions of a national faculty. The live Q&A session in effect brought the entire United States diabetes treatment community together in one big town meeting.[11]

■ Merrill Lynch's broadcast of "One Year Later—Investing in a New Era" (an attempt to reassure investors in the stock market after the crash of 1987) was seen by 50,000 clients at 478 Merrill Lynch offices as well as more than sixty hotels and other sites. Brokers at each site answered investors' questions after they viewed the video.[12]

■ Eastman Kodak holds a series of videoconferences where the work of prominent photographers is shown and attendees at remote sites can call in to question the photographers about the techniques they used.

■ Instead of flying buyers from its many stores to New York for style shows, J.C. Penney beams the live production to regional centers. When IBM dropped a line of software, within hours one of it competitors, Wang, was setting up a videoconference at thirteen sites to talk with its sales staff and advise them how to use the information to win customers away from IBM. Texas Instruments uses video sales meetings to demonstrate new products to one of its biggest customers, Hewlett-Packard.[13]

Even when rooms have been dedicated to videoconferencing, the public relations staff must do considerable detail work. If members of publics outside the organization—stockholders, the press, legislators—are to be included, invitations must be sent. Follow-up calls are needed to make final arrangements and to be sure that the facility is large enough for the number of participants. Information kits must be assembled and sent to participants ahead of time so they can plan the kinds of questions they'll ask and prepare for fruitful discussion. Panelists or experts may have to be brought to the videoconference site early for rehearsal, briefing, and perhaps even a professional makeup job.

When an organization owns the buildings that will serve as videoconference sites, installation of satellite dishes is no problem. But if some of the sites are in locations where the organization rents offices, landlords may not permit antenna installation. Or, they may charge sky-high rents for space on the roof. In such cases, the organization may want to use a nearby hotel or convention center. Most major hotels built since the early 1980s have permanent dishes and connections into their meeting rooms.

The videoconference can be taped, and the footage can be edited for management training modules, or even for use as an item in the next edition of the video magazine shown to employees.

Tailoring the Video Magazine to Employee Needs

Every organization must analyze the needs and interests of its employees—as well as the conditions under which video programs will be viewed—before deciding on the length and format of a video magazine. A few companies make the video "required viewing" and expect supervisors to arrange for screenings in the office. The majority, however, make the video available to employees in areas where they go when they leave their office. That means that video magazines must be kept short—rarely longer than twenty minutes—and they must be as interesting as entertainment television.

LTV Corporation's quarterly *LTV Report*, which is shown in employee cafeterias and is publicized in plant newspapers, rarely runs longer than fifteen minutes. It aims to allow workers to view their counterparts in other LTV locations—for example, showing office workers what happens in a steel mill or on an oil rig. Another objective of the video magazine is to give employees a chance to "meet" corporate executives they have known by name only.[14]

Merck, the pharmaceutical giant headquartered in Rahway, NJ, also has a video magazine. But because so many of its employees live in the immediate vicinity, the firm airs its taped program on local cable television, thereby reaching an audience beyond its own employees.

The Ball Aerospace Systems Group in Colorado also feels that its *Aeronews* employee communications video show is of interest to a wider audience, including the families and neighbors of employees, as well as suppliers. So it arranged with the public broadcasting station in Denver to air selected programs. Two anchorpersons host the show, making it like the news programs viewers are accustomed to seeing. Items are kept short and visual, just like the network news. The PBS station presents the firm an opportunity to reach an audience of about 300,000.[15]

New York Life usually includes four or five stories in each issue of its video magazine. In order to make the items interesting to employees, humor is used liberally. When the decision was made to devote a 10-minute segment to explaining the objectives for a new management system, the public relations department racked its collective brains to find a way to keep employees watching what essentially was a lecture with flip charts or slides. The solution was a parody on the old television situation comedy "Get Smart." New York Life even arranged with the producers of the original show to use their opening credits. Then actors mimicking secret agent Maxwell Smart and his cohorts "broke the case" of the new management system. The obtuse Maxwell Smart character needed to have everything explained to him, and he then parroted the information back in his staccato voice—just as in the original show. The viewers found the takeoff amusing, and the device worked well to implant the basic concepts of the new management system in their minds.

New York Life's feature on ways to obtain information from the personnel department—another potential yawner—was enlivened by a sequence in which a frazzled employee climbed a never-ending staircase past other workers who had obviously been waiting for days. Some were playing cards, others building model airplanes. Finally, the protagonist discovered that getting employee information at New York Life isn't all that difficult, if one knows the proper place to go for the answers.

TAKING ADVANTAGE OF THE ELECTRONIC WORKPLACE

Business communication has been revolutionized in the last decade because the computer has gone from a specialized tool in the hands of a few to a piece of standard office equipment found on virtually every desk. The computer you use on the job may be one of three types:

■ A freestanding minicomputer with a selection of software programs, including a word-processing system that allows you to compose, arrange, and print out text, and perhaps a graphics package that gives you the capability of adding drawings, charts, and other art to your document;

■ A minicomputer with the same capabilities, but linked through phone lines to other computers. These connections allow you to send information and receive information prepared by others; or

■ A station that is connected to your organization's mainframe computer. You can get access to information prepared for many employees to use simultaneously, and also move the information you created out of your electronic files and into storage for access by others.

Whatever the system, the effects are threefold:

1. You have access to more information than ever before;
2. You can gather information more rapidly; and,
3. Once you have created information, you can deliver it more efficiently to those you want to inform.

USING THE DATABASE IN PUBLIC RELATIONS

If you have used your computer only to write articles and papers, or to design and lay out a brochure, you're probably convinced that word-processing and graphics are the greatest features of the personal microcomputer. Much more awesome, however, is the ability of the computer to link you instantly with the world's information.

Databases are libraries at your fingertips. But there are some important differences between a database and a library:

- Through the system known as computer time-sharing, many users can have access to the same information simultaneously;
- Nothing is ever "in circulation" or "at the bindery"—it's always available; and,
- There's no wandering around from department to department because every level of information from listings (the equivalent of a card catalog) to full text comes up on the screen in front of you, ready for reading and printing out.

At first glance, cost would seem to be the only drawback of a database. There is a monthly charge to subscribe to the service, plus telephone charges for linking your computer with the service, and extra charges for the minutes and seconds of time when you are accessing information. The savings come in time: instead of hours or even days in the library, an information search can be conducted in one or two hours, as we saw at the beginning of Chapter 1.

Setting Up a Database

Before we look at externally developed databases, we should mention that databases can be developed and maintained internally. Information on employees, customers, suppliers, or other active publics can be organized and stored in the computer for later use. Alumni databases maintained by universities, for example, code each entry by year of graduation, major, history of giving to the institution, address—in short, any way that a user might want to call up the entry in combination with other entries to give a profile of specific alumni.

Commercial Databases

To understand the use of commercial electronic storage and retrieval systems, it is important first to distinguish between a *database* and a *database service.*

A *Database* is a collection of information stored electronically and made available to other individuals and organizations who pay for access from their personal computers through the phone lines. Many databases are electronic versions of information also prepared in print form by the producer. Here are some examples of databases of particular interest to public relations people:

Academic American Encyclopedia. A standard reference work with more than 32,000 concisely written articles arranged in alphabetical order.

Adtrack, Advertising and Marketing Intelligence, and American Profile. Three bibliographic databases that are useful for preparing marketing campaigns.

Electronic Yellow Pages. Listings of almost twelve million U.S. businesses.

Lexis. Contains legal documents from state, federal, and international law cases that may affect public relations programs.

Nexis. Contains the full text of articles from over a hundred newspapers and other periodicals, including *The New York Times* and *The Washington Post*.

PR Newswire. News releases and features from hundreds of American companies. A source of news and story ideas for the media, but also an important source of information for organizations that want to see what other companies are doing. (PR Newswire will be discussed in a later chapter as a means of disseminating news releases.)

Telecom. Reports developments in all aspects of telecommunications.

Trade and Industry Index. A bibliographic index covering the entire field of business.

There are nearly four thousand databases available in the United States. Some are very specific, such as those that cover medicine or financial markets in depth. Others are very broad, such as those that contain general news and information on all academic subjects in the sciences or the humanities.

Rather than trying to locate each individual database producer and arranging to be billed for receiving that particular information, the consumer subscribes to a *database service*. The consumer makes the selection based on the variety of databases included in the offerings of the database service. (It is analogous to the many channels offered by a cable television company. But whereas you must subscribe to the cable company that has the franchise to serve your community, you can select any database service that meets your needs.)

Some database services cater to investors, entrepreneurs, and managers who are interested in business and the stockmarket. The Dow Jones News/Retrieval service, for example, contains economic information, up-to-the-minute stock quotes, news headlines, specialized market information, plus the full text of *The Wall Street Journal* and *Barron's*.

NewsNet carries over two hundred specialized wire services and newsletters from the field of business.

Other services, such as Dialog, which offers 250 databases, are more general and cater to information professionals and academics. CompuServe, one of the leaders in the field, provides a mixture of databases to interest both professionals and general consumers.

The basic CompuServe package includes:

Bulletin Boards. Electronic mail, want ads and classified listings, a public kiosk of announcements, and interactive online conferencing that permits a group of users to "converse" back and forth using their computers.

Personal Computing Support. Information from computing publications that can help users get more out of their computer and the database system, as well as forums where users with questions or problems can seek answers from others that have more expertise.

News, Weather, and Sports. The Associated Press news, sports, and business wires, as well as the National Weather Service city, state, and marine forecasts.

Electronic Shopping. Discount home shopping with catalog information from leading national merchants including Sears, Bloomingdale's, and Waldenbooks.

Financial Transaction Services. Banking, American Express services, stock portfolio evaluation, and online purchase and sale of stocks.

Travel Services. Information on hotels, resorts, tours, cruises, and air-line reservations.

Entertainment and Games. Trivia, sports, board, and fantasy games, as well as an entertainment newswire and interactive forums for hobby and special interest groups.

Home, Health, and Family. Fitness and nutrition information, recipes and party planning, wine tips, hobbies, and personal finance suggestions, including a list of free government publications.

How to Use the Database

Database manager Anne Weathersby, a database designer for Information, Inc., suggests that public relations people use databases

. . . to develop an historical perspective on issues . . . by reviewing all the news on that issue over a specific period of time. Trends also can

Many corporate public relations departments, as well as large public relations agencies, keep abreast of financial news by subscribing to the many electronic services of Dow Jones, including the News/Retrieval database. At 6 A.M. EST, the entire contents of The Wall Street Journal *can be received in a company's computer, where special software programs sort the information into categories of interest to the specific subscriber.*

Photo courtesy of Dow Jones, Inc.

be spotted by performing the same search periodically to see if new attention is being focused on specific issues.[16]

Some databases greet the user when he or she "logs on" by offering a menu that asks what general type of information the users wants. Each choice leads the user to a more specific menu, and eventually the desired item is located. In Dow Jones News/Retrieval, for example, the user might indicate that he or she wants information about a specific company. When the specific company is designated, the menu might offer: stock quote, stock history, recent news in capsule form, news stories in *The Wall Street Journal* for the last ninety days, or a consolidated balance sheet from the annual report. If the "news stories" category is selected, the user is given a list of articles from which to select.

When performing searches across vast databases that include literally hundreds of thousands of articles on any number of topics, the user needs to construct a *search strategy*. Manuals provided by the database services explain how to create one-word or multiword indices to use in a computer search. If you are interested in conducting a public relations campaign that would help your organization address a consumer public concerned with nutrition, you might format the computer's search to look for articles that include the words "food" and "nutrition."

It takes some training, either with the manual or through a workshop offered by a nearby university, to learn how to construct database searches that look for particular linkages of multiword phrases such as "corporate responsibility" and "environmental risk assessment." But the investment in training can pay off handsomely in computer searches that turn up ten or twenty relevant articles in a matter of a few hours of work.

The first round of database research is analogous to the time spent with the *Reader's Guide to Periodical Literature* or the card catalog in a library. That is, the computer shows you a list of articles with the key words you have asked for. If the computer indicates it has found 200,000 items, you probably will decide to fine-tune your index words and see if you can get the list down to 200 items before you ask for a printout of titles, author's names, and publications where the articles appeared.

After you comb the list of two hundred items the computer has found, you may decide to ask for short abstracts of perhaps twenty-five items, and then the full text of six or seven particularly pertinent articles.

In a library, of course, you would progress from one section of the building to the next to locate all of the items, and then on to a copying machine for the laborious task of making photocopies. With the computer database, every phase is completed at your workstation.

The final advantage, of course, is that since you are working on your own computer, you may choose to move the information you find directly into a file for later word processing into your own article, memo, or speech.

One of the most important tasks for public relations people is the writing and routing of memos, which will be treated in Chapter 18. Once a memo is completed, you would like to have quick responses from recipients—or at least some assurance that the message has been received and acted on. But if a secretary must type and duplicate the memo, distribute it through an internal mail system that depends on footwork, and then wait for each member of the distribution list to respond in writing, it may take a week or more before all the replies have been received.

OTHER ELECTRONIC PATHWAYS

Electronic Mail

Electronic mail—usually shortened to "E-Mail"—is a way of getting ideas out fast and receiving responses within twenty-four hours, whether the recipients are in one location or scattered across the country. Memos are created on the computer video display, then routed electronically through the computer network, with codes assuring security and proper distribution. Every worker who is part of an E-Mail network quickly gets into the habit of checking the E-Mail file first thing in the morning, when returning from meetings or lunch, and before going home at night.

Using a laptop computer small enough to fit in a briefcase, workers at remote locations can also take advantage of E-Mail. They simply plug into any phone with a pinch-type connector, dial the computer at the home office, and the E-Mail file will come up on the screen of the laptop computer. Thus members of an organization need not be delayed in receiving mail simply because their work has taken them away from the office.

Many systems allow the sender to note whether the addressees have checked their files, and at what time. If the sender notes that an addressee has not checked the file, a phone follow-up is in order.

Voice Mail

Voice mail, which also uses the telephone system, works like E-Mail but carries the speaking voice of the sender rather than a written memo. Anyone can phone into a voice mail system using any phone. The receiving system has the capability of routing hundreds of messages up to ten minutes in length.

The most important application of voice mail is in situations where public relations people need to get information quickly to someone, and they must explain it carefully but not necessarily in person. While it's similar to talking into a phone-answering machine, voice mail has much greater ability to interact with and guide the caller and then route the information to the proper destination in an organization.

Some members of Congress, for example, inform their constituents that assistance can be obtained by calling a number designated to route requests using voice mail. A tape asks questions of callers about the nature of their request. The callers respond by touching the appropriate keys on the phone. Their message is then routed to the staff member with the answer, or directly to the government agency that can help. Many consumer inquiries can be handled by voice mail, and the system is also an efficient way of handling questions employees ask about their pay, benefits, tax withholdings, and retirement system.

Computer Database Bulletin Boards

Computer database bulletin boards enable subscribers of computer database services, described in the preceding section, to "post" notices that will be seen by all other subscribers to the system. Any one of those subscribers can then choose to leave a return message—aimed at the individual inquirer, but seen by all who choose to read the bulletin board.

A hospital public relations department, anticipating problems with community relations during repairs to the facility's main parking deck, might use the bulletin board designated for health care organizations to ask for suggestions from other medical centers that have faced the same dilemma.

Facsimile Machines

Facsimile machines—now popularly called "fax" (used interchangeably as a verb and a noun)—were invented early in the century, and by the 1920s they were carrying weather maps and wirephotos for newspapers. For decades, national magazines have used facsimile transmission to move page layouts from one place to the other in minutes.

The fax machine scans information electronically, looking at each dot of space for a millisecond. It converts all dark marks to digital pulses that then are converted to audible information for transmission over phone lines. The receiving machine reverses the process and prints out a copy moments later. The cost of machines dropped in the 1980s, and fax usage skyrocketed. Fax phone numbers now are printed on letterheads and business cards under ordinary phone numbers, suggesting two ways to communicate with the individual or office.

When fax machines became commonplace in every office, including those of the news media, public relations people who regularly send news releases and other items to editors quickly realized the advantages of the fax. In addition to speed of delivery, no envelope has to be opened. Thus the message is likely to catch the eye of the recipient.

The problem is, the recipient pays the cost of the fax paper and is billed for the time the receiving machine is connected with the phone system. Many new owners of fax machines have been angered to find huge quantities of paper used up by what has come to be called "junk fax." Some companies that were originating fax messages instructed their staff to send information only to those who requested it. But other firms eagerly assembled lists of fax numbers in order to increase their use of the machines as delivery systems for promotional messages. By 1990 three states had passed laws stipulating fines for those found guilty of sending faxes to those who did not request them, and the Telecommunications Subcommittee of the House Energy and Commerce Committee was considering a federal facsimile regulation act.[17]

Of course fax transmission is eagerly embraced by many publics as a quick means of receiving information. The investment community, for example, wants the releases from investor relations people as quickly as possible—and at the same time as all others are receiving them. A new service in the public relations industry is "broadcast faxing." The public relations person wanting to send dozens or even hundreds of faxes to a client list must be equipped with a broadcast fax machine, and must contract with a phone company to carry out the multiple transmissions. Public relations people today, in addition to their mailing lists, are likely to have "faxing lists" as well.[18]

The Workstation

The workstation represents the concept of bringing all of the electronic services available to the office together in one unit, managed by one computer. The workstation enables an individual to assemble an "electronic desktop" within the memory of his or her own computer that includes a directory, dictionary, files, documents in preparation, a calendar, a mailbox, and even an electronic wastebasket for information no longer needed. Information produced elsewhere is brought into the workstation computer, assigned a file number, and fit into the consumer's system of organization for later reference and use.

Computer-Aided Meetings

Computer-aided meetings put each employee at a terminal and require that participants, instead of speaking, type their comments and suggestions onto the document that the group creates. The document not only records the meeting, it *is* the meeting. IBM has built eighteen electronic meeting rooms at its sites and plans dozens more. Experience with the system shows that employees who attend computer-aided meetings are much more likely to participate. Even shy people who often are silent at regular meetings will participate, and with much more candor and assertiveness.[19]

Teleconferencing

Teleconferencing, like videoconferencing discussed earlier, has many applications in public relations. Instead of reporters coming to a central meeting place for a news conference, they may be linked to your conference room by phone. They can take turns asking questions of your CEO just as they would in person, and they can hear the Q&A from other participants. Companies with crisis communication problems find that setting up an 800-number system to handle the flood of calls from stockholders and consumers is another useful role for the telephone system.

In a later chapter, when we discuss the preparation of a professional-looking brochure, you will learn to work with a commercial printing house to achieve the results you want. When you are preparing a slick, four-color piece that may have special folds and inserts, using a commercial printer is absolutely necessary. But it often can be frustrating.

First there is the long lag time between sending off the material for a newsletter or brochure and getting the material back in the form of proofs that have to be read for accuracy. Then there is the disappointment when some things do not look the way you intended and others do not take up the amount of space you estimated they would. Changes are made, and then it all must be sent off again to the printer. Another round of anxiety awaits the return of the first page proofs. The process is not only time-consuming but expensive. There will be extra charges if too many changes have to be made in the text or the layout.

Computers and laser printers have changed the picture, enabling almost anyone to produce the "camera ready" layouts for simple publications. The results can be duplicated in the office using the photocopying machine or sent out for printing by a professional outfit. Routine publications such as fact sheets and reports can be produced literally on the top of a desk, hence the term "desktop publishing." (Recently the term "electronic publishing" has been in vogue.)

Software programs have been developed for the personal computer that will produce book-quality type set in neat columns. The columns then can be arranged into pages with the desired margins, borders, numbers, and other graphic elements, including headlines and grey shading. Fancier devices called sheet image scanners can take photographs and other images and fit them electronically to page layouts. The best-quality laser printers (as opposed to the daisy wheel printers used for simple office work) turn out crisp, high-contrast work equivalent to that produced by a print shop.

The rise of desktop publishing doesn't threaten to run professional printers out of business, because they specialize in quality papers, odd folds, plus stapling, gluing, and assembling operations that cannot be duplicated in the office. Instead, the effect of desktop publishing has been to "dress up" reports, internal publications, small newsletters, and flyers in a way that tends to impress the mass audience accustomed to lesser quality in "homemade" information. While content still is important, the impressive packaging achieved with the personal computer has helped bring credibility and impact to information produced by the consumers themselves.

We'll look first at the hardware and software needed for desktop publishing, and then at some ways to set up and make maximum use of your own operation. Specific applications of desktop publishing will be discussed in Chapters 11 and 12 when we look at the preparation of newsletters, brochures, fact sheets, and other print communications.

DESKTOP PUBLISHING: DO IT YOURSELF

The Basic Equipment

The basic personal computer is the centerpiece of desktop publishing. In the 1980s, the Macintosh, produced by Apple computers, was the leader in the field because of its "user friendly" system that provided on-screen guides to making the available tools work with ease. Other manufacturers have caught up and offer similar systems today, and software packages are now available that work on both Apple/Macintosh and IBM or IBM-compatible systems.

Beyond the personal computer, these are the basic elements of a desktop publishing system:

A Hard Disk   in the computer is virtually a must, because the complicated information necessitated by the graphics packages—especially those that adapt photos and drawings to the computer—take large amounts of storage space. A hard disk can be installed in any computer by the supplier of the original equipment.

A Word-Processing Software Program   is used to prepare the type elements of the message. "Macwrite" is the Macintosh system, and WordStar or WordPerfect are the basic IBM-compatible programs. Word-processing capability is included in "super programs" that cover both the text and graphics portions of publishing.

Graphics Software Programs   are used in combination with word-processing programs to add borders, drawings, charts, and other artistic elements. MacDraw is the all-purpose tool for Macintosh users, and a host of programs are available for those who use IBM compatibles.

Printers   translate what has been created on the computer screen to images on paper. Letter-quality printers are good enough for memos and reports, but laser printers have the resolution and sharpness of image needed to create "camera-ready" printouts that can be used by photocopiers or commercial printing companies to make sharp reproductions. Printers are rated according to the number of dots per inch (dpi) they produce. A 300 dpi output is sufficient for most publications, 500 dpi yields even sharper images, and some of the newest systems offer an astounding 1,000 dpi.

A Scanner   is needed to convert a photograph or drawing electronically so that it will be fed into the computer, brought up on the screen, and then printed out along with the text and graphics created by the software programs. While you're at it, you can use the scanner to alter the image. You can make a photograph look more like a sketch or line

Corporate support for non-profit organizations takes many forms and results in colorful publicity meant to generate "goodwill" for the sponsors.

Former San Francisco Forty-Niner quarterback Joe Montana joins Tony Bennett on a cable car ride with young people who have benefited from United Way programs as the Bay Area kicks off its annual fund drive. Bennett is honorary chairperson of the United Way, and Montana represents the National Football League, which provides television spots supporting the United Way.

Source: Photo courtesy of the National Football League

With their colorful balloons and "Leader of the Pack" banner, a thousand employees of The LTV Corporation line up for the start of the March of Dimes TeamWalk in Dallas. The banner refers to LTV's five-year record for producing the largest number of participants and raising the most money for the annual charity event. As a major part of its community relations program, LTV actively supports and subsidizes year-round employee volunteer efforts at all of its plants and facilities.

Source: Photo courtesy of The LTV Corporation

In Hill and Knowlton's MediaCom studio, clients learn techniques to help them communicate more effectively to their key audiences through television and radio news interviews. The agency's production facility creates video tapes that help promote client products, services or issues.

Source: Hill and Knowlton Photos

Hometown news releases accompanied by photos posed with Minnie Mouse are Walt Disney World's way of publicizing its College Program that brings interns to the theme park to gain experience in promotion and publicity. The colorful setting gains extra attention for Disney when the photo is run in college and hometown papers read by the friends and families of the interns.

Source: © The Walt Disney Company

Spectacular shots of the Navy's Blue Angels add excitement to the IMAX wide-screen film shown to visitors at the National Air and Space Museum in Washington, D.C. (See page 294.)

Source: Photo courtesy of Conoco/Du Pont

The Cover

On this page and the next three, you will see many of the key sections from the 1990 annual report distributed to its stockholders by Johnson & Johnson in the spring of 1991.

The Cover A striking photograph—two scientists studying computer-generated images of molecular structures at the R.W. Johnson Pharmaceutical Research Institute—introduces the "theme" of the annual report: *Focus on Innovation.*

Contents Page In addition to the table of contents, the first page carries the most basic sales, earnings, and dividends figures so that shareholders know what the "bottom line" is before they begin reading the annual report.

Management Letter Spread over three pages, the Letter to Stockholders is attributed to the three top managers pictured: the chairman and CEO, and the

ANATOMY OF AN ANNUAL REPORT— JOHNSON & JOHNSON

Three Years in Brief — Worldwide

(Dollars in Millions Except Per Share Figures)	1990	1989	1988
Sales to customers	$11,232	9,757	9,000
Net earnings	1,143*	1,082	974
Cash dividends paid	436	373	327
Stockholders' equity	4,900	4,148	3,503
Percent return on average stockholders' equity	25.3*	28.3	27.9
Per share			
Net earnings	$ 3.43*	3.25	2.86
Cash dividends paid	1.31	1.12	.96
Stockholders' equity	14.71	12.45	10.52
Market price (year-end close)	71	59⅞	42⅜
Average shares outstanding (millions)	333.0	333.1	340.8
Stockholders of record (thousands)	64.6	60.5	54.5
Number of employees (thousands)	82.2	83.1	81.3

*1991 earnings and earnings per share include after-tax 1-after America restructuring charges of $110 million, or $.33 per share in 1990. Before these restructuring charges, 1990 net earnings and earnings per share increased 27.2% over 1989. The percent return on average stockholders' equity in 1990 before restructuring charges is 27.6%. For a detailed discussion of the non-recurring charges, refer to Management's Discussion and Analysis, page 32.

Contents

Contents Page

Letter to Stockholders

Worldwide sales grew to a record $11.2 billion in 1990 and we are pleased to report that it was a good year for Johnson & Johnson, both in terms of financial results and in setting the stage for future profitable growth.

Net earnings were $1.1 billion — a record high level — which was achieved despite our decision early in the year to close down some operations and write off assets in certain Latin American countries — principally Argentina — where economic turmoil had become intolerable.

Our objective continues to be to make Johnson & Johnson the best and most competitive health care company in the world. We are fortunate to have a base of deep and solid strength from which to pursue this goal.

Our pharmaceutical companies now market more than 80 drugs in a wide range of therapeutic categories, and the number of compounds and medical fields they serve are both growing steadily. Our professional products are used in hospitals, clinics, surgical centers and offices by health care professionals in every medical specialty and field. To these pharmaceutical and professional capabilities, we add a high level of competence in consumer products that are trusted throughout the world and to which we bring substantial medical knowledge.

With these three pillars of strength, we are rapidly developing a fourth. Our diagnostics business is one of our fastest growing, both in products used by blood banks and physicians, and in products used at home for self-diagnosis and monitoring.

Another important characteristic of our business is its extensive global reach. More than half our revenues last year came from outside the United States, and we now sell our products in more than 150 countries. This allows us to expand our new product introductions quickly and efficiently around the world.

We are clearly well positioned for substantial growth in the years ahead. We remain convinced that our future lies in an unwavering commitment to research and development. We invested more than $830

Ralph S. Larsen, Chairman and Chief Executive Officer

Management Letter

two vice chairmen who are his main operating officers. Great care goes into the preparation of the letter, because it represents management's analysis of the health of the company—a statement that will be scrutinized carefully by financial analysts, not to mention government regulators.

Theme Section Opener   The photo of a scientist and his test tubes and a brief introduction prepare the reader for a 23-page section that depicts research and development in several key areas of the parent corporation and its worldwide family of more than 170 companies. It is no accident that the photo features one of J&J's main affiliates in Europe: the Janssen Research Foundation.

Year in Review   Three pages are devoted to new-product introductions.

Management Discussion and Analysis   Eight pages of bar charts

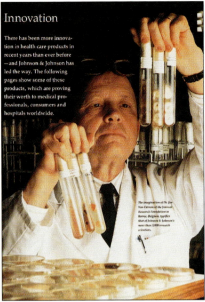

Theme Section Opener

Year in Review

Management Discussion and Analysis

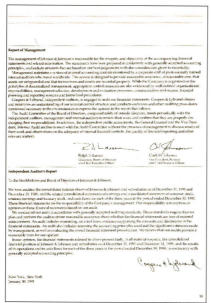

Consolidated Balance Sheet

present key data on sales and earnings, costs and expenses, and management's explanations of those figures.

Consolidated Balance Sheet The heart of the annual report is the 15-page summary of data reported to the SEC. Here it is presented in a straightforward manner, unembellished by art or graphics.

Auditor's Report Both management and the outside auditors attest to the validity of the figures presented and the methods used to obtain those figures.

Subsidiaries Seven pages are devoted to identifying franchises and companies associated with the corporation. In addition to informing target publics, these pages also serve to help stockholder-consumers patronize brands that will benefit their investment.

Auditor's Report

Subsidiaries

Sample Spread Three areas of innovation in research and marketing are highlighted in a two-page spread with color photographs.

Corporate Officers/Board of Directors Consistent with SEC requirements, those responsible for running the corporation are identified.

Corporate Information Items on this page enable the shareholder to obtain additional information. The description of the company is mandated by the SEC.

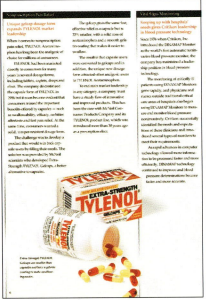

Sample Spread

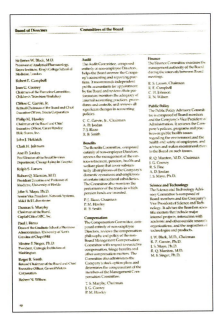

Corporate Officers/Board of Directors

Corporate Information

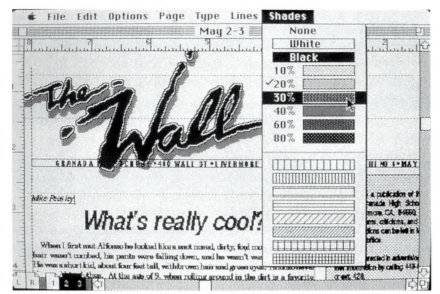

A state-of-the-art newsletter layout can be created on the computer using software programs designed to proportion type and position art. Here, a pull-down menu has been selected on the screen of the Macintosh computer, which enables the newsletter editor to select the desired shading for a border or boxed item.

Photo courtesy of Apple Computer, Inc.

drawing, and you can add grey shading to line drawings to make them look more like photographs.

Pagination Systems enable the desktop publisher to assemble all of the type and graphics into a full page of information. Aldus introduced the revolutionary Pagemaker system in the mid-1980s. Its Pagemaker 4.0 software package, introduced at the beginning of the 1990s, offered a powerful array of features that include: the ability to set any type size; extensive editing capabilities along with index creation; the ability to build tables and charts for easy integration into the page layout; the ability to build book-length publications; the ability to accept graphics created in other systems and place them in a layout; and the ability to integrate information created in other computer systems. A pagination system takes considerable practice to master, which means that it is practical only for organizations that prepare frequent publications.

Document Creation: A Complex Task

When you create a simple document such as a memo or a report, you have several decisions to make: margin width, linespacing, type size, heading format, page numbering format, indentations, and symbols to be used for items included in lists. You must also choose whether to use boldface, italics, or special typefaces to dress up the document.

When you move to a higher level of sophistication and use the desktop publishing system to prepare a newsletter, flyer, advertisement, or brochure, the task becomes infinitely more complicated. (All these issues will be revisited in later chapters that examine specific formats and types of messages.) Here are some of the steps in the process:

Analyze the Format   to decide whether to use a horizontal or vertical presentation. The decision often depends upon the art (photos or drawings) that you have available, and the style or "feel" you want. You also have to analyze how the publication must fit with other publications prepared by your organization.

Develop the Grid   means to design the basic page structure that will appear throughout the publication. In addition to the usual decision about margins, you'll have to decide on the number of columns, the width of those columns, the space between columns, and the spacing between lines of type. These decisions may be based partly on the type of art you're using and the best way to show off your photographs and drawings.

Select Typefaces   to give your publication a certain "feel." The tendency when using software programs with a variety of typefaces is to go crazy like the proverbial "kid in a candy store." Instead, the designer must select a basic "family" of type (one standard typeface and one or two variations on it) that conveys the style and purpose of the organization. Variety typefaces are used sparingly on special stories or items that warrant novelty or imaginative graphic treatment.

Dress Up the Layout with Character Lines and Borders   so as to visually separate items, thus contributing to the particular style or feeling you wish to convey. As with type, the standard software programs offer lots of fancy treatments. The designer of a desktop publication must choose wisely in order to achieve the desired results without crossing the line into "circus makeup" that stuns the reader with every typographical trick in the book.

If desktop publishing is beginning to sound rather complicated, the reason is that, if it's done properly, it *is* complicated. It's only cost-efficient if an organization can use it regularly and is willing to develop the necessary expertise. Even the most fervent enthusiasts of desktop publishing suggest that it shouldn't be used in some public relations situations where cost or the characteristics of target publics do not warrant the expenditure of time and energy.[20]

Throughout the rest of this book we'll point out situations where in-house preparation of documents presents a decided advantage over using outside suppliers.

NOTES

1. Adam Shell (Ed.) "IR Pros Bullish on Faxes, Videos, Databases," *Public Relations Journal* (February 1990), p. 14.

2. Ronald Anderson, Joey Reagan, Scott Hill, and Janine Sumner, "Practitioner Roles and the Uses of New Technologies," paper presented to the International Communication Association, San Francisco, May 1989.

3. Christopher Policano, "The Road to High Tech," *Public Relations Journal* (January 1985), pp. 12–15.

4. Judith M. Brush and Douglas P. Brush, "Corporate Video: Burgeoning Role for PR," *Public Relations Journal* (October 1977), pp. 14–16.

5. Brush and Brush.

6. Interview with members of Johnson & Johnson Public Relations Department.

7. Karen W. Arenson, "Anatomy of AT&T's Offering," *The New York Times,* June 10, 1981, pp. A–1, D–5.

8. Barbara Frankel, "Company Annual Reports, Once Dull, May Be Brightened on Cable TV," *The Home News,* November 25, 1980, p. 20.

9. Brush and Brush.

10. Ronald S. Posner, "A/V Comparisons: Video vs. Film and Slides," *Public Relations Journal* (September 1978), pp. 45–48.

11. ———, "Videoconferences in Health Communications," in *New Technology and Public Relations* (New York: Foundation for Public Relations Research and Education, 1986) pp. 139–141.

12. Celia Kuperszmid Lehrman, "Videoconferencing Comes Down to Earth," *Public Relations Journal* (April 1989), pp. 23–27.

13. David Neustadt, "Action! Camera! It's Time for a Video Meeting," *The New York Times,* November 10, 1985, pp. 6–7.

14. Julie Price, "Employee Video Magazines," *Public Relations Journal* (May 1986), pp. 11, 14.

15. Adam Shell, "'Channel 12' Delivers Company News Into Employees' Living Rooms," *Public Relations Journal* (March 1990), pp. 10–11.

16. Anne Weathersby, "Commercially Available Data Bases," in *New Technology and Public Relations* (New York: Foundation for Public Relations Research and Education, 1986) p. 13.

17. ———, "Legislation Affecting Faxes," *Public Relations Journal* (April 1990), p. 12.

18. ———, "Broadcast Faxing Gaining Popularity," *Public Relations Journal* (April 1990), p. 12.

19. Jim Bartimo, "At These Shouting Matches, No One Says a Word," *Business Week,* June 11, 1990, p. 78.

20. Judy A. Gordon, "Desktop Publishing: Separating Dreams from Reality," *Public Relations Journal* (November 1989), pp. 24–30; Suzanne Poor, "Desktop Publishing Report: It's Nifty, But Is It Necessary?" *Creative New Jersey* (May/June 1990), pp. 8–9.

ADDITIONAL READING

Cooper, Michael, "In the Stretch: Electronic Mail," *Public Relations Journal* (January 1985), pp. 21–24.

Felici, James, and Ted Nace, *Desktop Publishing Skills: A Primer for Typesetting with Computers and Laser Printers* (Reading, MA: Addison-Wesley, 1987).

Kleper, Michael L., *The Illustrated Handbook of Desktop Publishing and Typesetting* (Blue Ridge Summit, PA: Tab Books, 1987).

McCatherin, E. Zoe, "Beyond Employee Publications: Making the Personal Connection," *Public Relations Journal* (July 1989), pp. 14–20.

Parker, Roger C., *Looking Good in Print: A Guide to Basic Design for Desktop Publishing* (Chapel Hill, NC: Ventana Press, 1988).

Seybold, John, and Fritz Dressler, *Publishing from the Desktop* (New York: Bantam Books, 1987).

Stecki, Ed, and Frank Corado, "How to Make a Video," *Public Relations Journal* (February 1988), pp. 33–34, and *Public Relations Journal* (March 1988), pp. 35–36.

Winkleman, Michael, "Video Age," *Public Relations Journal* (April 1989), pp. 24–25, 28.

10

Preparing to Speak

Speaking and speechmaking are as fundamental to public relations as writing. Reaching *mass* audiences often means using written messages, but reaching *targeted* publics often means speaking to them. Mass audiences must be spoken to through the electronic media, but targeted publics often must be spoken to directly at meetings, rallies, banquets, and even impromptu settings in the workplace.

The same person who supervises the preparation of news releases and broadcast messages is likely, at any given time, to be working on one or more of the following nonmedia tasks:

- Preparing the head of a department to brief the press on a new program.
- Writing a "stock speech" for delivery to any visiting group before beginning a plant tour.
- Rehearsing the president of the firm for an appearance before the Chamber of Commerce.
- Setting up a speaker's bureau to provide presentations on nontechnical topics of interest to community, professional, and educational groups.
- Drafting the question format for interviewing employees' children who are candidates for company scholarships.
- Making arrangements for a dialogue session that will bring company officials together with community members to discuss problems of pollution and waste disposal.

All of these events have one thing in common: Someone will have to be prepared to speak on behalf of the organization.

SPEAKING VS. WRITING: DIFFERENCES AND SIMILARITIES

It is useful to understand the ways in which speaking differs from other communication skills, and the ways in which it is similar. First, two important differences:

■ While a written message such as a newsletter, brochure, or advertisement is somewhat impersonal, the spoken word carries the credibility of the speaker. Enthusiasm, concern, tolerance, understanding, and empathy are all best demonstrated through the verbal and nonverbal act of meeting an audience in person.

■ The speaking situation is flexible and can be altered to fit the response of the audience. With the print or audiovisual message, you fire your shot and hope it hits the target. In a speaking situation, you can make mid-course corrections.

But, in some very important ways, the speech is similar to other public relations messages:

■ It must be consistent with other messages disseminated by the organization. The speaker must be familiar with positions taken in written communication, and must strive to articulate them in a personal style that is consistent with the view of the organization.

■ Careful and complete preparation is necessary in order to avoid embarrassment. The speaker must have all the facts straight. He or she cannot hope to merely "wing it" on personal charm alone.

■ The speaking situation poses the usual "packaging and delivery" questions for the public relations department: Is this the best forum for reaching the target audience? Will it help us to achieve our goals? Is it the best use of resources? Should it be reinforced with other channels of communication? Will we be able to measure the effect?

Which Programs?

Speeches and interpersonal communication skills have a place in all of the programs aimed at specific publics, especially when the programs have the two-way symmetric model of public relations as a framework. Some examples:

■ You and your managers prepare to meet personally with the press and hold press conferences—essential to symmetric media relations.

■ Members of your organization give speeches to community groups. They also have face-to-face interviews and dialogue sessions with community leaders and other citizens.

- You speak at tours and open houses, help dedicate community facilities, visit school classes, and put on events for scouts and other youth groups.
- Public relations practitioners and managers meet directly with members of activist publics, trying to negotiate compromise solutions to conflicts with consequences for the organization.
- Government relations specialists meet with officials and members of key constituencies to present their organization's positions on policy issues. They also give numerous speeches to civic, professional, and political groups.
- Specialists in educational relations and economic education set up speeches and small group sessions to facilitate interaction between students and organizational representatives.
- Financial PR specialists talk with stockbrokers and give speeches to members of the financial community. They also plan the extensive spoken communication that takes place at the annual stockholders' meeting.
- The fund raiser finds that personal contacts, speeches to alumni and supportive publics, and telephone calls are essential for raising money.

RESEARCHING AND ORGANIZING THE SPEECH

In a perceptive article on the "Care and Feeding of Speechwriters," Westinghouse public relations manager Jean Pope, formerly a speechwriter for Hill and Knowlton, offered a scenario of what too often happens.[1]

The chief executive officer tells the secretary, "I'm speaking to the Management Club March 14 on the future of business–labor relations in Britain. Have Bob prepare a speech for me by next week." The secretary dutifully calls the vice president for public affairs, who passes the job to the public relations manager, who assigns the task to a second-stringer in his department, who fails in her attempts to get an appointment with the CEO. Laboriously and without direction, she comes up with something she hopes is satisfactory. When the CEO finally gets around to reading the speech, he reworks it and gives it to the secretary to type half a day before he delivers it.

The speech, needless to say, is lackluster and completely forgettable. Says Pope: "The writing-by-committee has mangled the best parts of the speech. What's more, unrehearsed, it comes across flat and lifeless."[2]

The moral of the story is that:

1. Adequate planning must precede speechmaking.
2. Writing and reviewing it are important group tasks.
3. The speechwriter must have access to the speaker.

4. Presentation of the speech should be rehearsed to assure that it will have the desired impact.

Let's look at the many facets of the job in greater detail.

Research

Anyone who has prepared a term paper has experienced the first phase of speechwriting: library research. Statements made about the topic should be reviewed in order to know what the main arguments are and what raw data are available. In addition to books and periodicals, make sure you check professional or trade journals and government publications for statistics and informed opinions that can lend credence to your presentation. Your own files are also important: You should be able to put your hands quickly on everything your organization's managers have written or said on the topic.

What's the "Big Idea"?

After you've gathered the data, but before you prepare an outline, the all-important question is, What is the main point we want to make with this speech? Just as the advertising copywriter must be able to reduce the entire message to a phrase, a slogan, or a headline, the speechwriter should be able to summarize the big idea of the speech in a single line: "XYZ Corporation believes high property taxes are driving business out of Central Valley" or "The main goal of the state Environmental Protection Agency during the next year is to clean up the air in our cities."

Deciding on that single thrust will help you to weed out information that may be interesting but that does not support or illustrate the main point. It may cause some tension with your spokesperson, since there may be pressure to "tell them about all of the wonderful things we're doing and all of the problems we think are important to overcome." Certainly, you should try to work in some background about the organization and its many concerns, but as one professional PR speechwriter succinctly puts it, one of the simple but hard-and-fast rules is to "keep your eye on the ball" at all times.[3]

Organizing and Outlining

To say that a good speech has an introduction, a body, and a conclusion is to say that, once again, it must be outlined the way you would organize a term paper or article. The concept can be summarized by that old

Before writing the speech, make sure that speaker, speechwriter, and public relations staff agree on the purpose of the speech. That way you can judge whether every piece of information and every rhetorical device is serving the main purpose of the speech event. Speeches have these main purposes:

Persuade/Defend—Present your organization's point of view and defend its actions. Data should support the views of your organization. Especially in the two-way symmetric model, opposing views should be acknowledged.

Inform/Explain—Present information on what your organization is doing and explain the reasons for the actions.

Entertain/Welcome—Greet guests, represent your organization, and spread goodwill. May include some facets of *inform/explain* function.

Background—Similar to *inform/explain*, but without the urgency of breaking news event or public issues. Sometimes referred to as a "technical" presentation.

Pro-forma—Includes "welcome" speeches, award acceptance speeches, and other occasions where your organization is responding to the needs of others rather than serving its own communication needs. Should serve your purposes while fitting the scene and setting created by the sponsoring organization.

Exhibit 10.1
What's the Purpose?

saw: "Tell 'em what you're going to tell them; then tell 'em; and finally, tell 'em what you told them."

If a one-page outline—with the classical I., A., 1. a. format for arranging main and subordinate points—is submitted to the speaker for discussion and refinement beforehand, the writing task will be easier, and fewer alterations will have to be made on the completed script.

Working with the Speaker

By this point, it should be clear that the speechwriter must work with the speaker on every phase of developing the speech. The word choices, even the length and rhythm of the sentences, must be appropriate to the individual speaking style. The speaker must feel familiar enough with the supporting data to field questions and defend his or her views. And finally, the speaker must have a general confidence in the speech in order to give it with conviction. Ideally, the person selected to write a speech should have worked for some time in close conjunction with the speaker. If that is not the case, then the writer must have access to the speaker to

Exhibit 10.2
Speechwriting for
the CEO: A
Specialized Skill

Every good writer is not necessarily a good *speech* writer. Corporations know that, and they often use the consultant services of a specialist who writes major speeches for chief executive officers.

Speechwriters don't necessarily have to be experts about the business of the company whose CEO they are writing for. That's because their job is to take the information provided by the public relations department and shape it into easy-to-understand statements that are written for the ear, not for the eye.

The key trait for the consummate speechwriter is that he or she is widely read. In addition to absorbing the leading news media and business publications, the speechwriter also is familiar with the latest nonfiction books on a variety of public affairs topics, and probably also the current novels that deal with problems that affect society.

Part of the speechwriter's homework is to study the style of the CEO—observing the speaker in public situations—in order to choose phrases and expressions that will seem natural when read from a script. The speechwriter must have access to the CEO before the speech is written and when the first draft is ready for the speaker's comments, questions, and suggestions.

Sources: Mark R. Perlgut, "How to Write a Speech for a CEO," *Public Relations Journal* (April 1986), pp. 30–31; Brent W. Rosenberger, "How to Recognize and Work with a Speechwriter," *Public Relations Journal* (January 1988), pp. 31–32.

go over the information, and there must be at least one session in which the writer hears the script read by the speaker. That way, the words can be tailored to the speaker, and the speaker can develop the necessary trust in the writer.

The All-Important Introduction

"A funny thing happened to me on the way to the hotel tonight . . ."

Oh, yeah?

A funny thing happened to speechwriting in the past few decades: Speakers learned that audiences don't howl anymore over jokes lifted from books like *A Thousand and One Stories for Every Occasion*. We get enough formula jokes and canned laughter on television. And the contemporary audience is cynical enough to doubt that the quotation from Aristotle, Will Rogers, or John F. Kennedy is really one of the speaker's favorites, rather than something the speechwriter dug up for the occasion.

Exhibit 10.3
Use an "Oral" Style in
Speechwriting

In his guidebook for executive speakers, AT&T government relations manager Edward H. McCarthy suggests that the most effective speech is written in an *oral* style, meaning that the language is clear, vivid, and easy to understand, and the information is easy to retain. Specific suggestions include:

- Use short words.
- Use the personal pronoun *I* frequently.
- Use active verbs like *push, take, grab* and *move.*
- Use analogies that help the audience visualize.
- Use repetition and parallel construction to develop a pattern and cadence.
- Tell anecdotes that are memorable and illustrative.
- Provide examples, facts, figures, data to make your points.
- Sentence fragments are okay, if they give the speech more punch.
- Rhetorical questions get the audience involved.

Source: Edward H. McCarthy, *Speechwriting: A Professional Step-by-Step Guide for Executives* (Dayton, OH: The Executive Speaker Company, 1989).

"The rule of thumb concerning a joke is threefold: the speaker can deliver it effectively; it flows out of the experience of the speaker; it is appropriate to the subject."[4] If those tests can be met, then certainly a moment of levity is an effective way to gain the attention and the empathy of the listener. The speechwriter might draw out an anecdote from the speaker during the first interview and attempt to shape it into a lively opening remark. If it falls flat in rehearsal, or if the speaker wants to open with something ad lib that is appropriate to the moment, then the humorous story is best left out of the script.

If the speech is to be serious in tone, an ominous opening statement might be appropriate: "Central Valley may be a ghost town ten years from now . . ."

Intriguing, little-known facts can raise the curiosity of the listeners: "Every year, twenty-seven pounds of soot and dust particles fall on each of the citizens living in Central City. Fortunately, it falls a little at a time, and not all at once!"

Still another effective device is the revealing bit of personal history: "This is the first time I've been back to Bloomington since I was graduated from college, and I have to admit the circumstances are a bit happier this time. Now I'm working for the government. When I left, the government wasn't so happy with me—as a student, I ran up a small fortune in

Exhibit 10.4
Humor Provides the
Human Touch

Songwriter, television host, and humorist Steve Allen is renowned as a toastmaster, MC, and speaker on serious subjects as well as light-hearted ones. As a humorist, he knows that jokes can fall flat, and the best humor in a speech adds a human touch, not just a bellylaugh:

> *Far better than a formula joke, and even better than a funny story, is humor with the ring of truth to it. If you can relate an actual incident, whether it happened to you or to someone else, and if, furthermore, your listeners realize that they are hearing a true story, the results will almost invariably be satisfactory.*

The implication for public relations speechwriters is clear. Instead of pounding through old joke books or lifting witticisms from one of the newsletters that packages quips and quotes for use in speeches, sit down with your speaker and try to come up with an incident that really happened. The speaker will relish telling such a real story, and that will add to the audience's enjoyment.

Source: Steve Allen, *How to Make a Speech* (New York: McGraw-Hill, 1986), p. 109.

parking fines right here on Campus Drive." (If it doesn't get a big laugh from the audience, at least it may help put the speaker at ease.)

How Much to Say?

A professional speechwriter put it succinctly: "No one will get mad at a speaker who made a twenty-minute speech when he was scheduled for twenty-five minutes."[5] The tolerance level of the typical audience, conditioned by half-hour television sitcoms, is not what it used to be. Even captive audiences (employees, fellow professionals, students in classrooms) become restless when the big hand on the clock completes a full circle. If you've narrowed your topic sufficiently, you can be complete and still be brief. If you've been commissioned to fill an hour, why not plan to devote half of it to fielding questions?

DELIVERING THE SPEECH

When managers are going to address a friendly and familiar audience, they probably will not ask the public relations department for help in preparing the speech. On the other hand, many managers attained their positions because they were superb engineers, planners, or economic analysts, not because they have a knack for getting an audience in the palms of their hands.

Even when the manager is a competent speaker, making an effective speech is not merely a matter of turning on the charm or reaching into a bag of oratorical tricks. One of the most important contributions the PR department can make, for example, is to research the composition of the audience in order to advise the speaker who the listeners are, what their interest level is, what they already know about the subject, and what kinds of questions they are likely to ask.

Provide Coaching

Some executives welcome coaching and preparation. Others are insulted to think they must be rehearsed and trained in order to perform adequately. It may be advisable, therefore, to make it official management policy that all speakers undergo a "prep session." Professional speech consultants, using video tape, are available to conduct such training.

One consultant suggests that the checklist for preparing a speaker begins with a discussion of the proper attire for the occasion.[6] Perhaps the topic can be overlooked in the case of a senior executive who routinely dresses in a three-piece pinstripe suit and silk tie. But it may be necessary to suggest that a scientist leave his loud sportcoat in the lab and venture out to speak at a professional meeting wearing a dark blazer and coordinated slacks. The public relations department must do its homework: at certain conferences held in tropical resort areas, it is customary to wear good-looking golf attire, and the speaker in urban work clothes may make the audience and himself ill at ease.

Some managers allow that old bugaboo stage fright to become a self-fulfilling prophecy. They expect to be nervous and to stumble, and so they do. It may be so severe that the speaker experiences momentary paralysis. The public speaking volumes listed as Additional Reading at the end of this chapter all agree that a certain amount of apprehension is useful, because it gets the adrenalin running and pumps the speaker up to perform. If your manager has severe apprehension, a speech consultant may be used to teach him or her helpful relaxation techniques. (The two-page spread in the color section in the middle of this textbook shows Hill and Knowlton trainers preparing executives for speaking engagements and television appearances.)

Polish During Rehearsal

During the rehearsal of a speech, help the speaker to slow up delivery of the first few lines. Mark the script to indicate where a breath can be taken. Try to implant a substitute self-fulfilling prophecy: "You're going to do great, because this is a well-prepared speech tailored to your style, and it's got some information that the audience really wants to hear."

Give the speaker an opportunity to perform before an in-house group, such as a regularly scheduled department meeting. Some organizations routinely make use of their video studios to tape dry runs of presentations, thus providing the speaker with valuable instant analysis. Stored copies of trial runs can also be used to train speakers in the future.

USING VISUAL AIDS

Notice that we didn't discuss visual aids earlier as a device for helping the speaker to overcome stage fright. Visual aids shouldn't be thrown in to compensate for a mediocre speaker. They should be used primarily because they make the presentation clearer and because they can add interest and variety.

The time to decide whether a visual aid will be useful is after the research and first draft are completed. Then the speechwriter must analyze whether some data lend themselves to graphic display, or if a slide show, film, or video tape might make a major point come to life.

Another major concern is whether the visual aid will be appropriate for the meeting room where it is to be used. If you plan to show sales figures and research expenditures using graphics on slide transparencies, make sure the room can be fully darkened. If charts and graphs are to be used, provide the speaker with an easel and cardboard-backed signboards that are nonreflecting so that they can be read no matter how harsh the lighting. (The best professional easels have a light source hanging from the top.)

Misuse of Visual Aids

Nothing is more annoying than the misuse of visual aids. Does the one card left on the easel for thirty minutes carry routine information that the audience didn't need to "see" in order to understand? This kind of presentation can insult them and lead to boredom. Conversely, is there so much information on the cards that the speaker must flip them before the audience has had a chance to digest the ideas? This can be especially upsetting.

Do the audience members or the speaker have difficulty in seeing the graphics and interpreting them from where they sit or stand? Maybe using a flip pad of blank paper and a felt tip pen to create fresh material would make the audience feel that the presentation was geared especially to its interests.

Exhibit 10.5
Get Out from
behind the Lectern

In his deliciously irreverent book, *I Can See You Naked: A Fearless Guide to Making Great Presentations,* speech-making consultant Ron Hoff points out the problems with making entire speeches from behind lecterns or podiums: They hold the manuscript nicely, but they usually light the speaker in a way that makes him look like Frankenstein, Dracula, or worse. Worst of all, they literally put a physical barrier between the speaker and the audience.

The best presenters may stand behind the lectern or podium for a few seconds, then—as if freed by some cosmic force—move into a pool of light, probably closer to the audience. This well-thought-out piece of business has some salubrious effects. It says you are more confident of the material than previous speakers who have remained rooted behind the podium. It also suggests a desire to cast aside all foolishness and get down to the nub of it.

If your spokesperson has the ability to remember the outline of a speech from a hand-held index card with major topic headings, hold a rehearsal that gives the speaker practice in breaking down the barrier by stepping away from the podium.

Source: Ron Hoff, *I Can See You Naked: A Fearless Guide to Making Great Presentations* (Kansas City, MO: Andrew & McMeel Books, 1988).

And remember, if your speaker is a dynamic person with a personality that can rivet the attention of the listeners, visual aids may actually detract from the presentation.

With speakers who are so mechanical in their presentation that they can't or won't vary a word, then the PR department might as well use video tape to disseminate the message. One of the principal benefits of using a live spokesperson is that feedback received from listeners during the speech can be acknowledged and used to improve the audience's understanding of the topic.

During rehearsals, note whether the speaker is able to read perplexity on the faces of the audience. Help the speaker learn to stop and say, "Are you all familiar with the concept of 'front-end-loaded' funds? Let me explain briefly." Some speakers also need practice in order to avoid unwanted interruptions by perpetual question-raisers. Teach them a phrase such as, "I know this is a complicated subject, but I think it will be much clearer when I explain step by step, so I'll ask you please

FEEDBACK AND EVALUATION OF THE SPEECH

CHECKLIST ✔ Speech Evaluation Form

Speech Evaluation

Date: _____ Audience: _____

Speaker: _____ Evaluator: _____

Room was properly set up for presentation.

Introduction of speaker was clear and adequate.

Speaker's dress and bearing were appropriate to occasion.

Voice level was satisfactory to the audience.

Speaker established rapport with audience.

Credibility of speaker was established.

Eye contact was maintained.

Overdependence on prepared script was avoided.

Opening section got attention.

Topic area and main point were clearly established.

Main points were repeated and emphasized.

Topic was clearly summarized and point driven home.

Ending section elicited desired reaction.

Audience was engaged throughout speech.

Feedback was acknowledged and corrections made.

Opportunity for questions was provided.

Visual aids were properly set up and used.

Visual aids provided emphasis and clarity.

Speaker was comfortable using visual aids.

Audience reaction to visual aids was positive.

Additional suggestions:

to hold your questions for just a few moments." These may seem like obvious devices to the practiced speaker, but it's surprising how many people have to be coached in order to master them.

PR students who have taken public speaking courses know that a speech-evaluation checklist can be a useful analytical tool. While it may not be politic to present your CEO with a "report card," the checklist can help the PR department to evaluate the speeches it prepares. Extra space or wide margins should be left after each item, so that additional specific comments can be added by the evaluator.

The sample speech evaluation form provided on the opposite page can be modified to fit your organization's specific needs. One or more evaluators may be used. A check is placed in front of every item that was satisfactory. Comments are written in the space below each item if there was a deficiency or if the evaluator has a suggestion for improvement.

Rarely will feedback be useful unless it is provided immediately and in an organized way. That's why the speech-evaluation form often works better than the verbal briefing you never seem to find time to hold until too many days later.

You may have followed every suggestion to the letter, and your speaker is ready to dazzle an audience . . . when an unpredicted ice storm makes travel hazardous, and two-thirds of the expected guests stay at home. If the speech was your total PR message, then you probably will end up far short of your objectives. But if you have planned multiple uses of the prepared material, success can still be yours.

GETTING MORE MILEAGE FROM THE SPEECH

As soon as the speechwriter has completed the final draft, for example, preparation of a simultaneous print press release should begin. (One speechwriter even suggests that the press release should be written before the speech, in order to force the speaker and the speechwriter to come up with key thoughts that can be packaged as news.[7]) The release, along with a text of the speech, can be provided to the wire services and other news organizations in the area ahead of time. The PR person should be prepared to put the speaker in phone contact with the media immediately after the speech, especially if reporters who had expressed an interest in attending were not able to be there.

And don't forget the reprint value of a speech. If the names of those attending a convention where your spokesperson appeared are available from the sponsors, you may want to send a reprint to each, with a cover letter reminding them of the impact the presentation had on the convention. A device that has special impact is the reprinting of the speech in a quality booklet format, with a picture of the speaker preceding the text. A commencement speech by your CEO, or a keynote address to a professional or trade meeting, might warrant such prestigious treatment.

Exhibit 10.6
Sample Page
from Speech Script

THANK YOU!

WHEN I WAS INVITED TO SPEAK TO THE SOCIETY OF PROFESSIONAL JOURNALISTS, MY IMMEDIATE REACTION WAS "WHY NOT?" AFTER ALL, IN MY POSITION AS INFORMATION DIRECTOR FOR THE STATE COURTS, I DEAL WITH JOURNALISTS ON THE PHONE EVERY DAY. SO WHY NOT CONFRONT THEM IN PERSON? WHY NOT LET THEM SEE THAT I AM NOT AN OGRE WHO PREVENTS THEM FROM TALKING WITH THE CHIEF JUSTICE AND HIS STAFF?!

SERIOUSLY, I VIEW YOUR JOB AS IMPORTANT—INFORMING THE PEOPLE. I VIEW MY JOB AS EQUALLY IMPORTANT—INFORMING YOU IN TIMELY AND ACCURATE FASHION ABOUT THE WORKINGS OF THE COURT SYSTEM SO THAT YOU CAN INFORM YOUR READERS AND YOUR LISTENERS.

SOMETIMES WE MAY SEEM LIKE ADVERSARIES. BUT I VIEW OUR RELATIONSHIP AS A PARTNERSHIP . . . AND AN IMPORTANT PARTNERSHIP AT THAT. WHEN WE WORK TOGETHER IN A CLIMATE OF MUTUAL UNDERSTANDING, THE PUBLIC WILL INDEED BE SERVED.

    The script is written in capital letters—as high as one-quarter inch—for ease of reading. Care is taken to avoid confusing breaks at the ends of lines, and paragraphs are always completed on one page with no continuation. The speaker then will go through the transcript of the speech and highlight words and phrases for emphasis. Some speakers prefer to have cue words such as (PAUSE) and (BREATHE) written into the script they will read.

ORGANIZING A SPEAKERS' BUREAU

At some point it's going to hit you: "We're sending somebody out there to speak to some organization almost every week." Maybe it's time to set up a speakers' bureau. Here's what it takes to set up an ongoing service for presenting your organization's ideas to other organizations through a team of trained speakers:

■ A program to identify managers in your organization who are willing speakers. They must not only do the job well, they also have to enjoy going out to meet with Kiwanians, Daughters of the American Revolution, or the Association of Professional Whatevers.

- A set of topics suitable for any and all groups: "The New Technology" . . . "The History of Mining" . . . "How to Prepare for a Job in the Aerospace Industry" . . . "Why We Must Explore Outer Space." All of these topics, of course, must relate to your organization's goals and interests. The target group expects some sort of "sell," although they expect it to be "soft."
- A system of publicizing and promoting the speakers and their topics. In most parts of the country, the phone company's bill-stuffer newsletter includes an occasional item about "interesting programs for your club—just call your local Bell office to arrange a speaker." Utilities, along with the monthly bill, also promote "science magicians" and experts in various fields for school and club appearances. Another good device is to mail flyers to school superintendents and principals, who are always looking for free educational programs. National headquarters of professional and fraternal organizations usually are willing to provide mailing lists of presidents or program chairpersons of local chapters, making it easy for you to get your descriptive brochure to them.
- A booking person. One secretary or administrative assistant in the public relations department should be responsible for handling all speaker requests and assuring that obligations are fulfilled.

Most universities maintain a list of professors and their interest areas, so that groups requesting presentations on very specialized topics of interest can be matched with speakers. Large corporations provide speakers in wholesale quantities: the Western Electric Company has five hundred speakers working out of fifty-two local bureaus around the country.[8]

Dealing with Brushfire Topics

Sometimes a special speaker service is set up to deal with a very limited public relations situation. When the state legislature is considering a bill that would limit duck hunting, sportsmen's organizations may set up a special task force to go around the state speaking on "Our American Heritage: The Sport of Duck Hunting." Whenever First Amendment guarantees are threatened, journalism and public relations groups usually field speakers to address civic and school groups about "Our American Heritage: Freedom of the Press."

When the speakers' bureau is set up on a "brushfire" basis, phone contacts with school administrators and civic groups listed in the telephone directory can be used to arrange several quick bookings for speakers.

Use by the Military

Speaker materials are provided to all military commanders in order to increase the visibility and reputation of the military in the community. Each service branch has an information office that prepares stock speeches and speaker materials for use on Veterans Day, Memorial Day, the Fourth of July, and other special occasions when military personnel may be called upon to speak. While many college students may never have had an opportunity to hear such speeches, they are regular fixtures of public gatherings in thousands of communities around the country where military bases and large government contractors are prime employers.

PREPARING MANAGERS FOR PRESS CONTACTS

Given the choice between speaking to five hundred Rotarians or just half a dozen reporters, most managers would choose the vast audience of five hundred. There may be an awful lot of them, but at least you know they won't bite.

As awesome as a major speaking engagement may seem, the speaker has a great deal of control over the situation. The press, on the other hand, insists on making its own rules. And, the impact of speaking to a half-dozen reporters is potentially much greater than addressing a huge hall full of people. It can be even riskier than a formal debate, because the rules seem to be made up as the interview or press conference goes along.

Frederick Knapp, president of a consulting firm that specializes in preparing executives to appear in public, calls the media interview the most challenging of speaking appearances because of the probing questions and the necessity of thinking clearly under pressure.[9] Keeping the main point in mind and avoiding getting sidetracked takes concentration.

Another key problem is the fact that most managers can't visualize what a story will look like in print or sound like on the air. The PR practitioner should keep clips showing the results of interviews where the spokesperson for an organization understood the task and provided quotes that worked well for the organization, along with other articles that illustrate how the speaker's ineptitude led to embarrassing coverage in the press.

After reviewing the clips, you can stage a mock interview or press conference for your manager, using PR department personnel as reporters. Throw a little of everything at the speaker: rudeness, interruptions, hostile questions, no-win questions ("When is your company going to stop polluting the river?"), and incessantly returning to previous topics the speaker feels have already been addressed. If you try everything imaginable on the speaker in practice, the actual interview may seem more tolerable and manageable.

Before and after the mock interview, try to impress the following guidelines upon your spokesperson:

1. Be brief. Print reporters who take longhand notes will choose quotes that are succinct and to-the-point. Broadcast reporters need to tape only a few sharp sentences for use. Interviewees who ramble on will be "paraphrased" instead of quoted directly, if they are quoted at all.

2. Avoid being "cagey" about information. Don't ask that something be "off the record"—nobody can guarantee it. "No comment" makes the speaker look evasive. Better to say, "I am not at liberty to release that information at this time," giving the reason, if possible. If you don't know something, instead of pretending to be secretive, tell the reporters you aren't sure of the facts or figures, but you'll have your PR staff check it out and get in touch with the press as soon as possible. Most important of all, don't get caught telling a half-truth. An enterprising reporter may check it out and find that you were revealing only part of the story.

3. Maintain a firm but cordial stance. If the reporters are on a first-name basis with you, address them by first name, too. Otherwise use Mr. or Ms. Don't show favoritism to one reporter who is a friend or who represents a "friendly" news medium; the other reporters may unconsciously or consciously retaliate for being put on less-favored status. Above all, don't lose your temper, no matter how boorish a reporter may become. If you threaten a member of the press in any way, that fact will probably become the lead of the news story, not the information about your organization that you hoped to present.

4. When asked a negative question, don't give a knee-jerk, defensive response. Think quickly about the topic raised by the question. What relevant facts can you discuss about your organization's performance in this area? As we have stressed, in the symmetric model it is important to answer negative questions honestly, truthfully, and fully. If your organization has done something wrong, explain what happened and tell what is being done to rectify the situation. Without ignoring the substance of the question, try to turn the main substance of the reply into a "plus" for your point of view.

5. Keep calm and try to manage a smile. You're only doing your job, and the reporters are only doing theirs.

Exhibit 10.7
Interviewers' Questions:
An Opportunity

Some of the shortest and most effective speeches ever made may not appear to be speeches at all. They're the responses given by the leader of your organization to an interviewer like Robert MacNeil of the "MacNeil/Lehrer News Hour" on public broadcasting. These "answers" should not be ad-libbed. You can anticipate the question, craft a tidy statement, and rehearse your spokesperson to deliver the set speech at the proper time.

Newsman MacNeil, quoted by noted press relations expert Jack Hilton, even expects his interview subjects to take the ball and run with it: "Know what you want to say, and use whatever questions you are asked to say it. Just don't get so fixated by the questions you are asked that you forget to make your points."

Hilton explains why he prepares speakers very carefully to present the points they want to get across no matter the forum or the question: "Only a consultant with an IQ lower than room temperature would permit you to ad-lib in front of an important audience, particularly a TV audience."

Source: Jack Hilton, *How to Meet the Press: A Survival Guide* (New York: Dodd, Mead, 1987), pp. 33, 37.

NOTES

1. Jean Pope, "Care and Feeding of Speechwriters," *Public Relations Journal* (May 1979), pp. 6–9.

2. Pope.

3. Edwin F. Brennan, "Five Rules for Speechwriters," *Public Relations Journal* (May 1979), p. 10.

4. Pope.

5. Brennan.

6. Frederick J. Knapp, "Prepare Your CEO to Meet His Publics," *Public Relations Journal* (May 1979), pp. 11–13.

7. Nariman N. Karanjia, "The Nitty-Gritty of Speechwriting," *Public Relations Journal* (May 1980), pp. 17–19.

8. "Speakers Bureaus Can Amplify PR Impact," *IABC News* (December 1980), pp. 1, 5.

9. Knapp.

ADDITIONAL READING

Allen, Steve, *How to Make a Speech* (New York: McGraw-Hill, 1986).

Burns, Robert Edward, "Combating Speech Anxiety," *Public Relations Journal* (March 1991), pp. 28, 30.

DeVito, Joseph A., *The Elements of Public Speaking*, 4th ed. (New York: HarperCollins, 1990).

Hilton, Jack, *How to Meet the Press: A Survival Guide* (New York: Dodd-Mead, 1987).

Hoff, Ron, *I Can See You Naked: A Fearless Guide to Making Great Presentations* (Kansas City: Andrews & McMeel, 1988).

Koranda, Timothy J., "Writing Speeches with Impact," *Public Relations Journal* (September 1990), p. 31.

McCarthy, Edward H., *Speechwriting: A Professional Step-by-Step Guide for Executives* (Dayton, OH: The Executive Speaker Company, 1989).

Ross, Raymond, *Speech Communication*, 8th ed. (Englewood Cliffs, NJ: Prentice-Hall, 1988).

Tarver, Jerry, *Corporate Speechwriter's Handbook* (New York: Quorum Books, 1987).

11

Brochures and Direct Mail

When we discussed the preparation of materials to be included in press kits (Chapter 6) we highlighted the basic *fact sheet* as an important tool for getting information about your organization or program into the hands of reporters and eventually into their articles, columns, or news items.

Now we look again at the fact sheet and its fancier cousin, the brochure, in the context of direct mail as the delivery system. In the past decade, direct mail—sometimes called direct advertising—has risen to become the third largest marketing medium, right behind newspapers and television.[1] Its phenomenal growth can be attributed to the fact that direct mail targets specific publics and reaches them at the time and in the place where they make most of their decisions—in the home. That makes direct mail an extremely attractive message channel for public relations programs.

Advertising, promotions, posters, displays, and special events are used to alert the public to ideas and programs. Brochures and fact sheets are designed to go into greater detail about the issue. They provide information that can be saved, stored, referred to, and acted upon.

The mailing list is one of the most valuable tools a PR department can use. The mass media deliver thousands of unwanted members of subpublics that do not interest your organization. But mailing lists target much more precisely the audience you want to reach: homeowners,

OBTAINING OR BUILDING A MAILING LIST

Exhibit 11.1

Elements of the
Direct Mail Piece

When designing a direct mail piece—whether it's a solicitation for a charity, an invitation to support a public interest group, or a request to join an organization in its efforts to affect a piece of legislation—you must consider all of the elements that can have an effect on the recipient:

- *The envelope.* The return address in the upper-left-hand corner should intrigue the member of the target public. A "teaser" in spot color can intrigue the recipient into opening the envelope. A gummed first-class stamp can convince the recipient that the message is personal, not mass-mailed.
- *The letterhead.* It may introduce your organization, or it may be the letterhead of a celebrity who has agreed to be spokesperson for your cause.
- *The salutation.* It may be personal if you have used a mailing list and a direct mailing service, or it may be general but focused: "Supporter of the Arts" . . . "Fellow Taxpayer" . . . "Dear Concerned Senior Citizen."
- *The opening "grab."* A provocative question or statement compels the recipient to read on. "Jimmy was only nine when his life ended . . ." "If you can read this, count yourself lucky. . ." "Thank God you and I live in a country where we have choices . . ."
- *Underlining and highlighting.* Key phrases can be underlined or covered with color blocks that make them jump out of the text.
- *The signature and identification.* Celebrities can give special appeal to your message, or use of names that seem familiar and gain from identification: "Decorated World War II Hero" . . . "Member of Congress."
- *Enclosures.* Reply cards, testimonials on separate letterhead, and reprints of news clippings add to the evidence that may lead to desired behavior.

apartment dwellers, boating enthusiasts, hunters, coin collectors, registered voters, users of credit cards, opera patrons, senior citizens, supporters of gun control, opponents of gun control, conservationists, and left-handed bowlers.

Some mailing lists cost thousands of dollars, especially those that identify high-income families with special characteristics. Other lists can be bought more cheaply from magazines aimed at hobbyists or regional audiences. Many organizations, such as noncompeting arts and cultural organizations, routinely exchange mailing lists at no cost to either organization. Commercial direct-mail houses, for a handsome fee, will take care of everything from obtaining the appropriate mailing lists to stuffing and mailing the envelopes for you.

Of course, any organization should carefully develop its own mailing lists by making sure that every person participating in an event sponsored by the organization, every citizen who writes the organization for information, every contributor, every customer, every personal friend of management, every elected official is put in a card file or on a computer list to receive mailings that fall in his or her interest areas.

Now let's look at formats that will deliver your messages effectively and discuss how they are produced.

DESIGNING THE MAILING PIECE

Varied Names

The range of names for direct-mail items suggests the variety that is possible: circulars, folders, booklets, pamphlets, monographs, tracts, catalogs, packets, portfolios, bulletins, broadsheets, manifestos—not to mention pseudo-magazines, pseudo-newspapers, and pseudo-newsletters. Because so many of these terms are associated with the hoopla of marketing and promotion, public relations practitioners working for government departments, public utilities, and regulated industries often prefer to use the more dignified term "fact sheet" to identify any printed matter that provides background information about the organization and/or one of its projects.

Some examples of fact sheets:

- The state government of South Dakota distributes a four-page brochure at meetings of senior citizens to describe a special phone service that enables the elderly to call the state capital on a no-charge 800 number for information about Social Security benefits, consumer fraud, homemaker services, taxes, Medicare, and legal services. As shown in Exhibit 11.2, included with the brochure are a wallet card and a gummed sticker so that the number can be affixed to the telephone.
- Branches of the armed services issue fact sheets in convenient, three-hole-punched, looseleaf format, on such varied topics as "The Chaplain Service" and "Burial in a National Cemetery."
- The National Bureau of Standards issues regular bulletins on the progress of research and development on such projects as cardiac pacemaker batteries, natural gas pipelines, and resistivity standards for silicon power devices.
- Federal and state health agencies, as well as hospitals, health-maintenance organizations, professional medical organizations, and insurance companies, offer printed material on every disease, physical ailment, or mental problem imaginable.

Exhibit 11.2
Brochure for the South
Dakota Tie-Line

*The brochure is shown with
related materials rendered in
similar graphic style.*

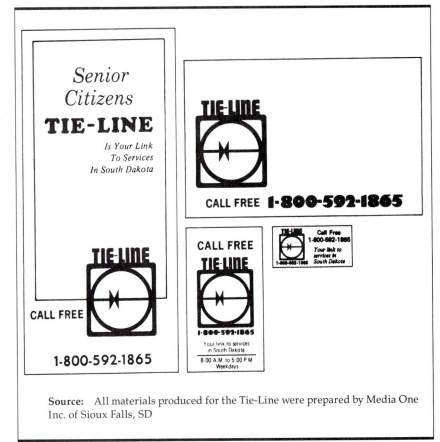

Source: All materials produced for the Tie-Line were prepared by Media One Inc. of Sioux Falls, SD

Common Formats

The format you decide on depends upon the needs of the occasion, the creativity of the PR department, and, of course, the size of the budget.

Because the standard "legal-size" mailing envelope is approximately $4\frac{1}{4}$ by $9\frac{1}{2}$ inches and the most common precut sheet size used in duplicating and quick-print processes is $8\frac{1}{2}$ by 11 inches, it is not surprising that the most popular mailer is what printers call a "two-fold folder" consisting of six panels, each $3\frac{5}{8}$ inches wide and $8\frac{1}{2}$ inches high. When a standard printing press and the standard 23-by-45-inch paper stock are used, a printer can neatly fit ten such brochures per sheet with a minimal loss of paper through trimming.

A common variation is the four-panel, single-fold brochure. Another configuration favored by the travel business is the $8\frac{1}{2}$-by-22-inch sheet, which appears to be the standard six-panel format until it is fully opened to reveal a "poster-sized" inside spread. Still another option is the two-fold, six-panel folder with one of the end panels trimmed to as little as 1½ inches so that it forms a "teaser" flap that partly overlaps another page. Price information or copy that intrigues the readers enough so that they will continue reading inside, might be placed on this small surface. Exhibit 11.3 shows the common brochure formats, how they fold, and how the panels can be numbered for easy reference.

Typically, the right-hand panel on one side of the 8½-by-11 sheet is designed as the cover. The left-hand panel on the same side of the sheet folds around to become the second panel seen by the reader after opening the cover. The middle panel of the same side of the sheet thus becomes the "back" side. Because it occupies the least advantageous position, it may be used for supplementary information. Or it may be left blank, except for a return-address section, so that the brochure can be mailed without an envelope.

The three panels on the reverse side of the sheet read in one of three ways:

■ As a single "poster" spread.
■ As a left-hand single page seen first in conjunction with the inside cover flap, then in conjunction with a two-panel spread at center-right.
■ As three separate and individual panels reading left to right.

The decision, of course, depends on the amount of information, the personality of the design, and whether or not you want the information to be presented in a linear or random fashion.

When the object is to keep the cost down to between five and fifteen cents per brochure, and to present the reader with a familiar artifact, the formats above work best.

If you wish to intrigue the reader or achieve a lavish feeling with your message, you may decide to work with a printer to develop a nonstandard format. A particularly intriguing, if expensive, format is the standard two-fold brochure with an extra flap glued on the right-hand inside panel to form a pocket that holds a sheaf of single sheets in varied heights and colors.

The single-sheet, unfolded broadside is preferable for meeting announcements, grand openings, sale promotions, and handbills to be passed out at rallies. The uncomplicated format suggests a certain directness, urgency, and lack of pretense. Conversely, any multipage format that is glued, stitched, or stapled at the back becomes a booklet and has a sense of permanency. Having attracted an audience to a meeting with handbills, you might then put a durable pamphlet into their hands for more careful consideration.

Exhibit 11.3
8½ × 11 Brochure
Formats

Here are some standard formats for brochures, all using 8½ by 11 sheets of paper. The two-fold, six-panel format may be horizontal or vertical. When the one-fold, four-panel format is used horizontally (bottom), an off-center fold provides a "teaser" that is visible when reading page 1 as well as when viewing the pages 2–3 center spread.

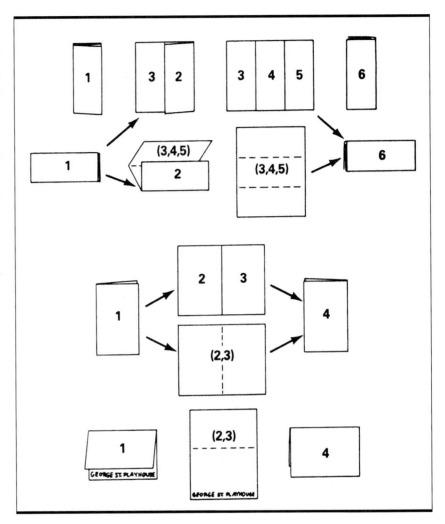

DEVELOPING THE LAYOUT

Arranging information for multipanel presentation creates many design situations that don't occur when you're dealing with the single rectangle of the poster or advertisement. If the brochure is to be disseminated from a rack or holder where it shares space with similar messages, the front cover must be arranged with the title or "teaser" on the top third of the front panel—just as magazine cover designers have to put intriguing information at the top, where it can be seen peeking out over its competitors for attention. While the cover should be unique in some respect, the designer cannot forget that it must be related stylistically to the remaining panels through consistent use of a related type and art materials.

Organizing the text presents another challenge. Essentially, you write the copy to make a complete message in linear form, as for a news release or a feature article. Then it must be divided into suitable segments for each panel. Key sentences should be highlighted by placing them in display type instead of regular text. Care must be taken to keep the presentation balanced, with approximately the same number of titles or headlines on each panel, or a multipanel overline holding the text together.

Selecting the Art

Depending on how many appeals or how many examples you want to provide in one publication, you may decide to use several small pieces of art—line drawings or photos—or you may feel that the impact of a single picture will carry the entire message. For a leaflet decrying the fact that many unwanted pets must be put to death each year because nobody will adopt them, the startling statistic ("One out of three cats in Ourtown will be 'put to sleep' this year") might be most effective if reversed (light lettering over dark image) and placed right over the picture of a cute, furry little kitten.

Will you need to include a coupon, so that the reader can request more information or mail in a contribution? Ideally, it should be on a separate slip of paper so that the main message will not be mutilated once the coupon is removed. Make sure that the type, the art, and the slogan of the main brochure are echoed on the insert. That way they will relate stylistically when they are together, but each also can stand alone. If the budget dictates that the coupon must be torn from the brochure, put it on the flap farthest from the cover, and make sure no important information is removed from the main message when the coupon is torn out.

Some Do's and Don'ts

There may always be good reasons for ignoring accepted rules and practices of design. Nonetheless, the following advice can spare you considerable trial and error:

- ■ Resist the temptation to design an entire brochure so that it reads sideways—that is, so that the 8½-inch measure is the width and the pages are flipped from the bottom. The format is useful when you must present statistical information in tables that are wide because there are many columns of figures. But, ordinarily, it is perceived as "odd" and rather annoying. Never mix horizontal and vertical makeup if you want the reader to get all the way through the multipanel layout.

Exhibit 11.4
Brochure Gets
Wide Distribution

Perhaps the most widely distributed brochure of the 1990s is "A Profile of Older Americans," prepared by the American Association of Retired Persons (AARP) in cooperation with the Administration on Aging (AOA) of the U.S. Department of Health and Human Services.

Printed in two colors (black and burgundy) on a long sheet and folded accordion style (so that the entire brochure can be laid out flat), the piece uses U.S. Bureau of the Census figures and charts to document the number of Americans over sixty-five, their living patterns, income, housing, health care, and other demographic information.

The cover letter transmitting a sample copy of the brochure to educators, civic leaders, business leaders, and media people indicates how multiple copies of the brochure can be obtained for distribution to groups. The same message is found on the last panel of the brochure. The brochure makes no argument or appeal for anything—it serves merely as a data base for those who want to know who and where the elderly are.

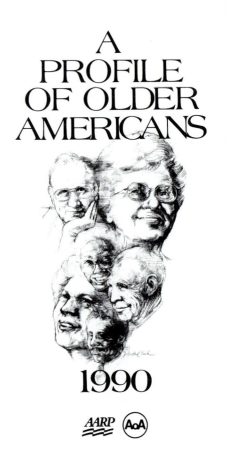

Source: Copyright 1992, American Association of Retired Persons. Reprinted with permissiion.

Bringing lifetimes of experience and leadership to serve all generations.

Dear Colleague:

Older Americans are increasing in impact upon our lives in many ways. And their influence will be felt increasingly in the days ahead--they are currently the fastest-growing group in our society. We will be wise to keep abreast of the changing needs, trends, and lifestyles of this dynamic part of our country's population.

One way to gain a great deal of insight in a short time is to review the publication enclosed, "A Profile of Older Americans: 1990." Statistics, maps, charts and graphs under headings like Marital Status, Living Arrangements, Racial and Ethnic Composition, and Geographic Distribution provide snapshot information at a glance.

"Profiles" is packed with essential data about people aged 65 and older, it's a handy brochure to keep for reference, and it's updated every year so you can always have current information.

If you'd like additional copies, simply write to the address shown on the back panel. Please allow 6-8 weeks for delivery.

"Profiles: 1990" is one of more than 250 publications produced and/or distributed by AARP. For information about the Association and it's programs, services, activities, publications and audiovisual materials, write to the Program Resources Department at the address shown below.

We look forward to hearing from you.

Sincerely,

C. Anne Harvey
Director
Programs Division

Enclosure

American Association of Retired Persons   1909 K Street, N.W., Washington, D.C. 20049   (202) 872-4700

Robert B. Maxwell *President*   Horace B. Deets *Executive Director*

Exhibit 11.5
Preparing the Dummy
for a Brochure

*To prepare a rough dummy
for a brochure—in order to
make a presentation of the
concept to the client, and in
order to show the printer
what you have in mind—use
these standard elements: (1)
a pair of lines, or closed pairs
of lines, to indicate the
headline; (2) a rectangle or
an irregular shape with an
"X" in the center to indicate
art (photo or line drawing);
(3) open or blocked sets of
lines to indicate a block of
text; and (4) a rectangle or
irregular shape marked
"logo" to indicate the name
of the sponsoring
organization. This way the
"feel" of the brochure can be
given even though specific
copy has not yet been
written.*

■ Don't tilt the main title on the cover panel ninety degrees, unless it is one or two simple and easy-to-recognize words such as "We need you" or "Go Navy!" A complex title such as "Ten Reasons Why You Must Support Land Reform" should be run in orthodox fashion. At most, tip it at a thirty-degree angle if a bit of excitement is desired.

■ The information on the cover should either intrigue the reader or clearly label the topic of the contents. The development of the concept begins through the text that is inside. Usually, the cover is most effective if it is approximately one-third type and two-thirds illustration or visual relief (white space). Sometimes, of course, impact is achieved by totally filling the cover space with super-sized type that boldly confronts the reader: "The five minutes you spend reading this pamphlet could save your life!"

■ Some element on each and every panel should "pull" the reader on from the previous panel: an illustration, a headline, a boxed item, a statistical table, or a variation in the layout. Reading an all-text message is hard work; the reader needs incentive.

■ Strive for equilibrium. A brochure should not be top-heavy, bottom-heavy, right- or left-heavy, front-loaded, or crammed at the back. If your only copy adds up to the equivalent of three pages of text, use white space and wider margins in order to spread it out evenly. Avoid the device of dumping a gratuitous piece of art in at the end in order to fill.

■ Is this one of a "family" of messages from your organization? If so, don't forget to use devices that will make the family resemblance obvious: the organization's logo and slogan, distinctive color or border devices, and familiar typefaces.

■ Liven the presentation with separate boxed or bordered items such as maps, directions, "how-to" explanations, and lists. A brochure is supposed to have a longer lifetime than other messages. Nothing assures longevity more than the inclusion of vital information that the recipients realize they may need to use at a later date.

■ The question-and-answer format never seems to outlive its usefulness. It is just about the simplest and most recognizable way to draw the reader in to the material. It is especially effective when the Q. lines appear in larger or bolder type. Questions should be written in an intriguing, punchy style, with a "What if?" or "How come?" aspect that the reader absolutely must resolve before going on. The Q&A format may fall flat, however, when the questions are loaded or petty. ("Why don't the conservatives care about the little man?")

■ If you can afford to spend a bit more, spot color will dress up a brochure—unless you splotch it around with wild abandon. Try using a dark-blue ink throughout for instance; render a title in red for emphasis; or obtain a shading effect by having the printer back one entire panel with a halftone screen to give the brochure extra snap. Restraint and good taste are usually preferable to gratuitous excitement, however. When in doubt, have your printer show you examples of work done in the past. If it has a quality look, you might want to try colored paper stock or spot color on some of your text.

Exhibit 11.6
Avoid Common Pitfalls

Management consultant Howard Upton warns that three common mistakes can negate the value of a costly brochure:

- *Built-in obsolescence.* If information in a brochure is too specific, such as listing all your officers or managers or customers, it may be obsolete soon after your order of five thousand copies is delivered. The remedy: design the brochure so that it can be revised easily from time to time without redoing the whole thing.
- *Ostentation.* Turning the brochure into a tribute to your organization's leader and leading off with a letter or extended quote allegedly from the leader's mouth or typewriter can sink the brochure in a sea of pomposity.
- *Awkward format.* Designers love to play around with odd dimensions and strange folds. That may give "visual impact," but it also can necessitate special envelopes for mailing the brochure. And the odd brochure is less likely to be filed and saved.

Source: Howard Upton, "Manager's Journal: How to Make Your Company Brochure Picture Perfect," *The Wall Street Journal,* November 28, 1988, p. A–12.

WORKING WITH THE PRINTER

Since almost every PR practitioner must design print messages, a working acquaintance with typography and printing is helpful.

It is a waste of both your time and the printer's if you have not sufficiently thought out what it is you want printed. It helps greatly if you have in hand rough layouts or samples of jobs similar to what you are looking for. On the other hand, the worst approach you can take, unless you have an unlimited budget, is to come to a printer with the job so firmly worked out in your mind that you are totally inflexible. Printers will accommodate you, but it may mean jobbing out parts of the project that they can't handle, and you will pay a premium price.

Contact three or four printers far in advance of the time when the work must be done, and obtain samples of their work. You may find one printer who is already doing jobs similar to what you want, which translates into cost savings. Find out what typesetting and other services each printer handles in the shop and what has to be sent to an outside supplier. Time is lost and the price increases every time something must be sent outside. The printer may not want to divulge this information, but if you obtain two or three competitive bids, it will show up in disparities between fairly standard items such as typesetting and binding.

Be sure to let the printer know if it's a one-shot job or whether you will bring similar work periodically. You may get a better price on return business, especially if the printer can save certain graphic materials you intend to reuse.

The printer will need a day or two to work up the bid. Estimating is a fairly exact business, taking into account the normal office and plant overhead that must be apportioned among all the jobs, plus hourly costs of running each piece of machinery involved in your job. It is always useful to ask for a "break-down bid," which indicates how the price differs depending upon the grade of paper, the type of ink, the number of pictures, the multiples of thousands of copies, and the use of spot color. If you have a limited budget, you may have to play off one item against another: Take a better grade of paper and sacrifice the second color of ink, for example.

Write a Careful Contract

Before signing the printer's contract, check three important areas:

1. How much time will it take from the day you deliver all the copy until you receive the printer's proofs? How long will you have to correct and return the proofs? Make sure you will have an opportunity to make a final check of the corrected material before it goes to press. To guarantee that you and the printer understand what you expect in terms of turnaround time, work out a production schedule that shows how many days each of you has for each step in the typesetting, layout, and checking process.
2. How much material can you correct or change without paying extra? Some printers allow up to 10 percent without penalty. Others charge for everything. You should be able to make "normal" corrections, plus a few changes of headlines that don't please you, without paying extra.
3. Where is the job to be delivered? If the contract doesn't specify, then the probable answer is the end of the printer's loading dock. If your publication is to be mailed, you may wish to contract with a printer who has the capability of preparing material for postal delivery and mailing it, thus saving you the bother.

Learn the Basics

You'll be able to work much more closely and effectively with your printer if you learn the basics of typography and printing by taking a

Exhibit 11.7

The Organization-at-a-Glance Brochure

For journalists, fact sheets are most useful if presented on standard 8½ by 11 pages that they can spread out on their desks. For other publics, the facts that present your organization at a glance may be put in a multipage booklet-type brochure that can be mailed, slipped in a larger folder, or handed out to people as they begin a plant tour or enter a meeting.

In its twelve-page fact booklet, revised every year, Warner-Lambert describes itself as "a worldwide company engaged in the development, marketing and manufacture of quality health care and consumer products." Other categories of information in the brochure are:

- Financial highlights. (The balance sheet reduced to its simplest form.)
- Segments of the industry in which the firm is a major player.
- Brief descriptions of major subsidiaries.
- A listing of corporate officers.
- Names and affiliations of the board of directors.
- The Warner-Lambert Creed.
- Key facts about the number of stockholders and employees.
- The address of the company, for those who might desire more information.

Source: Warner-Lambert, *Facts*, 1991 edition.

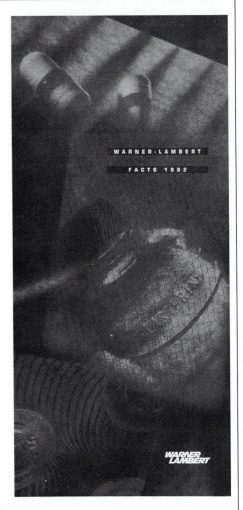

DESCRIPTION OF BUSINESS

Warner-Lambert is a globalized company devoted to developing, manufacturing and marketing quality health care and consumer products. The company's ethical pharmaceutical business is focused on the major therapeutic areas of cardiovascular disease, anticancer and anti-infective chemotherapy and central nervous system disorders. The company's broad range of consumer products includes over-the-counter pharmaceuticals, health care-related personal products, confectioneries including chewing gums and breath mints and shaving products including razors and blades. Warner-Lambert employs some 34,000 people in its operations in more than 130 countries.

FINANCIAL HIGHLIGHTS

	1991	1990
	(Dollars in millions, except per share amounts)	
Net Sales	$5,059.0	$4,686.9
Net Income	34.8*	484.9
Net income per common share	.26	3.61
Cash dividends per common share	1.76	1.52
Research and development expense	423	379

Includes a nonrecurring charge of $418.0 million after-tax or $3.11 per share and a charge of $106.0 million after-tax or $.79 per share to adopt SFAS No. 106, "Employers' Accounting for Postretirement Benefits Other Than Pensions."

CONTENTS

Corporate Headquarters: 201 Tabor Road, Morris Plains, New Jersey 07950 (201) 540-2000

INDUSTRY SEGMENTS

Warner-Lambert produces hundreds of products for sale throughout the world. These products are organized into three distinct lines of business.

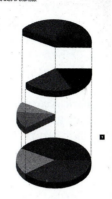

PHARMACEUTICAL PRODUCTS
1991 Sales: $2.0 Billion (40%)
■ Domestic
■ International
Consisting of prescription pharmaceuticals, biologicals, specialty chemicals and empty hard-gelatin capsules.

CONSUMER HEALTH CARE PRODUCTS
1991 Sales: $2.0 Billion (39%)
■ Domestic
■ International
Including over-the-counter health care products, razors and blades, pet care products and Novon specialty polymers.

CONFECTIONERY PRODUCTS
1991 Sales: $1.1 Billion (21%)
■ Domestic
■ International
Consisting of chewing gums, breath mints and chocolate/caramel candies.

LEADING PRODUCTS

Products and product lines with 1991 sales exceeding $100 million

(Dollars in millions)

LOPID	$487	CLORETS	$140
HALLS	360	CERTS	127
LISTERINE	280	ROLAIDS	122
SCHICK	280	BENADRYL	120
TRIDENT	229	TETRA	114
CAPSUGEL	199	PONSTAN/PONSTEL	103
DILANTIN	184	DENTYNE	102
CHICLETS	142		

To develop, produce and market its products to a diverse global audience, Warner-Lambert structures its business into various operating units. The following pages provide an overview of these operations.

graphics course while you are in college. You can teach yourself the basic nomenclature using the additional readings at the end of this chapter.

You'll want to have a working knowledge of printing methods, artwork reproduction, typesetting, and type characteristics.

Printing Methods   Offset, the predominant method used today, gives a flat, even image, and reproduction of art is inexpensive. Letterpress, which some specialized printers still provide, gives a sharper, glossier look. Gravure is used for large jobs where high-quality reproduction of color photographs is important.

Artwork Reproduction   Line drawings, which have no intermediate tones of gray, can be reproduced quickly and cheaply in photo offset, and they can be put directly on the final layout. However, continuous-tone art, including photographs, must be made into a halftone screen, so that the image is created by a pattern of dots that will ink properly.

Typesetting   Some special display types are still set mechanically or even by hand. But most text and display type today is handled through an electronic process called phototypesetting. The material is typed into a computer, which takes care of all spacing and word division, and the finished type comes out of a printer on strips of paper, ready to be pasted directly onto the layout sheet.

Type Characteristics   Every typeface has special characteristics: plain, fancy, bold, light, italic (slanted), or Roman (straight up and down). Each has a "personality" as well: masculine, feminine, humorous, serious, pompous, dignified. And most types belong to a "family" that includes bold, bolder, boldest, light, lighter, lightest, italic, and Roman variations on the same basic design.

NOTES   1.   *Advertising Age,* statistical table: "U.S. Advertising Volume," May 14, 1990, p. 12.

ADDITIONAL READING

———— *Producing Flyers, Folders and Brochures* (Chicago: Ragan Communications, 1984).

Craig, James, *Designing with Type: A Basic Course in Typography* (New York: Watson-Guptill, 1971).

Hanson, Glenn, *How to Take the Fits out of Copyfitting* (Ft. Morgan, CO: Mul-T-Rul Co., 1967).

Hodgson, Richard S., *The Dartnell Direct Mail and Mail Order Handbook* (Chicago: Dartnell, 1990).

International Paper Pocket Pal, 14th ed. (New York: International Paper Co., 1987).

Jones, Gerre, *How to Prepare Professional Design Brochures* (New York: McGraw-Hill, 1976).

Miller, Allen, "Workshop: How to Develop a Direct Mail Piece," *Public Relations Journal* (April 1988), pp. 31–32.

Nelson, Roy Paul, *The Design of Advertising* (Dubuque, IA: Wm. C. Brown, 1977).

Turnbull, Arthur, and Russell Baird, *The Graphics of Communications* (New York: Holt, Rinehart and Winston, 1975).

12

Newsletters and Magazines

Industry and government have long appreciated the need to inform their workers, their customers, and their fellow professionals about what they are doing. They do so through publications modeled after the most successful public media, particularly newspapers and newsmagazines.

Organizations such as the International Association of Business Communicators are working to improve business, industrial, and government publications through workshops, professional meetings for editors and writers, and newsletters. (In fact, the IABC's *Communication World* is a newsletter that carries articles about how to improve newsletters.)

NEWSLETTERS TARGET SPECIFIC PUBLICS

Today, almost every company and organization publishes at least one newsletter or magazine, and some have as many as a dozen aimed at various internal and external audiences. The "house organ," or employee publication, is a newspaper or magazine designed principally for an internal audience. Industrial publications, company publications, and "the business press" are terms usually associated with vehicles packaged primarily for external audiences. Trade publications are aimed at segments of the professionals in a specific area of manufacturing or service, such as *Toy Trade News, Hardware Age,* and *Office Products Industry Report.*

Publications issued by nonprofit organizations usually must manage simultaneously to look competent and yet not too extravagant.

Their editors often prefer merely to call them newsletters. Typically, they have an audience composed of a combination of alumni, academics, contributors, legislators, lobbyists, bureaucrats, industrial leaders, and clergy.

Often the word *News* or *Newsletter* is simply appended to an organization's name to create the publication title. Or the word *Weekly* or *Monthly*. Other commonly used names strive for generality, universality, or all-inclusiveness: *Update, Outlook, Overview, Action, Perspective, Reporter, Scene,* and *Review.*

Whatever the name, the publication usually has two well-defined roles:

1. To present special information to a special audience (the term "special-audience publication" is used by some magazine specialists).
2. To positively reinforce cognitions and attitudes about the sponsoring organization.

SELECTING THE FORMAT

Many PR departments have been putting out their special-audience publications in the same formats for so long that they haven't considered the options. Not that change for the sake of change alone is good. But each format has its strong points.

Newspapers

The tabloid four- or five-column newsprint format is relatively inexpensive and easy to produce. It is well suited to organizations that have plenty of "hard" news items to report, and a single staff member responsible for most of the writing, photography, and editing. If advertising and notices, as well as columns of information concerning the activities of employees or members, are to be carried, the presentation may be modeled directly after the standard weekly suburban newspaper.

Magazines

When longer articles of a feature nature are to be illustrated with color photographs, or when a more durable and prestigious product is desired, the commercial magazine printed on slick, heavy paper is the model. In most states, the external publication circulated by the local or regional Bell System company to leaders of business, industry, education, and government contains photo features in full color, illustrations by area artists,

Exhibit 12.1
Targeting the
Customer

The newsletter format lends itself well to marketing public relations, as demonstrated by *Update*, published by IBM to inform customers about new products and services as well as other advancements made by IBM in computer technology. The four-column tabloid format is "busy," but effective use of white space, color and grey shading makes each item stand out.

(Reproduced courtesy of the International Business Machines Corporation.)

and articles on progress in the state or area, often with no discernible tie-in to Bell's products or programs. The so-called *Time* magazine size is most common—approximately 8½ by 11 inches, but some firms go to 9 by 12 for more impressive impact. Often, the magazine is mailed in an envelope or brown paper sleeve, rather than having a gummed mailing sticker affixed. Again, the special treatment is part of the prestige factor of the magazine.

Minimags

The half-size (approximately 5½ by 8½ inches) magazine says, in effect, "Go ahead, give me a look. Even though you didn't plan on receiving me, a quick browse will be easy." *Everybody's Money*, circulated to federal credit union members throughout the nation by the Credit Union National Association, looks like a particularly bright and colorful slim edition of the *Reader's Digest*. The compact two-column format means that half a dozen short features on personal and family finances can be included in each thirty-two-page issue, along with two or three easily read columns and regular features. The Grumman Corporation's *Overview* packs four or more 500-word features with dramatic black-and-white photographs into a tidy sixteen-page minimag directed at stockholders, subcontractors, and government officials. It is also a handy and effective vehicle for the firm's quarterly report. *Voter*, sent quarterly to all members of the national League of Women Voters, is a two-column, digest-sized magazine printed in black-and-white with spot color. The format includes articles, a news column, one-page reports on important issues, a photo spread highlighting a national or regional meeting, and a regular report from Capitol Hill on developments in important legislation.

Maganews or Magapapers

An imaginative and flexible hybrid format that has emerged in recent years is the maganews or magapaper. With its magazine layout (at least on the first few pages) and generous use of white space, it presents engaging modern graphics. Usually printed in black-and-white offset on newsprint or quality white stock, it blurs the line between both of its typographical antecedents by mixing newspaper column presentation with the more open magazine layout. The *St. Regis News*, employee publication of the paper company, leads with a full-page picture on the cover, then reverts to a fairly orthodox four-column newspaper format inside. *Perspective*, published for the employees of the Prudential Property and Casualty Insurance Company, also leads with a full-art cover. Inside, the features and employee news items are presented in a wide-open style

Exhibit 12.2
Flexible Format

The "magapaper" format provides a clean design when plenty of white space and spot color are used to separate information. *MSM Quarterly*, published by a nonprofit regional planning organization, uses small photos next to headlines on a magazine cover front to draw attention to articles. Inside, the tabloid-sized newspaper format continues the use of such magazine-style design features as blocks of "teaser" copy and generous use of white space to keep the eye engaged and draw the reader into the text.

(Reprinted courtesy of the Middlesex Somerset Mercer Regional Council.)

Exhibit 12.3
Many Formats Serve
Varied Publics

A single employee may receive several newsletters from the company, depending on location of the workplace and status within the organization. A manager at the Morris Plains, N.J., headquarters of the Warner-Lambert Co. would receive the daily *Morning Line* (prepared by a different public relations staff member each day) that summarizes major trade news and national and international events of interest to managers. As an employee at the company headquarters, he or she also would receive the bi-weekly *Plains Talk*, which is produced in-house using desktop publishing. All Warner-Lambert employees throughout the country receive the *WL World* and the special health-oriented publication *Life Wise*, both produced by the corporate public relations staff and printed commercially.

(Reprinted with the permission of Warner-Lambert Co.)

patterned as much after modern corporate advertising as magazine or newspaper layout. Tipped type and generous use of white space are complemented by stark black-and-white photography and drawings.

DESKTOP PUBLISHING OFFERS MANY BENEFITS

For middle (and especially middle-aged) managers, the advent of desktop publishing has meant learning new skills and an entirely new nomenclature—*cursor, icon, pagemaker, megabyte, text-graphics merger, laser printer,* and *electronic clip-art.** For the college student who has been using the Macintosh computer to produce not only term papers and reports, but flyers and announcements for extracurricular activities, desktop publishing comes more naturally than working with a commercial printing service.

Some organizations have moved to desktop production of all publications. Other organizations continue to use commercial printers for their prestige publications intended for a wide range of publics, but they use desktop publishing for "local" newsletters that go only to the employees in one facility, or only to a few hundred managers with common interests.

At Chase Manhattan Bank's international communications division, desktop publishing is used for all internal communication. The main reason is that considerable time is saved because there is no wait while an outside vendor processes material. When material will go to external publics, the rough work is done in-house, and then it is sent to outside graphic artists for polishing before it is printed by an outside vendor.[1]

---

* *Cursor* The blinking dot, line, or arrow on the screen of a computer monitor that shows you where you are working on a document.

Icon A pictorial representation of a function that you might wish to use. Example: a trash can, for information you want to discard.

Layout Package A software program such as Pagemaker or Quark Express that enables you to lay out an entire page of type and graphics for use in a newsletter.

Megabyte A unit for measuring computer memory or information storage capacity.

Text–Graphic Merger A software system for arranging your newsletter text in columns and positioning your art where you want it in relation to the text.

Laser Printer A moderately priced to expensive printer that uses laser technology to achieve the crisp black images needed for high-quality reproduction of text and graphics.

Electronic Clip-art Software packages that include a selection of standard line drawings of every category of information; the electronic equivalent of print clip-art books.

Exhibit 12.4
Quick . . . and
User-Friendly

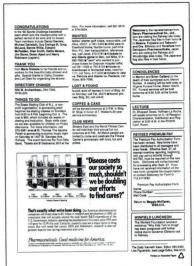

Ask people what they want in a computer system, and the answer is simple: I want information quickly, and in a format that serves my needs.

The same applies to company publications. That's why Merck & Co. went to a daily, two-sided, one-page publication. It's a quick read for busy managers when they come to their desks in the morning.

Page one summarizes developments that affect the company, personnel changes, new-product introductions, and research findings.

Page two features employee news, announcements, and the most popular item of all: classified ads that employees can place for free, either to seek or sell goods or services. Because many employees own company stock, the previous day's closing price is posted in a box on page one.

(Reprinted courtesy of Merck & Co.)

Important Questions to Ask about "Desktop"

Desktop publishing has caused a rush of excitement through the world of public relations. The very phrase suggests ease of preparation as well as savings realized by the elimination of outside vendors. But desktop publishing is not a panacea; it may not be useful for all organizations. Ask the following questions if your operation is considering a move to desktop:

- *Will it pay for itself?* The computer with the power to handle sophisticated software programs, the programs themselves, and laser printers are an investment for your organization. They should pay for themselves within a few years, because new systems will come along and you will want to move on to them. Get fresh bids from your outside vendors—let them know you're considering desktop publishing—and then calculate the savings, if any. Remember that outside vendors now are using the same systems, and so their costs may be lower and their service faster than it was in the past.

- *Will we use it often enough?* An organization that puts out a single monthly or quarterly newsletter may find it hard to justify the expense of the system. Desktop publishing makes the most sense when you are putting out several frequent publications, especially if you put out daily or weekly newsletters.

- *Do we have the expertise?* Even with the most sophisticated and "user-friendly" software, designing and executing a desktop newsletter for the first time takes about as long as building the Great Pyramids. Someone in the organization has to become the resident expert, figure out the shortcuts, and develop the formats for producing a publication on desktop. If you have that person, and if that person has enough work to make desktop publishing a day-in, day-out task, then moving to desktop can make sense.

- *Can we do parts of the job in-house?* If complete desktop publishing isn't the answer, is it possible to cut down on charges from outside vendors by doing part of the work for your publications? Can you prepare all of the text, then give it to the printer on disks? Can you prepare your charts and other graphics using the same software you use for making overheads and slides?

Use a Consultant

Some organizations "luck out" when anybody from the principal in the agency on down to the mail clerk is a computer nut who just loves to spend entire weekends putting together a desktop publishing system. If you don't know such a person, the money charged by a consultant will be well spent. Be prepared to tell the consultant what is important about your publications, what changes you have been contemplating, what flexibility is possible, and what publications from other organizations are models for what you would like to do. Make sure the consultant is not only part of the decision to purchase equipment, but also part of the set-up and start-up phase of switching to desktop publishing.

The "additional readings" section of this chapter includes a large number of resources for those interested in learning more about the technical requirements of setting up a desktop publishing system.

LAYOUT

Designing, or laying out, a print publication is a challenging job. It can be vexing because so much information must somehow be fit in limited space. But it also can be rewarding when the results are pleasing to the eye and focus attention on the desired pictures and articles. We will discuss newsletters in this section, but the principles apply also to magazines and other print formats.

Placing the Basic Elements

Your printer or office-supply firm can provide layout sheets marked off in fractions of inches, so that you can plan each page or spread (pair of facing pages). The lines on the layout forms are blue, and the editor makes all of the sketches and notations with a light-blue pencil. Why? Because light blue does not photograph in the offset process, and thus the color is "invisible."

Layout means placement of the four basic elements of typographical design:

1. Body type (text)
2. Display type (headlines, titles, "teasers")
3. Art (photos, drawings, graphic elements)
4. White space (air, or "visual freedom")

Each page or two-page spread goes through three phases of preparation:

1. Rough layout, or dummy, in which the editor sketches in the four basic elements to help visualize the final product.
2. Comprehensive layout, or "comp," which is a mock-up precise enough for the printer and the editor to measure the exact space needed for each item.
3. Mechanical layout—a paste-up of the type and halftones into a camera-ready layout suitable for photographing and making into a printing plate. If you have a light table, cutting and pasting tools, and a supply of graphic materials, you can develop the skills necessary to prepare your own mechanicals. Most editors, however, prefer to let the printer take over once the comp has been approved.

Exhibit 12.5
Working with a
Newsletter Designer

Because most public relations people don't have extensive experience with design, and because clients expect good-looking newsletters and magazines, you may find yourself working with a designer—an expert at typography, layout, and graphic arts. A professional designer brings visual communication savvy to the job, but you'll still have the responsibility of making sure that your client's objectives are being met. The designer has the "look" in mind; you have to keep the target public's interests in mind.

Editor's Workshop, a newsletter for newsletter editors, suggests that the person assigned to work with the designer should read books about layout and production, tour a printshop, even take a course at a trade school to become conversant with design concepts and terms.

The editors of *EW* warn that designers sometimes get carried away, so it's important to establish a careful budget at the same time you're giving the designer your plans. At the same time, you'll want to allow the designer creative freedom to try colors, shapes, and sizes that you might not have known you would like.

Most important, you have to make sure the designer meets your deadlines. The key is learning how much time a designer needs to develop a concept and, if necessary, he or she must be willing to re-do the work to your specifications.

Source: *Editor's Workshop* (February), 1991, pp. 10–11.

How Many Columns?

When you first sit down to design the format for your newsletter, the initial decision involves the number of columns per page. A single full-width column of type is difficult to read. The single-column newsletter format is only feasible for "news-flash" business letters and economic forecasts, which break the text up into short, one-paragraph items.

The two-column format allows plenty of room for type, since only a small amount of space is lost to the "gutters," or white space between columns. But there are few layout variations in two-column format, and it will be difficult to make each issue of the publication look fresh. That's why the three- and four-column formats are so popular. They permit all sorts of combinations of one-, two-, and multiple-column items. Following the lead of the major national newsmagazines, which reintroduced thin lines called "rules" between the columns, some newsletters have gone to four-column format with slightly smaller type.

One reason so many editors prefer the three-column format is that the editor can use one-column "mug shots" for pictures of individuals, two-column shots for a small number of people, and three-column display for special art that is worthy of major attention. The choice of three headline widths also helps the editor to "grade" the news better and to offer greater variety in sizes of type.

Another currently popular layout development is basically the three-column format modified to a "one-and-two" style, with the outside column (left on a left-hand page, right on a right-hand page) run as a single column, and the other two columns set double-width. *Hope News*, the quarterly publication of Project Hope, follows basically a two-column format, but uses three columns for picture spreads and news-notes sections on the top two-thirds of single pages—proving that an editor can even mix-and-match formats with success.

The three-column format has also been transmuted into a kind of one-column format where the single main column is at least as wide as two-thirds of the page, with all headlines and pictures stacked in the free column at the left. It's an idea that calls for generous use of white space and careful planning, but it pays off as an attention-getter. Whenever the editor goes to multiple columns, white space must be added, and thus there is shrinkage in the amount of copy that can be included in the standard number of pages. The narrower columns can lead to more hyphenation and odd spacing of letters. But most editors feel the flexibility gained makes the tradeoffs worthwhile.

As the layout for an issue of a newsletter takes shape, the editor must assure that the edited material precisely fits the assigned space on the layout sheet. "Copyfitting" means developing a counting and estimating scheme for headlines and text. Several of the additional reading suggestions at the end of this chapter explain the systems for estimating type.

Graphic Elements

The logo, slogan, and proprietary color selected to represent the organization (Kodak's yellow and Campbell Soup's red-orange, for example) should appear prominently in every publication's nameplate. In fact, the announcement of any changes in such corporate identity elements usually is made first in a newsletter article and picture.

If your organization publishes several publications for special audiences, the family tie should be apparent in typeface and graphic styles. People who come across a publication for which they are not the usual audience should nevertheless recognize the organization's personality and style.

Don't underestimate the ability of such basic graphic elements as cutoff rules and border treatments to create the style and "feel" of your publication.

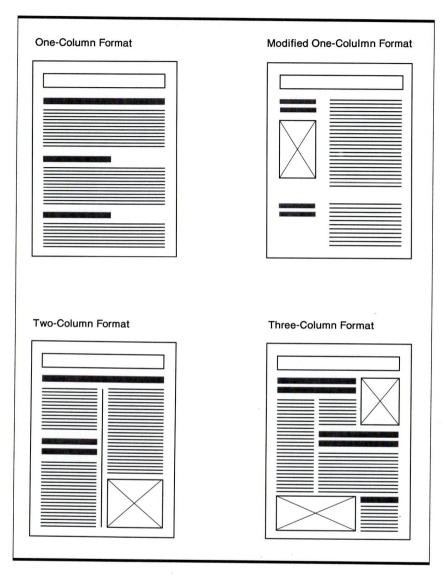

Exhibit 12.6
Basic Formats for
$8^1/_2 \times 11$ Newsletter

The publication editor must develop a production schedule to assure the organization's ability to publish one or more periodicals on time. The lead time for a publication—the time needed to develop article ideas, make assignments to writers and artists, and allow the printer to set type, make up pages, and do the complete printing job—typically is two to three months. This means that an editor may be working on the phases of three different issues of a monthly publication at any one time.

Of course, the production schedule for a weekly newspaper may be as little as ten days, while the annual report's preparation literally

**SETTING THE
PRODUCTION
SCHEDULE**

CHECKLIST ✔ Proofing Your Newsletter

Before signing off on a printer's proof of your newsletter and approving the job for printing, make sure you check for the following common errors:

✔ *Nameplate* Update the volume number and the date—printers tend to leave the information from the last issue in place.

✔ *Folio lines* Go through the publication and make sure that the proper page numbers are in place and that the sequence is correct.

✔ *Photo cutlines* Read each cutline carefully and make sure it matches the picture. Pictures that are the same size sometimes get dropped into the wrong "hole" in the makeup.

✔ *Headlines* Read each carefully, and look for heads that have been switched because both are the same size and font.

✔ *Names* Check all names of people against the original copy; no error causes as much grief as a misspelled name.

✔ *Continuations* Match all swing-arounds on the same page (bottom of one column to the top of the next column) to make sure the text reads right. Check all jumps (from one page to another page) to make sure that the "to" and "from" lines correctly identify the other page.

✔ *Widows* Look for ugly lines of type that got separated from the rest of the paragraph when the printers put the text into the assigned space. If the printers can't bring a lonely word or phrase (called a "widow") around to where it joins the main block of type, then strike out words or a sentence to achieve the clean look of an unbroken paragraph.

✔ *Rules* Scan through the entire publication to make sure that cutoff rules at the ends of columns, rules between columns of type, and any other lines around boxes and under headlines are in place and used consistently.

✔ *Greyness* Flip through and make sure that each page has some variation in tone. If you find a page with no art and no graphic interest, have the printer add a light grey "screen" behind one short item in order to get some depth and variety on the page.

✔ *Broken or tipped material* Be on the lookout for letters with broken parts (especially the ascenders and descenders) or lines that have come unstuck and are not perfectly horizontal.

---

takes an entire year. Whatever the period of time, the editor must spell out which activities take place, in what order, and with what time separation. Here, for example, is an abridged production schedule for a monthly magazine (numbers indicate how many days prior to the mailing date, which is the twenty-fifth day of the month preceding the month of the issue):

Exhibit 12.7
Make Use of a
Mailing Service

If your newsletter is distributed internally, to employees, don't depend on a "bundle drop" system, where bundled copies of the newsletter are placed near the time clock or in the lunchroom. Employees may not make the effort to take a newsletter, and they won't consider a newsletter fetched from a pile on the floor to be an important source of information. Distribute newsletters through your organization's mail system, preferably with the name of each employee on his or her own copy.

External mailings are a different matter. In order to take advantage of the post office's discounts for bulk rate mail that is pre-sorted by ZIP code (including the ZIP + 4 codes that get the best rate), you'll want to use a mailing service. In effect, the mailing service pays for itself, since its rates for attaching labels to your newsletter, bagging by ZIP code, and delivering the bags to the post office, gets you a discount of as much as 80 percent. The postal rules are so confusing, and the systems for preparing a mailing so complicated, that the experts attend workshops and refresher courses to keep up with latest trends.

Freed of the overwhelmingly specialized job of preparing a mailing, your staff still has an important role: maintaining an up-to-date mailing list with ZIP + 4 codes. As a manager, you'll want to make sure that those who receive your newsletter find a reminder and possibly even a form in every issue for notifying you of address changes. For a fee, the post office will return undeliverable newsletters with correct new addresses if you put the words "Address Correction Requested" in the address area of your publication.

90—Story list completed. Assignments to writers.

70—First drafts due from writers. Conferences.

60—Assignments to photographers and staff artist.

50—Final drafts due from writers. Editing.

40—All art must be in. Prepare rough dummies. All material to printer for typesetting by now.

25—Proofreading. Prepare comprehensive.

10—Printer prepares mechanical. Final corrections.

0—Distribution.

GENERATING STORY IDEAS

Reader surveys may help the editor to know generally what the readers like. But it is the editor's job to generate specific ideas. It is extremely easy for a periodical to get in a rut, to become predictable—and thus irrelevant. This is especially true when the publication runs a scant

Exhibit 12.8
Insurance Newsletter
Serves Special Functions

Focus

Published Bimonthly for Employees of the Agency & Brokerage Group

Mass Marketing Department Aims At Increasing Agent, Broker Generated Business

In July, 1990, fueled by the rapid growth of mass marketing of insurance through third party sponsors, Continental Insurance began broadening and focusing its approach to this market segment by merging the forces of Agency and NBS into one mass marketing department for the Agency and Brokerage Group. And with premium volume up by 26% during the first quarter of 1991, the department is well on its way toward its year-end goal of $88 million in written premium.

"Our strategy has been one of controlled growth," explains Dan Sherlock, Vice President and head of the department, "and the field force of both Agency and NBS play a critical role in the execution of our strategic plan. We want to become recognized as an innovative company within the mass marketing arena, and we'll accomplish that by working closely with key producers who aggressively participate in group business."

Teamwork is the key. The department is comprised of four home office account executives, each of whom is responsible for a particular section of the country, and one account executive to coordinate internal underwriting and administrative functions.

In the field, regional mass marketing coordinators help develop their respective territories by working closely with producers and tracking down leads. "I work as a coordinator between all parties involved, including the administrating agent, the sponsor, underwriters in the regional office and home office staff," explains Ron Ratliff, Mass Marketing Coordinator, Agency Great Plains Region. "I'll even make a physical

inspection of numerous risks with the producer involved."

Adds Joel Parise, Mass Marketing Coordinator, Agency Rocky Mountain Region. "We don't just look at new mass marketing programs, but ones that have already been developed by a competitor. We examine where we can improve upon what an account has ... provide better service and expanded coverages, and often times accounts will roll over to Continental. Plus, we want to maintain our existing programs ... constantly review and analyze to make

certain the match is still good."

Still, 1991 plans call for the writing of 29 new programs. How will these new accounts be developed? Either one of two ways. "When we find a class of business we want to write, we'll select a producer and work with them to develop the program," explains Ratliff. "We prefer, however, for producers to follow our lead and develop the contacts ... the ideas. The nature of their jobs puts them in contact with many prospects. For example, we recently developed a program for the National Cable Television Operators Association. One of our agents knew the head of the association. We reviewed the needs of association members, added a few enhancement coverages, and put a program together for them."

"The key is getting out and talking to producers, and showing them the success we and other producers have had," explains Jim Titus, Home Office Mass Marketing Account Executive, with responsibility for the Great Lakes, Great Plains and Gulf Coast Regions. "We need to point to the results ... that this is a profitable, stable class of business."

Parise points to the success the unit has had with the American Horse Show Association. Begun as a local program in Denver, it has since been rolled out in the Great Plains Region, and will gradually be expanded to other regions as it's rolled out countrywide.

"We recently held a meeting in Florida (for the Central Zone) that was attended by Farm Directors from several regions, area Territorial Office Managers, and numerous local agencies," details Parise. "We conducted a presentation on how the mass marketing program works, and it went

over very well."

"The meeting was a unique approach in that we brought staff in from other territories," explains Helena Grebis, Home Office Mass Marketing Account Executive, responsible for the Central Zone region. "Most agents are very interested. We point out that in the future, a large portion of consumers will be purchasing their insurance through these third party groups. Now when they see similar opportunities, they'll think Continental."

How does it all come together? "More often than not," explains Linda Sproule, Mass Marketing Coordinator, New England Region, "a producer will have an 'in' with an association, usually due to an individual policy they've written for a member of that association. For example, an agent came to us wanting to write a golf program for the Massachusetts Golf Association. Based on information the agent provides us with — What the association's current program looks like. What their requirements are. Loss history, and so on — our regional team will review and determine if it's a program worth pursuing. If so, the information is sent to Doug Treiber, our account executive in Cranbury, for further review. Sometimes, we'll bring the agent into Cranbury to provide additional information on a particular risk we might not be familiar with. If it's accepted, we put together a proposal which is first presented to the agent, and then to the association. We explain how the program will be marketed and the support materials Continental provides, who Continental Insurance is, and, above all, what program coverages and ser-

Continued on page 6

Getting Involved	**Continental Kudos Program**		**Special Inserts**		**Expanded Authority**
Agency and Brokerage Group's action volunteers help generate positive public relations	Now it's our producers' chance to say "thanks" to Group employees for a job well done.		Continental Style... Use the special order form insert to purchase merchandise containing the Continental logo.	We'd like to know your thoughts on *Focus*. Please take a few moments to fill out the enclosed Readership Survey.	New advance technical training seminars help expand field expertise and authority levels.
2	**3**				**6**

Unlike general-purpose employee newsletters, *Focus* is published specifically for the Agency and Brokerage Group of the Continental Insurance Company and it aims to stimulate employee involvement in marketing programs. Publications like *Focus* that are aimed at the special interests of a target group are more likely to be read than newsletters aimed at all employees.

Teaser boxes along the bottom of the front page feature articles inside the oversized newsletter, which folds out to triple width. The box with spot color overlay ("Special Inserts") calls attention to two items stuffed into the main publication. One enables employees to order shirts, caps, jackets, and pens with the company logo. The other is a readership survey. This single package shows the many functions that can be performed by an employee publication.

Technical notes: *Focus* is produced in-house using Quark software on a Macintosh computer, and a laser printer with Linotron unit and cameras. It is sent to the printer "camera-ready" on film, meaning that the printer's only job is to reproduce the publication prepared by the public relations department.

(Reprinted courtesy of Continental Insurance.)

four pages, and several reports, columns, and departments are "must-run" matter, leaving precious little space for enterprise material.

Here are some ways a good editor gets story ideas:

■ All meetings held by the organization are potential "story sessions" from the editor's point of view. Most meetings are called to discuss problems and their solutions, new programs, or ways that an organization is responding to its environment. All of these topics can generate articles.

■ The editor should meet frequently with department heads and committee chairpersons to become familiar with the workings of the organization and to learn about new developments.

■ An occasional walking tour of the plant or premises will help the editor to see things from an outsider's point of view. Often, physical changes are made without thinking about their news value. Department bulletin boards can yield stories.

■ Distribution of a simple form for reporting news items can bring in some worthwhile information. It is useful to set up a network of "stringers"—one worker in each department who is responsible for reporting on human-interest items or developments that may not have been discussed in meetings attended by public relations personnel. If the editor can pay $25 for each short article used, the stringers probably will be fairly productive.

■ The editor should read related publications for story suggestions. A consultant for state dental association newsletters suggests that editors of county and regional dental newsletters might read the state and national journals, then think of ways to "localize" topics by interviewing dentists in their area. Many editors exchange subscriptions in order to keep up with what others in the field are doing.

■ The editor should affiliate with organizations dedicated to improving house organs, such as PRSA, IABC, and the American Business Press. There are specialized associations for editors of banking publications, Defense Department organs, medical journals, etc. Most hold occasional workshops in major cities.

■ A postpublication critique, in which the entire PR staff analyzes the effectiveness of the current issue, should generate ideas for the next one. A quarterly planning meeting should be used to generate ideas for the next three or four issues. Both of these devices can enhance the reputation of the newsletter editor within the organization, since outsiders such as department heads can be invited to help strengthen the role and the quality of the publication.

1. Suzanne Porter, "Desktop Publishing Report: It's Nifty, But Is It Necessary?" *Creative New Jersey* (May/June 1990), p. 8.

NOTES

Beach, Mark, *Editing Your Newsletter* (Portland, OR: Coast to Coast Books, 1988).

Beach, Mark, Steve Shepro, and Ken Russon, *Getting It Printed* (Portland, OR: Coast to Coast Books, 1986).

Bivens, Thomas, "Newsletters and House Publications," in *Handbook of Public Relations Writing* (Lincolnwood, IL: NTC Business Books, 1988).

Bove, Tony, and Cheryl Rhodes, *Desktop Publishing with Pagemaker* (New York: Wiley, 1987).

Brigham, Nancy, *How to Do Leaflets, Newsletters and Newspapers,* (Somerville, MA: Economic Affairs Bureau, Inc., 1982).

Davis, Frederic, and John Barry, *Newsletter Publishing with Pagemaker* (New York: Dow-Jones-Irwin, 1988).

Hudson, Howard, *Publishing Newsletters,* 2d ed. (New York: Scribners, 1988).

Lichty, Tom, *Design Principles for Desktop Publishers* (New York: Scott-Foresman, 1989).

MacGibbon, John, "Publishing Comes of Age: Pagemaker 2.0," *Communication World* (November 1987), pp. 30–32.

Maxwell, Linnea, "Taking Desktop Publishing One Step Further," *Communication World* (November 1988), pp. 30–32.

McGowan, Andrew J., and Josephine Curran, "How to Create Desktop Publications," *Public Relations Journal* (March 1986), pp. 35, 37–38.

Nelson, Paul R., "How to Use Graphics and Printing," in *Lesly's Handbook of Public Relations and Communications,* 4th ed. (Chicago: Probus Publishing, 1991), pp. 503–524.

Nelson, Roy Paul, *Publication Design,* 3d ed. (Dubuque, IA: Wm. C. Brown, 1983).

Pavlik, John, "Why Employees Read Company Newsletters," *Public Relations Review* (Fall 1982), pp. 22–23.

Rose, Douglas, "An Update on Desktop Software," *Communication World* (November 1988), pp. 14–18.

Spiegelman, Marjorie, "Eye-Catching Pages," *Publish!* (September 1986), pp. 34–35.

Wales, LaRae H., *A Practical Guide to Newsletter Editing and Design,* 2d ed. (Ames, IA: Iowa State University Press, 1978).

ADDITIONAL READING

13

Photographs and Illustrations

We noted in Chapter 8 that the ability to supply or arrange exciting "visuals" increases the chances of placing a story on television. In truth, every medium needs photographs and illustrations. Presented with two articles of equal value, the magazine or newspaper editor is more likely to choose the one that is accompanied by "art."

Since preparing photographs for dissemination to the media is a skill most PR people need at one time or another, we'll examine the ways in which practitioners place art. First, however, let's look at the important task of selecting which visual medium fits your objectives best. Then we'll discuss management considerations and the basics of setting up an in-house photo operation. Finally, we'll see how to prepare pictures and illustrations for layouts and displays.

SELECTING THE VISUAL MEDIUM

The danger in public relations is that "the tool available is the tool used." That is, if a department or an agency has the capability to make slides or a unit that does video or a manager who loves still photography, the preferred visual medium will be selected without considering carefully the objectives for the public relations program. The visual media are not interchangeable; each has its strengths and weaknesses. Before we look at still photography in this chapter and other visual media in the chapter that follows, let's analyze the "upside" and the "downside" of the most popular visual media.

Still Photography: The Benefits

Photo displays are a familiar and safe medium. The audience likes to look at pictures on the wall, and individuals particularly like the fact that they can proceed at their own pace. In that sense, still photography is the most personal of the visual media, since the viewer can edit the time of exposure to each picture. Unlike other visual media where "what you see in the viewfinder is what will appear on the screen," still photographs can be cropped to eliminate parts of the picture that detract from the message, and they can be trimmed for unusual shapes or proportions that fill well in a layout of type, graphic art, and photographs.

Still Photography: The Drawbacks

Granted that still photographs are familiar and safe, they may lack the novelty and excitement of moving images for an audience accustomed to television. We noted that the viewer is the final editor. With displays of still photographs, that may mean that some persons skip over sections or move through so fast that important parts of the message are not retained. Finally, believe it or not, quality photography can be expensive to obtain and mount properly for display—more expensive than the basic slide show, and costlier even than some simple video productions made with the most popular equipment. The best photographers are paid well, and prints of the size used in displays may cost $25 to $75 each, contrasted with a few dollars per transparency used in a slide show.

Slide Shows: The Benefits

Most public relations people find slide presentations the easiest to produce. Anyone with practice using a 35 mm camera can take passable photos and select those that will tell the story and have positive impact. Slide shows are easy to assemble using an inexpensive illuminated organizer and then inserting the pictures in a standard carousel for projection. It's easy to change a show by adding slides as new information is available and taking out shots that don't get the desired audience reaction. The pace of the show can be varied—slower for audiences that are interested in all the information you have; faster for audiences that just want to touch on the main points or that appear to be getting restless.

Slide Shows: The Drawbacks

Boredom is a risk if the audience members have been overexposed to too many dull or poorly organized presentations of shots that weren't

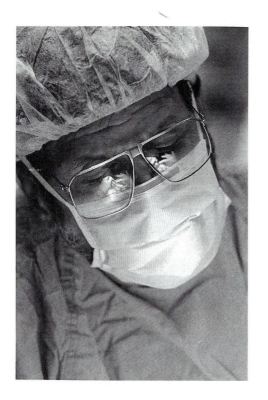

Pictures here and on the next page by photographer Nat Clymer demonstrate the artistry, imagination, and care that professionals demand for quality publications such as company brochures, employee newsletters, and annual reports.

Top left:
Cropping tightly to the physician's face increases the viewer's appreciation of the tenseness of the operating-room situation. The reflections of the operation in the lenses of the subject's glasses is a stunning way to illustrate the extreme care necessary in a medical procedure.

Top right:
The construction shot uses backlighting to create a silhouette and a dark-and-light counterplay that increases the drama of small figures working on a big project.

Bottom:
The portrait of two owners of a printing company with their new press could have been ordinary if the photographer had not chosen an elevated vantage point and assured that the entire pressroom was in focus and adequately lighted.

The shot of a mother picking up her child from the corporate daycare center is informal and looks unposed. But the photographer has controlled very carefully for lighting and focus so that the viewer readily absorbs the entire context of the situation.

carefully selected. Consistency of presentation can vary greatly from one performance to another, especially if various spokespersons take turns doing the narration. Lack of preparation by the presenter may lead to miscues of sound and visual coordination—the wrong slide may be shown on the screen as an unrelated part of the script is recited.

Film: The Benefits

Today most "film," even if it was shot using film equipment, is transferred to video for showing, because of the ease of using video playback equipment. For larger audiences, the full-screen film presentation in a totally darkened auditorium still has the greatest visual impact and is most likely to completely capture the attention of viewers. That's why films are still used at major exhibitions such as world's fairs, commercial museums, and pavilions at EPCOT Center in Florida's Disney World.

Film: The Drawbacks

Projecting a film calls for specialized equipment and a trained operator. The proper room must be found. Projection equipment can malfunction, disrupting presentation of the message. The costs of preparing a sound film greatly exceed the costs of producing a video, because picture and sound are recorded separately and must be joined through editing and post-production in a film laboratory. Thus films take longer to process and prepare than a video.

Video: The Benefits

Video (discussed in Chapter 9) is produced on versatile, easy-to-use electronic equipment that records sight and sound simultaneously. Almost every institution, from hotels to hospitals to universities, has plenty of playback equipment available, and most anybody can figure out how to use it in a few minutes. Video can be shown in a lighted room, making it easy for viewers to take notes. The tape can be stopped for discussion, answering questions, or simply to break up the presentation with spoken commentary.

Video: The Drawbacks

The available playback system may limit audience size. It is offputting to try to view a tape on a nineteen-inch monitor in a square room with fifty people. The quality of the visual image often is less sharp than that found in other visual media, and frequent use of the tape may have left it scratched. Poor playback equipment may further deteriorate the quality of the visuals and the sound. Video messages that aren't up to the quality of shows seen on networks or cable may suffer in comparison, and the attention of the audience may wander.

At some point, every public relations department is faced with a decision: Do we commission our photos to be taken by outside photographers, or do we set up our own photo operation, including a fully equipped darkroom? Freelance photographers may seem expensive, since their charges must reflect considerable overhead and the cost of getting one good print out of scores of shots and dozens of trial prints. Top-flight commercial photographers do not blush at charging $1,000 for a single photograph, when getting it involves half a day of shooting and countless hours in the darkroom working to achieve the perfect print. With experience, a PR department learns to appreciate the value of a good freelance photographer.

There can be good reasons for setting up an in-house photo operation. In a fairly small public relations department, a staff member who has an interest and expertise in photography can add a much-needed dimension to the print media effort. In a larger shop, there may be enough regular work to warrant employing a full-time photographer.

ORGANIZING THE PHOTO OPERATION

CHECKLIST ✔ Working with a Photographer

If you use an outside photographer, make sure that your contract—written or otherwise understood—covers the following important items:

✔ Who owns the photographs? If you pay the minimum rate for shooting the photos, the photographer may retain the rights to the photos and may require additional compensation each time you request copies. If you wish to retain rights, you must pay the photographer accordingly and stipulate that negatives are to be turned over to you for your use.

✔ What credit will be given for the photographs? Most photographers stipulate in their contracts how they are to be credited for their photos. If your organization does not wish to credit the photographer, that must be stipulated in the contract, and extra payment may be required.

✔ Who has the right to approve the photographs? Absent any other stipulation, the photographer may demand payment upon presentation of proofs or prints that fulfill the assignment. Provisions for re-takes, delays because of weather or other cancellations, and re-processing for special reasons may be written into the contract.

✔ Cancellation fee. If the client decides not to use any of the photos after viewing the proofs, a cancellation fee may be paid, according to the contract.

✔ Who pays expenses? If the photographer incurs expenses while taking the photos, your organization should pay the costs if you expect to retain exclusive rights to the photos. On the other hand, the photographer may be liable for the expenses if the photographer retains the right to make further commercial use of the pictures.

✔ Who has final approval of the pictures? Your organization should designate a representative to attend the shooting of the pictures and to select from the proofs the shots that are to be reproduced. Absent these provisions, it is up to the photographer's judgment.

The small department probably will need $3,000 to set up a basic darkroom, and it will be worth it. The big-time operator will need $15,000 to set up a darkroom, but it will be worth it. Just consider the $50 to $100 or more per shot that a freelancer must charge, and you will see how quickly a staff photographer can pay off.

Whatever the source of photographs, the public relations department must be prepared to organize and keep track of the many photographs it commissions. A numbering and cataloging system should be instituted so that every single picture has its own identification and can be found in the proper place. As each roll of film is shot, negatives are placed in plastic holders, contact sheets are made, and each strip of contacts is serially stamped—92-24 identifies the twenty-fourth set of negatives filed during 1992. The code number 92-24-15 written on the back of a print indicates that it is frame 15 from the 92-24 set. This is the only way to keep track of individual shots in an operation where thousands of pictures are taken each year.

Editors of newspapers and magazines usually begin laying out their pages by selecting the pictures that will "anchor" each display. Photos, in other words, are given the best display on the printed page. And that is why they are so important in public relations plans.

SUPPLYING PHOTOS TO THE MEDIA

Whether a photograph accompanies a story or stands alone, the following specifications are fairly standard:

- The 8-by-10-inch photo is the preferred size for submissions to newspapers and magazines that use black-and-white photos, although the 5-by-7 is sufficient for a head-and-shoulders shot of an individual; some public relations operations stretch their budget by using the 4-by-5 for mug shots. The larger sizes ensure that the picture will be reduced for publication rather than enlarged, which is easier for the editor and results in better engraving quality. The 35 mm color transparency is the most common format for submitting photos to a magazine that uses color shots.
- The photo should be glossy for submission to any print medium. For television, however, provide a matte-finish print that will not reflect into the television lens. (For glossy finish, dry a photo against a smooth metal surface; for matte finish, dry it pressed against woven cloth.)
- Your chances of placing a picture, especially in smaller media with low engraving budgets, are enhanced by providing "camera-ready" halftone reproductions of photographs already cropped to standard two- and three-column newspaper widths. That means you go to the extra expense of having a printer make the halftone and reproduce multiple copies of it on slick paper. But if it induces more editors to use the material because it can be pasted right onto their layouts, the expense is worth it.
- Cutline information is typed double-spaced, just like the news release, and duplicated on white paper. Glue or tape is applied to a one-inch fold of the sheet, which is then affixed to the back of the photograph. The remainder of the sheet is folded over to protect the surface of the glossy photo, which is unusable if it becomes scratched or soiled.

Two kinds of photos are submitted to trade magazines. The first may be a straightforward shot of the product, with brand name visible. The second is more dramatic or intriguing—in this case, a photomicrograph showing the crystal clusters of alpha-2 interferon produced by Schering-Plough Corporation using genetic engineering technology. The product is used by leukemia patients to self-medicate.

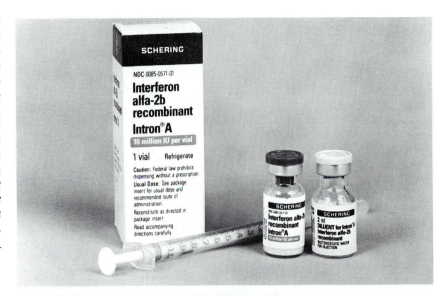

Photo courtesy of Schering-Plough, Corp.

Public relations photos do not normally carry a credit line for the photographer, unless the shot is provided by a well-known artist with the agreement that credit be given. It is assumed by the receiving news media that actual or tacit permission has been granted by all identifiable persons in the photograph to use their likenesses for publicity purposes. The public relations value of the photograph would be negated if complications later arose because of a failure to obtain these permissions. (See Exhibit 20.1 in Chapter 20 for an example of a photographic release form.)

Exhibit 13.1
Getting It on the
Wire Services

Hitting the wire services with a picture means reaching hundreds of outlets and millions of people with your visual message. That's why it's important to understand what the Associated Press, United Press International, and other more specialized services are looking for. Approximately 25 percent of the photos they use are suggested or supplied by public relations people who know how to target the wire services.

First make a call to the editor of the wire service and, in a few brief sentences, explain why your photo situation will interest the widest possible audience. The editor will tell you immediately whether it is worth assigning a photographer, and what the deadline is for a photo.

The requirements are basic: The photo must be timely. It must interest a large number of people. The content has to be interesting, and it can't look like it is a staged event. The photo must be of the highest quality, and the explanation of what is happening must be simple. Product names and "plugs" must be downplayed. The wire service expects a contact number of someone who can answer questions about the photo at any hour of the day, on deadline.

Meet these requirements, and you can document millions of exposures for your client's message.

Source: Kate Walter, "Moving Your Photos on the Wires," *Public Relations Journal* (March 1989), pp. 33–35.

SELECTING THE SUBJECT

The alert PR person walks through the plant, the office, and the community with an eye toward subjects that will make good photographs. That may mean taking scouting trips to locations such as outlying plants and research areas, visualizing what will make a dramatic or storytelling shot. It means thinking of ways to avoid the standard head-and-shoulders mug shot: How can we show the subject in context, naturally, in an appealing way that doesn't suggest the scene was staged?

Another important skill to develop is selecting shots from the contact sheets. If you look at the contacts along with the photographer who took the shots, try to remain dispassionate. Look at the shots one by one in progression, seeking the single photograph that summarizes the idea found in the series of shots. Determine which picture has the most human interest or emotional appeal—a close-up of a face registering happiness, a gesture that telegraphs the subject's reaction to the situation. Next look for supporting shots that might make a multipicture spread. Then check to see that the pictures you selected are consistently excellent in tonal quality, with proper focus and contrast.

The dilemma of selecting the best picture is this: How can you avoid the cliché that will make the editor groan, yet hit upon the ready appeal

Exhibit 13.2
Services Provide
Stock Photos

Need a picture of King Kong on the Empire State Building? (It relates to a point in your article on mankind's relationship with animals.) How about photos of early presidents, some of whom were involved in the activities of your nonprofit organization? Or maybe you just need a shot of a desert to make a point about life in dry places.

The answer to your quest is a photo syndicate. These services stock every photo imaginable. Describe it and they'll find it and arrange for you to receive a print. The cost usually depends on your description of the use you intend to make of the picture and the number of impressions you plan to make.

Leading suppliers of stock photos and historical pictures include:

Associated Press News Photos, 50 Rockefeller Plaza, New York, NY 10020

Bettman Archive, 136 E. 57th St., New York, NY 10022

Black Star, 450 Park Avenue S., New York, NY 10016

Globe Photos, 275 Seventh Avenue, New York, NY 10001

Newspaper Enterprise Association, 200 Park Avenue, New York, NY 10166

Wide World Photos, Inc., 50 Rockefeller Plaza, New York, NY 10020

of what interests people? The line is fine: A photo of a child discovering the wonder of a small animal is either downright corny or utterly charming. In fact, the corny one and the charming one may be found side by side on the contact sheet—if only you can decide which is which.

Editors despair of receiving the same kinds of pictures that have been crossing their desks since shortly after the camera was invented. Here are some standard shots that you should try to avoid:

- Person at desk talking on telephone.
- Group of retirees (honorees, appointees) standing in semicircle beaming at camera.
- One person handing a check (certificate, trophy, plaque) to another.
- Speaker standing at microphone on podium, with standard meeting hall decor including drape and potted palm in the background.

We have all seen these shots so many times that they hold no interest for us. The photographer must be instructed to try for candid shots that catch the subject more naturally than the stock poses ever can. This can be a problem when the chief executive officer always seems to have one eye cocked on the camera, ready to strike a properly presidential pose. Press photographers know that the secret is to shoot dozens, even scores, of pictures in quick succession, in order to capture that moment when the guard is down and the subject appears "real."

When the cutline is written for a picture that accompanies a news release, the information is kept to a minimum. The meaning of the action in the picture is described in a few words, and all identifiable persons are named, unless it is clear that they are merely "models." For example:

WRITING THE CUTLINE

> *The terminal of the new computer that enables the company to monitor all traffic in the tri-county area and flash instant reports to police and area news media is operated by Fairbanks Corp. technician Fred Paltzman.*

When the picture stands alone, the cutline must give all of the pertinent information that would appear in a short news story:

> *TRAFFIC MONITOR. The Fairbanks Corp., located in the Beltline Industrial Park, has completed installation of a new computer that will enable the firm to electronically monitor traffic under a recently awarded federal Department of Transportation grant. Here Fairbanks technician Fred Paltzman operates the console, routing information to computer terminals at area news media and local police departments. Fairbanks President Ronald E. Glazer said the computerized traffic monitor should lessen jams and delays in the tri-county area.*

Since the public relations department cannot always be sure whether the news media will prefer to use the picture in conjunction with the full press release or let it stand alone with the longer cutline, frequently the practice is to provide both versions on the same cutline sheet.

Photographs are mailed in manila envelopes with a cardboard liner to provide protection. That extra stiffness, along with a "Photo Do Not Fold" warning on the front of the envelope, will ward off all but the most punitive of postal employees. Because of the extra value of photographs, it is also common for public relations firms to have them hand-delivered by courier. Do not expect unused photos to be returned, however. The news media just don't have the time or resources. At best, they may file a timeless photo in the library for possible later use.

**CROPPING
FOR EFFECT**

Every photo gets its first "crop"—cutting away of extraneous information—when the photographer frames the subject and eliminates unwanted background. When making a print from the negative, the photographer usually improves the picture by cropping still tighter, in order to make the central subject as large as possible. Then the public relations specialist, acting as editor, decides whether to make still another crop—either for aesthetic reasons or because a picture of a certain size or proportion is needed for use in a specific layout.

Reasons for cropping a picture include:

■ To highlight a specific object or to focus on detail. At the time a product promotion picture is ordered, the photographer may be told to provide a shot of "a woman modeling the new line of jewelry." When it comes time to select the photos that will be sent along with the news release, you may decide to crop to the hand and arm, eliminating the model's face—perhaps because other photos in the same group have smiling faces, and they are getting a bit repetitious.

■ To reduce ambiguity or remove distractions. Details that enhance a single photo may be extraneous when the photo is to be used with other shots. Sometimes the line of a hand or leg may lead the viewer's eye away from the most important element of the picture. Or, on a multipicture spread, a hand in one picture may seem to be pointing to something in an adjacent picture, with humorous results. These are situations in which the photo editor exercises the prerogative to chop the person off at mid-torso.

■ To fit a scheme. The editor may want to make a particular point by juxtaposing two pictures to call attention to similarities or differences. If so, the pictures may need to be cropped to make the parallel clear and to keep subject size consistent. It looks odd, for example, if the head size of the person in one photo is just 10 percent larger than the head of the person in the adjacent shot.

■ To highlight shapes or direction. The photographer tends to compose within the camera frame, achieving balance and unity. The designer who uses the photograph must work with a new frame: the page, the "spread," or the display background. New horizon and boundary lines may be created by blocks of type or the architectural environment. Thus, it is sometimes necessary to crop a perfectly fine picture in order to bring its shapes and directions in consonance with external elements.

Crop marks may be made by the photographer or designer right on the contact sheets or the glossy print, using an orange or white grease pencil.

The simplest device for estimating and planning the crops before making the marks is a pair of cornices—L-shaped cardboard pieces that can be manipulated to create instant frames of any size or shape. In fact, any two sheets of paper lying handy can be used to perform a quick crop.

When the editor of a newsletter or other public relations publication works with a staff photographer, prints of pictures often can be made to fit the precise space on the layout. But more often than not, available pictures have to be adapted to fit the space. That means "sizing" the photo—determining how much the shot must be reduced or enlarged during the engraving process.

SIZING PHOTOS FOR REPRODUCTION

Usually editors work with standard column widths, and pictures routinely are ordered two or three columns wide by so many inches "deep." In other words, the width is a common one, and the depth of the picture is the variable. Let us look at a typical sizing situation:

Known quantity:	width of cropped picture	$= 8\frac{1}{4}$ inches
Known quantity:	depth of cropped picture	$= 6\frac{1}{2}$ inches
Known quantity:	two-column width on layout	$= 5\frac{1}{4}$ inches
Unknown quantity:	picture's depth on layout	$= "x"$ inches

The unknown quantity can be found by stating the problem as an algebraic problem and using a calculator to solve it:

$$8\frac{1}{4} \text{ is to } 5\frac{1}{4} \text{ as } 6\frac{1}{2} \text{ is to } x \ (x = 4\frac{1}{8})$$

Fortunately for editors who are not mathematicians, printing-supply houses sell (or give away as a promotional device) a marvelous little gadget known as the proportioning wheel, which anyone can learn to use. By lining up the known numbers on the two rotating wheels, one finds the unknown quantity lined up opposite the depth of the cropped picture. Another versatile gadget for proportioning pictures is the Scaleograph, which can be used simultaneously for cropping and sizing. The device consists of two clear plastic cornices with ruled scales. The two pieces slide on an aluminum bar and can be tightened into a fixed relationship, once the desired crop is made by framing the desired portions of the picture. When the knobs are tightened, the plastic pieces slide along the aluminum bar. In effect, the Scaleograph mechanically performs the same function as the algebraic equation.

CHECKLIST ✔ Before You Mail That Photo

Things to ask about a picture before you send it to the media:

✔ Is it really *visual?* Does it have action, or is it just a static shot? Avoid sending out the "grip-and-grin" picture of stuffed shirts holding a plaque or a check.

✔ Is the cutline information lively? Do the verbs pick up on the action in the picture? Do the words add to the excitement in the photo?

✔ Are all people in the photo identified with full names, identifications, and in proper order from left to right?

✔ Do the photo and cutline stand on their own, so that they tell the story and accomplish the public relations objectives, even if the accompanying article is not used by the editor?

✔ Are the composition and the photo quality up to the standards needed by the media? If all of the preceding questions have been answered positively but the picture is of poor or marginal quality, it will not be used.

If you have only a ruler (plus a dread of both mechanical devices and mathematics), use a window or light table to shine through the picture so that you can make both your crops and your proportions on the back of the picture with soft pencil. Once you have drawn a full frame around the desired part of the picture, draw a diagonal line across the frame from corner to corner. Place the ruler so that "0" touches the left or right side of the frame, and the desired reproduction width touches the diagonal. (In the example above, place the ruler so that $5\frac{1}{4}$ touches the diagonal line.) Make a mark at that point on the diagonal. Now all you have to do is to take the vertical measurement from the mark you made on the diagonal line to the bottom margin of the cropped area, and that is your "unknown quantity"—the depth of the picture when it is reproduced.

MOUNTING PHOTOS FOR DISPLAY Prints of photos that are to be published can be used even if they curl or get bent slightly at the corners. But pictures intended for display need more protection. Generally speaking, every print benefits from being dry mounted—laminated to stiff backing material—before it is framed, attached to a display card, or suspended in any manner. Dry mounting assures that the picture will stay flat. If done correctly, it prevents buckling, creasing, bubbling, or other imperfections that can decrease the impact of the photo.

A photo operation of any size should include a mounting press and associated materials. If yours is a small operation, you'll find that many photography- and art-supply houses provide free use of their press to their regular customers. Supplies you'll need are mounting board and dry-glue tissues, which form the adhesive bond when heat is applied. Also necessary are a small tool called a tacking iron, and a good-quality paper cutter for cropping the photo and the supporting mounting board. Personnel at the supply house where you obtain your equipment will show you how to make a "sandwich" of photo, adhesive tissue, and mounting board, and how to apply just the right amount of heat and pressure to cement them together.

Store mounted pictures in envelopes until you are ready to display them. The same dry-mounting process may be used to attach individually mounted shots to a larger board for a photo essay or display. However, since wrinkling is not a problem when attaching board to board, any other adhesive, such as rubber cement, is satisfactory.

PHOTO STORY LAYOUT

Whether you are planning a two-page magazine spread or a photo display for an exhibit, you will want to try to group the individual pictures so they make a statement greater than the sum of the parts. The editor or designer increases the impact by intriguing the viewer with patterns and positioning, leading the eye.

As you recall from our discussion of how to choose shots from a contact sheet, the goal is to find the all-purpose picture, some emotional human-interest shots, and photos that show the steps leading to the culmination of an event. To these we may add the context-setting shot, which documents the environment in which the events take place, and the reaction shot, which indicates how observers other than the main subject react. These categories are generalizations, of course, but they represent the basic elements of good visual storytelling.

Having selected the shots, rank them in terms of visual effect and storytelling ability. The photo you rank highest is your "anchor" picture, which you probably will make twice as large as any other photo in the essay. Place it in the grouping so that the viewer begins and ends by looking at this crucial picture. After all, a photo essay has to have a beginning or end, just like any other story. In order to achieve the public relations objective of making a point, the essay must be more than merely a collection of individual shots.

ARRANGING FOR ILLUSTRATIONS

There are many good reasons for deciding to use illustrations—anything from simple line drawings to reproductions of famous paintings—instead of photographs. They include:

- You want to get a different feel, or style, or tone for a layout, and an illustration accomplishes the task better than a photograph.
- You want variety in your publication, and you already have made extensive use of photos.
- You're under deadline pressure, and there isn't time to shoot a photo and process it; you have to grab for an illustration in a hurry.
- The cramped layout won't display a photo adequately; you need a small piece of art to fit in a precise corner.
- The situation calls for some humor, but the photo you asked for turned out to be merely corny. A witty line drawing injects just the right level of lightness to the spread.
- You have exceeded your budget and can't afford more pictures; you need artwork that is inexpensive or free.

There are three main sources of illustrations: artists, clip-art services, and computer graphics. Let's look at how each is used.

Staff Artists and Graphic Arts Freelancers

In a large operation, you may have the services of a staff artist. The advantages are threefold: (1) as a member of the team, the artist works only for you and therefore works to meet your deadlines; (2) as your regular artist, the graphics specialist develops a shared language with you, and thus you can communicate your art needs more effectively; and (3) using the same in-house artist gives your publication a noticeable style that adds to its personality.

Freelancers, if used regularly, offer many of the same benefits as staff artists, but your organization doesn't have to pay for their fringe benefits. Other freelancers are called in sporadically because of their specialties: portraits, drawings of wildlife and nature, or perhaps a special technique for rendering complicated technical charts. Freelancers may have trouble meeting your deadlines, and they may not pick up on your organization's publication style. Finding and developing artists who understand your needs is a major accomplishment, which is why editors stick with a stable of regulars and fight for the budget to pay them well.

Clip art—in this case "ClickArt" available for the computer—helps designers to incorporate drawings into their layouts.

Clip-Art Services

For a monthly subscription fee, clip-art services will send your publication voluminous books of simple line drawings of every subject matter available. Because they are rendered in black-and-white with simple shading or a single spot color, these illustrations can be pasted directly onto the camera-ready offset layout without engraving or special preparation.

Your one-time fee when you purchase the service takes care of the copyright. You can use as many of the illustrations as you want, as often as you want.

There are two drawbacks to using clip-art: (1) much of it looks like clip-art to anyone with any sophistication, so you might want to use it for flyers and internal publications but not in an advertisement or an external publication, and (2) there is no exclusivity on the use of clip-art; the same illustrations you use might show up in a tacky advertisement run by a competitor or by the manufacturer of a product with which you don't want to be associated.

Computer Graphics

Software now available for use on personal computers enables you to prepare basic pie charts, bar graphs, and other standard information formats that are programmed into the computer. The programs permit you to label the charts, enter your own figures, select colors or shadings, and print out the graphics in precisely the desired dimensions.

Similarly, other software programs offer you hundreds of basic images that you can rework to fit your layout. Clip-art has come to computers, and you can order special packages of business cartoons, seasonal designs, or drawings of items and objects common to your particular industry (see illustration). For under $3,000, you can purchase a scanner that converts any piece of art you find into a "captured image" that you can incorporate in your computer layout. (You are, of course, responsible for compensating the owner if the art is protected by copyright or trademark.)

Graphics Services

Just as you may have decided to "farm out" your typesetting and/or the printing of your publication, you may decided against investing in computer software and peripheral equipment. After all, you or someone in your organization has to learn how to use it, and if you don't use it regularly the system may not be efficient or cost effective.

Look in the Yellow Pages and you'll discover that many entrepreneurs have set up graphics services businesses in areas where there are many communication organizations. Many offer one-day service on preparation of graphics and illustrations. For many firms, this is a cost-effective and time-saving solution to publishing needs.

Alexander, Michael, "Picture-Perfect Photographs Help Sell Story Ideas," *Public Relations Journal* (July 1985), pp. 5–7.

Baus, Herbert M., and Philip Lesly, "Publicity in Newspapers," in *Lesly's Handbook of Public Relations and Communications*, 4th ed. (Chicago: Probus, 1991), pp. 367–392.

Cherry, David, *Preparing Artwork for Reproduction* (New York: Crown, 1976).

Douglas, Philip, *Pictures for Organizations: How and Why They Work as Communication* (Chicago: Ragan Communications, 1982).

Kobre, Kenneth, *Photojournalism: The Professionals' Approach* (Somerville, MA: Curtin & London, 1980).

Morton, Linda, "Use of Photos in Public Relations Messages," *Public Relations Review* (Winter 1986), pp. 16–21.

Rivelli, William, "Photography: The Key to a Successful Annual Report," *Communication World* (December 1984), pp. 32–34.

Seybold, John, and Fritz Dressler, *Publishing from the Desktop* (New York: Bantam Books, 1987).

Sklarewitz, Norman, "Custom Photos for Stock Shots," *Communication World* (February 1987), pp. 23–25.

Swedlund, Charles, *Photography: A Handbook of History, Materials and Processes* (New York: Holt, Rinehart and Winston, 1981).

Walter, Kate, "Moving Your Photos on the Wires," *Public Relations Journal* (March 1989), pp. 33–35.

ADDITIONAL READING

14

Slides and Films

Because television is such a large part of our daily lives, we are not just exposed to visual images, we are *overexposed* to them. As a result, we can walk into a room where the screen shows one World Wrestling Federation hulk dressed head-to-toe in neon spandex throwing another across the ring (while a woman in a black hood fondles a python) and we hardly notice it all.

Despite this visual overkill and overexposure, we still respond when the lights in a theater or viewing room go down and a well-crafted audio-visual presentation is shown. In this chapter we look at the venerable slide show, which still has impact in many situations and settings. Multimedia presentations combine slides with other media, or bombard the viewer with multiple still photographic images. And film, now generally packaged for viewing on video playback systems, remains a high-impact medium when it is projected on oversized screens in theaters designed to immerse the audience in sight and sound.

Slide shows still are produced by public relations departments in many organizations—especially those with the capability of using computer graphics to produce their title slides. But multimedia and film presentations are so technically specialized that outside firms usually are engaged to produce them. This chapter aims to help you understand what makes a good visual presentation and what you should strive for in planning one, whether you produce it yourself or work with an outside production firm.

PLANNING AND SCRIPTING

And now . . . let's turn off the lights and see the slides.

If your skin crawls whenever that sentence is uttered, you probably have watched one too many slide shows that were poorly organized and accompanied by a droning commentary of interest only to the narrator.

And yet, the slide show is one of the most useful systems of public communication available. Prepared and presented properly, it can be a solid public relations device that doesn't need an apologetic introduction.

When your objectives have been established, outline the major points of the presentation, still not worrying about the exact visuals to be used. The list of main points is the equivalent of an outline for a speech or any other form of mass communication. In other words, the content of the message should be decided before selecting the form. If one starts with visual images, the danger is that objectives never will be set down. The result may be a presentation that is somewhat pleasing aesthetically but that fails to make specific points.

The outline must be broken into two parts:

1. Individual pieces of information—single ideas or concepts.
2. The visual images or series of images that will illustrate those concepts.

At this point, it is helpful to borrow a technique from television production: the split script. Place the concept (single piece of information) on one side of the planning sheet, the visual images on the other side:

Points to be Made	Visuals
Pelham Corp. is located in Centerville and is part of the business community.	Skyline of Centerville, with successive shots closing in on Pelham's rooftop sign.
Pelham is a clean place to work, a nonpolluting neighbor.	Views of lawn, flowers, and picnic tables in employee outdoor lunch area.
Pelham is not a cold, impersonal place.	Shots of executives meeting with group of employees.

Eventually, you must come up with a suggested shot or series of shots for each of the major and minor points in your outline.

Once the outline script and the visuals have been decided upon, the next task is writing the narration. But first, you'll have to make some more important decisions, based on your objectives:

■   Will the narration be live, which can make the presentation more personal? Or will it be recorded, which ensures accuracy and proper coordination of sound and visual?

- Will the narrator be an authoritarian figure, a professional-sounding announcer, or perhaps a "realistic" protaganist, such as an employee?

When the script has been written, it will become apparent if more shots are needed in order to fill out some sections of the show. Condensation of the visuals may be necessary in order to prevent "stalling" in sections where there is insufficient narration to cover the series of slides.

It should be noted that, on rare occasions, satisfactory results have been obtained merely by gathering together available slides and having someone write a sharp script to read as their accompaniment. A slide may pop up on the screen at the moment when the narrator is making a corresponding point. But, just as likely, a strange juxtaposition of visual image and verbal statement may occur: the narrator talks about the organization's mascot, a mongrel pup, just as the photo of our illustrious president comes up on the screen.

The professional-quality show is arranged so that a verb or noun in the narration corresponds to an action or an event on the screen. That "cue" word may be underlined in the script so that the narrator will accentuate the word, making the connection between the visual and the aural:

Narration	Visuals
"Youth in our community need adult guidance."	Counselor with hand on shoulder of teenager.
"Someone must show them useful skills for living."	Counselor holds up copy of auto-repair manual.
"And they need to learn for themselves."	Two young men puzzling over broken auto part.

A slide show should place demands on two key senses, sight and hearing. When both are working in coordination, the chances are greatly enhanced that the intended points will reach their mark.

In order to visualize the slide show before the script has been written and the photographs have been shot, it is helpful to prepare a planning board, which serves the same function as the storyboard in television or film. Using index cards, sketch each individual shot and write below the sketch what point is being made by the visual image. By putting these sketch cards on a board the entire planning team can view, it becomes easier to detect areas of omission or repetition. This device is especially helpful when different people will prepare the script and the transparencies. Gathered around the planning board, the members of the team can arrive at a better consensus on what the finished product will look like.

Large corporations have the facilities to take slides and film made for sales promotion, the annual meeting, or employee training and combine them in video productions with a variety of audiences and objectives. Here the director of the video operation supervises a staff technician and a contract graphics specialist as they assemble a multimedia production.

Photo courtesy of Johnson & Johnson

EVALUATING THE ROUGH PRESENTATION

Before showing the completed presentation to a preview audience for reaction, schedule a few run-throughs for the public relations staff. Look for these common faults of slide shows:

- *Show is too short.* A selection of only a dozen slides, with each held on the screen for two or three minutes, is likely to be boring unless each slide has a great amount of detail to be studied. Audiences do not like to sit in the dark listening to what is obviously a lecture accompanied by a handful of visuals. If there is too little visual information for a slide show, use posters or wall charts instead.
- *Show is too long.* An hour-long slide presentation is successful only if a great amount of information is dispensed, or if the narrator is able to keep the audience interested with lively commentary. Ordinarily, a slide show of ten to twenty minutes, followed by a question-and-answer period, is more enjoyable. Not infrequently, the duration of the show is dictated for the wrong reason: "We can only start the tour every half hour, so the slide show must be twenty-five minutes long." The audience can detect padding and will grow restless.
- *Pace is too slow or too fast.* An audience does not appreciate slides that flash by so rapidly that important details are

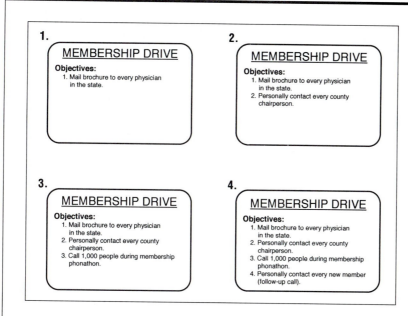

Exhibit 14.1
Build Your Idea with
"Build Slides"

To keep an audience interested, and to bring your viewers along through a complex set of ideas, use the "build slide" concept. Start a section of the slide show with a major heading: "WHAT WE EXPECT FROM OUR SALES FORCE."

Each successive slide in the series builds on the first. As the speaker adds more points to the series, subsequent slides add to the outline. You can branch off into specific points under subheadings and even offer photographic illustrations by way of examples, as long as you return regularly to the main point that is being explained and built.

Color coding of the main point and subpoints helps the audience pay attention and remain involved.

missed. The presenter who thinks that a shotgun approach to projection will assure visual excitement may really only be causing headaches and inviting the audience to tune out. The audience also may grow restless if the pacing is relentless— precisely fifteen seconds for each shot, for example. The pace should be varied from time to time by alternating slides that call for a longer attention span with groups of slides that can be shown in rapid succession. (Self-activated or continuous slide shows in display booths often are programmed at set intervals. In that context, however, the dynamic is different, because the audience is not held captive.)

- *Slide selection is redundant.* A dozen views of a building shot from slightly different angles may keep the information on the screen changing, but it will not necessarily be effective. Twenty shots of children at a playground do not convey the message of "successful youth program" as well as two or three technically excellent and well-chosen shots. If one cue word or one line of narration has to account for more than just a few pictures, the entire show may need overhauling.
- *Major points are inadequately illustrated.* Each major point in the script should be illustrated by a cluster of related visual information. Repetition of key slides may help solve the problem, but the audience feels cheated when multiple use is made of the same images.

TITLES, CHARTS, AND GRAPHICS

Title slides and other graphics such as tables and charts add professionalism to a show. The titles also divide longer shows into manageable sections, provide transition from one subject area to another, and help reinforce major points.

Some graphics-supply houses offer blank slides that can be written or typed upon to create simple titles and tables. However, they usually look so crude that they should be used only in emergencies. If you plan your slide presentation carefully, all titles and graphics should be accounted for from the beginning. One index card goes on the planning board for each title, color coded so it can be retrieved in a group and handed over to the person who will make the titles.

All titles and graphics should be shot at the same time, with the same camera and lighting, to assure consistency of color, brightness, and tone. Background colors, typefaces, and other design elements should be harmonious with the photo transparencies. For a show on state parks, use greens and browns, for example. For a new-product introduction, pick up the colors on the packaging or colors associated with the rest of the company's line.

As we mentioned in an earlier chapter, computer-generated graphics are now the "state of the art."

Keep the Audience in Mind

Never forget the makeup of the proposed audience. A leading midwestern newspaper assembled an informative show on display advertising, with an intended audience primarily of advertising salespersons and retail advertisers. A jaunty little stick-figure character was used on the title cards, pointing at the numbers and grinning at the audience. That was an effective device for the middle-aged male target audience.

But when the slide show was shown to college advertising classes, the students burst out laughing at the little man and his antics, which they described as "corny" and "old-fashioned." One instructor remedied the problem by removing most of the slides featuring the silly salesman.

Keep Preparation Simple

Hard-to-read titles and charts defeat their purpose. Cluttering the slide with too much information, not leaving sufficient borders for visual relief, and choosing type that is too small to be read are common reasons for illegibility. The Kodak booklets listed as suggested reading at the end of the chapter offer several guidelines for setting the proper ratio between type height and viewing distance. Overly fancy typefaces and insufficient contrast between the graphic elements and the background may also be detrimental.

Some of the points in this section appear to be painfully obvious, and yet the same flaws persistently mar slide shows. The public relations practitioner cannot afford to treat any principle of visual communication as "too elementary."

As we noted in the previous chapter, outside freelance photographers can be hired to shoot pictures. However, the PR department that anticipates making slide shows regularly for training and promotion will want to buy some basic equipment.

BASIC SLIDE-SHOW EQUIPMENT

- *Camera.* Transparencies usually are made with a 35 mm reflex camera. The through-the-lens viewing of a reflex camera permits precise composition of the frame when shooting. You'll want to equip the camera with a close-up lens, which is indispensable for making titles. A wide-angle lens will solve the problem of making good interior shots in cramped spaces. Also plan to buy a tripod and cable release: Both help ensure a steady, focused shot.
- *Copying stand.* For making titles and charts and for copying still photos, the copying stand is a must. It holds the camera steady in relationship to the flat surface upon which the photos are placed, and it may also hold lights in the proper position so that there is no reflection from the material being copied. Kodak's Ektagraphic Visualmaker is a relatively inexpensive copying outfit. However, if price is no object, you'll want a professional model that comes with guides and masks for pinpoint cropping and

positioning of material, as well as holders for transparent sheets of plastic upon which lettering may be placed for superimposition over background photographs.

■ *Lights.* For titling and copy work as well as close-ups and shots taken in confined spaces, you'll need photoflood bulbs and reflectors mounted on their own small tripods. One light can be used to enhance general illumination, while the other fills in shadows around faces or other details.

■ *Editing and viewing stand.* An editing stand is merely an inclined translucent surface, lighted from behind, with narrow ridges that hold slides in rows for viewing and rearranging. It is worth getting the largest model you can afford, so that you can edit as many as eighty to one hundred slides at one time.

■ *Storage.* Heat, dust, and temperature extremes are the enemies of the transparency. Slides should be stored in their projection trays in a metal cabinet. Out-takes, duplicates, or slides that have not yet been organized into a show may be stored conveniently in compartmented pages of clear plastic, which are indexed and placed in a heavy-duty three-ring binder.

■ *Projectors and accessories.* When shopping for projectors, you'll want to base your decision on the availability of features and accessories that can improve the presentation. Remote-control systems free the operator from standing next to the projector. Fade-dissolve mechanisms coordinate two or more projectors working in tandem (see next section). Other add-ons permit sound/visual synchronization with a tape recorder. Kodak's well-known Carousel series is preeminent in the field, although other manufacturers offer similar equipment to industry and educators.

MULTIMEDIA PRESENTATIONS

Slide shows used to be characterized by the constant clicking and blinking of the single, manually operated projector. Films, on the other hand, offer a continuous and smooth montage of shots. The distinction has been blurred by the development of fade-dissolve mechanisms and projection of multiple still images. Slide projection is greatly enhanced by using one of many multimedia approaches:

■ *Dual-projector, fade-dissolve twin projectors,* linked with a device such as the Kodak Carousel dissolve control, produce seamless shows in which one slide comes into view as the previous one is fading out, sometimes giving the illusion of a moving image. After a show has been edited, odd-numbered slides, including an opaque blank at the beginning, are placed in one unit. Even-numbered slides, including the opening title, are placed in another. The projectors are placed side by side or one above another in a rack that positions them properly. The frames then are perfectly overlapped, using two trial slides in order to assure a perfect match at the borders. The dissolve-control mechanism switches from one projector to the other automatically when the remote switch is depressed.

■ *Slide-tape synchronization.* In contrast to what you might think after enduring some slide shows, it isn't necessary to hear an annoying "beep" on a taped sound track every time the operator is supposed to click the projector switch. The cue for the next slide can be laid on the silent second track of a stereo (dual-track) tape recorder that carries the narration and background music on only one track. In addition to the recorder/playback unit and the projector, you'll need the Kodak Carousel sound synchronizer, which links the equipment and automatically coordinates the show. (If you are planning to distribute copies of your show to users who do not have the additional equipment, it may not be feasible to make a sound-slide synchronized version.) A console unit housing the tape recorder, projector, and synchronizer is used for displays and exhibits where the show is to be repeated over and over again, in which case an automatic-rewind mechanism must be added.

■ *Mosaic presentations.* If creativity, patience, and adequate budget are all found in your media operation—and, most importantly, if you have experienced professional audio-visual technicians on your staff—you might decide to dazzle your audiences with a multipanel, wide-screen presentation involving as many as eight projectors. By lining up four pairs of projectors, each pair fading and dissolving to account for one-fourth of the screen area, you can present a quadrant mosaic. With careful editing and timing, you can prepare a panoramic sweep across the entire screen—depicting your organization's headquarters, for example—and then move a version of that same shot to a single quadrant, while the other sections of the screen carry a fast-moving montage depicting the various activities that go on in the headquarters building.

If you have projectionists who can follow a multipart script and operate equipment with split-second timing, you may even use moving pictures in one or more of the quadrants during part of the show. If your organization has the means to consider such a complicated concept, you should consult with your audio-visual suppliers for the latest in computer-coordinated multimedia presentations. It now is possible to preprogram all projector and sound cues into a microcomputer that effectively and consistently runs the entire presentation for you.

Exhibit 14.2
New Lease on Life for the
Overhead Projector

One of the old chestnuts of the audio-visual closet has been the overhead projector that enables the speaker to drop transparencies with notes and charts on a glass surface for projection onto a screen. As every college student knows, "overheads" can be snooze material. When the lights go down, the poorly typewritten material goes up on the wall, and eyelids begin to droop as the voice of the lecturer drones on and on and little of visual interest occurs.

Computer graphics available in the basic Macintosh computers used widely on campus and in industry have breathed new life into overhead projections. With some care and preparation, it is possible to put together a lively and interesting overhead projector presentation that involves interesting typefaces, borders, illustrations, charts, and even line drawings that are capable of keeping your audience from becoming comotose. Colored highlighting pens also make it possible for the speaker to add flair to the presentation by splashing color on the projections where it will serve to emphasize major points.

Before putting what might better be a straightforward speech on transparencies, however, it is best to analyze the interest level of the audience and the adaptability of the information to projected transparencies. If you cannot demonstrate to yourself that the overhead projections actually clarify and sharpen the information to be presented, you may be using the audio-visuals merely as a crutch for a speaker who can't be trusted to interest the target audience.

Computerized or not, a complex multimedia show takes hundreds of hours of preparation and practice. You even will learn to put fresh lamps in all of the projectors for an important showing—expensive, but it ensures consistency of projection image across the screen! It can all be worth it if you really want to impress an audience.

FILM STILL HAS A ROLE IN A VIDEO WORLD

In an earlier chapter, we looked at the use of video, which included such diverse subjects as employee training and marketing tapes. Now, when we discuss "film" we refer to special productions that are shot on film, often for projection in theaters equipped with wide-screen equipment and sound systems that guarantee the greatest possible impact.

Increasingly, however, the "film" that is shot will be projected as video, simply because video playback systems are becoming the technology of choice in industry. The two media are converging to the point where some are predicting that the "movies" we watch in theaters by the twenty-first century—only a few years from now—will be video tapes.

As the United States and the rest of the world move toward higher standards for video images, the distinctions between the moving picture media are dissolving.

We refer to "film" in this section to mean top-quality visual productions created on film, for dissemination in whatever medium is most appropriate to the campaign. If multiple copies are to be sent out for showing at company plants or in classrooms, video probably will be the medium of distribution. If a single print is to be shown on a large, wide screen at an exhibition or show, film projection still is considered the medium that guarantees the greatest impact because of the sharpness of image in a large auditorium.

A Medium with Impact

The newly created New Jersey Sports and Exhibition Authority had a problem. The citizens, investors, banks, and other institutions of the state were wary: Was it really possible to build a new stadium, racetrack, and arena in the New Jersey Meadowlands, practically in the shadow of New York City? The press and the state legislature were skeptical.

The Sports Authority felt that its ambitious development plan was well conceived. It commissioned a 16 mm color film to tell the story. The producers wanted the film to project an overwhelming sense that the mammoth undertaking was both feasible and necessary. They also tried to appeal to the pride of New Jerseyans, a quality often thought to be in short supply.

Beginning with a horizon-to-horizon view of the site, the film dazzled the viewer with the feeling of an expanse of beautiful land, accessible by modern highways and rail links. New York City's towering skyscrapers were visible on the right, and the major urban centers of the Garden State could be seen on the left. When the camera panned over models of the football stadium and the racetrack, the motion—enhanced by stirring music—excited the imagination of the audience far more than a still photo representation could.

Similarly, the film's graphic elements, which explained the funding and outlined the expected economic growth of the area, were animated in vivid colors. This added excitement to the factual discourse on the numbers of persons served, the expected revenue, and the employment dollars to be generated. Even at the press showings, where skeptical reporters wanted to know the hard facts, there was a noticeable appreciation of the effectiveness of the filmed message. In fact, the high quality of the film stood as symbolic evidence of the commitment and the professionalism of the Sports Authority management.

(The film was always preceded by a short presentation from a member of the Sports Authority public relations staff, who also solicited

Exhibit 14.3
Super-Films Reap Super
Benefits for Sponsors

"Sponsored communication" refers to any message that has general interest to a wide public, but which is made possible through the support of a corporation. Increasingly, wide-screen historic documentary films shown at major public expositions have been examples of "sponsored communication."

Millions of visitors to the National Air and Space Museum since 1976 have viewed the epic film *To Fly!* sponsored by Conoco, a subsidiary of Du Pont. The wide-screen chronicle of the development of flight was shot in the IMAX system first demonstrated at the Fuji Pavilion at the Osaka Exposition in the early 1970s. Johnson Wax, Lockheed, and other corporate sponsors have underwritten similar film epics.

Using a 70 mm motion picture film, the IMAX system projects an image up to seventy-five feet high and one hundred feet wide that envelops the viewers. The definition of the image is so clear that the audience feels present at the events that are documented by the film. (See the photo in the color section in the middle of this textbook.)

Super-films have the capability of dazzling people who think they have seen it all on television and at regular movies. As such, they are powerful tools for associating a company's name with history, progress, and innovation.

Source: Robert M. Finehout, "Public Relations Film: Larger Than Life," *Public Relations Journal* (January 1985), pp. 4–6.

questions from the audience immediately following the film showing. The public relations department understood that a flashy movie alone might be seen as an attempt to overwhelm the audience with an emotional approach instead of a rational one.)

Today, the Meadowlands Sports Complex is a reality, home of the football Giants, basketball Nets, hockey Devils, and harness racing's top event, the Hambletonian. Film played a significant part in the success story.

Everybody loves the excitement when a movie projector begins to roll, the lights are turned off, and images flood the screen. And yet, for all its novelty, film has been used in promotion practically since the beginning of the century. In 1913, Hampton Institute, a college established to educate former slaves, made a film documentary depicting college life in order to recruit young blacks for the school.[1] The U.S. government used films as early as World War I to facilitate recruiting and to marshall those on the home front for activities ranging from recycling to buying war bonds to resisting foreign propaganda.[2]

Almost every American has seen McDonald's All-American High School Band marching and playing in the Rose Bowl or Macy's Thanksgiving parades. In order to get music teachers, principals, and students involved in the nominating procedure, the hamburger chain distributes an exciting film, *The Musical All-Americans*, which depicts auditions, practice sessions, and highlights from performances.[3]

Industrial films sponsored by large corporations range from relatively hard-sell messages that detail a company's involvement in exploration for new energy sources, to soft-sell messages that celebrate mankind's history or ingenuity, with only the sponsoring firm's name on the titles and credits to act as a promotional tie-in. The award-winning *Why Man Creates*, produced for Kaiser Aluminum and Chemical Corp., is an example of soft-sell, as are many of the special 360-degree or wide-screen films shown at world's fairs by industrial giants such as Kodak and General Motors.[4] Films that deal more openly with the relations between industry and governments or consumers include Monsanto's *The Chemical Facts of Life*, Procter & Gamble's *Is Anybody Listening?* and Texaco's *The Big Job*.[5]

Countering the messages of big business on issues such as pollution and nuclear energy are the films prepared and disseminated by activist organizations such as the Green Mountain Post, which distributes such documentaries as *Lovejoy's Nuclear War*, which details one man's act of civil disobedience against a utility's attempt to build a nuclear power plant. The films are publicized in a quarterly bulletin and rented or sold to conservation and political groups.[6]

Most films begin as a general idea, and that idea is first set on paper in the form of a synopsis:

FILM: THE PLAN AND THE SCRIPT

> *This ten-minute film depicts a trip down the Delaware River by two canoeists. They put in at a secluded point north of the Delaware Water Gap, and the first part of their trip is peaceful, beautiful, and uneventful, capturing the spirit of man enjoying nature. But as they draw closer to the Philadelphia metropolitan area, pollution and water hazards increase, and the abandonment of the journey at a point where industrial wastes are being poured into the river is a comment on how man has spoiled his most precious natural resources.*

Even a major epic first must be boiled down into this 100-word format in order to summarize the main point of the film and to indicate the style and mood. When the synopsis is approved, you will next need to prepare a "treatment," which is a scene-by-scene (but not necessarily shot-by-shot) explanation of everything that will happen in the film. In the above example, the treatment would begin:

> *Open with two canoeists driving past a Delaware Water Gap sign to establish location. Their car bumps along a dirt road leading to the water.*

Exhibit 14.4

"Down the
Delaware"

Scene I/Shot 1   (Long shot)   10 seconds

Car with canoe on top is moving along highway with trees and boulders in background. Camera pans left to right until "Delaware Water Gap" sign comes into view at the right.

Scene I/Shot 2   (Medium shot)   (approx) 5 seconds

Stationary camera. Sign fills right half of screen, and highway fills left side. Shot begins with empty highway and lasts as long as it takes the car with the canoe on top to pass the sign.

Scene I/Shot 3   (Close-up)   10 seconds

Tracking shot taken alongside moving car at right angles, framing the two canoeists in the passenger side window. They are talking animatedly, and the person on the passenger side gestures, pointing through the windshield.

Scene I/Shot 4   (Medium-long shot)   3 seconds

View, through windshield, of dirt road leading down to river from main highway.

Scene I/Shot 5   (Close-up)   5 seconds

Same as I/3. Passenger is nodding head to indicate "Yes, that's the place."

They stop, get out, stretch, breathe the fresh air, and point at ducks bobbing on the water. They spread a map out on the hood of the car and trace the route of their voyage down the river . . .

Like the synopsis, the treatment is a planning tool that enables PR managers to visualize the film. When it has been approved, you will then prepare a script like the one in Exhibit 14.4, complete with camera directions, times, and, if appropriate, dialogue.

In addition to a script, it is useful to prepare a storyboard comprised of a sketch of each shot in the film. That way the relationship of each object in the frame can be shown, along with the movement of each character and the motion of the camera as it tracks the subject, zooms in, pulls back, or pans. Most public relations films are group efforts and require the approval of a top manager who may not have any film experience. The storyboard enables the filmmaker to present the manager with a visual representation of the story early in the planning process.

Included in the storyboard should be all title cards, credits, still pictures, and charts or graphics. These are prepared by the art department or a typographer, filmed with studio lighting, and edited into the finished film. (When the Bell System used historic black-and-white still pictures as part of a documentary on the history of the telephone, it instructed the laboratory to add sepia tone and other tints to the pictures in order to give the old prints more life and to make them fit better into the full-color film.)

PROMOTIONAL TIE-INS

While the film is being processed and duplicates are being made for distribution, the public relations department should plan the promotion of the film. Posters and brochures can be printed to publicize showings. Because the information in the film cannot be stored and retrieved by the audience, you might want to prepare a fact sheet for distribution at the film showing.

Is the film to be used in schools and colleges? Most teachers say they want to have lesson guides, bibliographies, background information, and other print materials to use in the classroom in conjunction with the film showing.[7] The Phillips Petroleum Company distributes its "American Enterprise" series of high-school-level films on the economic development of the United States complete with minicourses, discussion guides, and suggested projects for students.[8]

DISTRIBUTING THE FILM

Once prints of your film are "in the can," how will you get them to the intended audiences? Most public relations people almost automatically think of maximizing the number of people who will view a film. Too few think of whether they have successfully distributed the film to their target public. You can measure the communication objective by keeping track of how many members of the target public see the film. Don't, however, equate general distribution with "reaching a target public."

Below are just a few of the ways that public relations departments have put their film messages into circulation. Can you think of the kinds of publics that might be reached with each distribution channel?

Audiovisual services and film distributors prepare and disseminate wide-ranging catalogs of industrial and promotional films. Educators

Exhibit 14.5
Classroom Films:
Sponsored by Industry

If you saw an interesting film in a journalism, speech, or communication class recently, the chances are that your teacher arranged for the showing by ordering the film from the Modern Talking Picture Service catalog sent to all college instructors. Despite the archaic title of its service, "Talking Picture" distributes film not only in 16 mm, but in videocassette format as well.

And where does the service get the films it distributes to teachers at no cost? From industry, associations, and nonprofit groups that have a story to tell. The film service operates as a middleman between those seeking free information and those willing to sponsor its distribution in return for credit.

Philip Morris, Inc. pays for the distribution of films about history, including titles dealing with black American art and the achievements of women. The Communication Workers of America trade union sponsors films about the nature of work and communication in the information age. The Aluminum Association has produced a dozen films specifically on facets of aluminum production for use in technical studies programs. The American Red Cross documents its assistance in the U.S. and abroad in the areas of health and welfare. Carnation Inc. documents black women in sports, with an emphasis on nutrition—a subtle linkage to the company's dairy products.

Indeed, all of these films, once they have captured an audience's interest with color, motion, and narration, depend on a soft sell and the goodwill of sponsorship to garner support from the target publics.

and program chairpersons of clubs and service organizations can arrange for free loans of the films. Your organization pays a fee for each showing. In return, you get wide distribution and a careful record of how many viewers of various types saw the film.

Industrial shorts are also shown in movie houses. Film distributors and local associations of theater owners can provide a list of theaters and chains that use public relations films to fill out their programs. The Insurance Institute for Highway Safety, for example, convinced theater chains to show a ten-minute film that promotes the use of seat belts, automatic air bags, and safer windshields.[9]

If your organization has the resources and the desire to handle its own advertising, booking, mailing, and maintenance of films, you can obtain mailing lists of educators and club officers from the national offices of school and professional associations.

Your own employees are the first audience for any film, and they can be your organization's connection with an entire network of local organizations such as PTAs, fraternal groups, churches, and professional groups. (Your lawyers belong to the bar association, your accountants belong to state and national associations, and your public relations people should belong to a large number of journalism and public-service organizations. All are potential audiences.)

Cable television has an insatiable appetite for free films, as we noted in Chapter 8.

If your organization regularly bills its customers, use a bill-stuffer brochure to seek audiences. The telephone company's miniature newsletter frequently lists available films on communication, technology, and American history. The best time to promote films is in the late spring and again in late summer, when teachers and club program chairpersons are planning for the upcoming year.

Anywhere people congregate is a good place to show a film. Trade exhibitions, county and state fairs, airports, and train stations are all good locations for minitheaters, which attract crowds of people who are bored, waiting for someone, or need to take a load off their feet.

Whenever possible, of course, you should control the presentation of your organization's films in order to ensure reliable and aesthetically pleasing projection. Use this checklist to obtain the best results:

PROPER PROJECTION

1. The room in which the film is to be shown should be totally dark for best image quality and minimal distractions. For clear and undistorted viewing, do not seat any viewer at more than a thirty-degree angle from the center of the screen. (Kodak customer service pamphlet AD-43 lists optimum projection distance for various screen widths and lenses.)

2. Make sure in advance that stable support is available for the projector, along with adequate heavy-duty power cords. Use wide plastic tape to secure power cords to the floor as far from the traffic pattern as possible.

3. Make sure you have a replacement projection lamp. If they are going to blow out, it usually happens when the projector first is turned on. Sound projectors call for a second lamp as part of the optical sound system, and each projector has a fuse that could blow out or go bad. Back-ups for all of these should be in your repair kit. You'll also want to have a few emergency splices in case the film breaks. Masking tape will do in a pinch.

4. Use a short roll of unimportant film to test the projector before loading it with the main film. If you have plenty of black leader on your roll, the projector will destroy that instead of your precious film if there is a malfunction when the "on" button is pressed. A good projectionist advances the film to the first frame of the titles and then puts the projector on hold until the audience is ready.

CHECKLIST ✔ Audio-Visual Presentations

✔ Format (slides, film, multimedia) fits your organization's budget.
   Scale down production if necessary to assure professional product.

✔ Length of presentation is right for the audience's attention span.
   Consider make-up of audience and context in which show is presented.

✔ Most effective form of narration has been selected.
   Live narration connects best with audience, but may be erratic.
   Recorded narration may be on-screen host or actor.

✔ Style of presentation is consistent throughout the production.
   Titles and subtitles join the sections of the show together.
   Color scheme and graphics are all related in tone and style.
   Consistency of slides or footage is uniform.

✔ Presentation team is prepared for technical problems.
   Alternate mode of presentation ready if A/V cannot function.
   Spare lamps for projectors, extra extension cords.

✔ Supplementary print materials have been prepared.
   Brochures, handouts, or fact sheets that viewers can take away.

✔ Feedback is sought.
   Audience members may be asked to fill out survey form.
   Presentation team makes notes and suggestions for future showings.

---

5. Have a contingency plan in case the projection is interrupted. This usually means a person other than the projectionist who can ad lib for a few minutes and attract the audience's attention away from the projection problem. Rather than duplicate information that will be seen in the film, it is best to talk about a topic related to the film.

6. As soon as possible after the showing, the film should be rewound, cleaned, repaired, and properly stored in a cool, dry place, ready for the next showing.

The caution and preparedness are worthwhile, because a properly presented film carries the message that your organization has foresight, the ability to marshall resources, and a good knowledge of what it is working to accomplish.

1. Nickieann Fleener, "Using Sponsored Films to Tell the Story: A Contribution of the Hampton Institute to the Evolution of Public Relations Practice in Higher Education," paper presented to the PR division of the Association for Education in Journalism, Boston, August 1980.

2. Richard Dyer MacCann, *The People's Films: A Political History of U.S. Government Motion Pictures* (New York: Hastings House, 1973).

3. Carl H. Lenz, "How to Use PRint Power in Film," *Public Relations Journal* (September 1978), pp. 30–35.

4. Ott Coelln, "The Business Side of Picture Street," *Public Relations Journal* (September 1980), pp. 14–16, 34.

5. Will A. Parker, "PR Films: Populist Pressures and Cinematic Excellence," *Public Relations Journal* (September 1978), pp. 28–29.

6. Green Mountain Post Films Bulletin (Spring 1980).

7. Lenz.

8. Lenz.

9. Michael deCourcy Hinds, "Theater Chain Shows a Dramatic Safety Film," *New York Times,* January 28, 1982, p. A–15.

NOTES

Finehout, Robert M., "Public Relations Film: Larger Than Life," *Public Relations Journal* (January 1985), pp. 4–6.

Jowett, Garth, and James M. Linton, *Movies as Mass Communication* (Beverly Hills, CA: Sage, 1980).

Kieckhafer, Sandra, "Successful Slide Presentations," *Public Relations Journal* (September 1983), pp. 17–18.

Kodak Publication No. V1-30, "Effective Visual Presentations," available from Kodak, Rochester, NY.

Kodak Publication No. AA-6, "Slide Showmanship with a Kodak Carousel Projector."

Lee, Robert, and Robert Misiorowski, *Script Models* (New York: Hastings House, 1978).

Mercer, John, *The Informational Film* (Champaign, IL: Stipes, 1980).

Sutherland, Don, "Designing Audiovisuals? Just Think Backward," *Communication World* (January 1985), pp. 33–34.

Sutherland, Don, "Dueling Concepts: AV Soul vs. Glitz," *Communication World* (January 1986), pp. 2, 25.

Ward, John, "Slide Shows Turn Professional," *Audio-Visual Communication* (January 1978), pp. 62–64.

ADDITIONAL READING

15

Exhibits and Special Events

Most of the activity of public relations practitioners, especially those who are communication technicians, is office work: writing, editing, conferring with clients, and attending internal meetings to plan information programs. But their assignments and projects occasionally take them out of the office to do nonroutine tasks such as arranging a lobby display, setting up a booth for a trade show, planning an open house, or running the firm's annual meeting.

All of these special events require conducting site inspections, working with designers and other artists, anticipating logistical problems, and dealing with emergencies far from home base. Most practitioners consider these challenges a rewarding change of pace.

This chapter describes several formal ways you can make person-to-person contact with members of your publics: displays and exhibits, open houses, tours, and the annual meeting.

PLANNING THE DISPLAY

Placing a display in the lobby of your organization's building is a good way of commemorating a special occasion, calling attention to a new program, or soliciting employee involvement in a worthwhile project.

But only rarely does a display booth stand alone. Usually, along with the other exhibits at a trade show, career day, or information fair, it is assigned a standard space of so much front footage and depth. Unless a desirable freestanding center or corner space is obtained, it most likely will be jammed in between two other booths.

The first task is to obtain from those in charge of running the show a detailed outline of rules for displays, the available services (including electric power), and the precise dimensions of the space. Will back and side walls be provided, will there be curtain separators, or does the space consist merely of marked-off floor space? Convention and trade-show facilities are fairly standardized in terms of services, but hotels, motels, and government agencies often leave it to you to figure out what to do.

Before designing the display, decide whether it will be used once only or reused as a standard exhibit. Single-use means the display can be built to the specifications of the one place and the one message. The multiple-use display must be adaptable to various spaces and applications. Because durable display materials are so costly, the display should be designed so that it can be updated and modified easily.

Portable booths constructed of quick-assembly, interlocking panels can be ordered from display-supply companies, along with such components as desks, brochure racks, railings, light fixtures, and storage cabinets that can be arranged in various ways to suit different locations. Most organizations that pack displays around to several locations spend anywhere from $5,000 for basic booth materials to $50,000 for custom-designed displays that can stand the transportation and yet be simple enough for a small team of workers to assemble in a few hours.

Visual Impression

A basic booth might consist of nothing more than a sign on the back wall and a table with literature, attended by a smiling person who is prepared to answer questions. But most successful displays are more sophisticated.

Consider the overall impression the booth will make on the audience. Will the display communicate a single concept, or several? It is possible to devote 70 percent of the impact and space to a major theme while also piggybacking related themes in the other 30 percent. For example, a company might give major emphasis to a new product line at a trade-fair booth while also offering information about established products.

Will the display encourage active audience involvement or only the passive soaking up of information? Will the viewer merely pass the display, or is there an opportunity to enter the space? At the annual Philadelphia Garden Show, the W. Atlee Burpee Company erects a greenhouse and a small vegetable plot with pathways so that visitors can walk right through and observe the plantings closely. Involvement increases interest in the company's products.

Will the mood be serious or fun? Several exhibitors at the annual Premium Show at the New York Coliseum display games and toys that can be imprinted with the sponsoring organization's name. But Wham-O Manufacturing of California steals the show with its promotion of

Exhibit 15.1
Try to Avoid Events
That Conflict

Once you have announced an event to your target publics, spent money on preparations, and invested your time and energy in exhaustive planning, it is dispiriting to find that your event competes directly with another one aimed at attracting the same audience. In some cities, arts groups join forces to publish a "cultural calendar." They coordinate through a central office so that nobody schedules an opening night or a benefit against another group.

Religious holidays are most important to avoid, not only because an event will lose some of its audience, but because some members of the target public may be offended. (Jewish holidays begin at sundown the previous day, so it usually is best to block out two days if many in your audience are Jewish.)

Programming expert E. W. Brody suggests that after you consult calendars for holiday observances and examine newspapers from a year earlier to discover which events are held annually at the same time, you should check with key personnel at several local organizations including:

- Local editors and news directors.
- Managers of stadiums, auditoriums, and convention hotels.
- Directors of tourist and convention bureaus.
- Sports and entertainment promoters.
- Government agencies that issue permits for parades and other events held on public property.

Source: E. W. Brody, *Managing Communication Processes* (New York: Praeger 1991), p. 166.

imprinted Frisbees. Everyone who passes the display is encouraged to try tossing ten Frisbees at the hole in a target. Get five through the hole and you win a cash prize. There aren't many winners, but the excitement assures that everyone attending the show gets Wham-O's message.

Sometimes the accent on prestige rules out pizzazz: The Beatrice Foods booth at trade shows is done entirely in gold, and attendants dressed in gold pass out gold-foil-covered pamphlets. The decor consistently carries out the concept that the Beatrice product line is of the highest quality.

Traffic Pattern and Lighting

Routes for approaching and passing an exhibit must be calculated. In a large public space, the flow down certain aisles may be mostly in one direction, owing to the places of entry and exit. That has several implications: Will the display be canted to one direction or the other? Where will the staff position itself? The width of the aisle may dictate whether people are forced to pass the booth at close range, or whether they can remain at distances from which they must be lured.

No matter how good the general lighting is in an exhibition hall, auxiliary lighting should be used to illuminate the main sign properly, to highlight products or other key objects, and to eliminate shadows. In addition to lights designed specially for the display, bring along inexpensive minispots to throw light on unforeseen dark areas.

Furniture and Floor Covering

Seating, surface display areas, writing space, and storage must be provided to encourage activity between exhibitors and audience. They should be an integral part of the design, incorporating the same style, tone, and colors.

An ugly floor can dull the effect of an otherwise impressive booth. When selecting the paint or fabric covering for the booth walls and furniture, obtain a carpet remnant in a compatible color. It will not only enhance the beauty of the display, it also can improve the acoustics, add a feeling of prestige, and make the job of staffing the booth less of a strain on the legs. Carpeting should be fastened down on all sides with wide, heavy-duty plastic tape in a matching color.

Audiovisual Equipment

Recorded sound can enhance a display, as long as it does not compete with a neighboring booth. If a booming public-address system is used, unhappy inhabitants of neighboring exhibits may complain—or else increase their own volume. If you incorporate sound in a slide-tape, film-and-tape, or video presentation, the visual image will tend to draw the audience in closer, so that sound can be heard at a reasonable volume. Hoods and panels of plywood, fabric, or insulating material keep sound under control.

If you use film loops or video, you may also need to plan for a hood, panel, or canopy to shield the back-projection screen from overhead lights and spotlights in neighboring displays. If you plan to make extensive use of audio-visual materials, check in advance with show coordinators to make sure there are adequate electrical outlets and sufficient power.

Maintaining the Display

Effective display design goes for naught if you fail to staff and maintain the exhibit properly. Two persons should be on duty in an active booth, and more may be needed if sales, recruitment, or complex demonstrations are taking place. Uniform dress, such as blazers with insignia or identification badges, should distinguish attendants. Consumption of food, drinks, or tobacco—unless you are providing it for your clients as well—should be forbidden.

A policy on who shall receive printed materials, samples, and premiums should be established in advance. If a display will be in place for a considerable duration, arrange for daily restocking of informational materials.

A display is not an end in itself; it is a way of opening a line of communication with prospective clients. Have a plan for taking names of interested visitors. Put them on a mailing list and assure them that they will receive follow-up materials shortly after visiting your exhibit.

There always will be unforeseen situations that call for repairing or altering an exhibit. Here is a minimal first aid kit for displays:

- Yardstick or tape measure.
- A selection of tapes—heavy-duty strapping tapes for structural repairs, cellophane tape for mending signs, extra plastic tape for the carpet.
- A small can of compressed air, available at photo-supply stores, for blowing dust particles from signs and samples without streaking them, and for cleaning A/V equipment.
- Felt-tip pens in various colors, and blank signboards, for the creation of instant signs to cope with audience behaviors you didn't anticipate. ("Please do not handle the diamond stylus" . . . "Available in several colors" . . . "Attendant will return in ten minutes.")
- Business cards, pens, letterheads, envelopes, stamps, and all the other things in the top drawer of your desk back at the office.
- Coins for pay telephones, a list of suppliers of anything your display might need if it runs out, and phone numbers of persons in your organization who can be called upon to answer the questions you didn't know people were going to ask.
- String, rope, or wire. Electrical extension cords. Extra bulbs or lamps for every lighting and audio-visual device. Batteries and fuses for A/V equipment. Dustrag, whisk broom, and spray air freshener. A bottle of water, aspirin, and cups.

Hospitality Suites

An alternative to the booth at a convention is the hospitality suite, perhaps adjacent to the exhibition hall, but more likely in a meeting room nearby. To some oldtime public relations people, the term hospitality suite conjures up images of free-flowing liquor at night after the main convention displays have closed up. Little more than supposed "goodwill" is accomplished in such a setup.

The trend is toward use of the hospitality suite as an alternative to the booth in the noisy hall where traffic and other exhibitors create constant distractions. Those invited to the hospitality suite for coffee and cookies usually have been identified as those with a special interest in your organization, not just "schmoozers" who will stop and talk with anybody. These are the people you want to get a commitment from to join your cause, buy your company's product, or use your services.

At the 1990 PRSA convention in New York City, for example, the hospitality suite operated on behalf of the city and businesses located there offered sightseeing and tourist brochures and sign-up sheets, members of the local PRSA chapter who could answer questions, information about companies located in the city, and a drawing for prizes donated by local merchants and public relations firms. The overall message of the room was that New York is a dynamic place, its businesses were proud to host the convention, and, most important of all, convention-goers should consider doing business with New York City-based firms. The average stay in the hospitality room was more than twice as long as the average stay at a booth in the main exhibit hall.

FAIRS ARE A PUBLICITY MEDIUM

Each year in the United States there are more than two thousand fairs, ranging from huge state fairs attracting more than a million visitors to trade fairs that target special-interest audiences.[1]

All fairs, even those famous for their midways, grandstand concerts, and stock car races, have education as a main objective. In addition to commercial exhibitors showing their wares, most fairs and exhibitions also have booths sponsored by organizations desiring to get a social message across to their publics. MADD and SADD—Mothers and Students Against Drunk Driving—find fairs an effective place to get their literature into the hands of ordinary citizens. Conservation and environmental groups recruit members and demonstrate "earth-friendly" habits and behaviors to interested passers-by.

One of the keys to deciding whether to place a booth at a fair is whether your exhibit will be in a high-traffic area or stuck in an information ghetto far from the churning crowds. Another consideration is whether your organization can muster enough volunteer help to staff a booth day and night for the duration of the exhibition. Literature costs also have to be weighed: Will the thousands of visitors who willingly take your brochures really read them or merely toss them away with the sticks from their cotton candy and taffy apples?

More than a century ago, companies began to open exhibits at their headquarters buildings or big city office buildings to display inventions and innovations for which they could take credit.

Henry Ford spurred the development of the Dearborn Museum, near the spot where his first assembly line once stood, to show succeeding generations not only the Model T and other Ford innovations, but everything else mechanical and manufactured that was the result of American genius. On the occasion in 1929 of the fiftieth anniversary of Thomas Edison's invention of the light bulb, Ford—with the help of public relations man Edward Bernays—got Edison, President Herbert Hoover, Luther Burbank, Harvey Firestone, and hundreds of other American businessmen and government leaders together at the Dearborn Museum to open a new exhibit that featured the actual laboratory in which Edison accomplished his feat. After decades of distrust, "Light's Golden Jubilee" marked the day when Americans' attitudes toward the contributions of "big business" became more positive.[2]

The corporate museum in America has evolved from the historical archive that merely shows off the company's products through the years to an important marketing device that helps the visitor to appreciate the firm's contribution to society, and thus encourages the public to value and trust the company.[3]

AT&T's InfoQuest exhibit at corporate headquarters in New York City depicts how telecommunications affect the modern family (see photos). Visits by school and recreations groups are encouraged. The midtown Manhattan location also makes it a place that office workers, shoppers, and tourists discover as a diverting and free attraction.

Other examples of corporate museums include:

- TRW's corporate headquarters exhibit demonstrating the broad range of technologies in which the company is involved— similar to the point made by its television commercials.
- The General Foods exhibit that shows how the firm fits into worldwide food production.
- The exhibit documenting the development of computers that is maintained in Boston by several computer firms located in that area.
- Squibb's art gallery at its Princeton, New Jersey, headquarters that has an impressive permanent collection in addition to itinerant exhibitions.
- The ground floor exhibit space purposely designed into the Lever Tower on Park Avenue in New York to provide space for arts and crafts shows.

THE CORPORATE MUSEUM

AT&T's InfoQuest Center in midtown Manhattan, where tens of thousands of tourists as well as hundreds of school groups visit annually, is an example of a permanent corporate museum exhibit. Providing a heavy dose of entertainment along with learning and interactive experience, it carries several messages to its publics. These include: technology is the key to the future, the communication industry is dynamic, and, of course, AT&T is a leader in developing the technology of the communication industry.

"Gor-Don" the talking robot greets visitors to InfoQuest and starts them on their tour through the dozens of individual exhibits within the center. Schoolchildren, after seeing a model of the Telstar III communication satellite, inspect screens that show how the complicated circuitry beams information back to earth. At the Lightguide Tower, visitors see how the image of a friend is carried by pulses of laser light, and they gain an understanding of how voice, data, and pictures can be transmitted simultaneously over the same system.

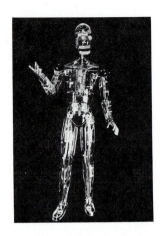

Photos courtesy of AT&T InfoQuest Center

Inviting someone in to look around, have a cup of coffee, and talk is as important for a large organization as it is for neighbors on any block. That's why most companies, government agencies, and nonprofit organizations that depend on public support regularly open their doors for tours. Visitors to tiny Aruba in the Caribbean are surprised to find that one of the serene island's most interesting attractions is the two-hour tour of Exxon's refining plant, which processes and transships much of the oil from Venezuela. After a slide show and talk in the Esso Club, the tourists ride buses through the huge refinery and watch supertankers being drained of their precious cargo. At the end of the tour, they enjoy light refreshments and have an opportunity to ask questions about the mammoth furnaces and storage tanks they have seen.

Visits to a facility by outsiders are considerably more complicated than when a neighbor drops in for coffee. Safety and security are considerations: Will guests have to wear hard hats? Will they be covered by the company's insurance? Will it be necessary to erect a tent or bring in trailers to provide protection from the elements? What measures will be taken to prevent unauthorized observation of manufacturing methods that must be kept secret? Will the tour or open house disrupt production or violate the rights of personnel? The labor unions may have to be consulted.

The company manual prepared by the public relations department of Johnson & Johnson for coordinating new plant openings suggests other areas for planning:[4]

- *Timing.* The facility must be ready and must look its best. Interesting activities should be taking place. The program must be long enough to make the trip worthwhile, but not so long as to be boring or redundant. An alternate date should be selected in case of inclement weather or emergency.
- *Invitations.* Send them out two weeks in advance. Make sure that if one politician, one academic, one subcontractor is invited, then all politicians, all other dignitaries in the area are invited. In other words, carefully work out a policy so that no one is offended. Whenever possible, involve employees and their families. Keep careful track of RSVP cards so that you know exactly who and how many are coming.
- *Transportation and parking.* Be assured that there is bus transportation to remote locations, and that there is adequate parking, clearly marked for visitors. For a large event, get the cooperation of local police in directing traffic.
- *Comfort and services.* Provide adequate restrooms, a checkroom for coats and parcels, public telephones, nursery areas for small children, and sufficient hosts and hostesses to guide guests and help out in case of emergencies.

OPEN HOUSES AND TOURS

■ *Greeting.* Assure that everyone is met by an official representative of the organization. VIPs should be met by persons of importance in the organization. Make certain that high-ranked officers of the organization make an appearance and participate in the program. Maps and printed programs should be provided to orient the visitor.

■ *Gifts.* A package of company products or some token gift imprinted with the company name is a gesture of goodwill that most visitors appreciate. Such a memento has lasting promotional value.

■ *Publicity.* Press kits should be prepared for every member of the media. A photographer should be hired to document the event. Media that do not send a representative should receive news releases and photos by mail or messenger to enable them to provide coverage. A press center should be set up to provide reporters with typewriters and telephones. A member of the PR department should be assigned to assist television crews with special needs for power and for specially arranged interviews.

■ *Refreshments.* Food and drink must be appropriate to the occasion. Liquor may be expected by a group of press or business individuals, while cookies and soft drinks are more appropriate for families. If the location is remote and the event is of more than a few hours in duration, a box lunch should be provided.

THE ANNUAL MEETING

Any incorporated organization must, according to its bylaws and the rules of the state in which it was incorporated, hold an annual meeting for the purpose of electing the board of directors and approving the financial report. The meeting must be announced in advance, and stockholders in attendance may speak and cast their votes. In practice, most votes are tallied through a proxy system. And the speakers often are perennial "gadflies" who berate the officers for not making sufficient profits, polluting the atmosphere, or otherwise mismanaging the company.

Nonetheless, most organizations believe that the annual meeting is a worthwhile ritual, because it affords the organization an opportunity to hear from its publics and, in turn, to speak directly to those who have a vested interest in the organization.

Does your organization have an auditorium or hall large enough to handle the expected turnout? Or should you rent space at a nearby theater, hotel, or other public facility? It may even be possible to use closed-circuit television to link the main meeting room with satellite rooms around the country, in order to get more people involved. Most of the concerns raised in our discussion of tours and open houses apply to the

Exhibit 15.2
Anniversaries: Advance
Planning Is Important

Anniversaries, whether the twenty-fifth, fiftieth, or one-hundredth, give your organization a good reason to point with pride to its history and accomplishments. For nonprofit groups, it's an opportunity for special development and fundraising. For commercial organizations, it's an opportunity to build employee pride and loyalty, and also to strengthen the reputation of the company and its products.

When Coca-Cola celebrated its centennial, facilities in the home city of Atlanta and in other major media cities were reserved as many as five years in advance. Actual planning of the events started in detail two years early. Three top company officers and a nine-member coordinating committee were set up to make sure that centennial objectives were central to all plans, including those carried out in various company locations around the world.

Even with the advance preparation, Coca-Cola felt that more planning and coordination would have made the events even better.

Source: Carlton L. Curtis, "Special Events: How They Are Planned and Organized," in *Experts in Action: Inside Public Relations,* 2d ed. (New York: Longman, 1989).

annual meeting. In fact, many organizations combine the annual meeting with a plant tour, social hour, or entertainment event.

Proxy materials and announcements in company publications are sufficient notice of the meeting place. However, special invitations should be sent to employees, members of the financial community, elected officials, dignitaries, and other special guests.

The annual meeting usually features speeches by one or two top officers. Unless your president is particularly inspiring, however, you may advise keeping the speeches to a minimum, and instead let a film or multimedia show tell the story of the organization's progress and plans.

Because public-interest groups concerned about pollution, energy, discrimination, and other issues have become increasingly vocal at annual meetings, PR departments today are called upon to draw up reasonable but firm rules regarding who may speak and for how long. It is also useful to use video tape to train company officers how to handle hostile questions.

Finally, PR may prepare a shopping bag full of printed materials and inexpensive souvenirs for all in attendance. This "bundle of goodies" is all it takes to satisfy many stockholders.

The annual report, which is distributed to stockholders at about the same time the annual meeting is held, is discussed in the following chapter.

NOTES
1. Baus, Herbert M., and Philip Lesly, "Direct Communications Methods," in Philip Lesly (ed.), *Lesly's Handbook of Public Relations and Communications,* 4th ed. (Chicago: Probus, 1991), pp. 490–491.

2. Warren Sloat, *1929—America Before the Crash* (New York: Macmillan, 1979).

3. Victor Danilov, "Museum Pieces," *Public Relations Journal* (August 1986), pp. 12–16, 30–31.

4. Johnson & Johnson, "Guidelines for Coordinating New Plant Openings," in-house publication, undated.

ADDITIONAL READING
—— *Good Show! A Practical Guide for Temporary Exhibitions* (Washington, DC: Smithsonian Institution, 1981).

—— "How to Determine Your Level of Exhibit Participation" and "Did Your Exhibit Pay Off?" *Public Relations Journal* (May 1978), pp. 36–38.

—— "Putting Pep in the Annual Meeting," *Public Relations Journal* (May 1978), pp. 22–31.

Berry, Elizabeth, "How to Work with Your Facility," *Public Relations Journal* (May 1978), pp. 18–19.

Brody, E. W., *Managing Communication Processes* (New York: Praeger, 1991), pp. 159–174.

Curtis, Carlton L., "Special Events: How They're Planned and Organized," in Bill Cantor and Chester Burgers (eds.), *Experts in Action: Inside Public Relations,* 2d ed. (New York: Longman, 1989).

Geier, Ted, *Make Your Events Special* (New York: Folkworks, 1986).

Widder, Frank, "Annual Meeting Check List," *Public Relations Journal* (July 1981), pp. 24–25.

Exhibitor Magazine : www. Exhibitornet. com/

www. oakridge. com/public-relations/

www. publicity. com/public-relations. shtml

www. salesplus. com/trade-shows. html
TENonline. org/art/nm. html

16

Annual Reports and Financial Writing

Read the trade journals and talk to public relations people: The impression you get is that the annual report is the tail that wags the dog.

"We begin work on the next one the day after this year's comes out," sighs one practitioner, partly from exhaustion and partly in awe of the mighty role the annual report plays in the public relations department's contribution to the organization.

A study of one hundred top corporations showed that 60 percent of annual reports are prepared in-house (the rest are prepared by outside consultants), the lead time for preparation is almost half a year, and virtually all companies consider the annual report to be an important marketing tool.[1] Another study used phrases such as "predictable," "entrenched," and "rut-bound" to characterize the standardization of the annual report format into a glossy color-photo magazine with emphasis on exciting graphics and readability.[2]

When you prepare an annual report or financial press release, usually you will be preparing information for active, information-seeking publics that need financial data about your organization. Thus, it's essential to provide clear and factual information.

Although financial publics appreciate attractive, four-color annual reports, they can be alienated if those reports do not contain the information they need. Too often, annual reports are written as though the readers are merely passive, information-processing publics.

Public relations practitioners using all four PR models produce financial information. Usually, the public information and two-way symmetric practitioners produce the most informative reports. The press agent/publicist and two-way asymmetric practitioners too often try to use annual reports to promote and propagandize. The symmetric model is ideal for financial reports that anticipate and address the concerns of stockholders and financial analysts.

WHAT'S "REQUIRED"?

Federal law requires corporations annually to file a Form 10-K with the Securities and Exchange Commission. Moreover, the SEC requires that an annual report to shareholders must precede or accompany delivery of proxy material. The stock exchanges require that companies deliver an annual report to stockholders as promptly as possible, and no later than fifteen days before the annual meeting. In order to assure interim flow of information regarding corporate profits and policies, the SEC also requires that a corporation make brief quarterly reports.

Beginning in 1980, the SEC required that more information be included in annual reports: financial data going back five years, and expanded discussion and analysis of financial condition as well as results of operation. In other words, the SEC required fuller disclosure than companies previously were accustomed to making to their stockholders.[3]

Beginning in 1990, the SEC required more disclosure and *clearer* disclosure in the section of the annual report called Management's Discussion and Analysis, where a corporation's management explains the financial data and puts the figures in context. Concerned that companies like Exxon, following the disastrous oil spill in Prince William Sound, contend that the company's operations are running smoothly, the SEC has begun to review Management's Discussion and Analysis sections. The federal regulators have required several companies to amend annual reports to give stockholders a more realistic picture. The SEC is considering requiring companies to describe in their annual reports the internal controls the firm uses to assure the accuracy of the figures given to stockholders and the financial community.

Today's PR departments must work doubly hard to satisfy federal reporting requirements and still keep the annual report lively and interesting enough to fulfill the marketing function.

Many stockholders, of course, merely look on the glossy and cheerfully positive annual report as an affirmation of the correctness of their decision to purchase shares in the company. But the more critical investors, along with investment analysts—the active, information-seeking publics—study a company's annual report in order to decide whether or not to purchase or hold the firm's stock. One company's survey of 200 stockholders and analysts showed that half of the readers of the annual report say they read the financial review and management discussion sections of the annual report—the dry, dull-looking pages full of figures and explanatory notes—because they consider evidence of good management to be the best indicator of a stock's potential profitability.[4]

Exhibit 16.1
Summary Reports Give
Only the Essentials

Stockholders, financial analysts, and companies all complain that annual reports often contain too many meaningless pictures and too much financial and legal jargon. It all adds to the expense of the annual report, and it detracts from the reader's understanding of the company's financial position.

In response to requests from General Motors and other companies, the Securities and Exchange Commission agreed in 1987 that firms can publish a *summary* annual report, stripped of the endless charts and footnotes that only accountants can understand. The result, it was hoped, would be more substance and less confusion.

A few firms have made the move to summary annual reports. But most have not, fearing that investors will be suspicious of a company that doesn't provide lots of data and will assume that a stripped-down annual report reflects poor earnings. Some companies cite surveys showing that investors want more information, not less. The summary annual report remains a rarely used variation on the standard format.

Source: Mel Wathen, "Just the Facts, Ma'am," *Public Relations Journal* (October 1987), pp. 20–26, 42.

You'll want to check annually with the SEC to learn what changes have been made in requirements for the contents of annual reports. Currently, the regulatory agency requires the use of at least 10-point type for financial statements and footnotes, so that companies can't "hide" information in tiny type. You must use the same system for reporting sales and earnings in the annual report to stockholders as you do in the 10-K report filed with the SEC; you must provide audited financial statements for two years and a five-year summary of operations; if different accounting practices are used in different company publications, you must explain the difference.

Certain content is mandated: the report of the auditing firm; a "brief description of the business," and a listing of all officers and directors with the names of their principal employers.

NONPROFITS ALSO ISSUE REPORTS

The corporate annual report has been such a resounding communication success over the years that nonprofit and service organizations have emulated the format, even though they have no stockholders to whom they are required to disseminate their financial records. The University of Minnesota's annual "Report to Investors" is actually aimed at individual, corporate, and foundation contributors whose private support augments the institution's state appropriation and earned income. The annual report of the American Field Service international intercultural program keeps former participants in the exchange program informed. The annual report of The Newspaper Fund, an educational foundation established by Dow Jones & Co., documents the career-information, intern, and training programs run by that organization in pursuit of its goal of furthering professional journalism education.

Some corporations use the annual report format to disseminate social reports or audits to their stockholders as well. For more than twenty years, General Motors has issued a separate "Public Interest Report" to discuss the firm's goals, programs, and progress in areas such as pollution control, safety, trade with communist countries, quality of life, equal employment, government relations, and philanthropic activities. Beatrice Foods has prepared a booklet depicting the identity marks of the more than two hundred brands it markets around the world, enabling stockholders to help their cause by patronizing stores and products owned by the company.

PLANNING THE CONTENTS

Since the annual report goes to substantially the same general audience each year, and since the financial data section is required information, planning for the next publication usually begins by critiquing the previous one. Just as a magazine editor builds the next issue on the framework of the preceding one, the PR department must figure out how to "top itself" with the next annual report.

Here are some questions the editors might ask in striving to improve and freshen the product:

- What audiences can we serve better next time? Are the roles of employees sufficiently highlighted? Do we show our impact on the communities where our plants are located?
- What is new this year? A good report is, in effect, a newsmagazine. Our treatment of developments in the company's organization and progress should be as exciting as a newsweekly's coverage of current events.
- Which of our tried-and-true staple items can benefit from a fresh approach? If we have led off each year with a letter from the chairman—literally a formal business letter on company stationery—perhaps this year an interview format could work better to humanize the chief executive officer. Instead of formal pictures of department heads, which make the report look like a high school yearbook, can we show company officers engaged in interesting workaday activities, or at least group them in lively pictures that don't make them look as if they're stuffed?

Exhibit 16.2
Keep the Audience's
Concerns in Mind

A Pittsburgh firm specializing in the design and production of annual reports counsels its clients in corporate public relations departments to prepare a positioning brief for management showing how the annual report will address the needs of the company's publics. If the audiences concerns aren't addressed, the money spent on the slick publication is wasted.

Writing in the annual report should be straightforward and honest, which means that bad news shouldn't be obscured or hidden. That means replacing a phrase like "income and sales were negatively impacted" with "income and sales dropped."

Lavish artwork during a lean year may send a subliminal message to the reader: the company doesn't know when and where to tighten its belt in tough times.

You don't have to wait until the report is published to find out whether you are meeting the needs of your publics. Focus groups, surveys, and other feedback mechanisms can get your audience involved during the design stage.

Source: Robert I. Denmarsh and Francis R. Esteban, "Workshop: How to Produce a Credible Annual Report," *Public Relations Journal* (October 1988), pp. 35–36.

■ Can we get a new graphic look by engaging the services of a different layout specialist, or by giving photographers free rein to experiment with innovative views of the organization's workings? How can we convince our readers to spend more time with the annual report when they flip through it the first time? The answer might be a running theme, or a "narrator" who conducts a tour of the organization.

■ Are the statistical summaries really as readable as we can make them? What will the introduction of color and helpful headings or marginal notes do for the readability of all those charts and tables?

(See the color section in the middle of this textbook for an analysis of the key sections in an annual report.)

"Theme" Gives Focus to the Annual Report

Early in the planning processes, the team responsible for the annual report will want to develop a *theme* for the book: a focus that interests the reader and differentiates the report from those in previous years.

Themes might include:

Growth—Expansion of the company's plants, increases in sales because of expanding markets abroad, new product lines.

Change—New leadership at the top, acquisition of new subsidiaries, a new organization of management functions.

Innovation—Results of research and development, scientific breakthroughs, products that open new markets.

Service—Participation in community affairs, corporate giving to cultural and charitable groups, programs to enhance employee education.

The Future—How the organization is preparing to fit the realities of a changing world and a different marketplace.

Excellence—How the firm is working to assure that quality is the prime concern of everyone in the organization.

History—In an anniversary year, a look back at how the organization evolved and grew.

The best themes grow out of management's enunciation of objectives for the coming year, which is why it is important for the public relations department to be included in management's planning sessions.

In 1988, the year that Allen H. Neuharth stepped down as chairman of the Gannett Company, Inc., and handed the reins over to John J. Curley, the theme of the annual report was "diversity." Pictures of Gannett personnel stressed the women and minorities in important roles throughout the organization. Equally as important was the "ties and jackets off" visual presentation. Neuharth and Curley were pictured informally in the *USA Today* newsroom, not dressed in corporate blue in the oak-paneled boardroom. Pictures of all executive officers of the corporation were taken at a management retreat at a resort, and so all the officers were wearing sports shirts open at the neck. The image was of real, hardworking people, not stuffed shirts. Gannett has continued the practice in subsequent annual reports, showing officers and managers in relatively unposed situations that make them seem human.

In the light of the SEC's requirements for fuller disclosure, some companies have gone beyond the usual platitudes in their reports. One firm devoted nine pages to the results of a public-opinion survey it conducted to determine the degree of risk people will accept in a complex society; one company made corporate governance the topic of its feature article; another firm laid out expansion plans, project by project, for the next five years, explaining the rationale behind each move.[5] Clearly, the annual report of the future will be less of an advertisement for past successes and more of an agenda-setter for future programs—a development that should provide a challenge to new practitioners

Exhibit 16.3
Employees Get Separate
Annual Report

Potential investors, analysts, and current stockholders are the main target publics for the annual report. But employees, some of whom also may own shares in the company, are another important audience. So important, that some firms prepare a separate annual report to explain to their employees how the organization's plans and profits will affect the workplace and their careers.

Most corporations are so large that employees in one branch or division don't know what is going on in another unit. The employee annual report gives them a better idea of how the parts of the organization work together to achieve goals and objectives.

Because employees tend to be suspicious of sugar-coated information provided by their employer, some employee annual reports feature guest articles by outside experts who discuss the economy, market trends, and how they see the company's chances of prospering in the future.

In addition to providing information, employee annual reports help workers to identify with their company and also improve workers' morale by making them feel appreciated by upper management.

Source: Laurie Sue Brockway, "Employee Annual Reports: Thriving Amidst Corporate Changes," *Public Relations Journal* (July 1989), pp. 21–24.

entering the field of public relations. You will remember from Chapter 9 that video is an optional channel for the annual report. Many Fortune 500 companies are taping reports for use on cable TV and for satellite transmission to groups of stockholders around the world.[6]

Target Additional Audiences

After stockholders and financial analysts receive their copies of the annual report, you'll want to have enough extra copies to add other publics to the distribution list. They might include:

- Your major customers and your suppliers.
- Community leaders in towns where your facilities are located.
- Legislators, especially those sitting on committees that can have an effect on your organization.
- Local media where your facilities are located; trade publications.
- Business publications, business writers, and columnists.
- Libraries.
- Teachers, college professors in subjects such as communication, business, accounting, and anything having to do with the nature of your company.

■ Financial institutions, including banks and brokerage houses.
■ Directors of government agencies, especially those having dealings with your organization, and including those with regulatory powers.

FINANCIAL WRITING: HOW DOES IT DIFFER?

The very term "financial writing" has a mystique about it, as does "science writing" or "medical writing." Everyone agrees that "we need better financial writing" and "a good financial writer is hard to find." So what is it that makes writing about the world of business exotic and mysterious?

In truth, it isn't the "writing" that calls for special qualities, it's the ability to understand the terminology and thinking of the business community. In other words, the jargon. Indeed, the qualified financial writer is one who can plow through the obfuscations of business communicating with business, then translate it into clear, interesting prose. The essence of good technical writing, no matter what the field, is the ability to read and understand specialized material, and not to forget the basic principles of effectively aiming your message at your audience.

Manage Your Financial Writing

Because financial publics are active, your objective should be to help them retain and understand financial information. You must understand what you write, or you can't help your reader. Evaluate your own understanding: Explain concepts to someone else before you write, and see if you can put together a coherent explanation. Use the signaled stopping technique yourself, on your own writing, to see where there are gaps in your understanding.

Research on technical writing has identified some critical techniques that promote message retention and understanding.[7] Most importantly, you should use the active voice and sentences with subject-verb-object structure, rather than sentences with linking "to be" verbs. Always define terms that the reader will not understand without a dictionary. Use analogies, metaphors, and examples to relate unfamiliar ideas with ideas familiar to readers.

Pitch It to Different Publics

Earlier we enumerated multiple publics for annual reports. Most of the same audiences are targets for other forms of financial writing, including news releases sent to business editors, articles written for trade magazines by your public relations staff (but carrying the byline of your president), and even "bill-stuffers" included with regular correspondence to your customers. The insurance industry frequently uses bill-stuffers to explain the reasons for rising costs, or to encourage clients to influence the defeat of legislation that would regulate insurance companies and affect their ability to do business in the state.

Rarely does one article serve the needs of all your publics needing financial information. For that reason, you will first outline and write a standard piece that includes all the points you want to make. Then, with your mind on the capabilities and interests of various publics, you will add or subtract information to fit each audience. It is not unusual for a public relations agency or department to fashion half a dozen different articles out of one set of "boilerplate" information.

Improve Your Skills

The emphasis in training for financial writing should be on preparation and backgrounding in the fields of economics and business. The best place to start is with college courses on macroeconomics (the world order), microeconomics (the workings of specialized marketplaces), business administration, and marketing. The public relations practitioner who avoided such subjects as an undergraduate will find that many colleges offer night courses, summer seminars, and week-long workshops to help professionals learn about the workings of monetary and financial systems.

The reference shelves of most libraries are stocked with literally scores of handbooks that explain the special jargon, practices, and procedures of financial subfields: *The Accountant's Handbook, Handbook of Insurance, Marketing Handbook, Real Estate Handbook, Corporate Secretaries' Manual and Guide, Corporate Treasurer's and Controller's Handbook.* To learn about the size, role, and particular interests of financial institutions, look for the fact books issued annually by their trade associations. The United States League of Savings Associations, for example, issues both an annual *Savings and Loan Fact Book* and the yearly *Savings Association Annals.* The latter carries essays, reprints, and summaries of government actions affecting the savings industry, along with the reports of all association standing committees. The annual *Mutual Fund Fact Book* published by the Investment Company Institute in Washington offers data provided by mutual fund directors and underwriters.

The best advice to the would-be financial writer, then, is to build a reference library, keep current by reading business periodicals, take refresher courses, attend banking institutes, and, in general, associate with those whose activities you must understand and report. Once you have gathered and selected your information, refer to the principles outlined in Chapter 4 of this volume: Identify with your readers, write tightly, explain complicated concepts with simple analogies, and don't fall prey to the self-fulfilling prophecy that financial writing has to be complex and confusing. Successful, popular financial writers, such as columnist and author "Adam Smith," have shown that business and economics can be made comprehensible—if you're willing to work at developing the skill.

NOTES

1. Ronald Goodman, "Annual Reports Serving a Dual Market Function: Report of a Survey," *Public Relations Quarterly* (Summer 1980), pp. 21–24.

2. Janet Dyer, "Predictable: The Watchword for 1980 Reports," *Public Relations Journal* (August 1981), pp. 9–10.

3. Vincent Cannella, "Integrated Disclosure: Betwixt and Between," *Public Relations Journal* (August 1981), pp. 8–9.

4. George L. Fisher and C. R. Davenport, "What Investors Want to Hear," *Public Relations Journal* (April 1981), pp. 14–15, 18.

5. William P. Dunk, "28 Trends in Annual Reports," *Public Relations Journal* (August 1980), pp. 10–13.

6. Nancy L. Ross, "The Corporate Score Card Takes to the Airways," *Washington Post*, May 2, 1982, pp. L1, L6.

7. For a complete review of the literature of science writing, which is quite similar to financial writing, see James E. Grunig, "Communication of Scientific Information to Nonscientists," in Brenda Dervin and Melvin J. Voight (eds.), *Progress in Communication Sciences*, Vol. 2 (Norwood, NJ: Ablex, 1980), pp. 167–214.

ADDITIONAL READING

——— "Annual Report Credibility," *Public Relations Journal* (November 1984), pp. 31–34.

——— "Making Sense of Annual Reports," *Money*, March 1985, pp. 201–204.

Badaracco, Claire, "Smoke and Substance: Trends in Annual Reports," *Public Relations Quarterly* (Spring 1988), pp. 13–17.

Chandra, Gyan, "Disclosures in Summary Annual Reports," *The Ohio CPA Journal* (Winter 1989), pp. 18–25.

Graves, Joseph, *Investor Relations Today* (Washington, DC: Investor Relations, 1985).

Howard, Elizabeth, "Preparing Annual Reports in the 1990s," *Public Relations Journal* (May 1991), pp. 26–27.

Otterbourg, Robert K., "Annual Report Copy: Banish the Boredom," *Public Relations Journal* (July 1990), pp. 21–23.

Parker, Robert A., "How Do You Play the Annual Report Game?" *Communication World* (September 1990), pp. 24–28.

Schneider, Alan J., "Summary Annual Reporting: Has the Concept Been Accepted?" *Financial Executive* (July–August 1988), pp. 20–24.

Smart, Tim, "Annual Reports: The SEC Cracks the Whip," *Business Week*, April 10, 1989, p. 74.

Taylor, Anne Marie, "Put on a Happy Face," *Communication World* (September 1990), pp. 20–23.

Truesdell, Wesley E., "The Great Annual Report Non-Controversy," *Public Relations Quarterly* (Spring 1988), pp. 10–12.

Winter, Elmer L., *A Complete Guide to Preparing a Corporate Annual Report* (New York: Van Nostrand Reinhold, 1985).

Woodmansee, Lelan K., "The Video Annual Report," *Association Management* (February 1991), p. 164.

17

Public Relations Advertising

Nonproduct advertising by corporations goes by many names. Indeed, J. Douglas Johnson, former senior vice president of McCann-Erickson, the giant advertising firm, and later a marketing professor at Indiana University, identified more than a dozen labels for various nuances of corporate advertising, including "concept advertising," "general promotion advertising," "goodwill advertising," "image advertising," "issue advertising," "personality advertising," and "responsibility advertising." In the end, he selected "public relations advertising" as the term that covers the entire spectrum.[1]

Another major American advertising firm, Foote, Cone & Belding, created the FCB/Corporate Division to specialize in what it likes to call "corporate positioning." An advertisement for FCB/Corporate's services is headlined: "Companies sure know how to sell products—but they don't know beans about selling themselves."[2] Believing that a corporation can't tell securities analysts where it is heading unless it has a strong sense of its own distinguishing character and point of view, FCB/Corporate conducts in-depth interviews with the client and the client's customers, and then prepares a "positioning document" outlining an advertising campaign aimed at projecting the desired identity.

A survey by the Association of National Advertisers showed that the biggest single purpose of corporate advertising was to build recognition, especially for corporations that need "umbrella identification" for broadened and diversified lines, as well as "industries where there are

CORPORATE ADVERTISING IS GROWING

high levels of public criticism," such as petroleum and basic materials.[3] The president of one advertising agency believes that what she calls issues-and-causes advertising "may soon be as big as detergents or automobile advertising," and adds, "I believe that the business of ideas is beginning to look more and more like the business of products."[4]

All this is good news for the world of public relations, since PR practitioners play a major role in shaping corporate advertising policies, according to the annual surveys conducted by the *Public Relations Journal*. PR departments are the principal originators of concepts and themes for corporate advertising. More and more they are involved in media selection and placement of ads, taking over some of the responsibilities of advertising departments.

The primary goals of corporate advertising, according to the annual PRJ surveys, include:

Improving consumer relations,

Presenting stands on public issues,

Improving stockholder/financial relations,

Improving trade relations,

Community relations, employee relations, and

"Image" and reputation.

Most companies also expect product sales to be improved by corporate advertising, and thus consider it a marketing tool as well.

How useful is corporate advertising? Studies conducted on behalf of *Time* magazine by Yankelovich, Skelly & White, Inc., indicate that companies devoting substantially more of their advertising budget to corporate advertising than product advertising enjoy "recall" scores (i.e., the message-retention objective) almost equal to corporations that use mainly product advertising—and with substantially smaller budgets![5]

The researchers also found that corporate advertisers were more cost-effective in realizing "association with specific traits" (the objective of message acceptance), "favorable overall impressions" (the objective of affecting evaluations—attitudes), and "potential supportive behavior" (the objective of influencing behavior). Yankelovich concluded that corporate advertisers outperform noncorporate advertisers on all key measurements of effectiveness studied.

Examples of "Issues" Ads

The best way to get a feel for the wide range of topics and issues covered by institutional advertising, along with the techniques used to make a point, is to examine a portfolio of examples:

Exhibit 17.1
The "Image" Ads That
Saved a Company

*Chrysler Chairman
Lee Iacocca helped engineer
the turnaround of this
company by serving as chief
spokesperson in all
advertisements.*

In his autobiography *Iacocca*, then-Chrysler chairman Lee Iacocca re-calls that the decision to use paid advertising to carry public relations messages was the key to "setting the record straight" and convincing Congress and taxpayers, as well as consumers, that the auto company was asking for loan guarantees, not handouts, and that the company's management was capable of turning the firm around.

Iacocca said he went along with the decision to put his face in the ads and his signature at the bottom because he realized that the main message had to be: "I'm here, I'm real, and I'm responsible for this company. . . . We were inviting the public to write to me with their complaints and their questions. We were announcing that this large, complex company was now being run by a human being who was putting his name and his reputation on the line."

By using advertising to demonstrate his commitment to the two-way symmetric model of public relations, Iacocca helped engineer the turnaround of his company.

Source: Lee Iacocca, with William Novak, *Iacocca* (New York: Bantam, 1984), pp. 222–223.

■ Stung by the spate of anti-Japanese advertising messages at the beginning of the 1990s, the Toyota Motor Corporation began an extensive campaign to show that the company cares about America. Ads described scholarships given to American students, the sponsorship of a high school basketball team, and other acts of generosity toward America and Americans by the Japanese firm.

- Worried that environmental groups were spreading anti-business messages based on "doomsday" predictions of the effects of technological advances, United Technologies ran an ad that chronicled the now-laughable "dire warnings" through the ages about the effects of rail travel, horseless carriages, flight machines, jet propulsion, and other innovations that now are accepted by society.

- The U.S. Corporate Council on South Africa, headed by the chairman of General Motors, ran a series of ads pointing out that leading South African businesses had taken a stand against racial apartheid, and that leading American businesses stood behind that movement.

- Philip Morris Inc. sponsors a series of ads with the theme line "It takes art to make a company great" to call attention to the firm's long-standing support of museums and performing arts groups.

- "You'll forgive us a little flag waving" headlines the IBM ad picturing pennants from more than thirty American colleges and universities. The campaign highlights the firm's annual contribution of more than $82 million to college programs in computer science, engineering, and science.

- A coalition of automobile industry associations, including dealers' organizations and manufacturers, joined to sponsor a series of ads during the Iraq invasion of Kuwait in 1990. Their concern was that Congress would pass stricter laws on auto fuel efficiency based on emotions during the crisis. The campaign argued that dependence on foreign oil should be reduced through market incentives, not restrictions on automobile fuel use.

- When beloved comedian Danny Kaye died, his years as spokesperson for the United Nations Children's Fund (UNICEF) came to an end. The agency used an advertising campaign saluting Kaye's contributions to stimulate special contributions of money in his honor.

- Because many people associate the Teamsters union with truck drivers—and with corruption—the ad campaign designed to enhance the "image" of the Teamsters features appealing and emotional pictures of teachers, nurses, firemen, and flight attendants who are represented by the union.

- In an extraordinary two-page ad run in major papers after the Mexico City earthquake, American Express listed the names of all 701 of its employees in Mexico City to salute them for "being there to help" during the crisis by keeping offices open, working overtime, and going beyond the call of duty to help rearrange flights and get emergency funds to cardmembers.

- In a series headlined "We're Environmental Activists," Union Carbide detailed its achievements in air emission reduction, waste reduction, public education, and development of new technologies. The company also presented its objectives for the future in areas such as reducing spills and accidents.

- When a Roper poll indicated that most of its Delaware Valley neighbors didn't know what the Rhom and Haas Company did or was, the chemical company hired a public relations firm to design ads and other programs to make it a more visible member of the greater Philadelphia business community.

- W. R. Grace & Co. prepared a television commercial called "The Deficit Trials, 2017 A.D.," depicting a future world where a remorseful old man was on trial for failing to protect future citizens from the damage done by deficit spending in the America of the past. The hard-hitting ad, second in a series, was rejected by the networks on the grounds that it was controversial and opened the networks to providing time for response by those who disagreed with the highly political message. While Grace did not succeed in getting its message to the widest possible public, the debate that followed achieved the objective of putting Grace's ideas and concerns on the agenda of legislators, the media, and other opinion leaders.

JOINING THE PUBLIC DEBATE: ADVOCACY ADVERTISING

When he was vice president for public relations and advertising at Kaiser Aluminum, Ronald E. Rhody (now executive vice president for corporate communication at the Bank of America) stated that "issues advertising is an idea whose time has come" in America. Answering critics of Kaiser's aggressive use of advocacy advertising, Rhody replied: "We don't want to dominate the national debate—we just want to participate in it."[6]

Since all advertising involves advocacy, many companies prefer to call it "issues" advertising. For two decades, the Mobil Oil Corporation, spurred by vice president of public affairs Herbert Schmerz (who has now formed his own public relations agency specializing in issues management), has spent more than $4 million annually to let its publics know where the company stands on issues involving energy resources and government regulations and issues facing the nation. In one of the op-ed (opposite the editorial page) ads for which the company is noted, Mobil observed that "few seem any longer surprised that corporations have ideas and the right to express them." The company said it considers its ads to be "a running conversation with the public."[7]

In the "Memo to editors" ad shown here, Mobil ostensibly is speaking directly to journalists. Instead of criticizing them directly,

Exhibit 17.2

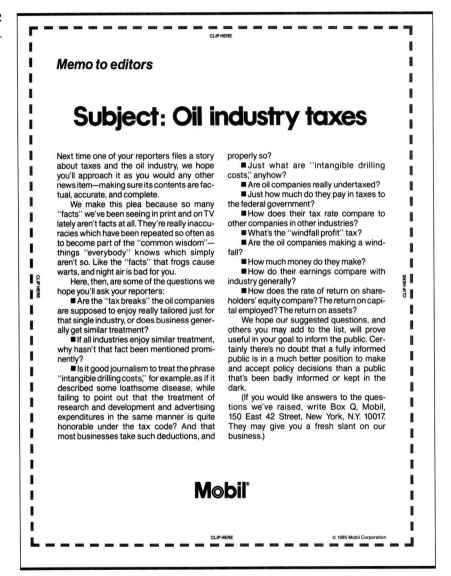

Courtesy of Mobil

the company suggests that editors should be more demanding of reporters who cover the petroleum industry. Of course Mobil is also talking to opinion leaders and readers of the newspaper, stimulating them to question whether or not they are receiving the full and unbiased truth from the news stories they read.

The U.S. government prepares print ads with AIDS information and urges publications to run them as a public service.

Courtesy of U.S. Department of Health and Human Services Centers for Disease Control and Prevention

Four Reasons for Using Advocacy Ads

According to S. Prakash Sethi, a University of Texas scholar of business policy, corporations use advocacy advertising for four reasons:

> To counteract public hostility to corporate activities that results from what corporations believe is public ignorance or misinformation.

> To counter what corporations believe is misleading information spread by critics of business, and to better explain complex business issues.

> To foster the values of the free-enterprise system.

Exhibit 17.3
Media Welcome Public
Service Ads

Spending on advertising for products and services was down in the early 1990s, owing to a sluggish economy. But the value of "free" advertising jumped a record 30 percent from 1989 to 1990, amounting to $1.35 billion of media time and space donated to public service messages.

The fact that media need to fill the time and space left empty of paying ads had something to do with the upswing. But another important reason was the increasing quality of public service campaigns concerning illiteracy, AIDS, drugs, and other social issues. Major ad agencies, donating their time and resources on a *pro bono* basis—for the good of society—are preparing campaigns that are as slick as those used to sell automobiles and perfumes.

Research indicates that major public-service ad campaigns have an impact. A Proctor and Gamble-sponsored Ad Council campaign to inform men about the dangers of colon cancer more than doubled the number of men who saw their doctors for an examination, and awareness of the issue quadrupled during the campaign.

Sources: Stuart Elliott, "Public Service Campaigns Ran at Record Pace in '90," *The New York Times*, August 12, 1991, p. D–9; Randall Rothenberg, "Study Shows Power of Public-Service Ads," *The New York Times*, April 8, 1991, p. D–1.

To gain access to the media, which many corporate leaders believe they have been denied, and to counteract what corporate leaders perceive to be media bias.[8]

Studies have shown that print is more effective than television as a vehicle for advocacy advertising, but television is effective as a tool for reminding people to look for the arguments contained in print issues ads.[9] Advocacy ads also appear to have a "halo" effect. That is, persons who read ads sponsored by organizations tend not only to respond favorably to the information in the ads, they also respond favorably when the same organization is associated with issues not discussed in the advertisement—suggesting that "goodwill" does indeed carry over from one message to another.[10]

PREPARING THE CORPORATE AD

As with any form of communication, the designer of a corporate advertisement should begin by determining the audience to be reached by the ad and the goals to be served. Next comes careful research to marshal the facts and select those that best make your points. Only then can you turn to the actual layout of the message.

Elements of the Print Ad

There are five components of a newspaper or magazine advertisement:

1. The headline, which grabs the reader's attention and poses a question or raises a proposition. The headline should entice the reader into examining the rest of the message.
2. The copy, the main block of text, which develops the premise of the headline and leads the reader to the desired conclusion.
3. The "art," or illustrative matter, which attracts attention to the ad and appeals to the emotions.
4. The signature or "logo" of the sponsoring organization, along with an address to which interested readers may write for more information.
5. White space, or "visual relief," which directs the eye, provides separation from adjoining messages, and relieves the cluttered feeling that could make the ad difficult to read.

Elements of the Broadcast Ad

All parts of the print advertisement can be viewed simultaneously, and the reader can decide how much time to spend absorbing each element of the message. Broadcast ads, however, are linear and unvarying—the creator of the message must decide exactly how many seconds should be devoted to capturing the audience's attention, developing and supporting a theme, and summarizing or calling for a specific responsive action. In addition, broadcast ads offer the realism of sound and, in the case of television, motion. Sound effects literally "grab us by the collar." Properly selected voices have the effect of annoying, surprising, or convincing us as we listen.

Television offers both action and print: at the end of a 60-second drama, the final frame freezes, and a logo, slogan, and address to write for more information can be superimposed over the image. Television also permits "layering" of information on top of information through the use of an announcer's "voiceover."

What makes radio potent as a communication medium is the fact that the audience creates the visual parts of the message. The listener who completes the picture in his or her own head is perhaps more likely to remember and embrace the ideas put forth. Because there is no visual presentation, however, radio spots are apt to have less recall unless they are repeated frequently. And because attention paid to the specifics of a radio message is low, the advertiser hopes mainly to plant a single fact or idea, which may later be augmented and reinforced by print messages. Radio advertising is flexible: A campaign that begins with 60-second spots later can be continued with 30- or 20-second spots.

Union Carbide counters public perceptions by claiming the high ground in the issue of environmental protection. Even if the reader only glances at the large type, the company has positioned itself as concerned and involved.

WE'RE ENVIRONMENTAL ACTIVISTS

Today's Achievements

Community Involvement — In nearly every community in which we operate, Union Carbide employees are leading the way to help local emergency planning committees execute their plans to meet or exceed U.S. reporting and communication mandates. We have also established programs at most of our locations to ensure continuing dialogue between our plants and local communities.

Air Emission Reduction — In the U.S., our Chemicals and Plastics Group has reduced the annual amount of chemicals released to the air by 19 million pounds — or some 50 percent — from our 1985 baseline.

Waste Reduction — In the past few years, Union Carbide Corporation's Chemicals and Plastics Group has cut annual generation of hazardous waste in the U.S. by 64 percent. Our Carbon Products Group has reduced waste generation by 60 percent. By recycling, our Industrial Gases Group has drastically reduced the need for waste disposal.

Public Education — We are working with communities, environmental groups, and other companies in support of public environmental education, including the funding of household hazardous waste education and disposal programs.

New Technologies — We are developing technologies and systems to eliminate undesirable chemicals.

Dioxin Destroyers — Linde "A" Burner, an advanced combustion process for cleaning up dioxin-contaminated soils.

PCB Removal — A proprietary chemical engineering system for the removal of PCBs from electrical transformers.

Ozone Protectors — A new polyurethane foam system that does not require the use of chlorofluorocarbons, which are suspected of depleting the earth's protective ozone layer.

Tomorrow's Objectives

Reduce Air Emissions — Control emissions of potentially harmful chemicals so that exposure levels in the community are at least 1,000 times lower than U.S. workplace standards. Ultimately eliminate emissions of known and suspect carcinogens.

Reduce Wastewater Discharges — Control discharges of potentially harmful chemicals so that levels in the receiving streams are lower than

any level known to cause adverse health effects. Upgrade technology and operating practices to ultimately eliminate discharges of known and suspect carcinogenic chemicals.

Reduce Process Waste — Establish a mindset that makes waste minimization a high priority. Eliminate, to the maximum degree practicable, the use of commercial land disposal for process waste and develop the

incineration capacity needed to manage our burnable chemical process waste internally.

Reduce Spills and Incidents — Create a "working creed" that seeks to eliminate all spills and incidents. Take precautions so that even major accidents will not result in serious adverse effects on our employees, neighbors, or the environment.

ADVANCING ENVIRONMENTAL EXCELLENCE

To learn more about Union Carbide's Health, Safety, and Environmental programs write:
Corporate Communications Department, Union Carbide Corporation, 39 Old Ridgebury Rd., Danbury, CT 06817-0001

Courtesy of Union Carbide

Exhibit 17.4
Develop the "Big Idea"

The first step in developing any advertising campaign is to come up with the "big idea"—the theme, slogan, concept, or creative spark upon which everything can be hung. To arrive at it, you and your entire staff have to brainstorm, jot down a thousand ideas both cosmic and trivial, study the field to see what others are doing, try those ideas out on family and friends, then rest for a while and see if the results of the first round of brainstorming hold up when you revisit them later.

Other basic requirements of a good advertising campaign: Keep the message simple and speak directly to your public. People don't have time to try to comprehend a complicated message. Boil it down to what they can understand, believe, and act upon in the few seconds or minutes they can devote to your message.

Source: Jan Lewis, "How to Write Corporate Ads," *Public Relations Journal* (September 1988), pp. 45–46.

Direct Advertising

If publics are expected to contribute to a cause, join an organization, send for information, or cast a vote, advertisements placed in the media of mass communication may not be sufficient to bring about the desired action. Direct-mail advertising is a necessary element of the campaign. The beauty of direct advertising is that few of the space and time limitations of the mass media apply. A successful "issues" mailing may include a multipage "personal" letter, a brochure, and a return envelope. With direct advertising, it is also possible to segment publics targeted for variations on the standard appeal, and to keep count of those who responded in the desired way to the message.

NOTES

1. J. Douglas Johnson, *Advertising Today* (Chicago: SRA, Inc., 1978), p. 247.
2. *The New York Times,* July 16, 1981, p. D–13.
3. Philip H. Dougherty, "Corporate Ads Show Growth," *The New York Times,* October 17, 1981, p. D–17.
4. Paula Green, "Huge Growth Expected in Issues-Causes Advertising," *Advertising Age,* November 13, 1980, pp. 66, 68.
5. *Corporate Advertising/Phase II* (New York: Yankelovich, Skelly & White, Inc., 1979).
6. Address to public relations and advertising divisions, Association for Education in Journalism and Mass Communication conference, August 9, 1981, East Lansing, MI.

7. *The New York Times*, September 25, 1980, p. A–21; see also "Why Do We Buy This Space?" *The New York Times*, April 1, 1982, p. A–27.

8. S. Prakash Sethi, *Advocacy Advertising and Large Corporations* (Boston: D.C. Heath, 1977), p. 57.

9. Robert Heath and William Douglas, "Issues Advertising and Its Effects on Public Opinion Recall," *Public Relations Review* (Summer 1986), pp. 47–56.

10. Heath and Douglas.

11. Robert C. Grass, "Measuring the Effects of Corporate Advertising," *Public Relations Review* (Winter 1977), pp. 39–50.

ADDITIONAL READING

———, "The Issue of Issues Ads: W. R. Grace, the Networks and the First Amendment," *Public Relations Journal* (October 1986), pp. 30–33, 42–43.

Alvarez, Paul H., "Corporate Advertising Survey: Magazines, TV Top '90 Media Lists," *Public Relations Journal* (September 1991), pp. 14–19.

Bivens, Thomas, "Print Advertising," in *Handbook for Public Relations Writing* (Lincolnwood, IL: NTC Business Books, 1988).

Garbett, Thomas E., *Corporate Advertising* (New York: McGraw-Hill, 1981).

Hagopian, Louis T., "Advocacy Advertising," in Joseph S. Nagelschmidt (ed.), *The Public Affairs Handbook* (Washington, DC: American Management Association, 1982).

Heath, Robert, and William Douglas, "Issues Advertising and Its Effects on Public Opinion Recall," *Public Relations Review* (Summer 1986), pp. 47–56.

Lesly, Philip, "Using Advertising for Public Relations Communication," in Philip Lesly (ed.), *Lesly's Handbook of Public Relations and Communications* (Chicago: Probus, 1991), pp. 452–470.

Nelson, Roy Paul, *The Design of Advertising*, 6th ed. (Dubuque, IA: Wm. C. Brown, 1989).

Reisman, Joan, "Corporate Advertising: Public Relations in Disguise?" *Public Relations Journal* (September 1989), pp. 20–27.

Sethi, S. Prakash, *Handbook of Advocacy Advertising Concepts, Strategies and Applications* (Cambridge, MA: Ballinger, 1987).

Welty, Ward, "Is Issues Advertising Working?" *Public Relations Journal* (November 1981), p. 29.

18

Business Communication

In the preceding sections, each chapter has looked at a medium or means of communication and described its use. What we have not sufficiently acknowledged as yet is that public relations practitioners using the various techniques of mass communication cannot disseminate their messages to target publics without first engaging in a great deal of coordination.

The participants involved in the discussions and the decisions that lead to the execution of an event, campaign, or program may include:

- the public relations department,
- the management of the organization,
- other internal departments that have a stake or an interest (including the legal department),
- outside agencies called in to help plan and execute strategies,
- research firms used to measure attitudes and responses,
- vendors and suppliers who prepare the message components, and editors or producers for the media where material is placed.

Coordination within an organization is achieved in a variety of ways. Only in the smallest departments and agencies, however, will the exchange of oral information be sufficient to assure that all interested parties know what is going on and what is expected. In any project that involves more than a handful of people, written communication is essential. The ability to write a memo that motivates people, a report that gets the attention of management, or a letter that persuades others to support your initiative is an important attribute of the successful public relations person.

Even supposedly oral communication situations—meetings and briefings, for example—have important written components such as the memo calling people to the meeting, the agenda, background materials, audio-visual aids, the record that is kept of what happened at the meeting, and follow-up reports.

Mastering business communication takes practice. The best way to learn is to pattern your work on successful models, and we'll provide some here. Once on the job, every student of public relations should maintain a file of formats particularly suited to the specific industry, trade, or sector where he or she works. Sales-related positions, for example, may call for heavy use of charts, balance sheets, and printouts. Technical writing has its special requirements for handling data. In some highly competitive fields, security of information is of particular concern.

Before we look at specific forms of business communication, it is useful to review the purposes of messages. We also will describe the purposes and parameters of an organization's policy manual, which usually contains a section on communication procedures.

WHAT'S THE PURPOSE?

It may seem trivial to pose the question "Why am I preparing this written message?" because often the purpose appears to be self-evident. But the careful public relations practitioner never takes anything for granted. That even includes raising the question: "Is there a downside—a negative consequence—of communicating to this audience in this format at this time?"

The following are some situations where it may be wise not to engage in written communication with members of your organization:

■ Goals and objectives have not been set—therefore memos and reports concerning execution of a program may appear premature and even presumptuous;

■ Distribution of a message from top management to all employees might undercut the role of the individual managers who have been charged with coordinating the activities of their departments;

■ A blizzard of paper has swamped members of the organization, and more written communication will only result in overload;

■ It has not been settled or decided yet which department will take the lead on a project, and thus it may not be "politically" expedient to issue written communications; or

■ Introducing a new topic may have the effect of giving it priority over more pressing projects already under way.

If none of these conditions precludes communication, then the next step is to analyze the purpose of writing a memo, letter, or report. Organizational communication expert Gerald M. Goldhaber suggests that each message has one of the following four purposes:[1]

To Help Accomplish a Task Task-related messages give employees the information they need to do their jobs. They provide orientation and announce objectives. Examples: A sales report that shows whether goals are being met. A job description given to a new employee by his superior. A description of procedures for using a new piece of office equipment. Announcement of the formation of employee "quality circles" to improve product or services.

To Help Maintain the Organization Maintenance-related messages pertain to policy and procedures, they aim to set norms, and they assure the continued functioning of the organization. Examples: Promulgation of a policy for taking unused vacation days at the end of the year. Announcement of a chain of command that must be followed when proposing changes in the procedures followed by the organization. Explanation of procedures for making budget requests and filling out quarterly or annual reports.

To Improve the Human Conditions in the Organization Human messages concern morale, the quality of life, job satisfaction, and the personal fulfillment of individual employees. Examples: Sign-ups for the plant bowling league. Announcement of free and confidential drug-counseling services for employees and members of their families. Meetings to inform senior employees about their retirement options. Presentation of achievement certificates to those who have completed training programs.

To Promote Innovation within the Organization Innovation-related messages are part of the process of adapting the organization to a changing environment. Examples: A "Benny Suggs" program, with the cartoon character of that name representing employees who receive cash payments for submitting beneficial suggestions on ways to improve production or working conditions. A retreat where middle-managers get out of the office and engage in an unstructured brainstorming session to come up with ideas. Briefings for various levels of employees to allow them to speak to top management without the presence of their direct superiors.

The public relations department needs to analyze the overarching purpose of each message. It also should consider the question "What behavior do we want from the recipients of this message?" Building from that objective, one can judge the clarity and effectiveness of a message by pre-testing it with selected audience members and determining whether the desired behavior is likely to occur.

Good managers learn to prepare a working draft of every memo, letter, report, or briefing plan. The draft is circulated to staff members in proximity to the writer—either the immediate superior or another employee familiar with the workings of the department. It may also be carried to one or two trusted individuals in other departments who can look at it without making the same assumptions the public relations department might make. Although this review process adds another day or two to the preparation of a written message, the payoff is usually worth it. Messages intended for external audiences usually benefit from pre-testing, and so do those intended for internal publics.

USING THE POLICY MANUAL

Public relations managers in new or small organizations often are on their own when it comes to making decisions about communication with their publics. But in established organizations, sooner or later managers realize the cost of "reinventing the wheel" and "doing your own thing" when it comes to business communication. Eventually the director of communication decides to oversee the writing of a communication policy manual for the entire organization—or at least for the public relations department.

Many policy manuals begin with a capsule history of the organization. They then provide an organization chart showing who reports to whom and where the communication department fits in the hierarchy. Names, phone numbers, and/or access codes for reaching key personnel on the organization's internal electronic mail system are listed. Mission, goals, and objectives of the organization are summarized, and related goals and objectives for the communication department are outlined. The balance of the policy manual sets down procedures for each type of communication in which the communication department regularly is involved. Often the sections are divided to account for the differences in procedures for dealing with internal and external audiences.

An organization can model its communication policy manual generally after that of another similar organization. But, to be genuinely useful, a policy manual must be tailored specifically to the situations each organization faces. To make that point, we'll provide two lists of sections from policy manuals. The first includes items useful to almost any type of organization. The second shows the special problems and needs faced by specific organizations.

Standard Section Headings from Communication Policy Manuals

- Employee Publications—Roles and functions of newsletters; assigns responsibility for gathering news items.
- Service Recognition—Awards and ceremonies accorded to employees who have achieved five, ten, fifteen, or twenty-five years of service.
- Press Releases—Formats for releases, system for approval of drafts, lists of general, business, and trade publications usually targeted by the organization.
- Photo Releases—Procedures for obtaining identification of persons shown in photos for internal or external use; form for obtaining release to use photos for publicity purposes; format for cutlines containing identifications; guidelines for purchasing rights from freelance photographers.
- Press Relations—Procedures for handling press inquiries, including system for recording the nature of the information requested and record of approval for all information released.
- Annual Report—Assignment of responsibility to department managers for submitting material needed for annual report; timetable for preparation of standard sections of annual report.
- Bulletin Board Policy—Regulations for posting official and unofficial items on organizational bulletin boards; departmental responsibility for posting official announcements; assignment of board space to unions, employee interest groups, and other non-management functions.
- Emergency Policies—Assignment of roles and responsibilities in case of fire, plant closing, strikes, weather emergencies, or civil disorders.
- Memos and Other Internal Messages—Formats for standard memos; routing codes for reaching segments of management levels and general list of employees; coding system for categorization of memos into standard headings.
- Employee Information Rights—Explanation of employees' rights to information about pay, benefits, labor regulations, tax information, performance ratings, job postings, equal opportunity requirements, and retirement options.
- Customer Relations—Policies for handling inquiries, complaints, and legal actions involving customers; standard letter formats for responding to inquiries, complaints, and suggestions.

Successful meetings depend on a variety of communication components—an agenda, written and oral reports, and supplementary information.

Photo © Mary Ann Fittipaldi

- Audio-Visual Services—Listing of services available in-house for preparing slides, videotapes, sound recordings, and graphic reproductions to support sales, marketing, education, or management programs; timetables for preparation of materials; in-house costs and approved costs for using outside vendors.
- Suggestion Box System—Mechanism for encouraging and rewarding employee input on improving communication within the organization; policy for protecting "whistle-blowers" who report wrongdoing or unethical conduct.

Special Situations Addressed in Communication Policy Manuals

- Advertising Guidelines—When advertising space or time is to be purchased for public relations purposes, the manual may stipulate limits on amounts to be spent; coordination with the department or agency that usually handles buying of advertising space for the organization may be required.
- Contributions and Matching Gifts—Many organizations spell out situations in which gifts by their employees are matched by

the company; both nonprofit and commercial organizations usually allow communication managers to make donations up to a certain amount to community groups; a committee may oversee grants of larger requests from cultural, educational, or social welfare groups.

■ Political Action Committees—Defense contractors and others doing business with government agencies are likely to permit and encourage formation of political action committees for the purpose of allowing employees to make contributions to political candidates and parties. The Federal Election Campaign Act and similar state statutes spell out strict rules, which the communication manual may require the public relations department to promulgate.

■ Relationship with Other Companies—As more and more companies become subsidiaries within a conglomerate structure, communication manuals spell out the protocol for handling information requests locally or referring inquiries to the parent company. Many companies prepare products which will carry the name of a major distributor or retailer; contracts with the other company stipulate how such relationships must be treated when dealing with outside publics.

In addition to the communication policy manual, large organizations have other devices for ensuring consistency of messages:

SPECIAL MANUALS AND FORMS

Style Manual   Patterned after the Associated Press Style Manual or other style manuals, this is usually a booklet that spells out forms and formats for capitalization, punctuation, handling names and titles, use of facts and figures, and ways to avoid libel. Each organization tailors the style manual to its own requirements. The *Writing Style* guide that the Amoco Corporation distributes to its communication staff throughout the nation shows the proper way of identifying all Amoco subsidiaries. The guide explains technical terms common to the petroleum industry, and provides the staff writer with a compendium of significant company and petroleum-industry dates and events for the purpose of providing background information for articles and presentations.

Graphics Manual   Many organizations provide managers with model formats for letterheads, signs, brochure covers—anything that will carry the organization's name. Samples of border treatments, logo designs, and proprietary colors are included, along with instructions for printers to follow in order to assure compliance with the official design of the group's "visual image."

Exhibit 18.1
Tips for Writing
Better, Faster

Frank Grazian, executive editor of *communication briefings*, suggests that managers can cut down on the time it takes to write a memo or short report:

- Keep a collection of good examples of reports, articles, and memos. Before beginning to write, prime your own pump by reading some good models.
- Don't delay writing until all your thoughts are collected. Good writers create thoughts while they write.
- Write with a minimum of pauses: get a full draft down completely before beginning to make small editing changes.
- Don't try to impress the reader with stylistic tricks. Strive for clear and concise writing.
- Get to the point right away. Your reader is busy and wants to know "What is this about?"
- Don't try to write about anything you don't understand. Learn first.
- Pretend that your memo is a telegram and you have to pay for every word.

Source: Frank Grazian, "Writing Better and Faster," *communication briefings*, Vol. 9, No. 5, undated, p. 3.

Forms   To ensure that procedures have been followed for responding to press inquiries, handling consumer complaints, and routing drafts of news releases up-line to superiors for checking, most organizations have forms that must be filled in, reported to managers, and kept on file. Use of the forms usually is mandated by the communication policy manual.

MAKING YOUR MEMO EFFECTIVE

A memorandum is meant to be quicker to write and easier to read than a letter. It often serves as a call to action requiring some specific response or behavior from the recipient, although another purpose—the "memo to the file"—will be discussed later. Memos can be sent up-line or down-line within the organization, and of course a different tone is appropriate depending on whether a superior is addressing the staff, or a staff member is providing information to a superior.

One can note at the bottom of a letter that copies are being sent to other parties for informational purposes. A memo offers even greater flexibility because it can be directed to a group of people, with others included on an "INFO" line under the "TO" address.

Categories and Purposes of Memos

Memos usually fall in one of three broad categories:

Informative memos transmit data that the addressees previously did not have. A superior may report the proceedings of a meeting he or she attended and explain the effects of decisions made at that meeting on future operations of the department. A manager may use the memo format to present new rules or procedures. With a simple one-line memo to the staff, the boss may announce that she is leaving the organization and that a new boss will be named shortly.

Persuasive memos present information and ideas with the aim of getting the boss to consider a new concept, or convincing a team of people to follow a certain course of action. A professor who hopes to see the journalism or communication curriculum made more rigorous in order to reduce the number of majors may circulate a memo to other professors in the department stating the rationale for the proposal. The person designated to be the United Way coordinator drafts a memo that explains why the organization wants each employee to donate a percentage of salary to support social services in the community.

Responsive memos are solicited or mandated by either informative or persuasive memos. The manager who is looking for fresh ideas may direct every subordinate to reply with a memo listing ten ways to increase productivity. The director who must make up a vacation schedule for the summer months requests a memo from each employee by April 30 in order to coordinate and assign leave times.

Formats: Free or Dictated?

Public information specialists in the military service must refer to a manual that spells out the correct format for a memo, including the numbering of paragraphs, citation of the military regulations that pertain to the subject at hand, and the proper way of routing the memo through the chain of command. Large corporations may model their internal correspondence after the military, especially in scientific or engineering divisions where lengthy memos detail important procedures for meeting contract specifications.

At a lower level of intensity, many organizations try to differentiate memos from other correspondence by giving them distinctive headings and sometimes their own particular paper color. In an attempt to encourage brevity, some groups provide half-sheet memo pads 8½ inches wide and 5½ inches high. In many offices today, a handwritten phrase or two on the trademarked Post-it brand notes made by 3M are an acceptable means of communication between staff members. Offices with electronic mail can make the job simple and efficient by creating files where memos are stored in such a way that the sender can monitor when the memo was received and whether action is being taken.

Smaller organizations, and those with looser administrative structures, leave the format for memos up to the individual, assuming that each will use standard elements that are recognizable to the recipients. In Exhibit 18.2 we've provided a model for such a standard memo produced on the typewriter or personal computer.

Elements of the Standard Memo

There are many variations, but the memo in Exhibit 18.2 is fairly standard in appearance and content. It is of the type and purpose we characterized as *informative*, but it has some elements of the *persuasive* memo in that it seeks to motivate staff members to do some low-level research, brainstorm a bit, and be ready to support the program that has been proposed.

The Heading   is simple and direct. If your computer has a choice of type faces and sizes, you might dress up the word "Memorandum" by making it bigger and bolder, but not so ornate as to appear frivolous. And avoid printing a memo out on letterhead or other cluttered formats meant for more formal or official correspondence.

The Date   usually comes first. Pre-printed memo forms may call for it to be written in directly under the heading.

To/From/Subject   usually appear in that order. "SUBJ:" or "RE:" are acceptable variations for the last line. "INFO" may appear after "TO" indicating secondary addressees who have an interest in the subject, although they are not required to take action, nor are they expected to return a *responsive* memo. When several staff members are to receive a memo, a superior may list last names only. However, it is courteous when addressing multiple addressees of varying status to give each a line and identify each by title or position:

> TO: John E. Rockwell, Vice President Administrative Services
> Mary R. Bushnell, Comptroller
> Elfridge Rambeau, Account Executive, Cox Public Relations

The subject line should be to-the-point, but not cryptic. The one here could have read merely "Casual Day." But what *about* it? There may be several memos over the next few weeks where the subject is the same.

Exhibit 18.2
Standard Memo

MEMORANDUM

November 10, 1991

TO: Communication/Public Affairs Staff

FROM: Anne Franklin, Director of Employee Communication

SUBJECT: Human Services Request to Support Introduction of
             "Casual Day"

I have met twice in the last week with Hal Renberg, Director of Human Services, to begin planning for the introduction of "Friday— Casual Day" after the first of the year. Management has approved the concept but wants to see a report from Human Services on the expected benefits and a report from our department on how the program will be presented to employees.

Attached is a draft of the Human Services report. Note that, in addition to improved morale, the most tangible benefit is expected to be increased productivity resulting from fewer sick days and personal days taken on Fridays.

Here are my main concerns at this point:

■ We need to determine the best way to inform our employees about the concept of wearing casual clothes to the office one day a week and management's expectation that they will use the day to catch up on office work, filing, report writing, and other tasks that will enable them to get a fresh start on Monday of the following week.

■ We need to advise management whether or not to inform other companies—especially clients—about the new policy. One of the questions concerning management is whether we will be seen by other firms as undisciplined, or as a place where happy employees roll up their sleeves to get the week's work done.

We'll make this the main topic at our regular weekly staff meeting set for 9 a.m. next Monday, Nov. 16. Please read the enclosure, talk with people around the company, and be ready to provide input and suggestions.

EmpComm/A44/11-10-91/af

The phrase on this memo is specific enough to differentiate it from the others. It also has a motivational phrase—"request to support"—that has the effect of increasing the addressee's interest and involvement in the subject from the start.

The Body of the memo consists of short paragraphs written in logical order. Background information is provided first. An attached report is referenced, and the attention of the reader is called to the most important information in that report. In the longest paragraph, where the writer is raising issues and explaining what work must be done, points are highlighted by using bullets (a printer's term for black dots). Numbers would also have been acceptable. Highlighting helps make certain that, in skim-reading long sections, the reader doesn't miss major points.

The Call to Action is highlighted with underlining in the final paragraph. The point is underscored that the subject of this memo has been made an agenda item and that certain behaviors—talking with employees, thinking up ideas—are required.

Coding at the bottom of the memo (it could just as well be at the top) tells the computer and/or the filing secretary that: this memo was generated by the Department of Employee Communication (EmpComm); it is the 44th memo of the calendar year issued on the topic of internal communication (A); it was circulated on 11-10-91; and, finally, its originator was Anne Franklin, whose initials complete the code.

The Style and Tone are direct and personal. The writer uses the same words and approach she would use in a face-to-face situation. Whereas letters usually adopt a more formal tone and style, memos are, in effect, substitutes for messages the sender would have preferred to make in person. Some managers use the technique of planned redundancy: announce information at a staff meeting and hand out a memo at the same time that covers the same information. By writing in a conversational style, the manager is able to use the active voice. That can pay off in terms of motivation. Without action phrases like "Note that" and "We'll make this the main topic," it would be easy for the reader to merely glance over the information without retaining much. Because the addressee can expect to interact with the sender on the subject, he or she better understands the level of involvement that is required.

Suppose that the director of employee communication had more than two or three concerns worth highlighting at this point. Should the memo have gone to two pages? Many managers would counsel that the memo should be kept to just one page so that the call to action at the bottom doesn't get lost. A solution would be to include a second attachment to the memo: a list of eight or ten points for discussion and a phrase or two about the director's concerns with each one.

The Sender's Initials are added at the end of the "TO" line, although some managers prefer to use their full signature. In any case, it is never put at the end, as on a letter. A good technique, however, is to personalize each memo, perhaps by circling the action line and writing something like: "Frank, I hope you will talk to the people in Operations about this before the meeting, just in case they see any problems with implementing the program."

Memos to the File

Sometime early in your entry-level job you'll hear the expression, "This reads like a memo to the file." That means that the memo doesn't appear to call for any action, but the writer apparently has a need to put something on the record. If one is cynical, or perhaps pragmatic, the memo to the file can be seen as an example of CYA (cover your . . . anatomy)! The purpose may be to set up an "I-told-you-so" situation.

To give the genre its due, many good managers follow up a meeting or an interview with a memo-to-the-file that serves at a later date to document actions and establish accountability. When seeking a raise, applying for a grant, or writing a history of the organization, file memos can prove useful.

Public relations agencies find it useful to document agreements with frequent memos-to-the-file. In doing so, they establish what was agreed upon, since clients are notorious for changing their minds.

One Idea per Memo

Do you have three different topics to share with the same group? Then you should write three different memos. Chances are each memo will call for a different action, go on a different pile, and be handled in a different time frame. If you send out a multitopic memo, you probably are dooming one of the topics to oblivion because it will get lost in the shuffle.

Aim for Tuesday

When buying a new car, the old *caveat* is "Never buy a car built on Friday or Monday"—as if the consumer could know on which day a car was built. The point is that on Friday workers are dreaming of their weekend plans, and on Monday they are exhausted from recreation and family involvements.

The same rule applies to memos: try to time a memo to arrive on a day other than Monday, when employees must face work not completed the previous week, or on Friday, when everybody is loathe to start a new project. By that reasoning, Tuesday would be the optimum day for distribution of a memo that calls for action.

Memos as Cover Sheets to Other Communications

Before we leave our discussion of memos, we should point out that they are also used as a means of calling attention to other forms of print communication. When General Motors mails its Social Responsibility Annual Report to stockholders, legislators, educators, and investment counselors, a brief memo from the chief executive officer is inserted as a way of explaining to the recipient what the report is and why it has been sent. Similarly, reprints of speeches are distributed to selected publics with a brief memo calling attention to the importance of the content. The versatility of the memo makes it a valuable management and public relations tool.

WRITING BUSINESS LETTERS

When you read the letter from the public relations agency to the head of a software firm in Exhibit 18.3, you may recall that we said business letters are more formal than memos, mainly because they are going to *external* publics—clients, consumers, regulators, suppliers—rather than *internal* publics such as managers and employees of your own company. However, the difference here is more in format than in style of writing.

As with a memo, the tone of the letter is not stiff or haughty. Stilted and old-fashioned phrases such as "in reference to our earlier meeting" and "we trust that you will give this matter your attention" have been avoided. That's because even the formal business letter today must get briskly to the point, and it should be written in familiar style that compels the involvement of the person you need to inform or persuade.

Our sample letter is, of course, an example of marketing public relations, which means that its purpose is to sell a service. (It is what public relations people call a "pitch letter" because it pitches the services of public relations to a potential client.)

The format and the techniques, however, differ very little from those you would use in a letter from a nonprofit group that was approaching a corporation for support, or from a social welfare agency that was seeking the help of a legislator for a project of importance to the community.

Exhibit 18.3
Business Letter

LETTERHEAD

April 20, 1991

Ms. Genevieve Lacourte, President
Lacourte Software Systems, Inc.
1489 Ridge Parkway
East St. Paul, Minnesota 55110

Dear Ms. Lacourte:

My partner Robert Lowell and I enjoyed very much talking with you at the recent Technology Exposition held by the St. Paul Chamber of Commerce. You mentioned that you are looking to expand distribution of your "Math Genius" software to school systems throughout the Upper Midwest and, eventually, the entire country.

As I explained to you, we think that there are many benefits from using public relations programs to achieve your goals. Certainly advertising will help make your product familiar to target audiences of the leading education journals. But advertising is expensive, and it may not go much beyond making teachers and administrators familiar with what "Math Genius" is and does. A good public relations program will enable you to listen to your target audiences. It can help you determine what your publics want and need. And public relations techniques can help you show your publics how "Math Genius" serves those needs.

We would like the opportunity to make a presentation to you and your associates on how our two-way communication program helps you tailor your product and services to the needs of the educators who can best use "Math Genius." Specifically, we would like to suggest how focus group interviews can help shape your public relations marketing approach. And we would like to suggest how an interactive display booth at the upcoming Minnesota Education Conference can show the product to educators and find out how they react to its potential in the classroom.

I'll call you early next week. We'd like to schedule our presentation wherever it is most convenient, at your offices or in our new multimedia viewing room. If you have any questions before then, please call me at 612-4190.

Sincerely,

John Cabot, Senior Partner

ENCL: Agency brochure

The Business Letter Format

The basic business letter consists of:

The Letterhead, including the name of the organization, the address, telephone and Fax numbers, and, for international firms, the cable address. Variations include the name and title or position of the sender (which means the title need not be repeated under the signature at the bottom) and, for most nonprofit organizations, a list of officers and directors.

The Date and Address, which should be the same as the address on the envelope.

The Salutation, which should be appropriate for the familiarity and relative rank of the addressee to the sender. In formal correspondence with a colleague, a nice touch is to have the secretary type "Dear Ms. Gompertz," and then, when signing the letter, the sender uses pen and ink to cross out the formal name and replace it with "Mary" in handwriting.

The Body of the Letter, flush left, with or without paragraph indentations according to personal or organizational style.

The Complimentary Close, such as "With warm regards," or the safe and relatively impersonal "Sincerely."

The Signature, along with the sender's position if it is not preprinted on the letterhead. First name only should be used for colleagues and friends.

Crafting the Letter

As with any communication situation, the letter-writer must begin by analyzing the audience, in this case the reader of the letter. Start by asking questions that include:

Is the reader expecting the letter?
Is the reader likely to have time to read the letter carefully?
Does the reader have all the necessary background on the topic?
Will the reader be favorably disposed to the information in the letter?
Does the reader have an obligation to respond to the letter?

If the answer to all of these questions is "yes," then the task of writing the letter is relatively easy. Perhaps a letter informing an associate that a favorable deal had been struck—pending only his or her approval—would fit in this ideal category.

More likely, the answer to one or more of our questions will be "no." Most of the people we must write in the course of business are busy, and they skim-read letters quickly to determine the "bottom line" of the content. ("What am I being asked to do? Can I do it? Do I have to respond to this?")

In some cases, the letter will threaten or anger the recipient and pre-cipitate an angry letter of response. If that cannot be avoided, then the sender of the original letter must carefully craft the original letter to make sure that it stands the scrutiny of management people, or even the legal department, when and if communication reaches an impasse.

One of the most difficult business letters to write is the one that re-quires presentation of considerable background information before a re-quest is made or an explanation is given for current actions. When you must write such a letter, think of your own needs in similar interpersonal situations. Most of us get edgy when we have to listen to a rambling, drawn-out explanation. In a letter, just as in face-to-face communication, it may be advisable to open by stating your intentions and explaining the need to provide an historical context. You might begin:

> As you will soon come to understand, my group is not likely to support your candidacy for head of the Development Board. I hope that what I am about to tell you will make clear to you and your staff why certain events in our dealings with the Board lead us to conclude that another kind of leader is needed at this time . . .

In choosing the correct tone for a business letter, the writer must again draw parallels between written communication and interpersonal style. People in the business world learn to reflect the organization in their choice of words and phrases. But most of us know that personal suc-cess within the organization often depends on an ability to convince an-other person that we are sincere, open, and concerned, not just robotic functionaries for the larger group. That delicate balance should be main-tained in written communication as well. The following passage person-alizes a corporate decision:

> Bob, you and I both know that Amalgamated prefers to take the high road in its dealings with suppliers, and that is why we are making a special ef-fort to open the bidding process to minority businesses. While we value our long relationship with your firm, we are obliged by the terms of our government contract to act in good faith with all bidders. You can be sure that, should your bid be acceptable, you will get your share of our busi-ness, and nothing could make me happier.

The preceding examples from letters that deal with fairly complicated situations may give the impression that business letters necessarily run more than one page because of the complexity of the issues they cover. In fact, the premium is on shorter letters. Effective managers know the value of letters that are only one or two paragraphs long.

The letter in Exhibit 18.4 is short and to the point for a number of reasons. The CEO of an organization wants to go on record as putting his organization into what we call a *two-way symmetric* communication situation, and he wants to lend his own credibility to the proceedings. But he is dealing with the lawyer for an activist organization, and he does not wish to overplay his hand or to appear to be compromising the interests of his stockholders. Also, he does not want to undercut the authority of his public relations vice president to manage the setting up of a conference; he merely wants to introduce her as the person authorized to represent the company.

The short letter can be used in a situation where the background that must be presented can be found in a previously prepared report. In that case, the letter may direct the reader to "familiarize yourself with the content of our position statement issued last year, in order that we can have a fruitful discussion when we meet to discuss the possible merger."

"Personal/Professional" Correspondence

Dear Kyle:

Congratulations on your promotion to Director of Media Relations for BNX Corp. I always knew when we worked together here in the media department that you'd get a top job in an up-and-coming company some day.

Dear Ms. Bowman:

I enjoyed your talk on "Learning to Negotiate on the Job" at last week's IABC meeting. Your research on "person perception" is especially interesting—is it possible to obtain a copy of your journal article that you described?

Ann-Marie:

I'm sorry that your firm didn't win the bid on our publications contract, but I just wanted to say that I thought your presentation was one of the most professional ones I have ever seen. I hope we get a chance to work together sometime in the future.

These are not excerpts from letters; each is the entire message. They were sent in formal business envelopes, but on personal half-sheets with just the name of the sender at the top. The one requesting

Exhibit 18.4
A Short Letter

LETTERHEAD

June 19, 1991

Malcolm R. Botchner, Esq.
Citizens for Clean Water
425 Market Street
Columbus, OH 43210

Dear Mr. Botchner:

Our firm agrees with your group's position that sitting down to talk over the issues is preferable to demonstrations and press conferences that result in the shedding of much heat but little light.

I have directed my Vice President for Public Affairs, Aileen Donovan, to work with you to set up a forum satisfactory to your organization as soon as possible. She will be in touch with you shortly.

Sincerely yours,

R. W. Tremayne
President and CEO

CC: A. Donovan

an article reprint was accompanied by a business card stapled in one of the upper corners.

We call this category "personal/professional" correspondence because, while each relates to the business of the organization, it also serves the purpose of helping to further the individual's career. The format is simple: what you see is what you get. Gearing up to do personal/professional correspondence is what takes some planning.

This type of communication is more effective if done by the sender rather than dictated to a secretary. Some even prefer to do it in longhand. In any case, a special corner of the top desk drawer should be set up with a supply of informal note paper to facilitate quick jotting of personal/professional messages.

The best time of the day for writing the notes is in the early morning, after reading the newspapers and trade journals that have come in that day. Often the impetus for a note like the one to Kyle above is an item you come across in the "Business Notes" or "People in the Business" columns of the specialized media.

Notes written in the early morning may catch the mid-morning first pickup of mail, thus enhancing the chance of next-day delivery in the same metropolitan area. The quickness and thoughtfulness of such notes may have a long-term payoff, or it may result in a response like "Thanks—let's get together for lunch" that may pay more immediate dividends in the form of useful information, new contacts, or even a lead on a new job.

PACKAGING A REPORT

The public relations practitioner who has just been told by the boss to prepare a formal report probably feels like the college student who has just been assigned to do a term paper: overwhelmed, and perhaps a little depressed at the thought of turning out a major piece of writing.

The assembling, writing, and packaging of a report need not be a task that brings the other functions of the public relations department to a standstill. The first and most important decision is what kind of report is needed, and, specifically, how formal it will be.

The Formal Report

The full, formal report includes some or all of these elements:

- A letter of transmittal to the person requesting the report.
- A cardboard or plastic protective folder.
- The title page.
- The table of contents.
- The body of the report.
- Charts, graphs, illustrations, computer printouts, tables, etc.
- Reprints of material published elsewhere.
- Copies of relevant correspondence.
- Samples of written messages prepared by the organization.
- List of resources, or a bibliography.

The Short Report

Many reports can be more informal than the full report, and they also are much briefer. The letter format can be used to report data to a superior, but the memo probably is the most practical format for a short report—especially if highlighting devices such as headings, underlining, and lists are used.

An example of a short report is the memo that informs staff members that "The following actions were taken at the April 7 meeting of the Committee to Plan for the Chelsea Plant Relocation" and then goes on to list what decisions were made, with a short explanation as to the reason for each action. A short data report might begin: "Here are the attendance figures for the seven community outreach programs held in St. Charles during the month of May, broken down by age, sex, areas of the city, and organizational affiliation." As long as every recipient of the report knows the context and the importance of the information, no further explanation may be necessary.

The Executive Summary

A hybrid form of report is the executive summary, which boils down the information from a long, formal report and presents it in the readable, condensed format of a memo. The executive summary may be an end in itself. That is, the top administrator may request that an executive summary only be prepared, with the understanding that all of the data discussed in the report exist in the files and can be produced if needed. Some administrators request a full formal report and an executive summary as well; they may plan to read the summary as a way of deciding what sections to read in detail.

What's the Purpose?

The length and format of a report may be dictated by the purpose. Some reports are *pro forma*, meaning that they are done regularly to satisfy the requirement of some person or authority. In this case, a format may be mandated, or perhaps a model has been developed over the years that serves well. If the purpose of the report is to get information to a superior who must make a decision quickly, the memo format is a good choice. If the purpose, however, is to analyze an issue and persuade an administrator or a deliberative body to take a new course of action, the longer, formal report may be needed in order to fully document the situation.

Assembling the Package

We said earlier that having to prepare a report needn't be overwhelming. The best way to make the task easier is to prepare and store data on a regular basis so that a large report can be "assembled" rather than created from scratch. In anticipation of report requirements, data created by the organization should be formatted for future use, stored in the office computer, and indexed for easy reference, with a hard copy kept in the files for backup. The main task, then, consists of writing an introductory section and transition sections that introduce pre-packaged data arrays.

For ease of reading, each new section of a report gets a fresh page, even if that means several blank half-pages. If the report is especially long, section dividers with tabular indices may help the reader to find and review sections of particular interest.

NOTES   1.   Gerald M. Goldhaber, *Organizational Communication,* 2d ed. (Dubuque, IA: Wm. C. Brown, 1979), pp. 125–128.

ADDITIONAL READING

Brusaw, Charles T., Gerald J. Alred, and Walter E. Oliu, *The Business Writer's Handbook,* 2d ed. (New York: St. Martin's Press, 1982).

Cross, Mary, *Persuasive Business Writing* (New York: American Management Association, 1987).

Goldhaber, Gerald M., *Organizational Communication,* 2d ed. (Dubuque, IA: Wm. C. Brown, 1979).

Hatch, Richard, *Business Writing* (Chicago: Science Research Associates, 1983).

Sandman, Peter M., Carl S. Klompus, and Betsy Greenleaf Yarrison, *Scientific and Technical Writing* (New York: Holt, Rinehart & Winston, 1985).

Starzyk, Lawrence J., and John R. Jewell, *Effective Business Writing* (New York: Macmillan, 1984).

19

Marketing Communication

Communication is an integral part both of public relations and marketing. It should not be surprising, then, that public relations practitioners often are called upon to provide communication strategy and techniques to support the marketing function. Advertising professionals also provide communication strategy and techniques to marketing, often in competition with public relations people. To avoid duplication and unproductive competition, many organizations and public relations and advertising firms have developed a strategy of integrated marketing communication—marketing communication programs that combine public relations, advertising, and sales promotion.

This chapter assumes that many public relations practitioners will at some time in their careers use the techniques described in this book to support the marketing function. Thus, our purpose here is to describe the techniques practitioners typically use to support marketing and to provide case examples of their use. Before describing these techniques, however, we begin by discussing briefly the relationship between public relations and marketing and the nature of "integrated marketing communication." It is important to understand when and why communication techniques are used in support of the public relations management function and when they are used in support of the marketing management function. The first section of this chapter, therefore, clarifies those relationships.

MARKETING,
PUBLIC
RELATIONS, AND
INTEGRATED
MARKETING
COMMUNICATION

In Chapter 1, we introduced this book by summarizing the managerial theory of public relations that is described in depth in our companion book, *Managing Public Relations*.[1] We also pointed out that the purpose of the public relations department is to help the organization as a whole as well as its subsystems—marketing, human resources, or finance—to communicate with people and groups of people both inside and outside the organization that affect or are affected by the organization or subsystem. Because public relations professionals help these other subsystems solve their communication problems, senior managers often confuse the public relations function with the other functions. They may also set up an organizational structure whereby public relations specialists report directly to the departments that administer those other functions.

In particular, employee communication often is managed by a human relations department and marketing communication by the marketing department. Organizations seldom place the entire public relations function in the human relations department, but many do place it in the marketing department.[2] In many cases, senior managers do not understand the difference between public relations as a broad management function and publicity as a narrow communication technique.

But public relations practitioners also sometimes choose to be sublimated to marketing. Many practitioners, especially those who are communication technicians with no managerial responsibility, also equate promotion and publicity with public relations. In a book on public relations in business, for example, Peake talked about "using the principles of public relations, publicity, and promotion (three terms for the same set of skills. . . .)"[3]

Most marketing textbooks talk about the four Ps of marketing: product, price, place, and promotion. Communication enters marketing through the fourth P—promotion—but most marketing managers have little training in communication or skill in using communication techniques. Thus, they typically contract with advertising agencies for advertising, and public relations firms (or an internal public relations department) to place unpaid publicity about their products and services in the mass media. Since different suppliers provide the techniques of advertising and publicity, they often compete with each other and fail to provide an integrated program of marketing communication.

Many public relations firms, especially the large ones, get a large portion of their income from marketing communication. For example, in 1982, Paul Alvarez, chairman of Ketchum Communications, told public relations educators at the convention of the Association for Education in Journalism and Mass Communication that half the business of his firm came from product publicity. By 1991, Thomas Harris, then a professor of public relations at Northwestern University and formerly president of Golin/Harris Communications, claimed that 70 percent of the billings of public relations firms are for activities related to marketing.[4]

Other studies and articles have shown that expenditures for "marketing public relations" are growing and that they are coming at the expense of advertising.[5] In 1992, Thomas Eidson, president and CEO of the Hill and Knowlton public relations firm, told the Public Relations Counselors Academy that 70 percent of total expenditures on advertising and sales promotion go to sales promotions and public relations, while only 30 percent go to media advertising. Twelve years earlier, he said, 54 percent of all expenditures went to media advertising.[6]

With so much money and attention paid to marketing support, it is easy for the marketing tail to begin to wag the public relations dog—that is, to assume that the total purpose of public relations is to support marketing and that public relations is a marketing function. Indeed, that is what most marketing textbooks seem to assume and what you will hear nearly always from marketing educators. For example, Philip Kotler, who is perhaps the best-known marketing educator and researcher, described public relations in his textbook, *Marketing Management,* as "another important marketing tool, which until recently, was treated as a marketing stepchild."[7]

Recently, however, Kotler seems to have realized that public relations is not a marketing function. In 1988, San Diego State University and the public relations firm of Nuffer, Smith, Tucker, Inc. sponsored a symposium on public relations and marketing. Kotler and William Ehling, the now retired head of the Public Relations Department of Syracuse University's Newhouse School of Public Communication, presented papers from the perspective of public relations and marketing. During the course of the symposium, Kotler apparently concluded that public relations and marketing are different functions. As quoted in an article on the symposium in the November 1989 issue of *Public Relations Journal,* Kotler said, "In my book on marketing management I put public relations in a chapter with sales promotion, saying public relations is 'another important marketing tool.' Based on our discussion, I think I need a chapter on marketing communication, but I won't be calling it public relations. I will have to make public relations a separate function."[8]

In a 1991 edition of *Marketing Management,* which is used in a large number of MBA programs, Kotler still said that public relations is a marketing function, but he pointed out the public relations department has duties other than marketing support: "The public-relations department is typically located at corporate headquarters; and its staff is so busy dealing with various publics—stockholders, employees, legislators, community leaders—that PR support for marketing objectives tends to be neglected" (p. 641). A few paragraphs later, he pointed out that "companies are setting up a *marketing PR group* to directly support corporate/product promotion and image making. Thus, marketing PR, like financial PR and community PR, would serve a special constituency, namely the marketing department."[9]

Public relations specialists most often support the marketing function by developing programs to communicate with consumers—markets—about products and services. These services are usually called marketing communication or product promotion. In this area, public relations practitioners have skills in communication techniques that marketing practitioners seldom have—especially in media relations, publicity, and promotion. Spicer, for example, surveyed a sample of public relations and marketing professionals and found that "marketing professionals *do not often engage in the kind of writing demanded of those in public relations.*"[10]

Spicer also found that members of public relations departments provide communication techniques to the marketing department more often than marketing provides skills to public relations. But he also found that practitioners with expertise in marketing communication and advertising do not work in other areas of public relations such as public affairs, community relations, media relations, employee communication, or issues management. As a result, Spicer's results support Harris's claim that "marketing public relations" is evolving as a separate discipline from other specialties of public relations.[11]

Obviously, then, "marketing public relations" should be integrated with advertising, sales, promotion, and direct marketing as "integrated marketing communication." Integrated marketing communication should be managed with the concepts of marketing theory. Thus, if you wish to specialize in marketing communication, you should study marketing theory as well as public relations.

Although public relations staffs most often provide product publicity for marketing departments, they also provide other critical support. In particular, public relations can help to build relationships with governments, regulatory agencies, communities, or other publics that block important markets. And public relations can help marketing to make more ethical and socially responsible decisions.[12] These public relations functions are discussed in detail in *Managing Public Relations.*

In the rest of this chapter, then, we will examine the public relations techniques used in marketing communication—the techniques that are used in communicating about products or services to consumers or users of those products.

SOME EXAMPLES OF PUBLIC RELATIONS TECHNIQUES USED TO SUPPORT MARKETING

Many kinds of organizations hire PR technicians to publicize themselves. For example:

Professional and college sports teams have directors of promotion to help fill their arenas or stadiums.

Theatres, dance companies, art museums, and orchestras promote concerts and shows.

Colleges and universities promote their faculty, facilities, and major fields of study to potential students.

Newspapers and radio and television stations have promotion departments to increase their audience, usually in the hope of securing higher advertising rates.

Park and recreation departments of local governments promote use of their facilities and programs.

Community groups hold special events—band concerts, community fairs, jousting tournaments, ethnic days, art fairs—that must be promoted if anyone is to attend.

Hospitals market their services and facilities through open houses, health and medical fairs, seminars and lectures, and health information provided to the media.[13]

Corporations have general promotion programs to establish a corporate identity. The most famous is the Goodyear Tire and Rubber Company's four blimps that help televise major sports events, attend air shows and community events, and help in studies of noise pollution, traffic, or marine life.[14]

Most public relations technicians, especially those with little or no training in marketing management, do promotions work with the press agentry or two-way asymmetric model as their guide.[15] The two-way symmetric model can work in marketing as well as public relations—and marketing theory stresses such a model using the term bilateral exchange.[16]

The two-way symmetric model is evident, for example, in the following passage from Nickels' book on marketing communication and promotion:

Too much of the marketing literature today emphasizes promotion management for *sellers*. This causes readers to think of marketing communication as something sellers do *to* buyers. Promotion is then viewed as one tool the seller uses to dominate the buyer. But marketing communication is something sellers do *with* buyers. Promotion, in reality, is a tool available to both buyers and sellers. Buyers may use promotion to convince sellers to change their policies and practices, and sellers may try to change buyers. Marketing is not a game to be won by being most persuasive. Rather, it is a technique for facilitating the creation and maintenance of mutually beneficial exchanges. Communication helps *both parties*, not just the buyer or seller.[17]

To give you some examples of the nature of product publicity, we will look at some cases before identifying the most common techniques that public relations technicians use to communicate about products.

The Genie Garage Door Opener

The Alliance Manufacturing Company, part of the North American Phillips Company, had dominated the market for home garage door openers with its Genie line.[18] Because of a boom in the market for garage door openers, however, other companies introduced competing products and gained more media attention than Genie.

Genie also had introduced a do-itself-yourself door opener—which could be installed in three hours—to complement its older model, which had to be installed by a professional. Genie hired the Cleveland PR firm of Hesselbart & Mitten/Watt to develop a promotional program for Genie. Here's what the firm did:

> Developed a press kit for use at a home center show in Chicago that was attended by members of the trade press.

> Established a consumer hotline number for do-it-yourselfers to call if they had trouble installing the Genie.

> Distributed drawings, photographs, and an informative article on how to install a Genie to more than one hundred newspapers around the country. Articles appeared in respected newspapers such as *The New York Times* and the *Denver Post*.

> Appealed to female consumers by sending the media a photo of actress Lily Tomlin installing a Genie opener in the movie *Nine to Five*. A story accompanied the photo explaining how easy it is to install the device and stressing that an automatic opener provides a woman more security near her home. The story quoted statistics that 32 percent of all attacks occur near the home. (The female angle to this promotion is clearly an example of the two-way asymmetric model: describing a product in terms that the potential buyer most wants to hear.)

> Tried to keep good relations with dealers who install Genie openers while promoting the do-it-yourself market. A Genie man—a giant, vivid blue character—was made available for dealers to use at special promotional events, such as the Pro Football Hall of Fame Parade in Canton, Ohio.

Burson-Marsteller Brings "Good Things" to GE

The General Electric Company gave the Burson-Marsteller PR agency the assignment of developing a public relations campaign to complement its advertising campaign, "We Bring Good Things to Life."[19] The Burson-Marsteller program did publicize products, but it also developed symmetric communication programs for consumers. First, the product publicity:

A microwave cooking contest that attracted several thousand entries.

A promotion for the twenty-fifth anniversary of GE's Toast-R-Oven.

A half-time cooking contest at pro football games with players' wives as contestants.

Videotaping joggers running on a treadmill before and after Tampa's Gasparilla Distance Classic to publicize GE's video camera and cassette recorder.

A 360-degree, multimedia presentation at major trade shows highlighting GE's solutions to consumer concerns.

In addition, Burson-Marsteller developed these symmetric programs for consumers:

A business leadership program to find out what information consumers need and how to simplify it for them.

A GE Answer Center, with a computer database on GE products, for consumers to call with questions or problems.

Designer Plugs, Sockets, and Switches

Most electrical plugs, sockets, and switches are plain white or brown, plastic or metal. One of the leading manufacturers of electrical wiring accessories in the United Kingdom, Volex Accessories, created an innovative set of accessories—its Designer Range—that broke out of this conventional mold. "Available in either Chamois (a light cream color) or Burnt Oak (a dark russet brown), the fittings came with a solid brass trim, slim flush plates which concealed screws, and large dolly switches."[20]

The launch of this new product provides an example of a fully integrated program of marketing communication, because it included media relations, advertising, direct mail, and extensive product literature. The public relations planners publicized the product in media read by electrical contractors and owners/managers of retail stores, as well as publications read directly by consumers. Specific techniques used were a press packet, personal visits to media, news releases, feature articles, high-quality photographs, and visits by journalists to the factory.

The public relations firm working on the project, Burgess Daring Public Relations, targeted such media as *Electrical and Electronic Trader*, *Electrical Retailing*, *DIY Superstore*, *Hardware Today*, and *Housewares* to reach retailers. To reach contractors, it targeted publications such as *The Builder*, *What's New in Building*, *Electrical Contractor*, and *Electrical Wholesaling*. Targeted consumer publications included *Good Housekeeping*, *Ideal Home*, *Do It Yourself Woman*, and *Practical Housekeeping*.[21]

Daring, whose firm worked on the project, said that the campaign was more successful in placing articles in the trade press than in the consumer press. He explained that there is intense pressure for space in consumer and women's media, and that public relations people must be careful not to inundate editors with information about products with little news value: "It is important to be honest with the client about the appeal of the product, particularly as they are often naturally excited about their new product and fail to appreciate how it will be viewed by a possibly jaundiced editor who is inundated with new product information releases. Careful media targeting is the key to a successful media relations campaign."[22]

Burgess Daring also tried to evaluate the effectiveness of public relations component of the campaign. It compared the value of the free space gained compared with the cost of the campaign—£59,633 compared to £36,797. Daring pointed out some of the limitations of this approach to evaluation:

> *Naturally such calculations must be treated with a degree of caution, not the least because variations in available rate card discounts can dramatically affect the calculation. Also, it can be misleading to compare the impact of editorial with paid advertising space, as the former tends to carry greater credibility and is hence worth more column inch for column inch.*[23]

Practitioners of marketing public relations often calculate how much the space they gained in the media would have cost if it had been purchased as advertising. As Daring pointed out, such estimates should be treated with great caution. The rates may be difficult to calculate, as Daring said. In addition, a public relations practitioner cannot control the time, place, or medium of exposure. Thus, it is entirely possible that few members of the target market are exposed to these messages or are affected by them. A well-placed advertisement, in contrast, could result in greater exposure by the target market with far less space. In addition, publicity and advertising generally complement each other—each makes the other more effective. For these reasons, estimates of the advertising value of "free publicity" have limited value in evaluating the effectiveness of a communication campaign.[24]

Daring also mentioned the concept of "third-party endorsement" or "third-party credibility"—the existence of which is cited almost as a matter of faith by most specialists in marketing public relations. According to Daring, people are more likely to believe a news story about a product than an advertisement because, supposedly, it has been "endorsed" by the journalist who chose to publish the story. We will discuss this concept later in the chapter, but one should treat the concept with caution. There is little research evidence to show that the free publicity is more credible than advertising.

Burgess Daring Public Relations also had difficulty separating the effects of the public relations techniques from the other communication techniques used. It was difficult to determine which techniques produced awareness of the product or purchase. However, the firm did use cards that editors and readers could use to get more information about the product as a way of determining exposure to the message and interest generated in the product.

E.T., Captain Crunch, and Friends

Product publicity can have dramatic effects on sales of products that are inexpensive and whose purchase often is a fad—what marketing theorists would call a low-involvement product.[25] Here are just a few examples:

E.T. and Reese's Pieces   Many companies try to place their products in movies either for free or for a promotional fee. Even the U.S. military services have an office in Los Angeles to cooperate in making movies featuring the military. When the Mars Company declined a request to provide product samples of its M&Ms candy for the movie *E.T., The Extraterrestrial,* the Hershey Company provided samples of its Reese's Pieces—which became the candy craved by the little creature from outer space in the movie. *E.T.* became one of the top-grossing movies of all time, Hershey followed up with a $1 million promotion of "E.T.'s favorite candy," and sales of the product soared.[26]

The Captain and Mikey   The Quaker Oats Company, with the help of the Golin/Harris and Hill and Knowlton public relations firms, integrated publicity, advertising, and sales promotion to get attention for two of its cereals, Captain Crunch and Life. For the Captain, Quaker Oats offered a $1 million reward that would be shared by all children who located the whereabouts of the Captain after his picture was taken off the cereal box. Publicists put detective kits in cereal boxes (sales promotion), placed advertisements on Saturday cartoon shows, and generated extensive publicity on the disappearance of the Captain through a syndicated radio series, a video news series, and news bulletins. A music video appeared on music video shows, and "Saturday Night Live" did a spoof of the search. After four months, the location of the Captain was revealed on a two-minute cartoon segment on Saturday morning television. More than 280,000 people entered the contest, and sales of Captain Crunch achieved record levels.[27]

You may also remember Mikey, the fussy eater who loved Life cereal. Well, Mikey grew up, so Quaker Oats ran twenty photos on the back of its boxes and invited consumers to send in guesses of which photo was the grown-up Mikey—an actor tracked down by Hill and Knowlton. Extensive media publicity supported the promotion. Although 100 winners got only $100 each, 750,000 Life buyers sent in their guesses. (Most of them ate Life to do so!)[28]

Cabbage Patch Dolls   Publicity alone cannot sell bad products, but it certainly can enhance the sales of good products. In his book on marketing public relations, Harris described the Coleco Toy Company's Cabbage Patch dolls as "an enormously appealing product concept"—a unique doll for each child, each doll with a unique name. Each doll also came with adoption papers.[29] The Richard Weiner public relations firm worked with child psychologists and did extensive research before promoting the product. Public relations techniques carried the marketing communication effort, and advertising played only a supporting role. The techniques included a press conference to introduce the product six months before Christmas, a media tour, media interviews, and appearances on talk shows. You know the rest of the story. Demand was so great that people stampeded toy stores. To counter the backlash that resulted from demand greater than supply, Coleco gave dolls to children in hospitals—well publicized, of course. Nancy Reagan even gave Cabbage Patch kids to two Korean children who were heart patients in a New York hospital.

Trivial Pursuit   The board game *Trivial Pursuit* was as popular as the Cabbage Patch dolls during the 1980s. The company that developed the game, the Selchow & Righter Company, sold 22 million games in the first year, sales that Harris said were achieved almost entirely by public relations techniques:

> *A first step was to send all living celebrities mentioned in the game copies of the card on which their name appeared. Word-of-mouth began in California and moved east to other celebrity centers like New York, Chicago, and Washington. Another tactic used by the public relations firm, Pezzano & Co., was to send Trivial Pursuit games to disk jockeys at radio stations throughout the country, with the suggestion that they be given away to listeners who correctly answered trivia questions from the game. The game's Canadian creators were booked as guests of talk shows on more than 125 stations. Finally, the PR program involved raising money for Easter Seals by scheduling Trivial Pursuit parties in 80 U.S. cities in November, a month before the Christmas selling season.*[30]

Keebler Cookies   The Keebler Cookie Company introduced a Soft Batch brand of cookies with soft centers six months after its larger competitors, Nabisco and Procter and Gamble. Because it was smaller than its competitors, Keebler wanted to avoid an advertising battle. Thus, Keebler used public relations techniques instead. Cushman described these techniques as "unusually effective media collateral, notably a

Public relations techniques carried the marketing communication effort for Coleco's Cabbage Patch dolls.

Photo courtesy of Hasbro

press kit designed as Keebler's 'Magic Oven.'"[31] Cushman calculated that the resulting exposure on television would have been worth more than $3 million if purchased as advertising and reported that Keebler gained 30 percent of the market as a result.

Pharmaceutical Marketing

Pharmaceutical companies have little difficulty using advertising to market nonprescription drugs directly to consumers, but they cannot market prescription drugs as easily because these must be prescribed by doctors. Thus, most advertising has been directed at physicians and is regulated by the Food and Drug Administration (FDA), which requires advertisements to be accurate and to balance their descriptions of benefits and side effects.[32]

During the 1990s, however, pharmaceutical companies broke away from this traditional method of marketing communication and used public relations techniques to promote prescription drugs directly to consumers—by "press conferences, media tours, video news releases, media coverage of scientific symposia, and drug research discussions with investment analysts."[33] Pharmaceutical companies used celebrity spokespersons such as baseball pitcher Nolan Ryan to promote the painkiller Advil for American Home Products Corp., and baseball Hall of Famer Mickey Mantle to promote the arthritis drug Voltaren for CIBA-GEIGY.

According to Harris, virtually all pharmaceutical companies employ medical experts to consult on products and to be available for press conferences and interviews—thus providing the endorsement of medical experts for their products.[34] *Newsweek* described the purpose of these endorsements in a story on the effect of public relations in promoting Retin-A, a product produced by Johnson & Johnson that seemed to reduce the wrinkling of skin. According to *Newsweek*, "Johnson & Johnson used public relations to go around the doctor to the consumer, and the consumer came back asking for the prescription."[35]

The FDA, however, has become concerned about abuses in such publicity campaigns. It was particularly concerned about "Mickey's drug," which apparently helped to reduce the effects of Mantle's arthritis, because all such drugs are effective when used for the first time for arthritis.[36] Thus, the FDA now applies the same criteria to publicity about drugs that it applies to advertising: both must be true, not misleading, and provide balanced information on both the benefits and side effects.[37] The FDA also has expressed concern about the contents of video news releases and has considered requiring pharmaceutical companies to submit the VNRs to its staff for approval before they can be released.[38]

To avoid the problems involved in marketing drugs directly, many pharmaceutical companies have turned to informational public relations programs that are not tied to a particular drug. Such programs provide valuable medical information without naming their own brands, although the name of the company providing the information usually is prominent:

> *Many of the public education or consumer health campaigns in our society are initiated, driven, funded, sponsored and organized by drug marketers. Osteoporosis, breast cancer and prostate cancer are examples of three conditions—once largely ignored—about which pharmaceutical companies have helped educate the American public.*[39]

According to Larry Wheeler, the vice president for communications at the Marion Merrell Dow Company in Kansas City, Missouri, these public relations programs "condition the market for the ultimate sale."[40] They build a strong reputation of caring and social responsibility for the company, which makes a difference to physicians, pharmacists, and patients when they prescribe or buy a product.

Public relations programs, as a means to build relationships with consumers and other stakeholders, may sometimes be more important than traditional marketing communication campaigns. In the pharmaceutical industry, corporate-wide public relations programs may help to market the product more effectively than the specific techniques of marketing communication.

Sports Marketing

During the 1992 Olympics in Barcelona, a controversy broke out when members of the "Dream Team" basketball squad refused to wear Reebok insignia during the medal ceremonies because they had contracts to promote competing brands of basketball shoes. Several players resolved the dilemma by draping an American flag over the insignia during the ceremony.

Tobacco companies cannot advertise on television, so they work around this restriction by sponsoring tournaments such as the Virginia Slims tournament for women's tennis—where their product names are displayed prominently for television audiences.

Most major college football bowl games now have corporate sponsors. L'Eggs pantyhose sponsored the Ice Capades. In 1992, Burson Marsteller had 200 clients come to New York to discuss opportunities for marketing connected to the Olympics. Sports marketing—promotion of events, endorsements, sponsorships, and sports teams themselves—are big business for public relations firms and organizations doing marketing communication. In 1991, that business amounted to nearly $2 billion.[41]

Repositioning a Bank and a Hotel

Many corporations and organizations use public relations techniques to change their identity, to reposition themselves after a change in strategy or a major rebuilding project. A bank and a hotel provide examples.

The Continental Bank of Chicago repositioned itself strictly as a bank for businesses in 1988. In 1989, Continental developed an integrated campaign of advertising and public relations to tell its target market of 400,000 corporate executives, money managers, and institutional investors about the change.[42] Advertisements announced Continental's new, exclusive focus on business banking and its customized products and services. Public relations contributed a four-color annual report produced in four editions, each aimed at a different kind of customer.

In a joint research project with the *Wall Street Journal*, Continental surveyed 1,100 CEOs of major companies about the competitiveness of U.S. business. The bank also helped to finance a quarterly *Journal of Applied Corporate Finance*, which featured articles on issues such as risk management and real estate written by financial officers of corporations, chief executives, professors of business, regulators, lawmakers, and Continental's own specialists. Public relations specialists publicized the survey in each issue of the journal to highlight Continental's expertise as a business banker.

The Delta Chelsea Inn had been a major hotel in downtown Toronto for many years, but new hotels increased the competition and reduced the advantage in price that the Chelsea had over its competitors.[43] Research on focus groups indicated that current and potential guests wanted a larger and better-equipped hotel. Thus, the management of the Chelsea spent $80 million to renovate the hotel: upgrades included 600 rooms in a new twenty-seven-story tower, a new lobby, more food and beverage outlets, and high-speed elevators. The hotel stayed open during the renovation. During this time, a program called *Please Bear With Us*—featuring a bear "chum" mascot—told customers about the project and apologized for the inconvenience.

After the renovation, the Chelsea wanted to appeal to a more upscale market, so it developed an integrated marketing theme of "Value on a Grand Scale." The integrated campaign included advertising in general and trade media, direct mail to prospective guests, trade shows, and promotions inside the hotel. Media relations also were used to promote the new hotel: free rooms were awarded to radio listeners and TV viewers in exchange for media exposure, radio stations broadcasting live from the lobby of the hotel, a media kit to announce the grand opening of the renovated hotel, and a gala opening party featuring food stations and casino games.

According to Nancy Arab, the director of public relations for the hotel, the result has been "nothing short of spectacular"—an occupancy rate in 1991 four times greater than the average for the city.[44]

TECHNIQUES USED TO PROMOTE PRODUCTS

We have placed this chapter at the end of the book for a reason. Most of the techniques of public relations described in previous chapters have been or can be used to support the marketing function as well as other public relations programs. The techniques that can be used to promote products, services, or organizations are limited only by the imagination and creativity of the public relations technician. In his book, *The Marketer's Guide to Public Relations*, for example, Harris has a chapter titled, "MPR Tactics from A to Z," in which he lists a technique for each letter of the alphabet. He acknowledged that he "cheated" only a little for the letter "x," for which he listed "expert columns."[45]

In a truly integrated program of marketing communication, it sometimes becomes difficult to distinguish public relations techniques from other techniques of marketing communication. Harris, for example, included T-shirts and sweatshirts, fan clubs, and symbols such as Ronald McDonald or the Keebler elf as public relations techniques—whereas most public relations people would consider them techniques of product promotion.

Many marketing textbooks, therefore, list all communication techniques used to advertise or promote products without distinguishing public relations techniques from techniques of advertising or product promotion. Lovelock and Weinberg, for example, distinguished between personal and impersonal channels. Personal channels include face-to-face and telephone contacts. Impersonal channels include advertisements on television and radio and in newspapers and magazines; publicity in those media; direct mail; displays, sales promotions and handouts; and signs and other cues.[46] Public relations technicians, of course, can and often do design messages and programs that use most of these tactics. Most are experts in interpersonal communication, media relations, publications, posters, and signs. Most also can write and design advertisements.

For most practitioners, however, marketing public relations consists of techniques designed to place material in the mass media, to get the attention of the media, or to service the media. Most practitioners also consider the use of journalistic skills to support marketing—such as the writing and production of newsletters, reports, or brochures—to be marketing public relations.

To give you an idea of the most frequent tools that public relations technicians contribute to marketing communication, we have constructed a list of techniques frequently used in marketing public relations. Footnotes for each of these techniques provide references to books on marketing communication where you can read more about the technique.

Media Relations. Public relations practitioners use the specific techniques that follow to place stories about products, services, or organizations in the media. We begin this list, however, by stressing relationships with the media. As Burnett put it, "the road to media respect is via honesty, accuracy, and professionalism."[47] You cannot place marketing-related stories in the media unless you respect and cultivate the news values and professional values of journalists.

Press Kits. Press kits often contain product samples. It is more important that they contain materials that the media can use directly—news releases, fact sheets, and technical information about the product or service, feature stories, photographs or drawings, biographies of key speakers, and background on the company.[48]

Product Releases. Product releases are news releases that introduce a new product or contain news about a product or service. Product releases usually complement or support the advertising program—that is, they are issued at the same time or just before or after advertisements are placed. They also may announce a trade show or special event held to introduce a product.[49]

Executive Statement Releases. Often organizations issue releases that do not specifically mention products but that quote executives or are based on interviews with executives. These releases are designed to develop confidence in the company that produces a product.[50] Companies issue such releases because many consumers buy products from companies they respect as much as they buy because they like the features of a particular product.

Feature Releases. Feature stories about a product are not pegged to a specific news event such as the release of a new product or a trade show.[51] Feature stores must build human interest in the product or users of a product so that both editors and readers are interested.

Customer Application Releases. These are a type of feature story describing how a customer has used a product or service. They also can be called "mini-case histories."[52] Case histories are especially good for trade publications. Mathews pointed out, for example, that, "A hotel that installs a new communication system to handle alarms, wake-up calls, billing, and maid service is a good candidate for a case study for publications in both the hotel/motel industry and the communication industry."[53]

How-to Releases. These releases are another type of feature story that describe how to use a product or service.[54] Such stories are a staple part of specialized and trade publications.

Factory Tours. Journalists, especially those working for trade publications, like to supplement interviews, fact sheets, and news releases with a tour of the factory where the product is made. PR people can supplement the tour with interviews with marketing executives, photographs, and opportunities for the journalists to take their own photos.[55]

Interviews. Journalists frequently want to gather their own information and to quote people in addition to using materials from news releases and press briefings that you may provide or set up.[56] Interviews allow journalists to make their story different from those of competing publications. Public relations people should help them by arranging interviews with marketing experts, researchers, executives, or customers who have used the product.

Press Conferences. Press conferences can be held to introduce new products, to deal with bad news about products, or to deal with inquiries coming from large numbers of journalists.[57]

Media Breakfasts. Journalists can be invited to breakfasts with key executives or to discuss a product or service with experts from the organization.[58]

Product Fairs. Journalists, as well as customers, employees, and investors, can be invited to fairs where products are demonstrated. Fairs can be held over several days to reach diverse audiences.[59]

Individual Briefings. If there are only a few journalists to deal with, a half- or full-day briefing may be an efficient way to provide them with information on the product and company. They can also interview researchers or executives and participate in a question-and-answer session.[60]

Trade Shows. If your company is an exhibitor at a trade show, reporters may wish to visit the exhibit and interview key people. Trade shows also attract large numbers of reporters, so they can provide an ideal opportunity to announce a new product.[61]

Press Seminars. For technical or scientific organizations, PR people may invite reporters to special seminars with scientists and experts to explain the product, the industry, a medical problem, or a new drug.[62]

Newsletters. Regular newsletters can be used to provide information about products to consumers, journalists, financial specialists, and similar audiences.[63]

Video Tapes. Video tapes can be used to provide information to reporters or consumers at seminars, product fairs, or trade shows. Or they can be sent to reporters who cannot attend.[64] Video tapes also can be prepared for dealers and sales representatives to help them convey information about the product.

Video News Releases. Video releases now are regularly used by television networks and stations.[65] They may not use all of your footage, but visuals used still will identify your product or organization.

Expert Columns. Columns by company experts often can be placed in newspapers or magazines. For example, the John Deere company used a Deere John column; Pearl Vision ran an Ask Dr. Pearl column.[66]

Books. Companies publish thousands of books or booklets describing how to use products or services or how to use them to solve problems.[67]

Photographs. All media want photographs to supplement stories. Print media may need either black-and-white or color photos. Visual media use slides.[68]

Created Events. You can stage all kinds of events to get the attention of journalists and consumers: examples are contests, birthdays, grand openings, special months or days, or landmarks in the selling of a product. You also can participate in national or local holidays, blockbuster sports events, or other special celebrations.[69]

Exhibits. Exhibits can be held at trade shows, but they also can be set up at fairs, professional meetings, shopping centers, museums, amusement parks, or company buildings.[70]

Road Shows/Media Tours. Company representatives can tour several cities, often in conjunction with special events, to gain media exposure.[71] The California Raisins, for example, gained national recognition after they went on tour.

Collateral Materials. Public relations technicians produce many journalistic products used by sales representatives or to support advertising. These collateral materials include descriptive booklets, brochures, manuals, videotapes, or displays. Public relations specialists also produce popular magazines that are distributed, for example, by dealers of automobiles, agricultural supplies, or insurance.

Official Endorsements. Endorsement by government officials or respected organizations lend credibility to a product or organization. Government officials can welcome touring representatives at a special event. Crest and other toothpastes have been endorsed by the American Dental Association.[72]

Product Placement. We have already heard about *E.T.* and Reese's Pieces. Placing products in movies and on television can stimulate sales and publicity.[73]

Trade Products for Publicity. PR people may donate products that radio or television programs can give as prizes in exchange for the publicity generated by the contest.[74]

Product Samples. Product samples can be given to reporters and opinion leaders.[75]

Thons. Telethons, marathons, bikeathons, and walkathons generate publicity and good will.[76]

Vehicles. We already have mentioned the Goodyear blimp. Hot-air balloons, automobiles, ships, and planes also generate publicity and attention.[77]

Youth Programs. McDonald's is famous for its All American Band. Companies sponsor Boy and Girl Scout programs, sponsor local events, and hold science fairs.[78]

Participation in Local Events. Organizations encourage their employees to serve on school boards, to lead charity drives, to head the Kiwanis or Lions Club, to be youth leaders, to participate in churches. All build the reputation that make consumers happy to buy products.[79]

Sponsorships. We previously discussed sports marketing. Sponsoring teams, sports events, as well as exhibits, television specials, or charitable events can create awareness of a product or company and a good, long-term relationship with consumers.[80]

Advertising to Create Publicity. The famous daisy commercial—featuring a little girl picking petals from a daisy while nuclear bombs exploded in the background—was created by Democrats to discredit Barry Goldwater in the 1964 presidential campaign. The spot appeared only once, but it generated an enormous amount of publicity. Apple Computers ran its *1984* commercial only once during the Super Bowl in January 1984, but the advertisement and the publicity it generated brought thousands of buyers into showrooms.[81] Sometimes advertisements can be so newsworthy that they only have to be run a time or two themselves to generate free publicity.

Many marketing communication specialists view their work as a form of the press agentry model of public relations. When they do, they tend to see their work solely as a creative function and lose sight of the marketing and communication objectives they are supposed to achieve. Naively, they seem to assume that publicity alone sells products. Burnett described the problem when he said:

MANAGEMENT CONSIDERATIONS

> Of all the components of the marketing mix, promotion is the most likely to get out of hand unless all the other elements of the marketing mix are carefully considered. Promotional strategy involves several different elements and usually a number of different individuals as well. It requires a considerable amount of specialized, creative talent that is difficult to direct and control. Moreover, designers of promotional material are often overimpressed with the importance of their function, while belittling the importance of others.[82]

Burnett then stressed the importance of choosing communication techniques to carry out a marketing plan:

> These factors tend to push promotional strategy away from the overall plan that has been selected. Promotional strategists often encourage the creation of more ambitious programs than are actually required. They frequently misdirect the promotional effort into areas not clearly related to corporate marketing objectives. The best way to make sure that the promotional strategy fits with the other marketing mix elements is to assess it carefully before proceeding with the final integrative process.[83]

Marketing managers should choose techniques of marketing communication after going through three types of planning. If you are involved in this managerial process, you will help with the planning. If you are involved strictly at the technical level of communication, you should understand the management planning that preceded your work. If none of this planning has occurred, you probably are wasting money and time if you choose to communicate anyway.

Howard described the importance of integrating one technique of marketing communication—a special event—with corporate and marketing objectives in the following passage:

> *Similar to an employee publication or news conference, a special event must have a specific purpose, be directed to a specific audience, and be part of an overall plan. It must be managed like any other part of the business. And it must support the organization's marketing and sales objectives.*[84]

Let's look, then, at how marketing communication fits into these three levels of management.

Strategic Management

Strategic management takes place at the corporate or organizational level. At this level, the organization defines its mission, selects its goals, defines a business portfolio (what businesses or products should make up the company), and plans how units such as marketing or public relations should contribute to the organization's mission and goals.[85] Although strategic management takes place at top levels of management, communication programs—including marketing communication—must be integrated into that process if they are to help the organization meet its objectives.

Marketing Management

Marketing managers contribute to this process of strategic management by identifying markets for products—market opportunities—that help to define the organization's business portfolio. (Public relations contributes to strategic management differently. See Chapter 1 for an explanation of the difference.) Marketing managers then develop programs to respond to the market opportunities by developing and selling appropriate products.

Marketing management, therefore, proceeds through four stages:

Analyzing Market Opportunities.

Selecting Target Markets.

Developing the Marketing Mix (**P**roduct, **P**rice, **P**lace, **P**romotion).

Managing the Marketing Effort.[86]

The planning of the marketing communication effort should flow logically from the Marketing Mix, so that the Marketing Effort (including communication) is managed to achieve both marketing and corporate goals.

Management of Marketing Communication

Once you understand the contribution of a program of marketing communication to the marketing mix, you can begin to plan a communication strategy that contributes to marketing and organizational objectives. Like most communication programs, this planning process generally falls into four stages:

Establish Communication Objectives.

Choose Messages, Techniques, and Channels.

Implement the Communication Plan.

Evaluate Results to Determine if Objectives Have Been Met.[87]

It can be tempting to begin the marketing communication process at the second stage—the choice of messages, techniques, and channels. Much more important is the choice of objectives—objectives that support marketing objectives and organizational goals. Chapter 1 described five objectives that communication theory and research suggest are possible objectives for communication programs—communication, accuracy, understanding, agreement, and behavior. Chapter 7 of our companion book, *Managing Public Relations*, describes these objectives in more detail and the theory and research behind them. Chapter 9 explains how to measure these objectives and the research methods that can be used to evaluate whether a communication program has met its objectives.

At first glance, you may think that the only appropriate goal for marketing communication is to affect the behavior of consumers—after all, you want to sell something. However, in his book, *The Marketing Imagination*, Levitt pointed out that marketing is a process of building a relationship with consumers[88] and that "people don't buy things, they buy solutions to problems."[89] Over the long term, you do want to sell products—affect behavior—but you may accomplish that goal better through symmetric, short-term objectives. With the objectives of accuracy and understanding you will help consumers solve problems while building a relationship with them.

Relationships are as crucial in marketing as in public relations. Public relations people can help marketing greatly because of their expertise in the building of relationships—a point made by Regis McKenna, San Francisco public relations counselor, in his book *Relationship Marketing*.[90] Thus, just as accuracy and understanding generally are the most important objectives for public relations programs, they usually will be the most important objectives when you plan and evaluate a marketing communication program.

When to Use Public Relations Techniques

Public relations technicians often find themselves competing with advertising, direct mail, and sales promotion for a place in the marketing mix. And technicians who work for public relations firms compete especially with advertising firms. Keep in mind that, although winning this competition may generate revenue for the public relations firm and help to pay your salary, it may not help the organization achieve its marketing objectives or organizational goals. That is why the concept of integrated marketing communication has become so popular. As Novelli put it, public relations is a wedge in the marketing pie that should be developed and integrated with the other wedges of the pie—advertising, promotion, and direct marketing.[91]

Nevertheless, it is important to understand the relative advantages of public relations techniques in marketing so that you know when they work best and when other techniques work better. Harris, for example, pointed out that some products have greater news value than others and that different strategies are needed to publicize products with different levels of consumer interest and news value.[92] Marketing communication experts, though, most often cite three reasons to use public relations techniques to promote a product or service. We list these advantages here but express caution about each of them. Publicity releases may have these advantages, but such claims are based more on faith and assumption than solid evaluative research.

Cost Publicity generally costs less than advertising—at least less than the costs of placing a story in each additional medium. As Goldman put it, publicity is virtually free after the initial costs of producing a press release or other message. "The cost of a few extra press releases or postage stamps is negligible compared with the costs of running ads in those additional media."[93]

However, one must be cautious about such a claim of cost effectiveness. Good media relations often require follow-up calls or visits. These follow-ups cost time as well as postage stamps. Sending press releases out indiscriminately also can have other costs, such as the loss of credibility with journalists when a release has no news value for a particular medium.

Credibility Marketing communication people claim that a story about a product, service, or organization that appears as a news or feature item has more credibility than a paid advertisement placed in the same medium.[94] Usually, they attribute this greater credibility to a "third-party endorsement"—meaning that journalists supposedly endorse a product when they run a story about it. Cushman expressed the claim this way: "The so-called 'disinterested third-person implied endorsement' carries credibility. And therein lies the strength of public relations."[95]

We know of little research evidence that people actually believe journalists have endorsed a product when they run a news story or that editorial copy has greater credibility than advertising copy. Harris, for example, based his claim of third-party credibility on the endorsement of Theodore Levitt, professor at the Harvard Business School and former editor of the *Harvard Business Review*. Harris quoted Levitt's book, *The Marketing Mode,* in which Levitt said that "when the message is delivered by an objective third party, such as a journalist or broadcaster, the message is delivered more persuasively."[96] Harris concluded, "Levitt's recognition gave added clout to a claim long made by public relations practitioners."[97]

Such an endorsement may add "clout" to the claim of third-party endorsement, but it provides no substantive evidence that editorial material has greater credibility or has other effects that advertising does not have. Cameron did conduct an experiment to compare the extent to which subjects remembered editorial material better than they remembered the same content in an advertisement and found a slight difference.[98] It also is possible that people are more likely to expose themselves to editorial material than advertisements. However, to our knowledge, that possible difference has not been researched.

As we have stated, advertising and public relations often complement each other. A reader or viewer might remember an advertisement better after having first read a news story with the same content. And advertisements themselves can create publicity. In short, it seems obvious to public relations practitioners that publicity has greater credibility than advertising. Yet, the evidence is so scanty that we recommend caution in assuming and claiming third-party effects. Rather, it would seem that each campaign, with different combinations of publicity and advertising, might have different effects. Each mix of communication techniques should be pretested and evaluated to see which technique or combination of techniques works best in each situation.

Use Publicity When You Can't Advertise   Marketers also turn to public relations techniques to publicize their products when there are legal regulations affecting whether and how they can advertise a product.[99] Cigarettes cannot be advertised on television, for example. Thus, the companies sponsor tennis tournaments and use other means to get their brand names in front of consumers. Similarly, as we have seen, marketers must be careful in advertising prescription drugs; thus they turn to media relations to promote the product. Again, however, exercise caution: Regulatory agencies look closely at the truth and fairness of public relations messages.

NOTES
1. James E. Grunig and Todd Hunt, *Managing Public Relations*, 2d ed. (Fort Worth: Harcourt Brace College Publishers, 1995).

2. This conclusion is supported by Lauzen's study of 168 organizations, which showed that marketing departments are more likely to take over public relations functions—"encroach" upon them—than are human resources and legal departments. Martha M. Lauzen, "Imperialism and Encroachment in Public Relations," *Public Relations Review* 17 (Fall 1991), pp. 245–256.

3. Jacqueline Peake, *Public Relations in Business* (New York: Harper & Row, 1980), p. 5.

4. Thomas L. Harris, *The Marketer's Guide to Public Relations* (New York: Wiley, 1991), p. 9.

5. Harris, pp. 5–7; Aaron D. Cushman, "Why Marketing Directors are Listening Now," *Public Relations Journal* 46 (May 1990), pp. 17–19; James Foster, "Working Together: How Companies are Integrating Their Corporate Communications," *Public Relations Journal* 46 (September 1990), pp. 18–19.

6. Reported in *pr reporter purview*, July 20, 1992.

7. Philip Kotler, *Marketing Management*, 7th ed. (Englewood Cliffs, NJ: Prentice-Hall, 1991), p. 643.

8. Glen M. Broom and Kerry Tucker, "An Essential Double Helix," *Public Relations Journal* 45 (November 1989), p. 39. Another report on this conference can be found in Glen M. Broom, Martha M. Lauzen, and Kerry Tucker, "Public Relations and Marketing: Dividing the Conceptual Domain and Operational Turf," *Public Relations Review* 17 (Fall 1991), pp. 219–225.

9. Kotler, p. 642. A similar discussion of Kotler's view of public relations can be found in his undergraduate textbook: Philip Kotler and Gary Anderson, *Principles of Marketing*, 5th ed. (Englewood Cliffs, NJ: Prentice-Hall, 1991), Chapters 16, 17.

10. Christopher H. Spicer, "Communication Functions Performed by Public Relations and Marketing Practitioners," *Public Relations Review* 17 (Fall 1991), p. 299.

11. Harris, p. 34.

12. These also are points made by Harris in his book on marketing public relations.

13. Dorothy L. Zutall, "How to Adapt Marketing Strategies in Health-Care Public Relations," *Public Relations Journal* 37 (October 1981), p. 15.

14. "Behind the Scenes with The Goodyear Blimp—Public Relations Ambassador Extraordinaire," *PR Casebook* 3 (May 1982), pp. 11–14.

15. Numerous examples of the press agentry model applied to marketing communication can be found in the book by Robert J. Wood and Max Gunther, *Confessions of a PR Man* (New York: New American Library, 1988).

16. See, for example, Philip Kotler and Alan R. Andreasen, *Strategic Marketing for Nonprofit Organizations* (Englewood Cliffs, NJ: Prentice-Hall, 1987), p. 71.

17. William Nickels, *Marketing Communication and Promotion*, 2d ed. (Columbus, OH: Grid, 1980), p. 15.

18. "Awakening Interest in a Well-Known Product," *PR Casebook* 3 (March 1982), pp. 3–5.

19. "B-M Brings 'Good Things' to GE," Marsteller, Inc./Burson-Marsteller *Viewpoint*, March 1982.

20. Bill Daring, "Case Eight: Volex Accessories Designer Range," in Danny Moss (ed.), *Public Relations in Practice: A Casebook* (London: Routledge, 1990), p. 112.

21. Daring, pp. 113–115.

22. Daring, p. 116.

23. Daring, p. 116.

24. For further discussion of how to evaluate communication programs, see Chapter 8 of Grunig and Hunt.

25. For a discussion of appropriate strategies for products with different levels of involvement, see Henry Assael, *Consumer Behavior and Marketing Action*, 3d ed. (Boston: Kent, 1987), Chapters 2, 4.

26. Harris, pp. 83–84; Carole M. Howard, "Promotions and Special Events: Integrating Public Relations into the Marketing Mix," in Clara Degen (ed.), *Communicators' Guide to Marketing* (New York: Longman, 1987), p. 189.

27. Harris, pp. 99–100.

28. Harris, p. 101.

29. Harris, pp. 135–137.

30. Harris, p. 137.

31. Cushman, pp. 18–19.

32. Marilyn L. Castaldi, "FDA Writing Tougher Rx for Pharmaceutical Marketing," *Public Relations Journal* 47 (August 1991), pp. 14–16, 19; Don Hyman, "Pharmaceuticals: Balancing the Demands of Diverse Publics," *Public Relations Journal* 46 (October 1990), pp. 22–25.

33. Castaldi, p. 15.

34. Harris, pp. 125–128.

35. As reported by Harris, p. 127.

36. Harris, p. 127.

37. Castaldi, p. 15.

38. Darren Bosik, "FDA Cautions Drug Firms and VNR Regulations," *O'Dwyer's PR Services Report* 5 (October 1991), pp. 1, 8, 10, 12.

39. Castaldi, p. 15.

40. Castaldi, pp. 15–16.

41. Adam Shell, "Firms Try to Pitch the Perfect Game," *Public Relations Journal* 47 (July 1991), pp. 10–12, 22.

42. "Continental Banks on Integrated Communications," *Public Relations Journal* 9 (September 1990), pp. 20–21.

43. Nancy H. Arab, "Integrated Marketing Repositions Toronto Hotel; Occupancy Soars," *Public Relations Journal* 47 (March 1991), pp. 22–23.

44. Arab, p. 22.

45. Harris, p. 91.

46. Christopher H. Lovelock and Charles B. Weinberg, *Marketing for Public and Nonprofit Managers* (New York: Wiley, 1984), pp. 397–399.

47. John J. Burnett, *Promotion Management: A Strategic Approach*, 2d ed. (St. Paul, MN: West, 1988), p. 437.

48. Wilma Mathews, "Marketing a New Product or Service," in Clara Degen (ed.), *Communicators' Guide to Marketing* (New York: Longman, 1987), p. 113.

49. Mathews, pp. 114–115; Goldman, pp. 15–26; Burnett, pp. 439–440.

50. Goldman, pp. 27–39.

51. Mathews, p. 115; Goldman, pp. 41–52.

52. Goldman, p. 19.

53. Mathews, pp. 115–116.

54. Mathews, p. 116.

55. Mathews, p. 116.

56. Goldman, pp. 53–56; Harris, p. 82.

57. Burnett, p. 440.

58. Mathews, p. 116.

59. Mathews, p. 117.

60. Mathews, p. 117.

61. Mathews, p. 118.

62. Mathews, p. 118; Goldman, pp. 58–61.

63. Mathews, p. 117; Harris, p. 83.

64. Mathews, p. 118.

65. Harris, p. 91.

66. Harris, p. 91.

67. Harris, p. 70.

68. Burnett, p. 442.

69. Harris, p. 79, Chapters 12 and 14.

70. Burnett, p. 444; Harris, p. 81.

71. Harris, pp. 85, 89.

72. Harris, p. 83.

73. Harris, p. 83.

74. Harris, p. 85.

75. Harris, p. 87.

76. Harris, p. 89.

77. Harris, p. 89.

78. Harris, p. 91.

79. Burnett, pp. 445–446.

80. Harris, Chapter 15.

81. Harris, pp. 93–95.

82. Burnett, p. 33.

83. Burnett, p. 33.

84. Carole, M. Howard, "Promotions and Special Events: Integrating Public Relations into the Marketing Mix," in Clara Degen (ed.), *Communicators' Guide to Marketing* (New York: Longman, 1987), p. 191.

85. Kotler and Anderson, pp. 29–41.

86. Kotler and Anderson, p. 41.

87. Kotler, *Marketing Management*, pp. 643–646. See also Goldman, Chapter 1; Harris, Chapter 6 for similar descriptions of the process.

88. Theodore Levitt, *The Marketing Imagination* (New York: The Free Press, 1986), Chapter 6.

89. Levitt, p. 127.

90. Regis McKenna, *Relationship Marketing* (Reading, MA: Addison Wesley, 1992).

91. William D. Novelli, "One-Stop Shopping: Some Thoughts on Integrated Marketing Communication," *Public Relations Quarterly* 34 (Winter 1989–90), p. 8.

92. Harris, Chapter 5; see his "Harris Grid" for each of four kinds of strategies.

93. Goldman, p. xvii.

94. See, e.g., Mathews, p. 111; Harris, p. 44; Lovelock and Weinberg, p. 435; Goldman, p. xvi; Cushman, p. 17; Foster, p. 18.

95. Cushman, p. 17.

96. Harris, p. 44.

97. Harris, p. 44.

98. Glen T. Cameron, "Does Publicity Outperform Advertising: An Experimental Test of the Third-Party Endorsement," paper presented to the International Communication Association, Chicago, May 1990.

99. This claim is made by the veteran public relations counselor Daniel Edelman in an article in *pr reporter.* "Marketing PR Can Outperform Advertising Says Long-Time Counselor Dan Edelman," *pr reporter,* October 30, 1989, pp. 3–4.

ADDITIONAL READING

Burnett, John, *Promotion Management: A Strategic Approach,* 2d ed. (St. Paul, MN: West, 1988).

Degen, Clara (ed.), *Communicators' Guide to Marketing* (New York: Longman, 1987).

Harris, Thomas L., *The Marketer's Guide to Public Relations* (New York: Wiley, 1991).

Kotler, Philip, and Alan R. Andreasen, *Strategic Marketing for Nonprofit Organizations,* 3d ed. (Englewood Cliffs, NJ: Prentice-Hall, 1987).

Kotler, Philip, and Gary Armstrong, *Principles of Marketing,* 5th ed. (Englewood Cliffs, NJ: Prentice-Hall, 1991).

Kotler, Philip, and Eduardo L. Roberto, *Social Marketing* (New York: Free Press, 1989).

Rice, Ronald E., and Charles K. Atkin, *Public Communication Campaigns,* 2d ed. (Beverly Hills, CA: Sage, 1989).

Salmon, Charles T. (ed.), *Information Campaigns: Balancing Social Values and Social Change* (Newbury Park, CA: Sage, 1989).

20

Legal Requirements

All of the techniques described and prescribed in this book involve the use of information and images. Sometimes those data and images are the property of other individuals or organizations. They just may cause someone to be held up to ridicule or to be publicly embarrassed. Sometimes they invade the privacy of individuals. And sometimes they are subject to rules regarding the timely disclosure of data that can affect the price of shares on the stock market.

In other words, the "simple" messages you create for your client or your organization may have legal consequences that could result in difficulties or penalties for your organization, and perhaps even for you as an individual.

Most students of public relations who take a campaigns course or a course in writing and message design have already taken a theory course—perhaps called Principles of Public Relations. The text in that course—such as our companion volume *Managing Public Relations*—covers laws and the reasons behind them. Another excellent reference source is *Public Relations and the Law,* by Frank Walsh, a PRSA-accredited public relations educator and attorney. It is available from the Institute for Public Relations Research and Education, Inc., 3800 South Tamiami Trail, Suite N, Sarasota, FL 34329.

As a quick reference and reminder, this chapter summarizes the main points in several areas of legal responsibility. The material is aimed at helping you to analyze whether a message you are creating might contain information that could get you, your organization, or your client in some kind of trouble. If in doubt, never rationalize that "I've seen things like this before, so it must be okay to do it." Seek legal counsel if you sense that the materials you are about to disseminate may violate one of the principles described in this section.

DEFAMATION: LIBEL AND SLANDER

Injuring a person or an organization by speaking (slander) or writing (libel) words that are untrue or that falsely cast a person in a bad light can lead to a lawsuit. The best defenses are that the injurious words or images are *true,* that the person involved is a *public figure* open to criticism, or that an individual gave (or implied giving) his or her consent to publication of the information. If injury was committed, the best defense against huge settlements in a court of law is proof of an *absence of malice* in committing the libel or slander.

However good your intentions as an individual, it is possible that the information you prepare may inadvertently injure someone. In a competitive business, the claims that one company makes regarding its products or services in comparison with those of another firm may cause injury and lead to a suit. It is difficult for a large organization to engage in commerce and public debate without offending others and, eventually, incurring a defamation lawsuit. The legal department is able to do its job better if the public relations people have exercised as much care as possible and can verify the information and images they have used as true, fair, and representative of reality.

Libel and slander laws differ from state to state, and local juries may be persuaded to give different interpretations to those laws. Typically, in order to constitute defamation, the information must *identify* a person or group, must *damage the reputation* of that person or group, and must be *published* by dissemination to an audience or public. To these basic tests are added many special situations, such as the following:

Mistaken identification. If you erroneously identify one person or group as another, and that identification injures their reputation, you are guilty of defamation, even though it may be "only" carelessness or an honest mistake.

Odious labels. If your information labels someone as a drunk, a deadbeat, a dishonest person, or if you characterize an organization as bankrupt, anti-American, or sleazy, you may be guilty of defamation.

Professional injury. If you damage an individual's means of making a living or if you cause an entire profession to be held up to ridicule (perhaps in a piece of promotional material that touts the benefit of your client's services over those of another), you may be guilty of trade libel.

"Per quod" libel. Libel "per se" is obvious on the face, but libel "per quod" is not. Intimating that an employee enjoyed a few alcoholic drinks at an office party is not necessarily libelous, but it may

qualify as "per quod" defamation. For example, a jury may be convinced that the employee—who happens to be a lay minister—has been injured by your characterization of him as a drinker.

Judges and juries can decide to award damages only to compensate a person or group for loss of reputation—so-called "general" damages. But in many states they can award special or actual damages where specific monetary losses can be proved, such as lost wages. And they can assess whopping "punitive" damages if they detect malice on the part of the communicator of information. Keeping careful records and offering testimony attesting to the care in preparation of information can go a long way toward convincing judges and juries not to go beyond the awarding of general damages.

COPYRIGHT, RELEASES, AND PERMISSIONS

Information, data, images, publications, and other messages are *property* in the eyes of the law—they belong to someone, and that individual or organization has the sole right to use them unless arrangements are made for another to use them.

When preparing messages for your client or organization, you may wish to protect them and identify them as your own, signaling to others that you expect credit or remuneration, or both, if they are used. When you first create the work, you are protected by *common law* copyright, which is easier to prove if you have labelled the information as to ownership, dated it, and kept orderly files. When you publish or disseminate the information, you may obtain the additional protection of *statutory* copyright by filling out a simple form, paying a small fee, and depositing a copy of the work with the Register of Copyright in the Library of Congress. Individuals thus can protect their work for their lifetime plus fifty years. In the case of the "work made for hire" produced on behalf of an organization such as a corporation, the copyright may run from seventy-five to one hundred years.

To obtain copyright forms, write The Copyright Office, Library of Congress, Washington, D.C. 20559. Stipulate what kind of work you wish to protect, because there are different forms for books, articles, photographs, etc.

When you are using photographs of people, especially photos of children and your own employees, make sure to obtain their signature (a parent's approval for a minor) on a *release form* like the one in Exhibit 20.1. A *permission form* is used to obtain approval for reprinting someone else's work. A *copyright authorization form* is used when a freelance photographer is willing to turn control of images over to the firm for which the photos were taken. (See Exhibit 20.2 for a sample form that covers several situations.)

Exhibit 20.1
Photographic Release

The photographic release form may be as simple as the one shown below.

PHOTOGRAPHIC RELEASE FORM

Date _____

I hereby consent to the use of the photograph described below for publicity and promotional purposes by (XYZ Corp.), and I waive all claims for compensation for such use, or for damages.

Description of photograph:

Signature _____

Name (printed) _____

Signature of parent or
   guardian if signing
   for minor child _____

Address _____

_____

Photographer _____

Never assume that it is permissible to use information or images you are familiar with. Watch out for these common pitfalls:

Public domain. The national anthem is in the "public domain" and may be used without permission. But "Happy Birthday to You" is not, and you must pay for its public use. Martin Luther King's famous "I Have a Dream" speech is copyrighted. When the copyrights expire, the works pass into the public domain and may be used freely. Check with a librarian or the copyright office if you are not sure. Similarly, popular images such as the Pillsbury Doughboy and the Peanuts characters are protected by trademark.

DATE: _____

A. Name of work (property): _____

B. Use (brief description of use: e.g., annual report, press kit, feature story, speech, presentation):
_____
_____

C. Ownership of copyright (check as appropriate):
  [ ] 1. We (user of form) own, because it is
    [ ] Work-for-hire because it was made by our own employee(s).
    Name of employee: _____
    [ ] Work-for-hire because:
      (i) It is a commissioned work, and there is a writing signed by the creator to that effect.
      Date agreement signed: _____
      Name of creator: _____
              -and-
      (ii) The work is for one of the following:
        [ ] a contribution to collective work
        [ ] a part of audiovisual work   [ ] instructional text
        [ ] a translation   [ ] a test
        [ ] a supplementary work   [ ] answers to a test
        [ ] a compilation   [ ] an atlas
  [ ] 2. We do not own, but we can use because:
    [ ] We have assignment of all copyright rights by written transfer, signed by copyright owner, that has been recorded with Register of Copyright in U.S. Library of Congress.
    Date of assignment: _____
    Name of creator: _____
    [ ] We have one or more of the following five exclusive licenses:
      [ ] 1. to reproduce (make copies)
      [ ] 2. to prepare a derivative work (sequel or prequel)
      [ ] 3. to distribute (sell) copies
      [ ] 4. to publicly perform
      [ ] 5. to publicly display
    Date of signing license: _____
    Name of copyright owner: _____
    [ ] We have the following nonexclusive license in writing and signed by copyright owner (briefly describe nonexclusive right; e.g., the use of photo as cover of annual report, use of statistical table in annual report):
_____
_____
    [ ] We have purchase order, unsigned by copyright owner, but received by copyright owner and containing the nonexclusive license thereon and paid pursuant thereto:
    Name and date of purchase order: _____
    Date of payment of purchase order and check number: _____
_____
    Nonexclusive license (describe): _____
_____
_____

Exhibit 20.2
Copyright Authorization (Sample Form)

Authorization of copyright when a work is "made for hire" by an employee or a freelancer may be complicated by a number of factors. Thus the form here offers several options. It was prepared by Harold Wm. Suckenik, Esq., an attorney specializing in public relations law, for a publication of The Institute for Public Relations Research and Education. The form is reproduced here with their permission.

Fair use. A scholar uses quotes and excerpts from the works of others and acknowledges the source with footnotes. When publishing information, it may be possible to use a small amount of a work without offering compensation under the doctrine of "fair use," particularly when quoting speeches or articles that address a public issue. But beware that no specific number of words constitutes fair use: as little as two lines of a poem, song, or speech may constitute the main idea of a message and may be considered protected by the owner.

Implied consent. Subjects may smile at you and wave while you're taking a picture, but later they may decide that you used their image without permission. Don't assume that you have permission; obtain it with a release form if you are using the photo for any commercial purpose.

PRIVACY, RIGHTS OF EMPLOYEES

Everyone with whom your organization or your client does business or has workplace relations expects personal privacy. You must consider whether you are merely giving exposure to an employee or a consumer in the normal course of events, or whether you are exploiting the image of the employee or the consumer for financial gain. The line is thin, but with care a lawsuit can be avoided.

In general, if you picture or describe employees in the workplace for the purpose of informing an internal audience, you have not invaded a person's privacy. If, for example, you have a new recycling procedure and you photograph several employees recycling materials in a photo taken for the plant newsletter, the chance of invading privacy is minimal. If the same picture is sent to the local newspaper, you may be showing an employee who is a bigamist or a debtor or a missing parent in the community, and the publicity may expose the employee to unwanted pressures from others. If you use the picture in an advertisement promoting your firm's recycling efforts, the employee may feel exploited without compensation. It is always advisable to obtain the permission of employees who are pictured or described in promotions or publicity, no matter how innocent the subject.

Similarly, consumers who willingly speak on behalf of a product or service or allow themselves to be photographed in public or private places, may feel that their privacy has been invaded when they see the public relations purposes to which you have put them. Again, gaining written permission is the key. Obviously when mass pictures of hundreds of employees are used, it is difficult for any one employee to charge invasion of privacy.

As a public relations professional—whether working in a corporation's public affairs department or for an agency assigned to a campaign of a publicly held company—you may receive information or data that could give you an advantage in knowing when to buy or sell a company's stock. Of course your involvement in the day-to-day affairs of the company gives you a sense of when to buy or sell stock. But if you or someone in your confidence—a relative or friend—suddenly buys or sells stock the day before the price changes dramatically, you can be assured that the Securities and Exchange Commission (SEC) will note the event and come calling for an explanation.

When an individual profits because of advance knowledge of a company's success or failure in a business endeavor it's called "insider trading," and the practice is prohibited by federal law. Computers readily reveal the identities of the culprits, and SEC investigators demand explanation. Public relations people should purchase stock in their firms at regular intervals, perhaps even through a payroll deduction plan, and avoid activities based on insider information.

Similarly, public relations people need to be able to demonstrate that they disclosed any and all information that could have impact on the price of their company's stock in a timely fashion and simultaneously to all of the financial news media. Failure to do so results in SEC penalties, including the voiding of sales of stock made when disclosure was not complete and generally publicized. Avoid management pressures to withhold material information about any development that may affect the price of the firm's stock.

FINANCIAL DISCLOSURE AND INSIDER TRADING

This section could have been headed "Ethics Codes" or "Ethics Standards," for there are written codes and standards, such as the Public Relations Society of America (PRSA) "Code of Professional Standards for the Practice of Public Relations" in Exhibit 20.3. But we prefer to focus on ethical *behavior,* because that puts the responsibility on each public relations professional to behave in a manner that is fair to all and does damage to none—in short, to perform in the two-way symmetrical model of public relations that supposes all parties work for the common and greatest good.

Each of us individually knows that it is possible to tell part of a story, or to focus on one aspect of a story, or to tell one story instead of another in order to put ourselves or our organization in the best light. To an extent, that is part of the charm of human behavior. But when selective use of facts becomes misleading, detrimental to society, and injurious to the cause of others, we label it a breach of ethics.

ETHICAL BEHAVIOR

Exhibit 20.3
Code of Professional
Standards for the Practice
of Public Relations,
Public Relations Society
of America

Declaration of Principles

Members of the Public Relations Society of America base their professional principles on the fundamental value and dignity of the individual, holding that the free exercise of human rights, especially freedom of speech, freedom of assembly, and freedom of the press, is essential to the practice of public relations.

In serving the interests of clients and employers, we dedicate ourselves to the goals of better communication, understanding, and cooperation among the diverse individuals, groups, and institutions of society, and of equal opportunity of employment in the public relations profession.

We pledge:

To conduct ourselves professionally, with truth, accuracy, fairness, and responsibility to the public;

To improve our individual competence and advance the knowledge and proficiency of the profession through continuing research and education;

And to adhere to the articles of the Code of Professional Standards for the Practice of Public Relations as adopted by the governing Assembly of the Society.

Code of Professional Standards for the Practice of Public Relations

These articles have been adopted by the Public Relations Society of America to promote and maintain high standards of public service and ethical conduct among its members.

1. A member shall conduct his or her professional life in accord with the **public interest**.
2. A member shall exemplify high standards of **honesty and integrity** while carrying out dual obligations to a client or employer and to the democratic process.
3. A member shall **deal fairly** with the public, with past or present clients or employers, and with fellow practitioners, giving due respect to the ideal of free inquiry and to the opinions of others.
4. A member shall adhere to the highest standards of **accuracy and truth**, avoiding extravagant claims or unfair comparisons and giving credit for ideas and words borrowed from others.
5. A member shall not knowingly disseminate **false or misleading information** and shall act promptly to correct erroneous communications for which he or she is responsible.
6. A member shall not engage in any practice which has the purpose of **corrupting** the integrity of channels of communications or the processes of government.
7. A member shall be prepared to **identify publicly** the name of the client or employer on whose behalf any public communication is made.

8. A member shall not use any individual or organization professing to serve or represent an announced cause, or professing to be independent or unbiased, but actually serving another or **undisclosed interest**.

9. A member shall not **guarantee the achievement** of specified results beyond the member's direct control.

10. A member shall **not represent conflicting** or competing interests without the express consent of those concerned, given after a full disclosure of the facts.

11. A member shall not place himself or herself in a position where the member's **personal interest is or may be in conflict** with an obligation to an employer or client, or others, without full disclosure of such interests to all involved.

12. A member shall **not accept fees, commissions, gifts or any other consideration** from anyone except clients or employers for whom services are performed without their express consent, given after full disclosure of the facts.

13. A member shall scrupulously safeguard the **confidences and privacy rights** of present, former, and prospective clients or employers.

14. A member shall not intentionally **damage the professional reputation** or practice of any other practitioner.

15. If a member has evidence that another member has been guilty of unethical, illegal, or unfair practices, including those in violation of this Code, the member is obligated to present the information promptly to the proper authorities of the Society for action in accordance with the procedure set forth in Article XII of the Bylaws.

16. A member called as a witness in a proceeding for enforcement of this Code is obligated to appear, unless excused for sufficient reason by the judicial panel.

17. A member shall, as soon as possible, sever relations with any organization or individual if such relationship requires conduct contrary to the articles of this Code.

Exhibit 20.3 *(continued)*
Code of Professional Standards for the Practice of Public Relations, Public Relations Society of America

Guidelines for ethical behavior, such as the PRSA Code, are just that: suggestive of the major areas of abuse, but in no way a complete guide to all of the nuances of fairness and justice to others. In the end, an individual's personal makeup, formed through family and community values, will help shape interpretations of what is and isn't ethical behavior. It is important to remember that small ethical lapses collectively chip away at the larger credibility of the public relations profession. Thus it is important for each practitioner to question every relationship and public communication in terms of its effect on the long-term viability of the profession.

APPENDIX

A Toolbox for
Planning and Analysis

Occasionally the text refers to a technique for planning a message strategy or for measuring the effectiveness of the message, followed by a notation to see this appendix.

Consider this a special toolbox. Each of the concepts or devices explained here in one-page format will enable you to decide what a message is accomplishing, or tell you how to improve the message.

(If you are interested in using these techniques on a regular basis, and if you are planning your public relations program with the use of a computer, we suggest that you investigate the use of PR PRO©™, the Macintosh software program developed by Don Bates and John Pavlik and available from The Bates Company, Inc., 156 Fifth Avenue, Suite 1134, New York, NY 10010 (Phone 212-675-4441). In addition to using material from this text and the companion text, *Managing Public Relations*, in its tutorial sections, the software program includes a readability test and several useful planning devices.)

Included in this appendix are the following tools:

- Hedging and wedging defined and explained
- The Gantt Chart
- Readership Survey Questions
- Content Analysis
- Readability Formulas
- The Signaled Stopping Technique

Choosing "Hedging" or "Wedging"

How do people manage to hold two incompatible beliefs, yet change their beliefs from situation to situation? Perhaps it is because they develop cognitive strategies for reducing ambiguity. Stamm and his coresearchers identified *hedging* and *wedging* as two such strategies.*

Wedging means rejecting one belief to make room for another. If you thought the police were corrupt, but a police officer saves your life, you may decide that law officers are wonderful guardians of the peace. If so, you "wedge out" other cognitions and become totally pro-police in your attitudes.

Hedging means making room for two conflicting beliefs. If you mistrust corporations because you think that they don't care about individuals, but if you then decide that XYZ Corporation in your town is wonderful because it supports your favorite charity, you will have to "hedge" to the extent that you remain largely anti-corporation while acknowledging that XYZ Corporation is a good citizen of your community.

We suggest in this book and in *Managing Public Relations* that it usually is more realistic to set an objective of having your publics *hedge* in favor of your organization rather than hoping that they will be able to *wedge out* all unfavorable cognitions they may have about your organization.

The Gantt Chart

The Gantt Chart, developed in the early 1900s by Henry L. Gantt, shows the activities to be completed on the vertical axis and the time required to complete those activities on the horizontal axis. The activities are sequenced from top to bottom, so that the activities at the top must come first and those at the bottom must come last.

If the time frame is open-ended, the Gantt Chart is built from the proposed starting date, and the ending date is thus forced. If the ending date is a given, then the necessary starting date will be forced. If both ending date and starting date are givens, the chart will suggest where extra resources need to be brought to bear in order to complete the process in the allotted time.

The Gantt Chart on the following page shows the steps and time frames needed for planning a typical public relations event: the press conference.

---

* See, for example, Keith R. Stamm and James E. Grunig, "Communication Situations and Cognitive Strategies in Resolving Environmental Issues," *Journalism Quarterly* 54 (1977), pp. 713–720, and James E. Grunig and Keith R. Stamm, "Cognitive Strategies and the Resolution of Environmental Issues," *Journalism Quarterly* 56 (1979), pp. 715–726.

A Gantt Chart for a Press Conference

Activities

Activities				
Arrange for room				
Arrange for phones, chairs, props, outlets for TV				
Arrange for person to greet reporters				
Arrange refreshments				
Invite reporters				
Prepare press kit				
Brief speakers				
Check arrangements				
Hold press conference				
	1	2	3	4	5

Duration (Days)

Readership surveys document whether anyone read the clippings that appeared in the mass media, whether employees read a publication, or, if a viewership study, whether anyone saw a television advertisement or news program. Readership studies may be done by personal interview, telephone, or mail questionnaire. If done in person, the interviewer shows the respondent the publication in which an article appeared and asks two self-perception questions:

1. Do you recall having seen this article on air pollution created by the Bethlehem Steel Co. in Baltimore?
   ( ) No (GO TO NEXT QUESTION)
   ( ) Yes ↓

     2. How much of that article would you say you read. Did you:
        ( ) Read all
        ( ) Read most
        ( ) Read some
        ( ) Not read it at all.

In a telephone or mail questionnaire, you would have to tell the reader a little about the story, or read the title: "Do you happen to remember a story that appeared in the *Baltimore Sun* discussing air pollution caused by the Bethlehem Steel Co.?" Then you would proceed with the same second question as above.

Sometimes, researchers ask readership questions about entire publications. For example, a study of employees at the National Bureau of Standards asked:

How Often Do You Read?	Always	Most of the Time	About Half of the Time	Hardly Ever	Never
NBS Standard	5	4	3	2	1
Technical Calendar	5	4	3	2	1
Dimensions Magazine	5	4	3	2	1
Bulletin Boards	5	4	3	2	1

Readership questions can also be asked about general types of content in publications. The same National Bureau of Standards study asked:

Next, would you indicate about how often you would read each of the following types of articles if it appeared in an NBS publication?

Would You Read It?	Always	Most of the Time	About Half of the Time	Hardly Ever	Never
News of appointments or awards	5	4	3	2	1
News about pay and benefit plans	5	4	3	2	1
Messages from the director	5	4	3	2	1

Content Analysis

Content analysis is a systematic, quantitative method of determining the content of the mass media, clippings about your organization, publications produced by the public relations department, speeches given by organization members, or other messages. It is a way of quantifying what we read and observe in these publications.

Content analysis goes one step beyond other indirect measures of the communication objective, in that it determines what the communication was about. It can be used to determine the themes discussed in press clippings about the company; to evaluate whether the clippings were positive, negative, or neutral; or to trace different content categories through time. It can be used as a check on editors of organizational publications to determine what they are including in their publications and to suggest that certain topics are being used too little or too much. Content analysis has many similar uses in public relations.

Content analysis has five major stages:

1. Select a unit of analysis. Will you examine entire articles, paragraphs, or sentences?
2. Construct categories. What themes, evaluational dimensions, or other units do you want to measure? The categories should be defined by what the PR program was designed to communicate.
3. Sample content. Not all clippings or articles need be examined. You may, for example, select articles randomly, take one entire week, or reconstruct a hypothetical week or month from a year-long period.
4. Code the units of analysis. You either do the coding yourself or train coders. Coders classify articles or number of column inches into the categories chosen. It is also important to check on coder reliability by having more than one coder code the same units and then comparing the results. If the two coders place the units into different categories more than 10–20 percent of the time, reconstruct the categories.
5. Analyze the results by computer or hand tabulation.

Source: Guido H. Stempel, III, "Content Analysis," in Guido H. Stempel, III, and Bruce H. Westley (eds.), *Research Methods in Mass Communication* (Englewood Cliffs, NJ: Prentice-Hall, 1981), pp. 119–131.

Readability Formulas

Readability research originated with education researchers as early as 1888. Readability researchers have attempted to develop a quantitative formula that indicates whether written materials are appropriate for audiences with different educational backgrounds. Researchers have also tested the ability of readability formulas to predict "listenability" of broadcast writing—writing read aloud.* This research shows that readability formulas predict listenability as well as readability.

All of the most widely used readability formulas today have two components: the difficulty of the words and the length of the sentences. Three of the frequently used formulas—the Flesch Reading Ease Formula, the Gunning Fog Index, and the Farr-Jenkins-Patterson formula—use the number of syllables in a word as a measure of word difficulty.

With the Flesch formula, researchers must count the average number of syllables in a 100-word sample of the writing. With the Gunning Fog index, they count the number of words with polysyllables (three or more syllables). With the Farr-Jenkins-Patterson formula, they count the number of monosyllables (one-syllable words). For the fourth formula, the Dale-Chall formula, the researcher measures word difficulty by counting the number of words in a 100-word sample that do not appear on a list of the 3,000 most common English words.

Let's take the Flesch formula as an example. As reconstructed by Powers, Sumner, and Kearl—to reduce its prediction error—the formula is:

$$R = (.0778)(ASL) + (.0455)(\text{syllables}/100 \text{ words}) - 2.209$$

where R = readability and ASL = average sentence length.[†]

To use the formula, take any continuous sample of 100 words, preferably not at the beginning of an article. Count the number of sentences and divide that into 100 to find average sentence length. (A sentence is considered to end with semicolons and dashes as well as periods.) Then count the number of syllables in the 100 words. Plug the two numbers into the formula to get a readability score. Interpret the scores as follows:

4.0–4.5—Very easy, like pulp fiction, drugstore novels

4.5–5.5—Fairly easy, like slick fiction, movie magazines

5.5–6.5—Standard, like newspapers or *Reader's Digest*

6.5–7.5—Quality, like intellectual magazines, *Harper's*

7.5–above—Academic, like learned journals.

To calculate the Gunning Fog Index, take a sample of 100 words, find the average sentence length and the number of words of three syllables or more.[‡] In counting polysyllables, however, do not include: (1) capitalized words, (2) combinations of short easy words (such as bookkeeper), (3) verbs that have three syllables because of "ed" or "es" at the end (such as created). Total the average sentence length and number of polysyllables and multiply by 0.4. The score approximates the number of years of education required to read a passage easily and to understand it. A score of 16 suggests writing for a college graduate. Most best-selling books test at 7–8. A score of 13 is the danger line for most readers. Try to keep your writing below that.

[*] Carl Jon Denbow, "Listenability and Readability: An Experimental Investigation," *Journalism Quarterly* 52 (1975), pp. 285–290.

[†] Richard D. Powers, W. A. Sumner, and B. E. Kearl, "A Recalculation of Four Adult Readability Formulas," *Journal of Applied Psychology* 49 (1958), p. 104.

[‡] Robert Gunning, *New Guide to More Effective Writing in Business and Industry* (Boston: Industrial Education Institute, 1963), pp. 2–15. Also Robert Gunning, *The Technique of Clear Writing* (New York: McGraw-Hill, 1952), p. 36.

The Signaled
Stopping Technique

When people read or listen to words, they put them together to construct ideas, or what Carter calls "pictures." These people stop, however, when they cannot process the information into a single idea,
when they get the idea and want to think about it, or when they agree
or disagree with it.

To use the SST, give people who represent your publics the message you have written. Ask them to put a slash mark anywhere in the
written passage where they feel like stopping. Then ask them to indicate their reason for stopping, using the following notation:

C—Because of confusion: You stop or pause in reading because
you feel you have lost the idea the
writer is trying to communicate

R—To reread: You stop because you have lost track
of the idea but you can get back on
track by reading a passage again

?—To ask a question: You stop because you feel that if you
could just ask the writer a question it
would help you to understand the idea
he or she is trying to communicate

T—To think about the idea: You stop to mull over what you have
read and try to put it all together

U—Because you understand: You stop because you do understand
the writer's main idea and want to
"let it sink in"

A—To agree: You agree with what the writer said

D—To disagree: You disagree with what the writer
said.

Write in any other reason.

A subject might, for example, make the following notations while
reading the first two sentences in this exhibit.

When people read or listen/^{C} to words, they put them together to

construct ideas, or what Carter calls "pictures."/^{D} These people stop/

, however, when they cannot process/$^?$ the information into a single

idea, when they get the idea/^{R} and want to think about it, or when

they agree or disagree with it./ "I'm bored!"

As you should be able to see from this example, the SST provides a detailed look at how readers construct the idea you want them to retain. It also shows whether they believe the idea and evaluate it favorably (two other PR objectives). Studying the various readers' reasons for stopping will suggest how you can improve the writing so that readers can grasp your idea.

If you go through the SST yourself on your own writing—especially the day after you write something—you'll be surprised at what goes through your own mind when you process the message you wrote. You can then use the codes you write to improve your writing, and that will spare the reader a lot of grief. The SST also can be used for spoken messages (speeches, radio, TV), if you have the subjects write down the codes as they listen. It is difficult to trace their reactions to specific parts of the message, however, for the spoken material.

The Signaled
Stopping Technique
(continued)

Index